Sheldon Amos

A systematic view of the science of jurisprudence [elektronische middelen]

Sheldon Amos

A systematic view of the science of jurisprudence [elektronische middelen]

ISBN/EAN: 9783742872456

Manufactured in Europe, USA, Canada, Australia, Japa

Cover: Foto ©ninafisch / pixelio.de

Manufactured and distributed by brebook publishing software
(www.brebook.com)

Sheldon Amos

A systematic view of the science of jurisprudence [elektronische middelen]

ANALYSIS OF TOPICS.

CHAPTER I.
GENERAL DESCRIPTION OF THE PROVINCE OF THE SCIENCE OF JURISPRUDENCE 1

CHAPTER II.
GENERAL VIEW OF THE HISTORICAL DEVELOPMENT OF THE MATERIALS OF THE SCIENCE OF JURISPRUDENCE 9

CHAPTER III.
RELATION OF THE SCIENCE OF JURISPRUDENCE TO ALL OTHER SCIENCES 16
  Physical and Psychological Science 29
  Ethical Science 29
  Science of Social Ethics 34
  Science of Political Economy 36
  Science of Legislation 37
  Science of Government (in the narrower sense) . 38

CHAPTER IV.
MATERIALS, OR CONTENTS, OF THE SCIENCE OF JURISPRUDENCE 40
  I. Description of the Original Fact of Law in Itself:
    Account of the Historical and Logical Genesis of that Fact:

Explanation of all the Leading Terms essentially involved in the Meaning of the Term *Law*.

II. An Investigation of the Possible *Sources* of Law (or Immediate Modes by which Actual Laws are, or may be, created), and of the Process of *Interpretation*, as severally Modifying the Operation and Nature of Law.

III. A Classificatory Arrangement of the Contents of all Possible Systems of Positive Law.

IV. An Investigation of Theories of Variation in the Quality, Number, and Mutual Relations of all the above Elements,—whether such Variation operates in Time or in Space] 44

CHAPTER V.

THE SOURCES OF LAW, AND THE INTERPRETATION OF LAW 50

[I. Judicial Legislation,—in its Several Modes . 52

II. Statutory Legislation,—or *Direct* Changes consciously introduced into the Existing Legal System by the Supreme Political Authority.

III. Statutory Legislation,—or *Indirect* Changes introduced through the Medium of Subordinate Legislatures of all sorts.

IV. Codification.

V. Scientific Reflection on the Nature of Law] . 58

CHAPTER VI.

DISTRIBUTION OF THE MAIN DEPARTMENTS OF A LEGAL SYSTEM 61

CHAPTER VII.

AN EXPLANATION OF LEADING TERMS 69
   State 71
   Law 73
   Right and *Duty* 76
   Person and *Thing* 79
   A Peculiar Class of Terms respecting the Possible Modifications of Moral Responsibility: as *Infancy, Sex, Idiocy, Insanity, Intoxication, Ignorance, Error, Compulsion, Fraud, Will, Intention* 85
   Act and *Event* 93
   Motive 95

CHAPTER VIII.

CLASSIFICATION OF LAWS 96

CHAPTER IX.

LAWS DIRECTLY RELATING TO THE CONSTITUTION AND ADMINISTRATION OF THE STATE (CONSTITUTIONAL LAW) 103
  A. Description of the General Nature, Province, and Limits of this part of the Law . . 103
  B. Meaning of the Phrase *Supreme Political Authority* 107
    I. Description of what is meant by the Phrase *Supreme Political Authority* generally.
    II. Description of the Modes in which such an Authority may be constituted in a given Community.
    III. Precise Determination of the Modes in which the Person, or all the Persons, representing the Supreme Political Authority, is, or are, Constituted 110

C. Legal Relations to each other and to all other Persons of the Persons (if more than one) composing the Supreme Political Authority . 110
  I. Rights of Each Constituent Portion of the Supreme Political Authority in its Corporate Capacity as against the Rest.
  II. Rights of Each Constituent Portion in its Corporate Capacity as against the Individual Members of it, and as against all other Members of the Community.
  III. Rights of Individual Members of Each such Constituent Portion, against (1.) all the other Members; against (2.) all other Persons in the Community 113
D. Modes in which Changes are brought about in the Classes of Persons composing the Supreme Political Authority, or in the Relations of such Persons to Each other and to all other Persons 113
  I. Limits within which the Constitution of the Supreme Political Authority admits of Change, whether in respect of, (1.) the Description of the Persons who compose the Several Parts of it, or (2.) the Rights of the Several Constituent Parts of such Authority in their Corporate Capacity as against Each other.
  II. Description of the Formal Machinery by which Changes of the above Limits may be effected 116
E. General Import of the Phrase *Executive Authority*. Legal Relations to Each other and to all other Persons of the Persons (if more than one) composing that Authority; and the Modes in which Changes are brought about in those Relations . . . 117

I. Precise Meaning of the Phrase *Executive Authority.*
II. Modes in which the Head or the Subordinate Members of that Authority may be Constituted, Suspended, or Removed.
III. Rights and Duties of the Several Component Members of the Executive Authority.
IV. Special Securities accorded to Citizens for their Individual Protection against Usurpation of Right, Neglect of Duty, or Malversation generally, on the part of any Member of the Executive Authority 121

CHAPTER X.

LAWS OF OWNERSHIP 122
  A. General Character and Purpose of Laws of Ownership 125
  B Things Owned. 128
    [1. "Natural Agents" as opposed to all other Things.
    2. Things set apart for the General Purposes of the State, as opposed to all other Things.
    3. Things Movable and Immovable.
    4. *Res Fungibiles* and *Non-fungibiles.*
    5. Things Corporeal and Incorporeal.
    6. *Singulæ Res* and *Universitas Rerum.*
    7. Sundry other Oppositions, as Things Divisible and Indivisible, Principal and Accessory, Existing and About-to-exist] 129
  C. Persons who Own.
    [1. Infants and Minors.
    2. Idiots and Lunatics.
    3. Felons and Outlaws.
    4. Aliens.
    5. Married Women] 143

D. Rights of Ownership 147
   I. *Dominium*, or Absolute Ownership, in which the Mode of User, the Duration of the Right, and the Facilities of Alienation, are Unlimited or Indefinite.
   II. All Lesser Rights, including Estates for Life, for Years, or upon Condition; Trust Estates, Copyhold Estates and Estates Tail in English Law, *Métayer* Tenancies, *Emphyteusis*, and Usufructuary Estates generally; Servitudes or Easements, and generally all *Jura in Re*, according to the largest Intent of the Classical Jurists, including the Rights of Carriers, of Depositaries, of Mortgagees, and of the merest Possessors 149

E. Facts (Acts or Events) which determine the Accruing of a Right of Ownership . . 154
  [1. Occupancy.
   2. Specification.
   3. Accession.
   4. Invention.
   5. Prescription.
   6. Alienation in Life.
   7. Alienation on Death.
   8. Adjudication.
   9. Forfeiture.] . . . .

F. Modes of Protecting Rights of Ownership.
   I. Summary Process, of the Nature of an Interdict or an Injunction.
   II. Action or Suit having in view the Compensation of an Owner for Injuries received.
   III. Action or Suit having in view not Compensation so much as actual Restoration or Restitution.
   IV. A Criminal Proceeding 174

CHAPTER XI.

LAWS OF CONTRACT 176
  A. Explanation of the Legal Term *Contract* . . 179
  B. Persons who Make Contracts 181
    [1. Infants.
     2. Lunatics and the like, including Drunkards.
     3. Persons under *Duress* of all kinds, Physical, Moral, or Legal.
     4. Married Women.
     5. Agents.
     6. Outlaws.
     7. Aliens.] 184
  C. Acts by which the Making of a Contract is signified.
    [I. A Mental state of each of the Persons professing to Contract, implying Acquiescence in the one and the same contemplated Course of Action indicated by the Purpose or Object of the Contract.
    II. An Actual and Physical Communication, having reference to the before-mentioned state, through the only possible *Media* for communicating a Knowledge of states of Mind.
    III. *Possibly*, a Supplemental Act insisted upon by Law for the Purpose of furnishing Evidence of the presence of I. and II. . . . .] 194
  D. Rights Accruing through the Making of a Contract.
    I. Rights to Performance of all the Acts Promised, and in the Mode, Measure, and Time Promised.
    II. Rights, in the event of the Non-performance of the Acts promised seeming probable, to do such Acts as may Minimise Loss.

xiv ANALYSIS.

    III. Rights to (by Judicial Process) (1.) compel Performance, or (2.) obtain Compensation for Losses sustained through the Non-performance of Acts Promised.
    IV. Rights to a Dissolution of the Contract on clearly ascertained Conditions 201
  E. Classification of Contracts 213
    I. Contracts in Aid of the Essential Relationships of Society.
    II. Contracts in Aid of Co-operation for Social and Industrial purposes.
    III. Contracts in Aid of Co-operation for more or less Artificial and Complicated Commercial purposes 216

CHAPTER XII.
LAWS AFFECTING SPECIAL CLASSES OF PERSONS . 230

A. Husband and Wife : Parent and Child . . 236
    I. General Description of the Moral and Legal Relationship of Husband and Wife.
    II. Authentic Signs that the Legal Relationship has been created 239
    III. Rights and Duties Accruing (1.) as between the Parties; (2.) as between the Parties, and each of them respectively, on the one hand, and the Children of the Marriage on the other; (3) as between the Parties and all other Persons . 243
    IV. Authentic Signs that the Legal Relationship has been terminated 252

B. Guardian and Ward 258
    I. General Description of the Legal Relationship.
    II. Events of different sorts on the happening of which the Relationship is demanded.

- III. Mode of Appointment of Guardians for different Purposes.
- IV. Rights and Duties of Guardians and Wards respectively.
- V. Duration of Guardianship and Modes of Changing and Supplementing Guardians.
- VI. Modes of Investigating and Redressing Injuries committed by Guardians 202

C. Trustees, Executors, and Administrators . . 202
- I. Description of the Legal Relations implied in the Fact of *Trusteeship* 267
- II. Modes in which the Relationship takes its Rise . 268
- III. Rights and Duties of Trustees 272
- IV. Modes of Enforcing the Duties of Trustees . . 275

D. Barristers, Advocates, Solicitors, Attorneys, Proctors, Writers to the Signet, Notaries Public, and the like 276
- I. Complete and generally Descriptive List of the Classes of Persons specially Authorised to assist Private Persons in the following respects :—
  1. Informing them as to the exact Nature and Extent of their Legal Rights and Duties, and of the Nature and Mode of Use of the Remedial Processes provided by Law for the Enforcement of the same.
  2. In case of Impending Legislation, Preparing the Subject-matter of Dispute for Judicial Investigation.
  3. Representing Litigants in a Court of Justice.
  4. Performing Public and Solemn Acts, demanded either by the Practice of Courts of Justice in the Course of Litigation, or by Mercantile or other Customs Judicially Recognised . . . 279
- II. Qualifications and Modes of Appointment through which Persons become Members of the Classes now under Consideration.
- III. Rights and Duties of such Classes of Persons severally in respect of each of the kinds of Functions enumerated in I.
- IV. Modes of Enforcing such Rights and Duties, whether by the Ordinary or the Extraordinary Processes of a Court of Justice.

V. Special and Arbitrary Provisions in Contemplation of the Possible Events of Sudden Change, Removal, Incapacity, or Death, of such Persons in the midst of the Performance of their appropriate Functions 280
E. Certain Classes of Corporate Bodies,—as those instituted for Ecclesiastical, Municipal, Educational, or Eleemosynary Purposes . 281

CHAPTER XIII.

LAWS OF CIVIL INJURIES AND CRIMES 283
    Grounds of Distinction between a *Civil Injury* and a *Crime* 283
LAWS RELATING TO CIVIL INJURIES. 287
   A. Injuries to Rights to (1.) Personal Security; (2.) Free Locomotion; (3.) Conditions of Health; (4.) Reputation.
   B. Injuries to Rights of Ownership.
   C. Injuries to Rights under a Contract.
   D. Injuries to Rights Appertaining to Special Classes of Persons. 288
LAWS RELATING TO CRIMES 297
   A. General Description of a Crime.
   B. Essential Constituent Elements of a Crime . 299
     I. The *Act*.
     II. The *Intention*.
     III. Grounds of *Exculpation*.
     IV. Distinction between *Consummate* Crimes and Crimes consisting in *Attempts* to Commit Crimes.
     V. Principals and Accessories.
   C. Classification of Crimes 300

1. Acts Directly or Indirectly Menacing the Constitution and Administration of the State.
2. Acts Directly Violating the Rights of Private Persons.
3. Acts Violating the Rights of Special Classes of Persons.

D. Enumeration and Classification of *Punishments* . 301
1. Enumeration of Possible Punishments.
2. Rules for the Application of Punishment.
3. Grounds of Extinction of Liability to Punishment.

SPECIAL DISSERTATIONS ON *MALICE, INSANITY*, THE PUNISHMENT OF DEATH, AND *EVIDENCE OF CHARACTER* 304

CHAPTER XIV.

LAWS OF PROCEDURE 317
  A. The Establishment of Courts of Justice,—Inferior, Superior ; Civil, Criminal ; Original, and of Appeal ; and for Local Matters . . 319
  B. The Formal Mode of Investigation of Alleged Breaches of Law, by :— 324
    I. Preliminary Process for the Purpose of Ascertaining the Real Matters in Controversy. (*Pleading* and its various Modes.) . . . 324
    II. Trial of Issue of *Fact*.
    (Distinction between *Direct* and *Circumstantial* Evidence) 329
    III. Trial of Issue of *Law*. 340
  C. Sentence, Assignment of Punishment or of Measure and Mode of Compensation, and Execution of Sentence 341
  D. Extraordinary Remedies.
  [*Interdict* or Injunction, *Mandamus*, "Commercial Tribunals," Bankruptcy, Distress.] 342

E. Limitation of Actions	346
F. Parties to Actions	348
CONFLICTING THEORIES OF CRIMINAL PROCEDURE	349
The "Litigious" and the "Inquisitorial" Theories	350
The Institution of a *Minister of Justice* or of a *Public Prosecutor*	351
The "Prerogative of Pardon"	352
Current Suggestions for a New Definition, or for New Methods of Trying the Crime, of Murder	356
The French Verdict of *Extenuating Circumstances*	358
Trial of *Political Crimes*	360
The Doctrine of *Extradition*	362
The "Unanimity of Juries"	363

CHAPTER XV.

PRIVATE INTERNATIONAL LAW	366
Nature and General History of *Private International Law*	366
A. Laws Relating to the Constitution and Administration of the State	372
I. Territorial Sovereignty	372
II. Citizenship	374
III. Domicile	376
B. Laws of Ownership	378
[*Lex Loci Rei Sitæ, Lex Domicilii.*]	
C. Laws of Contract	383
[*Lex Loci Contractus, Lex Loci Actus, Lex Fori.*]	
D. Laws Affecting Special Classes of Persons	384
[Marriages and Divorces Abroad.]	

E. Laws of Procedure 387
  [Bankruptcy, Limitation of Actions, and Foreign Judgments.]

CHAPTER XVI.

PUBLIC INTERNATIONAL LAW 391
  Nature and General History of *Public International Law* 391
  Distinction between International *Law* and International *Morality* 393
  The *Conditions* of the Creation and Growth of a System of Public International Law . . 395
  The *Sources* of International Law (Described and Enumerated) 404
  The *Sanctions* of International Law (Described and Enumerated) 409
  Conception of a *State* as a *Person* or Subject of International Law 414
  Limitations on the *Independence* of States . . . 416
  Rights of States (Described and Enumerated) . . 419
    [Modes of Acquiring *Territory*. Rights Under *Treaties*; and Obstacles in the way of Protecting such Rights] 422
  Limitations on the Exercise of the so-called Right of War 431
  Modern Aspects of *Neutral* Claims 432
  Modes of *Enforcing* Duties of *Neutrality* . . . 437
  Duties of *Belligerents*; the Treatment of *Non-Combatants* 438
  Geneva Conventions of 1864 and 1868, and St. Petersburg Convention of 1868 . . . 449
  Prospects of Permanent *Peace*, and Functions of International Law in Promoting it . . 451

CHAPTER XVII.

	PAGE
GENERAL PROSPECTS OF THE SCIENCE OF JURISPRUDENCE	457
CHANGES MANIFESTING THEMSELVES IN EUROPEAN SOCIETY; FUNCTIONS OF THE JURIST IN RELATION TO THEM	457
Demand for Political Reforms	458
National Church Establishments	461
Ownership of Land	462
Theories relating to the Legal and Political Consequences of *Difference of Sex*	464
CODIFICATION	471
Its History in Germany	473
Obstacles to its being effected in England	473
Written and *Unwritten* Law	475
Fusion of *Law* and *Equity* in England	479
State of Written and Unwritten Law in England	485
Suggestions as to Codification in England, and its Prospects	488
LEGAL EDUCATION	490
Functions of Universities	493
Lectures and Private Study	495
Topics of Study	499
GENERAL CONSIDERATIONS AS TO THE MUTUAL RELATIONS, IN THE FUTURE, OF LAW AND OTHER SOCIAL FORCES OR FACTS	500

There is scarcely a Topic in this Work which has not been the subject of repeated Lecturing, Teaching, and Conversational or Critical Disputations with Students. Thus the keen-minded members of the Author's successive Classes must have their share in the responsibility or the merit of attempted Innovations. It is to serious Students, Professional and Unprofessional,—Men and Women,—that this Book is addressed; though no Book,—if it serve its purpose as a Book,—can dispense with Oral Teaching,—if Oral Teaching also truly serve its purpose as such.

No English Writer, however, on Scientific Jurisprudence (be his temperament ever so cautious, self-restrained, and practical) can keep out of view the glaring demand for a Systematic Reconstruction of the Material Contents of English Law. The Possibility and the Modes of such a Reconstruction are discussed at some length in the last Chapter of this Work. In view of such a Task being one day,—or progressively from day to day, —undertaken, it has been essayed here to lay the indispensable Foundations by moulding a Precise

Terminology, by insisting on Logical Methods of Classification, and, above all, by drawing an unmistakeably clear Line of Demarcation between Ethical and Legal Conceptions.

In the Chapter on Laws of Procedure the passages with reference to Circumstantial Evidence are very slightly varied from some forming part of an Article by the Author on the same Subject which appeared in the Number of the *Westminster Review* for January, 1865.

In revising the Proof-Sheets, the Author omitted to notice that, on Page 300, " Principals and Accessories" appears as " Principles and Accessories." On the same Page, " VI. and VII." would be more properly printed as " C. and D.," as in the "Analysis of Topics." On Page 175, " Slander of Title" is accidentally made to appear as though it involved a Criminal Process.

THE SCIENCE OF JURISPRUDENCE.

CHAPTER I.

GENERAL DESCRIPTION OF THE PROVINCE OF THE SCIENCE OF JURISPRUDENCE.

THE Science of Jurisprudence may be said, broadly, to deal with the necessary and formal facts expressed in the very structure of civil society, as that structure is modified and controlled by the facts of civil government and of the constitution of human nature and the physical universe. This attempted description needs some expansion. To allege that Jurisprudence is a Science is to say that it is concerned with certain sequences of facts which, within the limits of recorded experience, are invariably the same for all times and places. As, however, the sequences of facts in question are those due to the existence of Law—that is, of a body of commands formally published by a Sovereign Political Authority—the times and places in which those facts are found must be such as admit of the presence of Law. In other words, the Science of Jurisprudence deals with certain sequences of facts invariably present at all times and in all countries not absolutely barbarous or without any kind of Government.

Now the existence of any kind of Government, even of the most inartificial and primitive, involves the presence of Law just as much as Law involves that of Government. Law and Government are born together, grow together, and die together. Furthermore, the presence of Law implies the opposition to each other of two different sets of persons in the community. There are, first, those who devise and impose the law; there are, secondly, those to whom the law is addressed and whom the first set of persons punish in the event of the law being disobeyed. Now the relations of these two sets of persons to each other admit of infinite diversity, and, in fact, may travel through the whole scale of State Constitutions which have existed or may exist on the face of the earth. But when once this relation of lawgivers and law-receivers is created, and whatever be its nature, there are some sequences which are permanent and invariable.

For example, every law contemplates the possibility of an act of disobedience to it, and every act of alleged disobedience to a law entails certain inevitable consequences. These consequences, implied as they are in the very meaning of the terms Law and Government, as interpreted with reference to the actual condition of the human beings for whose use they are provided, may be arranged as follows:—

(1.) Allegation by the Lawgiver, or his deputies the Executive, that the act complained of is an act specially forbidden by the law, or that it falls under the class of acts generally forbidden by the law. This involves

Interpretation of the law, with all the attendant distinctions as to the so-called *Sources* of Law, whether written or unwritten, and the production of the requisite *Evidence* as to the nature of the act.

(2.) Allegation of moral responsibility in the offender, that is, the assertion of his having known or having had imputed knowledge of the existence of the law said to have been disobeyed, of his having contemplated both the performance of the whole act and its immediate consequences when he moved his muscles in such a way as to bring it about, and of his having had the physical power so to move his muscles or to abstain from moving them; all this is gathered up in the allegation of *Intentional* breach of the law.

(3.) Adjudication, more or less formal.

(4.) Punishment in default of pardon at the hands of the Lawgiver, or the making of a fresh law productive of a like result.

Now it is to be noticed that in any imperfectly organised State several of these steps will be hurried through without their being judicially lingered over, and there may happen to be no Executive officer properly appointed to secure due attention to all of them. Nevertheless the very nature of a general command, addressed by one set of persons to another set, and enforceable by punishment, involves, by way of sequences as natural and as necessary as the fall of a heavy body to the ground on being disengaged from its support, every one of these stages. It is the province of the Science of Jurisprudence to discover what these inevitable stages are, and to bring them out into the light of day under as clear and obvious a system of arrangement as possible. By thus fixing the attention of the

Legislator upon them, the Jurist assists him in beneficially legislating in view of them. If the Legislator is thereby reminded that an alleged act of disobedience cannot be really such unless it is logically included among the acts forbidden by the general terms of a command, he will be cautious how he uses general language and in what terms he attempts to prevent the performance of individual acts. If, again, the Legislator is reminded that a law is only capable of being addressed to persons who are able to obey or disobey it at their will, and that therefore an alleged act of disobedience cannot be really such if it be purely accidental and in no wise intentional, he will arm his executive officers with every ministerial aid towards obtaining the best possible evidence as to the true mental conditions and surroundings of all acts forming the subject-matter of judicial enquiries.

This might suffice to establish that the Science of Jurisprudence is a real Science, and that the sequences with which it deals are independent of the special injunctions going to form the system of positive Law in any particular country. But, as this line of investigation has not been fully tracked before, it may be worth while to take another illustration of the universality of the Science of Jurisprudence from the region of Laws of Ownership.

It is an old and favourite diversion with moral philosophers to speculate as to the origin of the fact of Property, or, to use a less ambiguous and abused expression, of Ownership. Some have held that the idea and prevalent fact of Ownership are mere creatures of antecedent Law. Others have insisted upon their being coeval with Law, or have gone so far as to maintain that Ownership was one of the antecedent and ultimate facts which were the main occasion of the appearance of Law, and thereby of all further social development. The concurrent results of many recent investigations seem to indicate that the notion of individual Ownership, though always dormant, is in its clearer manifestations, of very slow growth. Furthermore, the notion of Ownership as between family and family long precedes the union of a number of families into such a society as admits of the existence of Law properly so called. There is no doubt that it is one of the main functions of early as of all later Law to precipitate social progress in the matter of Ownership by redressing the physical inequalities that exist between the social atoms: by protecting the weak against the strong; and by ensuring to the family, and afterwards to the individual proprietor, the secure enjoyment of such objects of the natural world as are held necessary to the support of life, or are otherwise recognised by the general sentiments of the population as matters of just appropriation by one family or individual person to the exclusion of all others. This rudimentary conception of Ownership, so embraced and fortified by the legal systems of all communities however primitive, implies the presence of certain permanent facts which, being independent of all the modifications introduced by particular legislation, are true materials for the Science of Jurisprudence.

Thus the fact of a Law of Ownership peremptorily involves the distinct contemplation of the following series of facts:—

(1.) Persons who own.
(2.) Things owned.
(3.) Events upon the happening of which the fact of Ownership commences or determines. (Title.)

(4.) Qualification of fact of ownership as to time of commencement and mode of exercise.

(5.) Exercise of Ownership, with or without actually recognised claim in the person so exercising it. (Possession.)

Each of these leading kinds of distinguishable matter in the whole body of the Law of Ownership involves still finer distinctions, which are quite as necessary and universal as the broader and larger ones. Thus—to take not more than one instance :—

The things to be owned may be either
Movable or immovable.
Perishable or imperishable.
Destructible or indestructible through use.
Divisible or indivisible.
Enjoyable at the same time only by one person, or by more than one person, or by all persons equally or otherwise.

It is the noting and classifying of such distinctions as these, treated as essential sequences of fact following upon the more general fact of the mere existence of a Law of Ownership, and wholly independent of the particular regulations of which the whole body of that law may be accidentally compounded, that constitutes the Science of Jurisprudence.

It is not necessary to insist further than has been done already upon the importance of the cultivation of this science to the practical Legislator. It is obvious that the Judge and the Advocate have a like concern in its successful prosecution. If the Statesman need the accurate mapping out of the whole field of necessary matter upon which the discriminating voice of the Legislature is called to pronounce, in order to his perceiving what are the gaps and defects in the existing system of Law, the Judge and the Advocate quite as much need to have those gaps and defects clearly illuminated in order to their being saved time, trouble, and misapprehension in vainly looking up and down for what, perhaps, nowhere exists. The Jurist has nothing to do with the relative political expediency of one or another method of filling in those gaps. He has only to show where they are, and what will be the necessary operation upon the whole existing legal system of filling them up in any assigned way. He will point out, for instance, that the death of an owner involves the inexorable consequence, either that the thing owned ceased to have an owner, or that it be owned by some fresh person, to be designated in accordance with some particular legal enactment. Such a legal enactment, the Jurist will go on to say, may either have the effect of giving the thing to the Lawgiver in the name of the State, or of allowing it to be owned by the first person who gets hold of it; or of giving it to one or another or all of the children or other relations of the previous owner; or of allowing the previous owner in his lifetime, or some one else, to point out by writing or otherwise who is to succeed to the vacant ownership. The Jurist will signify to the Statesman that such questions must needs arise, and will point out whether the existing legal system does or does not contain enactments to answer them, and so to prevent, by anticipation, public confusion and uncertainty. If, after due consideration of the different possible modes of supplying the want, the Statesman determines that a testamentary method is the best one to inaugurate, the Jurist again steps in and explains that a Will involves, as necessary sequences of fact, the following incidents :—

(1.) A person to make it.
(2.) Persons to carry it into effect.
(3.) Formalities to ensure its regularity, and to provide easily accessible evidence of its contents.
(4.) A time at which it begins to operate upon the matters purporting to be dealt with by it.
(5.) Formalities to determine the fact of its alteration, or revocation, if there be such.

Here again exactly the same process of pointing out gaps and describing the necessary consequences following upon any assigned mode of filling them is performed by the scientific Jurist. He stands by in tranquil possession of a calm and dispassionate spirit, as free from haste as from prejudice, from a disposition to favour any political project, however beneficial, as from one to cleave to any existing institution merely because it is time-honoured and precious.

CHAPTER II.

GENERAL VIEW OF THE HISTORICAL DEVELOPMENT OF THE MATERIALS OF THE SCIENCE OF JURISPRUDENCE.

THE Science of Jurisprudence has for its purport the noting and classifying of all the sequences of fact brought about by the contact of the fact of Law with all the other facts of human life, carried on as that life is in the midst of the actual and indestructible conditions of the physical world. It has thus been seen that, however rudely and imperfectly constructed a legal system in any community may chance to be, none the less does the operation of that system supply copious materials for the cognisance of the Jurist. The simplest form of Government, and the roughest principles of Ownership, afford a number of invariable sequences calling for exact description and arrangement. But, as moral sentiments improve, and intercourse between man and man for industrial and social purposes becomes more frequent and complex, new kinds of law are constantly demanded, and, however tardily it may be in proportion to the urgency of the demand, are gradually supplied. Thereby new sequences, due to the contact of these new laws with the permanent or the more transient facts of human life, are again brought to light, and the Science of Jurisprudence is constantly receiving a proportionate extension and enrichment. A Law of Entail, for instance, at once brings into view the persons made capable by Law of creating the entail, of the persons made capable of benefiting by it, and of the land or other things with respect to which the capacity given by Law may be exercised. Further limitations appear on the horizon as to the length of time during which the entail may continue, as to the modes by which the period of its natural efflux may be restricted or extended, and of the casual events upon the happening of which its enduring validity may be made to depend.

A Law of Bankruptcy is a further instance of the mode in which the facts with which the Science of Jurisprudence deals become multiplied as civilisation progresses. A law of this nature implies—(1.) a distinction of " acts of bankruptcy " from all other acts; (2.) a designation of what shall be the formal modes of making a claim to participate in the assets, and what the principles of distributing the assets among the rival claimants; and (3.) what shall be the rights and duties of the bankrupt after his discharge.

So, again, a Law of Divorce, when such a law comes to be enacted, involves a precise description of the acts or events which shall entitle the husband or wife to claim a divorce, and also an enunciation of the legal rights and duties of the divorced persons in respect of property owned or to be owned at any time by either of them, and in respect of the nurture and education of and provision for the children of the marriage. These cursory illustrations have been selected almost at random to make more unmistakably clear the truth that Jurisprudence is a growing Science, in the sense that the facts with which it deals are constantly accumulating as a more complicated social condition is being brought about.

It is not necessary here to investigate the problem as to whether legislation must always continue to be exhibited in this aggressive aspect, as striking out new lines of policy, and impressing with its imperious sanctions each novel mode of social intercourse and co-operation. It is possible that a "stationary" phase may ensue in Law as well as in industry and in social life, without involving retrogression or torpor. The purpose of the Lawgiver will then be confined to repealing useless or vicious laws, to facilitating the working of good ones, and to satisfying more just and refined moral sensibilities, instead of covering any new fields of human activity with his sometimes oppressively caressing wing.

However this may be, sufficient has been said to explain how it is that the mode in which special systems of Law have grown up in different countries has a most important bearing on the actual contents of the Science of Jurisprudence at any given period. The value of such speculations as those of Professor Maine and of the great German historical school is by no means to be measured by the mere amount of what they have contributed in the way of interesting antiquarian research. Those speculations owe their chief importance to the vivid apprehension they impart of new juridical conceptions, as they are progressively brought to light by the agency of actual legislation working in obedience to the higher moral aspirations of growing societies. For example, the process by which the Family became expanded into the Tribal community, at once the expression and the cause of a more intimate social intercourse, gave rise to the Law of Adoption. The existence of a Law of Adoption at once discovered groups of persons, events, times, and conditions needing demarcation in applying and interpreting the Law. The Science of Jurisprudence had thereby received a most fruitful extension. So, likewise, as social habits and moral sentiments admitted of the Legislator fixing attention rather on the individual than on the family interest in Property, and on the mental rather than the mechanical and formal elements in Contract, the Science of Jurisprudence itself obtained new and most weighty materials. The *person*, with his incommunicable and inseparable moral responsibility, became henceforth the integer from which all further conceptions of legal relationship were to start, and the correct analysis of such mental attributes, states, or habits, as *intention*, *negligence*, *motive*, *fraud*, *mistake*, *malice*, and the like, becomes one main department of juridical enquiry.

Broadly stated, the Science of Jurisprudence may be described as depending for its materials upon the growth of Positive Law, and the growth of Positive Law as determined by national progress expressed in such facts as improved moral notions and a more highly organised industrial life. Thus the Science of Jurisprudence is ultimately dependent for its comprehensiveness upon all the variable facts of human life and of the natural world. Some of these facts are universally present in every quarter of the globe, wherever man is found. Such facts are—birth, death, differences of sex, of age, and of mental and bodily health and strength, of language, of physical growth, of time, of place, and of that incalculable concurrence of events which is implied in the word "accident." Another class of facts is confined to such a condition of society as is found after the first step at least has been taken in the career of civilisation. Such are—Government, Positive

Law, Marriage, Ownership, and rudimentary Contracts. Another class of facts, again, is peculiar to societies making distinct moral and industrial progress, and struggling to adapt their positive laws to the necessities brought to light by the facts of that progress. Professor Maine has described with inimitable clearness the actual process by which a progressive nation strives to burst free from the swaddling clothes in which the Law appropriate to a primitive society has wrapped it. By the legal "fiction" the form of the old law continues to be maintained in procedure as a sort of tribute to the sentimental and unprogressive instincts of the bulk of the nation, while the wants of a nascent age are provided for through an artificial interpretation of that law. By "equity" a new series of legal principles, broader, of more modern hue, and of greater elasticity than the old ones, are developed side by side with their more rigid rivals, and are administered in different Courts of Justice by a new set of judicial officers and solely in reference to questions which fresh social facts have brought to the surface. This novel law-making authority encroaches more and more courageously on its antiquated predecessor, till finally it gets the upper hand, and is only arrested in its tendency to absorb the whole field of legislation by the apparition of a still more effective instrument—that of direct and conscious "Legislation."

From the time that a nation has acquired consistency enough to admit of a complete division of labour, the existence of a Profession wholly consecrated to the study and practice of the Law becomes one of the most momentous engines in the adaptation of Positive Law to national exigencies. No doubt the existence of such a Profession has, in some respects, a directly conservative bearing.

The habits of mind generated by a life-long devotion to the art of interpreting words used by others, and of straining the significance of particular instances so as to bring them into apparent harmony with recognised principles is, of itself, scarcely favourable to the development of a liberal disposition and intelligent political aspirations. A small and compact body of men, moreover, with minds better trained than those of the average members of the community, and directly interested in the maintenance of all the details of the system in learning which the best years of their life have been spent, are peculiarly exposed to the solicitations of indolence and political selfishness. The history of the English Bar up to the days of Romilly, Mackintosh, and Brougham, has been an unhappy illustration of the truth of these assertions.

Anomalous, however, as it may seem, the appearance of a Legal Profession is a necessary condition precedent to any large-minded reconstruction of the existing legal system. For the promotion of mutual understanding between the Bench and the Bar and among the members of the Bar, an accurate and unbending terminology is sure to be sought for, and to be more and more nearly approached. This itself converts the study of Law into a severe logical exercise, and predisposes the minds of the better class of students to scientific habits in the region of moral investigation. If the Law is in conflict with the moral requirements of the day, it will appear far more unmistakably to be so when it stands forth relieved from all complicity with the common moral sentiments, as colloquially expressed, and is arranged in the technical language generated among a narrow class of practitioners.

It may take long to close the gap between moral sentiments and legal axioms; it may be arduous to introduce piecemeal changes; it may involve a conflict with the united strength of a spirited Profession to introduce comprehensive changes; but when once a spirit of change has breathed upon a compactly organised legal system, the more completely that system is separated, through the attention for ages bestowed upon it by an exclusive learned Profession, from the language and common forms of ordinary social intercourse, the more unsparing will be the modifications it must finally undergo. The sagacious and almost revolutionary measures demanded by Bentham, and mostly carried out since his time, have been only rendered possible through the clear and isolated shape in which the whole legal system of England has stood apart from all other institutions in this country—moral, religious, and political. However, it must not be forgotten that a compact system of Law, cultivated by a close professional corporation, has at least the advantage of opposing a strong barrier to all inconsiderate changes, and of not taking the hue of each moral vagary as it comes uppermost in the country.

So much will suffice to show that one main instrument in developing Law, and thereby in supplying materials to the Science of Jurisprudence, is the rise of a Legal Profession. Briefly, the Science of Jurisprudence owes its growth to the mutual action and reaction of Positive Law and the facts of human life, as exhibited in the world constituted as it is. The more obvious intermediate instruments through which Positive Law is made to respond to the call of those facts of human life are, Judicial Interpretation operating by means (amongst others) of legal fictions, Courts of Equity, the rise of a Legal Profession, and direct Legislation.

CHAPTER III.

RELATION OF THE SCIENCE OF JURISPRUDENCE TO ALL OTHER SCIENCES.

A Science may be correctly described as "an organised body of permanent and universal facts, arranged in such a way as to exhibit their invariable relations to each other and to the whole body." It is now becoming a familiar idea that all the facts of the outer world, as well as all the facts of individual and of social human life, admit of being mapped out into different Sciences, however true it may be that some classes of facts have to wait longer than others for the process to be performed upon them. Of all classes of facts those appertaining to the life of man as a social being are the most complex, inasmuch as they include and presuppose all the rest, and they are the most reluctant to be brought into that clear and determinate relation to each other which the conception of a true Science demands. Nevertheless, certain of these classes of facts have already been presented in a strictly scientific form; such as those recognised by the Sciences of Political Economy, History, Social Ethics, and even General Politics. The slow progress of these branches of Science has been due, not more to the actual complexity and obscurity of the facts contemplated by them, than to the want of a discriminating and conscious logical power on the part of immature races, and to the slow and gradual way in which some important groups of social facts come to the surface. Thus in Political Economy, all the large department of the Science which treats of banks, of paper money, and even of rent and machinery, has no application whatever in a primitive, though partially civilised, community, such as Rome under the Kings, Greece under the Archons, and England in the time of the Heptarchy. The facts with which the full-grown Science deals have not yet made their appearance.

While, however, this last-mentioned obstacle to the progress of a Science is constantly and, as it were, spontaneously removing itself, the other obstacle, due to the obliquity and confusion of men's vision, is apt to be prolonged to a very late stage in the national life. The truly scientific habit of mind is so alien to the unanalysing, semi-conscious instinct by force of which the large mass of mankind must always do their work, and language is so constantly being reinforced from the common observations and feelings of the vulgar rather than from the keen and accurate conclusions of the Sage, that the separation of any one class of facts from all the rest is a matter of the greatest difficulty to inaugurate, and of lasting struggle to maintain. Furthermore, this provisional separation or isolation of social facts is always a violent, and, therefore, in some way, a false process. Each faculty of man is so controlled by all the rest, as well as so modified in its action and quality by the physical medium in which it works, that any hypothetical results drawn from contemplating it by itself must be peculiarly misleading. Even in a very primitive society there will be found present at once the germs of all the leading classes of social facts, hereafter to become the subject-matter of the several branches of Ethical and Political Science. In this is discovered the identity of the logical and historical methods in use for the investigation of all the facts of social life. The bare facts cannot be described, nor the terms in which that description is communicated adequately expounded, except by reference to the mode in which the facts have been historically evolved. On the other hand, the historical account of the generation of social facts can only be rendered interesting and intelligible by referring the process of such generation to the necessary action of the human mind working under special conditions, and in obedience to its own rules of action.

DEFINITION.—*The Science of Jurisprudence deals with the facts brought to light through the operation upon the fact of Law (considered as such, and neither as good nor bad) of all other facts whatsoever, including among these other facts the facts resulting in the creation, and expressing the historical and logical vicissitudes, of Law itself.*

It is quite impossible to contemplate Law as an isolated social phenomenon, standing alone among an indefinite number of other social phenomena. In no conceivable condition of mankind could it ever have stood alone. It is peculiarly the product of every social force existing at any moment in the community; it reacts back upon the social forces as being in itself the most potent force of all. Before a law attains its end through the processes of administration and interpretation it is directly qualified by every strong wave, and by all the multitudinous weaker waves, of thought and feeling by which, for the time, the community is swayed. The work of the Jurist is the evaluation and classification of these influences, so far as they react upon the pure fact of Law;

it is not for him to say what are the degree and mode of their operation at any particular epoch or in any particular country, nor how some kinds of Law are practically affected more than others. Such investigations are relegated to the historian, the statistician, the traveller, or the moral philosopher. The Jurist supplies each of these with the instruments for their investigations. He assists them in clearing the field from all irrelevant matter; he warns them against confusing the influence of what is partial and transitory with what is universal and everlasting; he teaches them how to lay hold, in Law itself, upon all that is essential to its very nature, and to suspend for a time all moral and political judgments with respect to its justice, its expediency, or its capacity of attaining its ends.

Professor Maine has rendered the greatest service to the Jurist in calling attention to the spontaneous modes in which Law gradually disengages itself, in primitive society, from a vague sentiment about the sacredness of customs, and of respect for a competent Authority publicly determining isolated questions of moral right or wrong. The growing fixity and distinctness which Law gradually assumes is only one of a large class of similar phenomena, which have the most complex modes of action and reaction upon one another. Thus the fact of individual Ownership— implying as it does a recognition, on the part of the whole community, of a person's claim to the peaceable retention of that of which he is in actual use, and next, of that of which he may at any moment wish to resume the use—must be treated as an organic element of social development, as well as a corollary from the other elements of Family Life and of the joint occupation of land which was undoubtedly bound up with that Life. So, likewise, this very fact of Family Life—implying as it does a steady recognition of the fixed relations of husband and wife, father and child, brother and sister, and of other bonds of consanguinity and affinity—is an independent mark of a growing sentiment of order and reciprocal duty, which, in conjunction with the fact of Ownership, leads on at once to the next and almost contemporaneous stage of Government and Law. Professor Maine has explained the formal creation of Government to have been due to the aggregation of families, coupled with the recognition of a Patriarchal Authority in one or some of them. This explanation is no doubt historically accurate; but the following account may appear, from a philosophical point of view, an indispensable complement to it.

An embryonic notion of man's true social nature has, by the supposition, been already developed through the facts of Ownership and Family Life. The maintenance of these great classes of facts implies the predominance of social control over individual caprice, and the subordination of the individual life to the ends of the social life, including in these ends the highest personal life of the individual himself as an integral member of the associated body. So soon as the bystanders learn to experience a shock of indignation or horror at an invasion of a customary claim of ownership or of the sanctity of the marriage-tie, and applaud the judgment of one who denounces the transgression, Government and Law have already begun. That the strongest and wisest (who, when the division of labour has advanced only a very little way, are likely to be one) should act as the permanent enunciators of the growing social Conscience; that they should be always ahead of the community in moral apprehension, but never very far ahead, and even generally very far behind certain individual persons in the community; that they should exhibit through their acts a constant personal struggle between their self-seeking tendencies and their prophetical and governmental functions; that in their conflicts with each other they should be ever turning to an ill account the influence they possess with the people, and that they should be supplanted from time to time by other more worthy and more conscientious exponents of the social aspirations; that, in default of such government being maintained, anarchy and barbarism instantly recur;—all this is strictly in accordance with anticipations based on the results of the best psychological and ethical inductions, as it also coincides in all respects with the actual facts.

Law, then, is the formal and outward expression of the moral order demanded by the joint spontaneous sentiments of a people and of its rulers. In order, however, to apprehend more precisely the relation of Law to all other classes of social phenomena, it is necessary to denote with greater particularity the stages travelled by a national community between the epoch at which the first moral crystallisation in the shapes of Ownership and Family Life is discovered and the epoch at which conscious Legislation and systematic Government begin. The union of families through natural, fictitious, and friendly ties, systems of village coproprietorship, the continuous satisfaction of a progressive tendency towards an effective division of labour, the necessities of self-defence and of the exercise of a rude Criminal Jurisdiction, are sufficient to account for the rudimentary forms of Government and Legislation which invariably characterise the lengthy period intervening between the epochs above noted. It is during this critical period that the most important Sources of Law, as it is afterwards truly developed, first make their appearance. It is then that the community is forming, in accordance with the physical and ethical conditions which envelope it and with its own historical antecedents, its habits of life, modes of thought, and peculiarities of sentiment, all of which combine with an indefinite number of other elements to make up what is called the national genius or character. As material expressions of such genius, certain customary forms and symbolic acts are reverentially preserved, quite as much from a sense of their antiquity and from the indefinite number of subtle associations linked with them, as from a belief in their utility or in the danger of admitting change. Furthermore, the authority of leaders of tried character and known desert serves to impress the moral maxims they enunciated with a stamp which, for ages to come, dispenses with all other more rational superscription. Lastly, the great similarity that marks all acts of violence in a society so uniform and so continuous begets a corresponding similarity in the modes of adjudicating upon them and of punishing transgressors.

All this time a number of concrete and complex institutions are assiduously taking their rise, supplementing the primary ones of Ownership and Family Life, and winning to themselves, like the symbolic acts aforesaid, the loyalty and reverence of successive generations. Such were the institution of the Roman "Familia" with all its offshoots, the "Feuds" of Middle-Age Europe, and the "Lex Mercatoria," (or " custom of merchants,") which has so profoundly modified the Positive Commercial Law of modern States. From this enumeration of the social elements which, in a progressive yet primitive community, are ever noiselessly making their way, it will be seen that there is contained in them, first of all, the main materials out of which a system of Formal and Positive Law will hereafter be built up; and secondly, a confession of the urgent need for such a Positive Legal System in order to prevent local order from degenerating into putrid corruption, to give uniformity and consistency to what is heterogeneous and scattered, and to substitute an effective national Sanction for the feeble and vacillating action of mere casual popular sentiment.

Thus everything will be prepared for the appearance of the scientific and conscious Legislator. Such a character will not be generally represented by a single man, as by a Solon, a Lycurgus, a Numa, or an Alfred, who were rather codifiers and reformers than original legislators, but in many men at once. Some of these men will be those who happen to be charged with the execution of the rude customary system of Law actually in force, and who, from contact with the real wants and modes of life of the people, being made practically aware of the insufficiency of the traditional system, will be the first to writhe under it. These men will spontaneously endeavour to amend that system by restrictive or extensive interpretation of written documents, by "fictions," by "equity," by inventing rules of orderly Procedure, and by gradually constructing an organised mode of mediation between general legal principles and the specialities of particular cases. At the same time other persons in public situations of authority and influence, as members of the governing body of the State, or of some out of several departments of that body, will also be daily confronted with the impotence of the mere accidental rules which have grown up through a series of irregular impulses, to determine the moral claims of citizens in all the multiplying intricacies of their family, industrial, and commercial relations. Conscious attention becomes fixed on the rules already in force; they are, partly, recognised and brought out to the light of day, and, possibly, couched for the first time in formal and unequivocal language; they are partly corrected, amended, and supplemented; they are partly abolished and a substitute found for them in new rules artificially prepared and systematically written down and published. At this epoch the stage of conscious legislation has been finally reached. It is then taken up by all the more advanced individuals in the community, who co-operate with the professional Legislator in laying bare abuses brought about through the operation of the judicial system, in inventing measures of reform, and, if the Legislator be indolent or incompetent, in employing such moral or physical pressure as may be at hand to force such measures upon him for immediate adoption.

From this brief review of the invariable phenomena that attend the development of Government and Law, however much the outward circumstances may differ from nation to nation, it will be apparent that the notion of Law itself, as the formal expression of moral order, overriding all the accidental deviations due to individual passion or caprice, is permanent throughout. It is, indeed, scarcely apprehended at first, except in the most tentative and desultory fashion; it continues for a long time only unconsciously grasped at, and, as it were, simulated in local institutions, ceremonies, symbolic forms, customs, and traditionary usages; it gradually becomes clearer and clearer, till at last it expresses itself distinctly and consciously to the whole community in the shape of "a series of formal commands of the Supreme

Political Authority, purporting to control the acts of all persons in the community."

So far as all the social facts above alluded to as operating on the complete development of Law become matters of strictly scientific investigation, as at this day they all are, the kind of relation which exists between the Science of Jurisprudence and all other Sciences is readily ascertained. The Science of Jurisprudence deals with the operation of all facts whatsoever, (and, pre-eminently among them, with all the complex facts which express the growth of human society,) upon the fact implied in the notion of Law elucidating itself ever more and more distinctly as a nation grows. If for the present purpose all the Sciences be classified as Physical, Psychological, Ethical, and Political, the relation between these and the Science of Jurisprudence will be at once deducible from the following considerations.

Every law strictly so called is in itself, and may easily be reduced to the form of, a command, purporting to control the acts of persons in the community. The acts which the command affects so to control may have reference in their immediate consequences to very different classes of Persons, as:—

(1.) To the persons publishing the command, as in the case of laws of treason, taxation, conscription or forced military service, judicial Procedure; (2.) to the agent himself who is directly addressed by the command, as in the case of laws forbidding suicide, sumptuary laws, and some sorts of sanitary laws; (3.) to a definite number of other persons, as in the large mass of all laws of Ownership, Contract, Personal Relationship, and Crimes; (4.) to an indefinite number of other persons, as in the case of laws generally forbidding Fraud and misrepresentation, public nuisances, blasphemous Libels, sedition, riot, and conspiracies of all sorts. It must be especially noted, that here only the immediate consequence of the act which the law affects to control is taken as the ground of classification, inasmuch as, in many or all of their secondary and ulterior consequences, the operation of each of these classes of acts upon the public well-being may be scarcely distinguishable.

Again, a further classification obviously suggests itself. One large class of acts which Law affects to control is directly and immediately concerned with visible and material *things*, detached portions of the medium by which *persons* are surrounded and in which they move and have their being. Such are the acts controlled by laws of Ownership, by large portions of laws of Contract and of laws of Civil Injuries and Crimes, as well as by certain portions of laws affecting Special Classes of Persons, of which last the rights and duties of trustees and of husband and wife in respect of material *things* is an instance. The other large class of acts which Law affects to control has no immediate reference to *things*, as is exemplified in the acts regulated by laws of service or hiring, of marriage, of slander and libel, of treason, and of personal injuries and crimes.

From this brief investigation it appears that all laws whatever admit of a twofold classification, based on the immediate consequences of the acts they affect to control. One mode of classification is determined by the quality of the *persons* involved in these consequences: the other mode is determined by the answer to the question whether a material *thing* is or is not looked upon as interposed between the act forbidden and its immediate consequences. All that has occupied so large and significant a space both in English and foreign Systems of Law with reference to the distinction between so-called *real* and *personal* rights, and the law of *persons* and *things*, has been due to an indistinct apprehension, groped after at the suggestion of a series of historical and practical necessities, of the validity of one or other of the two true modes of classification just indicated. The confusion has been all the greater from the lurking belief that somehow the several methods of classification can in the same legal system be carried out independently without interfering with one another. Thus, under the law of *persons*, in Roman law, *things* were supposed not to enter into consideration; while under the law of *things* the quality of the *persons* immediately affected by a trespass or by a breach of Contract was liable not to be brought into sufficient relief. The same confusion has communicated itself to all modern Systems of Law, though the practical necessities of daily life have restricted the field of its vicious operation.

From the above analysis it would appear that all the phenomena of Law, as they present themselves in a national society, may be distributed under three main heads, including severally :—

(1.) All the historical vicissitudes attending the formal communication of the will of the person or persons imposing the law.

[Under this head will be treated such matters as the history of the Growth of Law, the nature of its Sources, actual and possible modes of Legislation, the need and the modes of Interpretation, so far as the facts implied in the mention of any of these topics react upon the quality and operation of Law itself.]

(2.) An enumeration of the essential contents of any single law viewed as a command proceeding from a competent Authority and purporting to control the acts of persons in the community.

[Under this head a precise meaning is attached to such terms as "person," "acts," "commands," "control," and "political community." It is noted that variations in the meanings of these terms are brought about in two ways: first, by a change, due to national development, in the facts denoted by them, to a general recognition of which change a public appeal is made; secondly, by an arbitrary extension or restriction effected in the technical use of the term for merely logical purposes. Both these kinds of variations have a like effect on the operation of Law at the moment at which, in the course of actually administering it, the question arises whether an alleged command is or is not a true law.]

(3.) The logical arrangement or classification of all the particular and accidental materials of which all possible Systems of Law are composed.

[It has already been seen in what ways, among others, such a classification can be attempted. The founders of each System of Law, and each scientific Jurist, have hitherto contemplated a different arrangement. It has been suggested above that the most convenient mode to adopt is the one which serves the double purpose of starting directly from the complete definition of Law, and of keeping constantly in view the social purpose which all law-making, whether spontaneous or systematic, is intended to subserve. The immediate end of every law is to control the *acts* of *persons*; hence no simpler or more natural mode of distributing the materials of all possible legal systems can be arrived at than that of investigating the distinctive character of all the *acts* falling under the possible control of the Legislator. These *acts*—it has been seen—have generally a more direct bearing on some *person* or *persons* affected by them than on others. Furthermore, they affect the *person* who is the immediate object of them either with or without the interposition of a *thing* or detached portion of the material world. Hence the quality of the *persons* directly affected affords one basis of classification and the fact of the interposition or non-interposition of a *thing* between the agent and the *person* directly affected by the act affords another.]

The true functions of the Jurist in relation to all Sciences whatever are now coming gradually into view. It is the elaboration of these three divisions, dealing as they do with the whole range of legal phenomena, which is his appropriate work; and such elaboration implies the precise recognition of large classes of Physical, Psychological, Ethical, and Political facts.

Thus it is to *Physical* or to *Psychological Science* that the Jurist must recur when he is called upon to enumerate the characteristics of a " person," an " act," a " command," " will," and of the incidents implied in these names, as " birth," " death," " intention," " muscular action," " language," " time," and " space."

Ethical science, again, has a still profounder and less easily separable relation to the Science of Jurisprudence. The history of the growth of Law, and an account of its Sources, involve a recognition of some of the most embarrassing facts in the moral world. The obscure mental states which, in a highly organised society, become clearly determined into a sharp perception of right and wrong, justice and injustice, good and evil, and of all their several intermediate grades, have given rise to the bitterest and most irreconcilable conflicts which the tear-bedewed history of speculation presents. Either of the two main theories which have risen up again and again, enriching itself at each fresh Avatar with the latest achievements of its adversary, can account plausibly for all the most startling phenomena of the moral world; but neither of them alone, for all the more delicate ones, with such certitude as to merit the untarnished loyalty of speculative mankind.

It unfortunately happens that it is just with the epoch of man's history at which moral life throws out its earliest shoots, that the Jurist has pre-eminently to do. He is met face to face with customs, traditions, aspirations, sentiments, solemnities, of every degree of rationality and irrationality, as well as with occasional sparks of conscious direction and scientific prevision. And he desires to ascertain how all this mass of elements crystallised, in certain directions, into hard and formal Law. He is constantly tempted to cut the knot by resolving early Law either into nothing else than a body of more or less ingenious maxims, suggested by a keen sense of social expediency, or into the arbitrary dictates of an irresistible and irresponsible human authority, or into the mysterious promptings of some supernatural agency, providentially interposing in the affairs of men. Any of these theories is plausible, and will account for most of the facts, while none of them alone will account for all the facts. Thus the Jurist must, at the very outset of his work, have recourse to the teachings of a highly elaborated Ethical Science. It is this alone which can inform him what is the province of mere hope and fear as effective moral agents, how far the phenomena of Conscience are original or derivative, how far the education supplied by social intercourse, and by a growing experience of the order of the universe, creates faculties not existing before, or merely developes those already existing into their true and natural proportions by supplying them with their appropriate nourishment and functional activity.

The attention of the Jurist, thus directed to the facts implied in this primitive reaction between an individual and a social order, is not due merely to a frivolous spirit of historical curiosity or antiquarian research. The reaction itself, though changing its form, and ever growing less obscure and equivocal, is permanent and continuous through the whole history of a progressive national society. It is impossible to understand the intrinsic nature of Law, and to ascertain its relation to all other social facts, without having a firm hold on the main facts which it is the special province of the ethical enquirer to elucidate. The recurrent phenomena designated under such expressions as "equity," "fictions," "laws of nature," "law the perfection of reason," "natural justice," and the like, are unmistakable tokens of the incessant operation of ethical facts upon systems of Positive Law, and of the universal recognition of the truth of such operation.

Nor is it merely in the creation and amendment of formal Law that purely ethical facts tell so widely. No law can be administered in practice, even in a single case, unless the language of the law is at least believed to be clear, and the act forbidden by the law believed or alleged to have been done by the person who is on the point of being visited with the physical penalty. But in the interpretation of language all kinds of vague moral sentiments intrude themselves, which no amount of logical precautions suffice entirely to repel. It is only by estimating strictly the mode in which these sentiments produce their influence, whether through the minds of judges, jurymen, advocates, the public, or the Legislature, that language can be sufficiently fenced round by grammatical and other limitations in such a way as to reduce to the smallest possible amount variations in its meaning as it passes from the enacting to the administering body of persons.

In the interpretation of men's acts, again, however clearly a forbidden act may be denoted by the language of a law, a great amount of vacillation is still inevitable. This is due, partly to the ethical predisposition of the persons administering the law, partly to the ethical complications and individuality of every special case in which an infringement of the law is alleged to have taken place. The offence of killing a man in order to become the owner of what belongs to him may be taken as a specimen of acts forbidden by every system of Positive Law, and condemned by the moral sentiments of even the most rudimentary societies. But the strength of the indignation felt at different epochs of the national life, and by different persons living at the same epoch, admits of considerable variation. This becomes plain if the facts be supposed to be of a slightly more complicated character, as, where the person killed is one who has already on a former occasion severely injured the person who kills him, or where the *thing* on account of which the offence is committed has been previously abstracted from the person who now seeks to repossess himself of it, or where the person killed is notoriously a worthless person of whom a society is well quit. In all these cases individual persons, in accordance with their whole moral proclivities, attempt to strain the interpretation of the actual facts one way or the other, so as to make them accord with or be discrepant from those contemplated by the law in question.

But, apart from all accidental moral specialities in judges and jurymen and other persons concerned in administering the Law, the actual character of men's acts is oftentimes so composite and ambiguous in itself, or so open to misconstruction through the backwardness of the analytical branch of Ethical Science, or so difficult to be explained, that the same outward circumstances of one and the same complex act may involve an indefinite number of grades of legal liability. In other words, the act alleged to have been committed may be either an act forbidden by a law, or an indefinite number of other and like acts not so forbidden. This is manifest, for instance, in such transparent cases as those in which the state of the agent's mind in respect of Will and Intention calls for special discriminating power. Such are cases involving a consideration of the hypothetical presence of such circumstances as *ignorance, negligence, accident, mistake, fraud, malice, infancy,* and *lunacy.* In the investigation, on any particular occasion, of all the circumstances surrounding an act alleged to be one forbidden by Law, the facts of Ethical as well as of Physical and Psychological Science will all come on for recognition at once. The English law of murder, as laid down by all the judges in McNaughten's case, goes so far as to hold a man guilty of the crime of murder if it be proved that he knew at the time of the act that he was doing something morally *wrong*, even though, owing to inordinate ignorance or mental derangement, he believed the act of murder not to be forbidden by Law. So, likewise, the English Law shows peculiar favour to a Will made during a lucid interval by a person at other times seriously deranged in mind, if a recognition of the moral claims of relations or benefactors appear on the face of it. These are extreme instances of the general way in which the Administrators of Law, in order to discover whether or not an act is forbidden by Law, are compelled to enter upon grave ethical as well as physical and psychological enquiries. It is thus that a very backward condition of Ethical Science, especially on its analytical side, or a great ignorance of the results really attained, or a habit of confusing ethical with all other phenomena, such as is universal in all very early societies, where the mental elements and accompaniments of a complete act are depressed into comparative insignificance, reacts most prejudicially on the effectual operation of Law in the attainment of its ends.

There remains *Political Science*, in the largest sense of the expression, and as comprehending the Sciences of *Social Ethics*, *Political Economy*, *Legislation*, and *Government* in the narrower sense of the term.

It is a merely arbitrary and unreal mode of division to separate the Sciences of *Ethics* and *Social Ethics*. No ethical phenomena whatever can be exhibited out of a social condition, and it is solely through the development and organisation of this condition that any degree of ethical perfection in individual persons is attainable. On the other hand, the purpose of social life must ultimately be nothing else than the highest degree of culture and moral dignity of the individual elements out of which a social community is constituted. Nevertheless there may be a certain convenience in treating the two aspects of Ethics each independently of the other, according as attention is primarily fixed on the moral history, discipline, and attainments of the individual citizen, or upon those of the mass of individual citizens organised into a National Community. The latter branch of enquiry is the appropriate topic of the Science of Social Ethics, which is the leading department of the general Science of Politics. It is impossible to exaggerate the claims that Social Ethics have on the attention of the Jurist. The rudimentary appearance of Law at the first in a primitive society, the true nature of Law as an engine and symptom of national progress, the history of Law in all its stages up to that of its complete and self-conscious separation from all alien matter, the true and sole subject-matter with which Law can effectually deal, the vicissitudes due to varying fashions of administering and interpreting laws,—these all demand for their investigation a theory of Society at once to precede, accompany, and direct the whole course of the enquiry.

No one pretends to say, nowadays, that Law, in the shape of a body of commands, emanating from one class of persons however powerful, and addressed to other classes however weak, is the sole cause and creator of human Society. Scarcely anyone, again, is sanguine enough to believe that a time can ever come when the reserved physical force and expressed moral cogency of Law can be entirely dispensed with. Between the epoch at which there is little Law because men are so anarchical and the epoch when there is also little because men have become habituated to govern themselves, there is incessantly going on an interaction between the moral exigencies and aspirations of men on the one hand and the positive laws which affect to control their acts on the other. The latter are naturally and necessarily the outcome of the former, or rather of some past, if not present, condition of the former, though these operate back again as most powerful reagents. It is a critical problem for every Community to determine how the battle at every moment shall be fought out, inasmuch as there are periods when Law is the main civilising influence, and others when it is solely a retarding and depressing one. A Politician is never more wisely occupied than when he is learning to master the conditions of the political problem as presented in his own time, and to perceive whether, or at what points, the stringent force of Law needs to be tightened or relaxed. For the actual and reciprocal influences on each other of legal and moral forces generally, the Politician will be compelled to resort for aid to the Jurist, who, in turn, must have recourse to the teachings of the Science of Social Ethics.

The Science of *Political Economy* is only so far of interest to the Jurist as it compendiously embraces a review of all the industrial and mechanical agencies for facilitating which, in any given society, laws may be said chiefly to exist. Laws of Ownership, of Contract, of Civil Injuries, and of Crimes, can hardly be so much as understood, unless the social facts on which they are built are first of all recognised and catalogued. If the Science of Social Ethics touches more nearly the facts upon which " Laws directly relating to the Constitution of the State," and those "affecting Special Classes of Persons," repose, so does the Science of Political Economy deal with the facts more particularly concerned in the other leading branches of every system of Positive Law. Inasmuch, then, as the classification of the subject-matter of all possible laws has been seen to be one main function of the Jurist, the true ground of classification must be sought here, as elsewhere, in the actual nature of the matter classified, and hence, more particularly in the special Science the sole purpose of which is to investigate it.

The Science of *Legislation*, or, according to the meaning which will be here consistently adhered to, of the technical and formal publication of Law with a view to its most effectively attaining its ends, has so close a relation to Jurisprudence proper that the two Sciences have been constantly confounded together. Bentham, who was at once practical Politician, Scientific Legislator, and Jurist, and kept perpetually shifting from one of these capacities to another, is accountable for the confusion which has beset all his followers. Even Mr. Austin is not always consistent with himself in distinguishing between the Science of Legislation in the above sense and that of general Politics. While, however, the Jurist maintains unimpaired the integrity of his own Science as dealing with nothing but what is permanent and universal in the facts making up the whole phenomenon of Law, he will recognise that, among such facts, those due to different modes of formally publishing Law are some of the most influential. He will be induced, then, to investigate, in unison with the scientific Legislator, what are the main possible modes of publishing Law in such a way as to render it most secure of attaining its own appropriate ends. Judicial Legislation of all sorts, operating through the exposition of Unwritten rules, through the extensive or restrictive interpretation of Written rules, through Equity, legal Fictions, the adoption of Customs, the construction of rules of Practice, the naturalisation of Foreign Law, or the respect entertained for the opinion of the learned; statutory Legislation; systematic and comprehensive rebuilding of the whole legal system by what is called Codification,—all these modes of Legislation the Jurist will keenly scrutinise, in order to apprehend and estimate their several degrees of possible influence upon the attainment by Law of its appropriate ends. The Jurist will then be in a position to offer advice to the scientific Legislator how, in any given age or condition of Society, to clothe the policy resolved upon by the Statesman with that adequate legal dress which is most likely to secure for it practical sway throughout the length and breadth of the Community.

Lastly, the Science of *Government* in the narrower sense of the method of consciously determining men, through the use of certain kinds of influence, to seek, everyone, his own proper good and the proper good of all, cannot be foreign to the mind of the Jurist. In estimating the true nature and purpose of "Laws of Procedure" and of that large class of laws which falls under the head of "Laws directly relating to the Constitution of the State," attention must constantly be paid to the kinds of judicial and ministerial mechanism which the Science of Government treats of. The relative political value of what have been called the "litigious" and the "inquisitorial" modes of Procedure is not a question for the Jurist as such. But, in order to apprehend the true character of all the possible systems of Procedure which may chance to be the basis of laws of Procedure in different countries, an acute perception of the nature of those opposed modes, and of the other intermediate modes compounded of them in different measures, is indispensable. The same is the case with the possible functions of such officers of the Executive as Magistrates, Secretaries of State, Military officers, Revenue and Police officers, and other Government agents. A clear knowledge of the situation, responsibilities, and general political relations of all such persons is essential to the Jurist who would classify the laws directly implying a recognition of the existence of such persons, and who would note the amount of possible influence upon the operation of all Law whatever which is due to that existence.

CHAPTER IV.

MATERIALS OR CONTENTS OF THE SCIENCE OF JURISPRUDENCE.

The Science of Jurisprudence has for its purpose the investigation of all the possible modes in which the operation of Law is qualified by the existence of all the other facts which belong to the material or the moral Universe. This general description of the territory occupied by the present Science was assumed in the last chapter with the view of enforcing the plenary recognition of all those facts before attempting to ascertain in detail their bearing upon the fact of Law. It was also desirable to warn the juridical student that the fact of Law is so intimately interwoven in the way of cause and effect with the most apparently alien regions of human life and interest, that nothing can save him from endless embarrassments and practical errors but a clear mapping out, at the very threshold of the enquiry, of the provinces of the several Sciences which border on the Science of Jurisprudence. It is not, indeed, all the facts comprehended in Physical, Psychological, Ethical, and Political science that bear upon the fact of Law, or, at least, that can be obviously and immediately shown to do so. But the facts of those Sciences which do so bear upon the fact of Law cannot be understood, or separated from that upon which they operate, without a mastery of the facts as forming parts of organic wholes.

The purpose of the present chapter is to look at the

Science of Jurisprudence on the inside, as it were, rather than on the outside; to see of what facts it takes cognisance, rather than to expel and keep at a distance those which do not concern it. Of course in doing the first part of the work,—that of pointing out how far all other Sciences are distinguishable from that of Jurisprudence,—the second part, treating of the facts which alone are relevant to that Science, has been implicitly involved. However, by way of introduction to the detailed analysis which will form the bulk of this treatise, what has been hitherto suggested only implicitly must now be described with all possible explicitness.

There are two broad and universal aspects in which the fact of Law presents itself. There is, first, its historical generation as a political or ethical phenomenon, so far as Law has grown up in the midst of a people as the formal expression of the immutable order which invariably characterises a National Society in every one of its stages. There are, again, its formal modifications, whether as exhibited in the degrees of facility with which it attains its practical purpose, or in the several and different kinds of subject-matter with which it, from time to time, affects to deal.

The actual System of Law, then, in any National Society whatever, must needs surrender itself to an analysis attempting to distinguish these different features. In each such Society the fact of Law has originated in and through a distinct process of generation admitting of being brought to the light of day by historical, logical, psychological, or purely physical methods of investigation. In each such Society, again, and at any given epoch, the system of Positive Law then and there existing admits of more or less exact and elaborate distribution into compartments in view of the various purposes the System has to serve, that is, according to the various kinds of acts it affects to control. The System, moreover, effects those purposes with different degrees of precision according to the special modes in which it happens to be published to the people, and to the logical instrumentality ready to the hands of those whose function it is to interpret and administer the System.

Applying, then, this analytical process to any particular System of Law at any particular epoch, the results will fall under the following heads :—

 (1.) General account of the historical and logical genesis of the fact of Law as appearing in the midst of the National Society in question.

 (2.) A classified exhibition of all the actual laws composing the System; such classification being instituted either on the basis of the varying nature of the acts the laws affect to control, or upon some other basis.

 (3.) An enumeration of the several material modes through which the whole System of Law is published to the people, and of the logical provisions actually in use for the purpose of securing an accurate Interpretation of the Law.

Now it is by lifting this process out of its narrow and partial application to a particular System of Law at a particular epoch into its universal application to all Systems of Law whatsoever at all epochs that the work of the Jurist consists. It is by a process of rigid induction, founded on the particular examination of a variety of Legal Systems, as well as on the premises supplied by a number of related Sciences, that the Jurist finally obtains his great skeleton-grammar of Law into which the flesh, blood, arteries, veins, and nerves of every fresh System of Law must necessarily adapt themselves. He will so have ready to his hand an universal standard by which to test the formal and material completeness, the efficiency and the "*elegancy*," of every System of Law which happens to come under his notice; and, furthermore, to pave the way for that closer approximation, in form at least, between the Legal Systems of different nations on which a more frequent social and commercial intercourse, as well as a greater intimacy in public relations between those nations, hangs suspended.

The critical stage, then, in the construction of a Science of Jurisprudence is that of generalisation from the particular results obtained as above. Out of all the results which are presented by an indefinite number of particular systems and of particular epochs, those results have to be selected which are equally true for all systems and for all epochs. Thus the results selected will be more multifarious than those given by the examination of any one system by itself, but far less so and far simpler than the aggregate amount of the results obtainable by the examination of a number of systems in succession. The process of generalisation is especially simplified by a method similar to that in use in philological studies; that of evaluating separately the essentially fixed elements and the principles of variation in the number and nature of those elements. In this way the whole process by which the materials of the Science of Jurisprudence are finally brought into view may be regarded as of a two-fold nature, that is, at once *statical* and *dynamical*. The *statical* view determines what are the permanent and universal elements distributed as above, which characterise the fact of Law, wherever existing and at whatever time.

The *dynamical* view determines the nature, direction, and rate of change introduced into those elements, both through the mere passage of Time and through an enlargement of the purely National Conception in respect of Space.

Thus, on the completion both of the *statical* and the *dynamical* process, a true and finished system of Jurisprudence might be distributed into the following departments:—

I. A description of the original fact of Law in itself, an account of the historical and logical genesis of that fact, and an explanation of all the leading terms essentially involved in the meaning of the term "Law."

II. An investigation of all the possible *Sources* of Law (or immediate modes by which actual laws are or may be created), and of the process of *Interpretation* as severally modifying the operation and nature of Law.

III. A classificatory arrangement of the contents of all possible systems of Positive Law, whether on the basis of —(1.) the social purposes Law is destined to serve; or (2.) the particular benefits to private persons it affects to communicate; or (3.) the acts of private persons it affects to control; or upon some other basis. These several bases, namely, that according to the political object of laws, that according to Rights, and that according to Duties, may be combined in the same system of arrangement, one leading the way, and the remaining two subordinating themselves to the dominant one.

IV. An investigation of theories of variation in the quality, number, and mutual relations of all the above elements, whether such variation operates in time or in space.

It need scarcely be noticed, that where such words as

" possible " or " possibility " are used, or permanence and universality are claimed for any juridical phenomenon, nothing of a more absolute nature is asserted in favour of the Science of Jurisprudence than belongs to all other Sciences. The materials of this Science are wholly relative to the nature of man and to the constitution of the universe of which he is a part, and only to the extent to which the facts of that nature and of that constitution have been hitherto apprehended can permanence and universality be predicated of them. If these facts, in the march of ages, undergo any actual change, or if further experience and observation discover them to be less permanent and universal, the conclusions deduced from them will have to undergo a proportionate correction and adaptation. In the meantime it is sufficient to notice that during the whole period over which the history of Law, as derived even from its most antique monuments, extends, the facts of the Sciences, Physical, Psychological, Ethical, and Political, on which the facts of Law hinge, have either remained identically the same, or have changed according to fixed and generally ascertained dynamical principles. The same is true as observation has extended over space, and takes in societies of every degree of development.

It is true, nevertheless, that looking at the whole history of Law, there do appear to have been occasional breaks in the continuity of that history, which have been due to widely operating social causes of a nature more or less apparently spasmodic, and, owing to the brevity of the annals of human progress, tabulated in the form of rules. Instances of such startling social causes are the general abolition of Slavery and the growth of what is called " International Law." The effect of the first of these facts has been to clear the conception of a legal Person as opposed to a Thing, from all the ambiguities which attached to that conception so long as human beings were, either for all legal purposes, or for many and for the most momentous purposes, treated exactly as portions of the material world. The modern notion of a Person, for all legal purposes whatsoever, precisely coincides, both inclusively and exclusively, with that of a human being regarded as a subject-member of a Political Community.

Again : the incessant intercourse between modern States and the growth of humane ideas in respect of warfare and of international competition, has slowly introduced, for the purpose of controlling the acts of national Governments, an entirely novel Code of practical regulations closely analogous to a System of Positive Law. Some eminent writers, indeed, have rather insisted on the analogy of this Code to a body of mere moral prescriptions; but this analogy is far less close and real than the other one, inasmuch as the moral duties of States towards each other reach infinitely further than can or ought to be attempted by the most beneficial International Code.

Furthermore, the way in which such a Code has in fact grown up, the form in which it is couched, the methods of its Interpretation, and every other feature short of that of a Political Authority competent to enforce it, bear the closest possible resemblance to the phenomena of Positive Law. International "Persons," that is States, are a purely analogical development of the Persons known to systems of National or so-called Municipal Law. The Sources, however, from which maxims and institutions of International Law have emerged, are more vague, multifarious, and due to the convergence of different series of accidental, of moral, or of political sentiments and events than has generally been the case even with the Sources of National Law.

The application of the Sanction, again, is uncertain, and proceeds from an Authority up to the present day in the highest degree indeterminate, and such as at all times will be something less precise than that which is denominated a "Supreme Political Authority." But all these varying and more complex circumstances indicate nothing else than a growth in the materials of Jurisprudence, proportionate in its suddenness or in its graduation to the nature of the facts attending the social development of civilised mankind. When once these circumstances have been clearly and finally apprehended, they admit of being as exactly catalogued and classified, and as severely submitted to logical processes for practical use, as do all the simpler elements of systems of National Law. Whatever superior difficulties remain in the former case are due, not to the nature of the rules established or to any special perplexities in the way of their application, but to the doubt clinging to all Law in its earlier stages, as to whether, in any given case, there is any rule at all. Among other expedients for the removal of this class of difficulties, the most hopeful ones are to be sought in a multiplication of International Courts, each employing a similar Procedure, and each recognising the authority of all the rest; and in a comprehensive International Code, deriving effective support from the joint and truly sympathetic efforts of all existing States.

The abolition of Slavery and the growth of the sentiments expressed in International Law have been selected as instances of wide-spreading social causes affecting the fortunes of Jurisprudence, which, through their exceptional nature and their momentous magnitude, have no exact parallel in the past, and scarcely admit of repetition in the future. They may be said to have produced, as they were themselves the more gradual product of, a reaction of men's social sentiments, which has manifested itself in an entirely reconstructed notion of legal Persons, Rights, and Duties as well as of Law in itself. The actual mode in which these isolated causes have severally operated, and must yet operate, comes under the last of the above departments,—that dealing with theories of variation in the elements of Juridical Science. Under the same head, also, come all the more orderly and gradually manifested causes of variation, such as the improvement in the arts of human life and the progress of inventions; the growth of commercial credit; the increasing facilities and novel modes of locomotion by land and sea; and an increasingly developed sagacity in constructing and directing the mechanism of Government.

It is under the first of the above-mentioned heads (I.) that are contained all such speculations as those which have been adumbrated in the last two chapters as having for their purpose the linking together of the social with an unsocial state of humanity. The history of Primitive Law is the only unfailing key to the logical nature of Law in itself, and hence all enquiries into the historical and logical genesis of Law do in fact resolve themselves into one identical process. On the completion of this process the fact of Law will stand out as clearly distinguishable from all competing facts, and the token of the occupation of this distinct standing-ground will be a list of Definitions of all the leading terms implicitly or explicitly involved in the use of the term Law. The terms defined will be such universal ones as *Person, Thing, Fact, Act, Event, Inten-*

tion, *Ignorance*, *Negligence*, *Accident*, *Fraud*, *Malice*, and the like, some or all of which the conception of Law in its most rudimentary form carries with it, and the precise import of which no ulterior refinements in the form or material of Law can modify in the minutest degree. A sharp and clear intuition of the real meaning of terms of this nature is indispensable as an introduction to the treatment of all further juridical phenomena. Such an intuition, moreover, when transmuted into a sort of legal conscience, is the surest bulwark for the practitioner against fluctuations, as it is also a main and continuing help for all those who would systematise or codify a body of Law so as to preserve organic unity in the tumultuous press of the most heterogeneous details. Thus one leading topic of a systematic exhibition of the contents of the Science of Jurisprudence will appear under the head " Definition of Leading Terms."

So soon as Law exists at all in a National Community, it instantly begins to undergo a series of changes determined by the special physical, psychological, ethical, and political circumstances, in the midst of which its race happens to be run. These changes, as has been already hinted, reflect themselves in the actual history and form of Law on three of its essential sides. These three essential sides or aspects of Law are—(1.) The immediate modes by which it travels out of obscurity into consciously recognised existence, that is, its so-called *Sources*. (2.) The processes by which the general language of Law is explained and limited, so as to make it correspond with and cover a particular set of facts, that is, *Processes of Interpretation*. And (3.) the material topics which any given body of Law affects to handle, that is, its *Subject-matter* or *Purposes*.

E

CHAPTER V.

ON THE SOURCES OF LAW, AND THE INTERPRETATION OF LAW.

THERE are many reasons why it is expedient to consider the Sources and the modes of Interpretation of Law together instead of apart. The main difficulties of Interpretation owe their origin to the obscure and uncertain way in which the large bulk of every system of Law has come into being. It is mainly through an investigation of the historical genesis of particular laws that the meaning and purport of those laws must be sought. It is only through the practical necessity of Interpretation that it becomes of supreme importance to trace the early beginnings of particular laws. Thus any separation of one topic from the other is in the highest degree artificial and unnatural. By treating the two together, and thus making each throw light on the other, all confusion of the two topics will best be avoided, and the true place of each in the Science of Jurisprudence indisputably ascertained.

The expression "Sources (*Quellen, Fontes*) of Law," though in habitual use, is founded on the loosest of metaphors, and is, in a high degree, equivocal and vague. The phrase may be applied to express the original ethical circumstances giving birth to certain classes of laws, as, for instance—(1.) an instinctive sense of national self-preservation; (2.) a moral aspiration after a loftier civic life and a reconciliation of the claims of freedom and progress with those of stability and order; or (3.) a still more advanced demand for a corporate or truly national life, in which each individual citizen surrenders himself unreservedly to the service of the whole, and from the whole recovers his own individuality again infinitely enriched and intensified. These several and distinct mental conditions undoubtedly give rise in turn to different parts of every legal system, and so far might be correctly termed Sources of Law. But these operations are too obscure and commingled with each other, as well as with rival influences, to be used for scientific purposes with the precision such purposes require. Hence the only resource is to look for the more easily recognisable complex facts, or classes of complex facts, which become the proximate causes of different parts of the legal system. Such causes are—(1.) the *spontaneous practice* of certain habits of action towards each other on the part of some or all classes of the population ; (2.) *legislation*, more or less systematic, whether conscious or unconscious, whether written or oral, whether directly proceeding from the Supreme Political Authority or only indirectly so proceeding through the interposition of the Administrators of the Law, as these do their best to wrest its language and its forms to purposes conceived to be beneficial. But even this distribution of the Sources of Law into spontaneous and systematic is rough and unsatisfactory, inasmuch as the most systematic legislation is determined in the long run solely by the deep-laid, subtle, and innumerable tendencies of the whole population, both governing and governed ; and the most rational and universal customs can only attain to the cogent qualities of pure Law when the Supreme Political Authority has, by public recognition, stamped them as universally binding. Thus, in order to attach any practical value to the use of the phrase "Sources of Law," the term "Source" must be taken to mean nothing more than the *immediate group of circumstances through which a legal rule acquires its essential character as such.*

All the possible Sources of Law, as understood in this last sense, may be distributed as follows:—

I. *Judicial legislation,* conscious or unconscious, through

(1.) Extensive or restrictive Interpretation of written monuments of Law, whether existing or obsolete.

(2.) Equity, in the English and the Roman sense.

(3.) The amendment of old Law through the device of Legal Fictions.

(4.) The recognition and adoption of Customs.

(5.) The incorporation of portions or the whole of foreign systems of Law.

(6.) The giving validity to a traditional and generally unpublished collection of unwritten usages as expressed in concrete institutions, popular maxims, and habits of legal thinking and of interpreting language (English Common Law).

(7.) The framing of rules of Procedure.

(8.) Deference to the formulated opinions of authoritative jurisconsults, practitioners, text-book-writers, and commentators.

(9.) The compression of a long train of isolated decisions on particular combinations of facts into the form of a universal rule of Law.

(10.) Direct legislation, under the cloak of conforming to a so-called "Law of Nature," "Natural Reason," "Natural Justice," "Common Sense," or "General Utility."

II. *Statutory Legislation*, or direct changes consciously introduced into the existing legal system by the Supreme Political Authority.

III. *Statutory Legislation* through the medium of subordinate Legislatures of all sorts.

IV. *Codification*, or the conscious reconstruction of the whole existing legal system into a completely organised body of written Law, statutory legislation coming in to fill up existing gaps, and all other generative Sources of Law being excluded from further operation.

V. *Scientific reflection on the Nature of Law.*

Before dwelling particularly on the nature of these several Sources of Law, it will be convenient to interpolate some remarks on the theory of Interpretation. It matters nothing whatever to the real validity of a legal rule itself where it is to be found, with what ease or difficulty a knowledge of it can be arrived at, or whether the language in which it is conveyed happens to be unmistakable or ambiguous. The force and nature of the rule itself are quite independent of all the obstacles that may stand in the way of its being clearly disclosed and enunciated. So soon as it is finally brought to light it stands forth as a clear command, addressed to one or more or all persons in the Community, and directing or forbidding them to do certain acts. Thus the nature of the actual Source of the Law, to whichever of the above classes it properly belongs, in no way affects the quality or force of the Law when it has been determinately evolved for the purpose of immediate application. Nevertheless, inasmuch as between the moment of a law having been determined upon by the Legislator and that other moment of its final public recognition by a competent Judicial Authority, the law must needs have passed through the transitional condition of being effectually published, the mode of that publication does in point of fact very much colour and infect the purity and integrity of the law as originally conceived. Thus it comes about that the imperfection of the existing means of expression and the rude modes of communication between man and man as yet known to be possible, do by qualifying each law in itself and making it likely or certain to undergo a more or less perceptible variation in the course of actually being applied in practice, become some of the chief facts which are the appropriate materials of the Science of Jurisprudence.

Did legislators always interpret and apply their own laws in person, or were the executive judicial authorities they depute in perfect sympathy of mind and will with themselves or absolutely subservient to them, and were written or spoken language infinitely more potent, exact, and pliable than has ever yet been imagined, it is possible that Jurists might concern themselves little with the Sources of Law. But so far are legislators from interpreting and applying their own laws, that the large bulk of these laws are made in one generation and applied in numberless succeeding ones. Immense masses of Law, too, in every country, have never been under the distinct contemplation of any legislators at all, but have owed their being to some one or more of the Sources above enumerated other than those of Statutory Legislation and Codification, being only fictitiously imputed to the legislator of the day because with him rests the power of changing, repealing, ignoring, or enforcing them. So far, again, are Judges from being at one in mind and will with Legislators, that nothing is more noticeable in the general history of Law than the constant political struggle going on between the Judge, who is brought into immediate contact with a law in its practical application to a real set of concrete facts, and the Legislator, who only contemplates the concurrence of such a set of facts as a distant probability or possibility.

Lastly, as to the infirmities attaching to all methods of oral or written communication, the commonest experience teaches that there is scarcely a single word, still less any assemblage of words, which conveys precisely the same meaning to one mind that it does to another. When to this are added the changing significance of words as a nation progresses, the differing meanings of the same word in different parts of a country and among different classes of persons, and the very general language in which a command intended to bear reference to a large number of diversified facts needs to be couched, it can be no matter of surprise that the inherent difficulties of language are among the most insuperable of the barriers in the way of the Legislator's securing for his laws an infallible interpretation on the part of the Judge. The occasion on which the importance and difficulty of legal interpretation generally present themselves is that at which a Judge is called upon to pronounce whether or not an act, alleged to have been done by a determinate person, is or is not one of a class of acts forbidden by some rule of Law. Of course this enquiry may be anticipated by means of consultation with a private legal practitioner, who will have the question put before him in exactly similar terms, though it might be while the act was still undone. The simplest case is where there exists a distinct written rule forbidding in terms the particular act which is the subject of investigation. The next in simplicity is where there is a written rule forbidding all acts of the class or kind to which the present act belongs,—that is, all acts having certain common marks or signs which admit of their being included under a common name, and which marks or signs the present act has. To determine what are the true marks or signs which, in the mind of the Legislator, were really those forming the foundation for the common name for all those acts, and to discern whether these marks or signs are or are not to be discovered in the act under investigation, is the part of the Legal Interpreter, and may call for the highest exercise of logical skill. A corresponding sort and degree of logical skill is needed in the Legislator, to enable him to select, in the composition of his classes or general names, such marks and signs as shall best secure the inclusion of all acts he wishes to forbid and the exclusion of all he is willing to allow.

Thus Written Laws depend for their special value, that is, for the possibility of their being exactly apprehended with the least shade of variation on different occasions, on the logical skill of the Judicial Interpreter and the Legislator together. In proportion to the excellent technical construction of such laws does the Legislator control and restrict the Judge, and repel to the uttermost all the influences of judicial eccentricity, passion, or caprice. The main dangers to be provided against, as has been already indicated, are those due to the inevitable flux of meaning in single terms and to the ambiguities always likely to attach to composite sentences. Could the words of which every Written Law is composed acquire and retain a rigid fixity of meaning, so as not to admit a hair's breadth of change in passing from the Legislator to the Judge and from one Judge to another, and could

written sentences be so constructed as to reproduce the
exact intent of the Legislator without leaving any opening
for a twofold interpretation, the characteristic advantages
of Written Law would then be at their highest. It is
possible, indeed, that at some future period legal terms
may acquire something of this fixity of meaning, for the
accomplishment of which end a highly educated and
specially trained Bar and Bench are indispensable conditions. It is also possible that the art of precisely expressing in written sentences, all and no more than all, of
what is intended to be conveyed will hereafter reach a
pitch of perfection which it certainly does not possess at
present. This attainment of fixity of meaning in legal
terms and a corresponding development of the art of accurate expression are presupposed in, as they would be specially promoted by, all attempts to codify a body of Law.

In the meantime it may be assumed that terms used
by Lawgivers have at present, and at all former periods,
little of the stability of meaning here supposed, and that
the art of expression is in a very imperfect state. The
next case, then, that presents itself, on enquiry being made
by the Judge or the practitioner as to the conjectural
existence of a rule of Law forbidding a given act, is the
discovery of a practical persuasion on the part of competent authorities that some such rule exists, though it has
never been reduced to distinct outward form and shape.
The exact terms and extent of the rule in question might
in such a case have to be gathered, according to some
recognised mode of Interpretation, out of a number of
promiscuous but carefully defined sources. The evolution of the rule would then demand two distinct operations: first, the determination of the exact quarters in

which it is to be looked for; and, secondly, the process of its extraction from the quarters prescribed. In England the two main Sources of so-called " Unwritten Law," have been—(1.) legal or logical maxims and canons handed down by word of mouth from one generation of lawyers to another; and (2.) past judicial decisions upon special matters of fact brought into controversy, and which decisions either expressly declare or manifestly imply the existence of some determinate legal rule. Law, extricated out of these decisions, becomes what is called in England " Case Law." It is obvious that in order to elucidate the lurking rule, if any, it may be necessary to investigate the history, not only of the decision made in one Action at Law, but of those made in many. For it can only be by determining how far a modification of the facts induced a corresponding alteration in the decision, that the real principle or ground (called the *ratio decidendi*), which presumedly underlies the whole line of decisions, can be arrived at.

It might reasonably be supposed that if a sufficient number of cases involving very trifling variations of fact were examined and compared, and if they had each been properly decided in conformity with the true state of the Law, it would be possible thus to attain to a more exhaustive and discriminating knowledge of the general rule expressing that state of the Law than even were the rule written formally in a Statute or a Code. This might be so on the supposition that the number of cases exemplifying the rule, with all its attending limitations, were sufficiently numerous and varied; that the reports of the cases were accurate, unbroken, and readily accessible; and that it were easy or possible to distinguish infallibly between a case rightly and one wrongly decided according to the true rule of Law, assuming such a Law to exist. By collating these remarks upon the mode of extracting a rule of Law from an unwritten Source with what was said above about the obstacles in the way of apprehending the fixed meaning of a rule of Law formally written in a Statute or a Code, the relative values of these two leading Sources of Law can be easily understood. These values will be seen to turn very much on—(1.) the actual condition of the repositories of Law and on the bulk of the Legal System, from whatever Sources it is drawn; (2.) the degree of capacity for precise, exhaustive, and elastic expression existing anywhere in the Community; (3.) the state of Society, agricultural, industrial, or commercial, rendering the accessibility of a knowledge of Law an object of varying importance.

What has been hitherto said upon the subject of Interpretation, has only been on that side of it which is concerned with the import of terms and of sentences. But the term Interpretation has, for judicial purposes, a larger meaning than this. It is used to express the whole mental process by which the Will of the Legislator is ascertained, whether words and sentences have been employed to indicate that Will or not. In order, in the course of any particular judicial investigation, to discover the complete Will of the Legislator, his whole mental attitude and circumstances must as far as possible be reproduced. It must be taken for granted, for this purpose, that the imposer of a law had before his mind, when imposing it, the general habits, faculties, and nature of man, as well as the actual constitution of the outer world. Thus a Legislator may properly be supposed to anticipate an average amount of good sense, wisdom, honesty, carefulness, expertness, and respect for the claims of others, except in cases where the character of the Legislation distinctly supposes the opposite. In this way Lunacy, Infancy, Ignorance, Mistake, Negligence, Fraud, Malice, severally come under the cognisance of the Jurist, as facts introducing anomalies into the normal action of men in their average condition, and so presumedly provided against by the Legislator. The physician and the psychologist will here have to lend their aid, and, so soon as the qualifying abnormal facts are distinctly recognised, it becomes a mere logical process, based upon experience, to determine how far a given act is qualified by such recognition. The general process is facilitated by an habitual logical separation of the normal or average from the abnormal or exceptional conditions of men's minds and bodies, and by a classification of the latter conditions. This work belongs partly to the Jurist, and partly to the Psychologist, the Physiologist, and the Ethical Philosopher. In any case ready for Trial, the legal practitioner and the Judge are called upon to examine all the circumstances surrounding the act alleged to come within the purview of the Law, and to determine under what category the condition of the agent's mind as established by such circumstances properly falls. Thus, in relation to all the possible qualifications in human acts, as much as to all other matters of which it treats, the language of Law assumes a community of knowledge and sentiment on the part of the governors and the governed. Interpretation, in all its forms, is the process by which—(1.) a real and existing standing-ground, afforded by this assumed community, is determinately ascertained; and (2.) where accidentally no such community can be so much as even assumed, the most ready and practical devices for carrying out the general, social, and political purposes for which laws exist are provided.

CHAPTER VI.

DISTRIBUTION OF THE MAIN DEPARTMENTS OF A LEGAL SYSTEM.

It might be supposed that the social condition of nations differs so widely that no one universal mode of distribution could be adopted which could admit even the leading departments of all possible Legal Systems being fitted into it. The possibility of discovering such a mode is a question of historical fact and political observation. It is, of course, superficially true of the systems of Moses, of Ménu, and of Justinian, that each contains large chapters wholly disparate from any portions of either of the others. English Common-Law, again, differs from all the European Systems founded on the System of Justinian by all the breadth between the feudal and the family conception of the social unit. Laws of Procedure, again, always present an indefinite amount of variation and apparently capricious difference from one another. The notion of Crime and its separation from so-called Civil Injuries on the one hand, and from Sins or purely moral offences on the other, has a peculiarly sensitive dependence on the ethical circumstances of a people at any given epoch. Thus in order to attempt the formation of any comprehensive skeleton of a Legal System which shall be large enough to embrace all possible Systems without being so vague and indeterminate as to be valueless, certain leading principles, by way of concession, must be established at the outset. Some such principles are the following:—

1. For the purpose of framing, by a process of induction, an universal formal system of Law out of particular and actual systems, attention must be restricted to the characteristics of such Societies as have passed through a series of what may be called normal stages without permanent arrest, retrogression, or violent interruption. This rule will serve to include all National Societies whatever for the primitive stages of their growth, and to exclude all such as, in later stages, in place of a regular progress through an industrial and a commercial development up to the attainment of complete political and social freedom, have been fatally crushed by the weight of a priestly caste, of a despotic tyranny, or of a dissolute spirit of anarchy.

2. In contemplating the Societies to which attention is confined by the above rule, the history of each must be treated as an organic whole, and the determining facts of its civilisation, as they successively emerge, must be co-ordinated in every case with the similar facts occurring at a like stage in the evolution of all the others.

It is believed that the result of these two principles, when fully carried out and based upon an historical analysis which is the peculiar product of the present century, will be to give the following as the typical classes of facts or criteria of civilisation the history of which alone it is, for the present purpose, worth while taking into account:—

    (1.) Family Life.
    (2.) Ownership.
    (3.) Government.
    (4.) Contract.
    (5.) Crime and Civil Injuries.

It will be at once seen that the order of this arrangement, while immediately suggested by historical considerations, is in great degree misleading even from that point of view. The first three of the large classes of facts here mentioned present themselves in actual life not successively but simultaneously, and indeed obviously presuppose the existence of one another. The idea of Contract, again, though strictly a later development, even in its most embryonic form, is almost inherent in the idea of Ownership, inasmuch as both ideas equally imply an habitual moral reliance on the part of one person in respect of the future acts of others. Crime and Civil Injuries, again, have been placed in the last rank though they are in truth the background of all the other facts, and are involved in the very earliest consciousness of those facts. They presuppose the presence of sentiments favourable to personal security, to inviolate Ownership, and to social order, while the penal laws to which they give birth do much to invigorate the strength of those sentiments.

There is yet another difficulty, besides the chronological one, in taking the above-mentioned classes of facts as signs of common stages of development discoverable in all progressive nations, for the purpose of demonstrating the possibility of constructing an universal framework ready to hold all possible Systems of Positive Law. It is that each of these classes of facts is from the very first so closely implicated with the fact of Law itself, is to such an extent at once the child and the parent of Law, and so essentially dependent throughout its whole history upon the support of Law, that they are, one and all, exposed to the constant peril of being misrepresented as the mere products of Law instead of independent moral growths coeval with the history of Law itself. It thus becomes intimated that all the most solemn and mysterious facts of human and social existence are purely artificial or adventitious creations brought about by a conscious and more or less enlightened regard for the public advantage expressing itself in Law. The consequence of this view would be that the permanence and universality of the above facts would be no further argument for an invariable course travelled by all progressive National Societies than so far as the existence of Law itself is such an argument. Any distribution of the subject-matter of all possible Legal Systems would only be a dreary and more comprehensive reiteration of an oft-told tale of legislative cunning, instead of a compendious statement of the best results obtainable by a critical investigation of the most obscure moral facts underlying the outer fortunes of all actual National Societies.

Assuming, however, that the above considerations at least go so far as to point to the possibility of the construction of such an ideal framework for all Legal Systems, the same considerations at once suggest an answer to the second question, as to the basis on which such a framework would be best constructed. This basis is manifestly that of the social and political purposes for the accomplishment of which the different classes of laws composing a Legal System have come into being, and to subserve which they continue to exist, or are, from time to time, consciously amended. It happens, indeed, that hitherto, owing to the prevalence, in the region of Jurisprudence, of technical and logical over ethical and political studies, this has, in no case, been the actual basis in use among those who have digested the most celebrated systems of Positive Law. The main divisions have proceeded, as, notoriously, with the great Roman and English Institutional writers, from a regard to the technical peculiarities which are chiefly the products of Law itself rather than from a regard to the ethical facts and social actions which it is the province of Law to regulate.

All Laws whatever impose Duties, that is, they restrict the field of action of some person or persons in one direction or another; and most Laws, in addition, confer Rights, that is, they extend the field of action of some person or persons in one direction or another. Hence the contents of any Legal System are made up, in fact, of Rights and Duties, and upon the basis of these Rights and Duties, simply looked at in their technical aspect, it is possible to make a classificatory distribution of the whole system. By the expression "technical aspect" is here meant that these Rights and Duties are measured, not by their social bearings and purposes, but with regard to such coarser elements as—(1.) the description and number of the *Acts* to which they refer; (2.) the classes of *Persons* upon whom these acts operate; or (3.) the interposition or not of a material *Thing* between the acts and the Person or Persons upon whom they operate.

It has been said that some Laws only impose Duties without conferring Rights. This may, in some points of view, be said to be the case with sanitary laws; laws of treason; laws regulating taxation; laws forbidding cruelty to animals, and suicide; laws regulating dress, food, expenditure, amusements, and the like. Though, by the enactment of such laws as these, Rights of Action are conferred upon particular Persons, as on Government Inspectors, on Informers, on the police, and even on private members of the Community, yet such laws are imposed directly for the benefit, rightly or wrongly conceived, of the whole Community in its corporate capacity rather than, as in the case of all other laws, for the indirect benefit of the Community through the immediate advantage of particular Persons.

Some writers, in a violent attempt to make their whole scheme of classification proceed upon a basis of "Rights," have had to resort to a desperate expedient. They have treated all laws of Civil Injuries, of Crimes, and of Procedure, under the head of "Rights arising from the violation of a Right," calling the class that of "secondary" or "sanctioning" Rights. This would be tolerably unobjectionable, did there not still remain unclassed the peculiar laws mentioned above. These must be either placed in a special group of Laws conferring Rights vesting in the whole Community as such, or else must be relegated to the group of Laws conferring "Sanctioning" Rights; since, by an extension of language, it might be said that every member of the Community has an initial legal Right, capable of practical enforcement in a Court of Justice, to every other member's respecting the order of Society, not removing himself voluntarily from the Society, and not grossly violating the dictates of the public conscience in his dealings with the inferior animals. The violation of this last sort of Right might, in that case, be said to impart to every member of the Community a "secondary" or "sanctioning" Right against the offender. By this straining of technical language, the whole Legal System might conceivably be distributed under the head of Rights. Similarly it might be distributed under the head of Duties. But the inconvenience here would be even greater, since some of the most important classes of Rights, such as Rights of Ownership, Rights to personal Reputation and to personal Security, are precise and distinct, while the Duties corresponding to them are multifarious, vague, and defiant of all attempts at accurate enumeration.

All these considerations point to two conclusions; (1.) that if, for the distribution of the subordinate parts of a Legal System, a technical basis be adopted, that basis must be neither one of Rights nor of Duties singly, but must consist of both conjointly, looked at in view of the obvious and immediate purpose for which the laws are imposed. Thus, in some departments of the system, Rights will take the lead, and in others, Duties; the Rights always implying corresponding Duties, and the Duties generally (or, by an extensive use of language, always) implying corresponding Rights. (2.) For this very reason, as well as for other more potent ones, it appears that a social and political basis of distribution has for all purposes a transparent advantage over a technical one; and that the soundest of all classificatory methods is that in which a social and political basis is the ground of the main divisions, and a technical basis, consisting of Rights and Duties conjointly, is the ground of all the subordinate ones.

The different parts of the Legal System may then be exhibited under some such leading divisions as the following:—

I. Laws directly relating to the Constitution and Administration of the State.

II. Laws of Ownership.

III. Laws of Contract.

IV. Laws of Civil Injuries and Crimes.

V. Laws affecting Special Classes of Persons.

VI. Laws of Procedure.

Under each of these divisions the Rights and the Duties, which it is the immediate purpose of the Laws under consideration to confer or impose, will be treated under the heads of the several topics comprehended in the essential notion of such Rights and Duties.

Before proceeding, however, to this detailed investigation, it will be convenient to perform a task which has already been noted as a paramount object of a Jurist's labours, that of providing an Explanation of Leading Terms.

CHAPTER VII.

AN EXPLANATION OF LEADING TERMS.

On the very earliest appearance, among a portion of the Human Family, of the facts of Law and Government, a number of terms and expressions present themselves which henceforth constantly recur in every legal or judicial enquiry, and which, however much they may be multiplied, are never wholly superseded. These leading terms are very far from being invented for the occasion, and rather, being already in familiar use among the people, have a strict and sharply determined meaning put upon them for the purposes of Law. It is true that the smallest degree of national morality, and therefore the very existence of moral terms, presupposes, at least in their embryonic shapes, the facts of Government and Law; but these latter facts are unconsciously acquiesced in long before they are distinctly recognised and consciously reflected upon. In this sense only it may be said that all the most general Legal terms are nothing else than Moral terms created by the spontaneous sentiments and aspirations of the people. This is conspicuously true of such words as "*right*," "*duty*," "*person*," "*property*," "*promise*," "*fraud*," "*malice*," and the like. The fluctuating meaning, however, of all moral terms, which is due to the diversities of moral experience in individual persons, and to the peculiar susceptibility of such terms to the action of all kinds of varying influences—religious, social, and political, makes a precise terminology, as Moral become converted into Legal terms, a matter of the most stringent importance. An acquaintance with the meaning of some dominant Legal terms has, indeed, even in the preceding chapters, had to be presumed, and of others a brief definition had to be interposed by anticipation.

The word "Law," itself, is the best instance that could be taken of a thoroughly abused term, employed as it is in the Natural Sciences to express nothing else than an invariable sequence; in Ethical Science to express a rule, howsoever derived, imperative on the human conscience; and sometimes, in common speech, by a closer analogy to its true Juridical meaning, to express a command published by some potent though not political Authority, as in the phrases "Law of God," "Natural Law," "Moral Law," "Law of Honour." Whether all these different meanings of the term "Law" were originally borrowed by way of metaphor or analogy from the severe Juridical meaning of that term, or whether the Juridical meaning is only a narrowly circumscribed employment of a term already in familiar use, are problems touching upon a still more general historical enquiry as to the true mode in which a keen and conscious political sentiment severed itself from the vague moral sentiments current in primitive societies. It is sufficient for the present purpose to insist that, for the purposes of the Science of Jurisprudence, the term *Law* has a most precise and narrow meaning, the clear enunciation of which will shortly be proceeded with.

In the present chapter the strict Juridical meaning of the following terms, with that of all their correlated expressions, will be investigated, and, as far as possible, definitely fixed.

(1.) State.
(2.) Law.
(3.) Right.
(4.) Duty.
(5.) Person.
(6.) Thing.
(7.) A peculiar class of Terms respecting the possible qualifications of moral responsibility, as—Intention, Motive, Fraud, and the like.
(8.) Act.
(9.) Event.

1.—STATE.

The use of the word State has suffered, in this country and in Germany, from two opposite sources of laxity and indefiniteness. It has been crippled as much by the rude handling of an evanescent school of popular politicians in one country as it has lost all practical value and use in the over-refined and sometimes mystical philosophy of the other. In order to preserve unimpaired all that is at once most common and most precious in the term under consideration, the following elements in the conception of a State must be distinctly kept in view:—

(1.) A permanent Association of men, existing for definite ends, and looked at from a particular, and, in some respects, idealistic point of view.

(2.) Organisation; that is, a reciprocity of function and a mutual relation of all the parts to each other and to the whole.

(3.) A relation to Time—past, present, and future, indifferently; that is, to no one period exclusively of the others.

(4.) Relation to Things; especially to a definite portion of the earth's surface, named Territory.

(5.) Self-sufficiency, or Independence in respect of other like corporate associations.

(6.) Self-consciousness, as exhibited in such phenomena as patriotism, antiquarianism, conservatism, and in a general reverence for the past traditions of the Community as an organic whole, as well as in an onward looking towards the Future.

(7.) Concrete Government, with all its essential departments—legislative, executive, judicial, and the rest.

It is not pretended that everybody using the term State is aware that all these elements are properly contained in it. On the contrary, most persons, especially in England, use the term in the loosest possible fashion, making it synonymous now with "the person or persons governing a National Community at a particular moment," now with "all the members of such a Community alive at a particular moment," now with "the same persons looked upon as an organic body, whether as being of one race, as speaking one language, or as having one and the same set of historical antecedents," now with "a National Society looked upon chiefly in reference to the Past," and not as being organised and governed at the present moment, still less as having relations of the most transcendent importance to the Future. From one or other of these shallow and mutilated conceptions flow some of the most mischievous political theories and consequences. Thus from one conception it is readily concluded that no moral duties are owing to Posterity; from another, that no deference or veneration is due to the traditional unity of the Nation in the Past; from another, that no living principle or sentiment welds the members of a Nation together other than the hope of material advantages to be reaped through the union; from another, that Government is merely an accident, if not a superfluity, in a National Society, and may one day be dispensed with altogether.

Having, then, enumerated all the elements that constitute the true conception of the State, it will serve to fix the strict use of the term for Juridical purposes to give that term the following definition, or rather compendious explanation :—

A State is a permanently organised aggregation of a portion of the Human Family, occupying a definite Territory, and qualified by its magnitude and by the fact of Government for the complete satisfaction of all the material and moral necessities of Human Nature.

2.—Law.

A Law is a Command of the Supreme Political Authority of a State purporting to control the Acts of Persons in the Community.

The terms here used demand particular explanation.

A Command always implies a strong expectation on the part of the person issuing it, that it will be unhesitatingly obeyed. In this it differs from a mere wish, request, suggestion, or permission. In the case of the kind of Command which is called a Law, the expectation of obedience is founded on an assumed knowledge of human nature. It is either believed by the Lawgiver that the persons to whom he addresses his laws are themselves anxious to conform to them, and therefore only need direction as to the form which their obedience must take; or else the Lawgiver believes that the penalties he is enabled to attach to disobedience will be more certainly avoided than the advantages conceivably resulting from disobedience would be pursued. Every Law, so far as it is really a Law, is intended to be obeyed. There are, of course, periods during which a Law is, as it were, struggling into being; and there are other periods during which its vitality is departing. In both such periods it is not practically expected that it will be obeyed, just because it is not a true Law.

It is said that the Command issues from the Supreme Political Authority of the State. It is sufficient at the present stage to explain the phrase " Supreme Political Authority " to mean, " the Person or Persons in a National Community who, at a given moment, have unlimited and irresponsible power to control the Acts of all Persons in the Community." It is of the very essence of a State that there should be, at every moment in its history, some Person or Persons in whom this prodigious power rests. Every Command issued in pursuance of this power is a true Law; though it has been attempted in some quarters to limit the use of the term Law to such Commands as refer to a long series of acts, as extend over a longer or shorter period of time, or as affect a larger or smaller number of Persons. Such distinctions are wholly valueless and misleading. The most apparently isolated decree, if imperative and peremptory, is addressed to all the members of the Executive needed to carry it into effect, and to all Persons in the Community capable of interfering with its being carried into effect. Thus all distinction between some kinds of Commands and others, on the ground of generality, is as spurious as it is perplexing.

It is said above that a Law purports to control *acts*. In this it is distinguishable from all modes of influence which either purport to affect the intellect, the feelings, or the conscience of men on the one hand, or, on the other, to exert purely mechanical pressure on parts of the physical universe. Thus Law differs as much from all modes of merely moral persuasion, in one direction, as from all modes of material restraint in another. It is true that in order to make a Law effective, that is, to secure that it be universally obeyed, the state of mind which precedes men's acts must always be matter of the most careful consideration by the Legislator. It is sufficient in this place, before the full definition of the term *act* be proceeded with, to notice that every true *act*, that is, neither an *event* nor a mere *thought* or *desire*, is accompanied by certain mental or emotional states or operations, as Knowledge, Desire, energetic Resolution, final Design, or Acquiescence. The activity or strength of these various mental or emotional conditions will be determined by the kind of consequences, direct or indirect, of the *act* contemplated. The Lawgiver, by affixing a penalty to disobedience, gets certain of those consequences into his own power, and thereby reacts directly on the mental condition of all the Persons to whom his Laws are addressed. It is in this way that the proposition that Laws never affect to control anything else than the *acts* of Persons is reconcilable with the familiar fact, that Courts of Justice have no more frequent occupation than a searching scrutiny into the most recondite and intricate labyrinths of the human mind. All judicial investigations of questions of Intention, Motive, Infancy, Insanity, Fraud, and Malice, are nothing more than scrupulous enquiries into the state of mind of an agent with reference to the probable consequences, direct or indirect, of his *act*. The success of such enquiries depends partly on the prevalent knowledge of human nature, partly on the actual evidence forthcoming in the particular case. The whole judicial process is, therefore, invariably of a twofold nature: (1.) the ascertaining of the exact kind and quality of the *act* forbidden by Law; (2.) the determining whether an *act* of this precise complexion has been really done by the particular Person accused. It is customary to say, that the first part of the investigation is one of Law, and the second one of Fact.

3, 4.—Right and Duty.

Every Law is addressed to all Persons in the Community, inasmuch as all are commanded to take notice of it, and to abstain from interfering with its due operation. Every Law is also especially addressed to the class of Persons forming a department of the Executive who are commanded actively to carry out its provisions. But, furthermore, most Laws are also especially addressed to limited classes of Persons, whose capacity of control over the Acts of other Persons, either in respect of personal security, of reputation, of Things capable of being Owned, or of services promised, these Laws affect to regulate and prescribe. In this way the realm of action of one set of Persons in the Community is enlarged in exactly the same measure and degree that that of another is restricted. Such a capacity of control over the *acts* of another *Person*, so given by Law, is said to be a *Right*. The corresponding liability of the other *Person* to have his *acts* so controlled is said to be a *Duty*. Thus every Right presupposes a corresponding Duty. It has been questioned, however, whether every Duty presupposes a corresponding Right; in other words, whether there can be such a thing as an "Absolute Duty." Perhaps Laws relating to offences against the Existence or Constitution of the State, to taxation, to national defence, and the like, might be held to impose *Duties* upon some or all Persons without according corresponding *Rights*. The question is rather a technical and logical than a practical one, inasmuch as the whole Community has an interest in every Law being obeyed; and the most familiar notion of a legal Right is that of an advantage enjoyed by some Person or Persons more than by others, and capable of being made practically available by the Person interested through the use of special machinery publicly instituted for the purpose. In this stricter use of the term *Right*, it is evident that the Supreme Political Authority itself cannot enjoy Rights any more than it can be liable to Duties, though all the Persons who compose it, in their private capacity, can enjoy the one as they are liable to the other. Thus it is a mere courteous fiction to say that the English Monarch can do no wrong. It is merely a deferential form of imputing to him the attributes he had when he absorbed in himself the whole Supreme Political Authority, and now the antiquated phrase renders no other service than that of stamping the actual impotency of Courts of Law.

There are no terms in the use of which the confusion of Legal and Moral notions is at once so common and so dangerous as in that of *Right* and *Duty*. The sentiment of Right, however grounded, is so deep and penetrating, that it naturally imparts something of its own vivacity and mysterious significance even to the severely limited conception of a legal claim named after itself. This is only one instance out of many which shows that the real connection of Law and Morality is so intimate and profound that the only safeguard against endless perplexities is to be sought in the most anxious and decisive discrimination. The school of Bentham has done as much harm in allowing but a hair's-breadth of separation between Morals and Law as certain of their more ignorant opponents did and are doing in their attempt to deluge Law with Morality. The ambiguous meaning of the word Right was notably exemplified in the anti-slavery agitation, both in this country and in the United States. Most people are ready now to admit that there has been no time when a slave had not a *moral* Right to his personal freedom. Yet, in Sommersett's case, decided by the English Court of King's Bench in A.D. 1771, it took a lengthened argument to discover whether, by the law of England, a Negro confined in irons, on board a ship lying in the Thames and bound for Jamaica, had, or had not, a *legal* Right to his personal freedom. As to his *moral* Right, probably neither judges nor counsel had a shadow of doubt; and Lord Mansfield himself said that the state of slavery was so odious, that nothing could be "suffered to support it but Positive Law." However iniquitous and impolitic a Law may be, a legal Right enjoyed under it is just as perfect and available as if the Law were the product of the highest wisdom and benevolence. If a Law, in the face of every plea of moral justice, gives one Person the power of excluding another from the Ownership of land, ever so indisputably acquired, the Right of the new comer to possession, and the Duty of the evicted Owner to cede possession, must and will be recognised in every Court of Justice in the land; and all persons interfering with the due transfer of the property, or the full enjoyment of it, will render themselves liable to penalties, either criminal or civil.

Legal Rights and Duties, according to the explanation above given of them, are almost infinitely diversified and elastic in their character. They admit of classification with reference to—(1.) the Social Purposes which the acts affected to be controlled subserve, such as personal Reputation, personal Security, Ownership, services of all sorts ; (2.) the Time during which the control is to be exercised ; (3.) the Modes of legal Procedure by which the power of control is to be made practically available. The following may be given as a formal explanation of the terms *Right* and *Duty* :—

A Right is a measure of control delegated by the Supreme Political Authority of a State to a Person said to be thereby invested with a " Right" over the Acts of another Person or other Persons said to be thereby made liable to the performance of a " Duty."

Throughout this work the expression *legal relations* will always be used to imply an Aggregate of legal Rights and Duties.

5, 6.—Person and Thing.

The terms *Person* and *Thing* as used in the Science of Jurisprudence, owing to the incessant colloquial use of the same terms with the most lax and vague significations, present difficulties of exactly the same kind and degree as the terms *Right* and *Duty*. The Moral distinction has given rise to the Legal one, and, being much broader and deeper than the Legal one, always underlies it. Some writers have attempted to distinguish, for juridical purposes, a Person from a Thing, by describing the former as in all cases an end for which Law exists, and the latter as never more than a means to another end outside itself. According to this view, when a human being is degraded to the depth of being only recognised as a proper object for protection by Law so far as the interests of others are concerned, which seems to have been the case with Slaves in a very early period of Roman Law, such a human being falls under the class of Things and not of Persons. Other writers, nearly akin to these, have rather spoken of the capacity to be invested with Rights as the mark of Legal Personality. Others, again, have spoken of the capacity to be invested with Rights and to be made liable to the performance of legal Duties as the testing characteristics. According to one or other of these views the Roman Slave passed into the class of Persons so soon as he, or others on his behalf, could invoke the aid of any legal process against his Master or other Persons, or his Master or other Persons could invoke the like aid against him. Lastly, other writers have insisted solely on the criterion of what they call Moral Responsibility.

All these views are plausible, if no one of them is exhaustive. They each testify to certain essential elements in the conception of a legal Person as opposed to a Thing, and in a true definition no one of them can be entirely neglected. The following may serve as such a definition:—

A Person is a Human Being looked upon as capable of being invested with Rights, or made liable to the performance of Duties.

A Thing is a detached portion of the Material Universe, looked upon as an object mediate or immediate of the Acts of Persons.

By making the term *Persons* coextensive in its meaning with all Human Beings in the Community, all perplexing questions, arising in States which forbid by Law cruelty to animals, as to the quasi-Personality of animals, are avoided. The capacity of being invested with Rights or made liable to Duties sufficiently indicates the notion of Moral Responsibility, of which more will be said immediately, as inseparable from that of true legal Personality. The definitions above given of *Person* and *Thing* are, again, quite compatible with the two facts that—(1.) Human Beings are, sometimes, for special legal purposes, treated exactly as Things; and that (2.) Things, or aggregate masses of Things, are, for other legal purposes, looked upon as in some way capable of being invested with Rights and made liable to Duties, that is, treated as Persons. Of the first of these facts, the case of a Master having a Right of Action for an injury done to his Servant; a Husband, Father, or Guardian for an injury done to a Wife, Child, or Ward; Relatives or Insurance Companies entitled to compensation for negligence in the carriage of passengers, resulting in death, are notorious instances. Of the other of these facts, the familiar habit in all systems of Law of creating what are called "fictitious" or "artificial" Persons, is the most significant example. The "Hereditas," the "Fiscus," or Imperial Treasury, "Collegia" and "Juris Universitates" generally, in Roman Law; and Corporations, Sole or Aggregate, in English Law, are either assemblages of Things or of an indefinite number of Human Beings to which the Law attributes, for special purposes, a certain capacity of control over the Acts of Persons, or prescribes certain limitations in their proper or possible activity. They are, in other words, looked upon as capable of being invested with Rights, or made liable to the performance of Duties.

7.—A Peculiar Class of Terms respecting the possible Qualifications of Moral Responsibility.

For the purposes of the Jurist the use of the phrase "Moral Responsibility" must not be held to assume the truth of any Theory relating to the constitution of Man or to the government of the Universe. The phrase does nothing more than chronicle the products of experience with respect to the actual nature, habits, and faculties of Man. The possibility of Law wholly rests on the basis of this experience. If men's actions could only be determined in every case by special mechanical pressure then and there brought to bear, all use of a general Rule would be excluded. It is known, on the contrary, whatever psychologists may assert as to the liberty or the bondage of Man's Will, that he is practically affected in his conduct by the nature of the consequences which he foresees will ensue from it. These consequences the Legislator endeavours to control, and thereby he operates on that peculiar faculty of mental determination called the Will, which, in the absence of external control, is invariably followed by appropriate muscular motions. The juridical view, then, of Moral Responsibility involves the assumptions,— (1.) that average men have the capacity of forming an Intention, that is, of distinctly contemplating the immediate consequences of their own Acts, under the term *Acts* including all those muscular movements which, in default of external restraint or disease, are invariably followed by the sort of Desire denominated Will; (2.) that they have the capacity of Willing, that is, of conceiving the particular sort of Desire which is invariably and necessarily followed by Action; (3.) that they have the capacity of

Acting, that is, of making the particular kind of muscular movements upon which the Will has resolved.

Thus—

capacities of
{
1. Forming an Intention,
2. Willing,
3. Acting,
}
must all enter into the idea of Moral Responsibility.

Any one of these three capacities may be present without the other two. Thus a Person may form an Intention with respect to the Act he is at the point of determining upon, but, owing to some distraction or interruption, he never wills and never does the Act. Attempts to commit Crimes, and the English offence of "Compassing and Imagining the death of the King," are illustrations of this inchoate responsibility. So, again, a person may have that peculiar sort of Desire which, in the absence of all external restraint, is invariably followed by certain muscular movements, yet, owing to the introduction of some such restraint as sudden paralysis, capture by the police, or mechanical pressure, after the Desire has been fully conceived, the Act is never performed. In the same way the Will to perform a certain muscular movement may be present, and yet the consequences of that movement, direct or indirect, may never be contemplated. This is the case in extreme Infancy, or in equivalent states of inexperience, for certain purposes, in such peculiar conditions as those of Idiocy, Insanity, and Intoxication. The Will is present, but no Intention is or can be formed. One large class of exculpatory facts is determined wholly by the Mode in which the capacity of the Person relieved from legal responsibility may be trifled with, thwarted, or perplexed. *Fraud* relieves the Person pleading it on the ground that he was deceived with respect to the immediate consequences of his Act. He intended to do an Act to be immediately followed by a certain set of consequences which he foresaw. The real consequences of the Act were craftily concealed from him, or, by a slight legerdemain, a novel set of consequences were substituted for those he desired. He signed a Promissory note payable at six months' date for fifty pounds; by the *Fraud* of the Person to whom it is made payable, the sum is altered to five hundred pounds and the time to six days. Or a Person in a state of ill health signs what he believes to be a merely indifferent document, relating to one of the most every-day concerns. He has really signed his Will, by which all he owns will be transferred at his death to the Person who has, by fraudulently substituting one document for the other, disguised the real consequences of the Act of Signature.

For complete Legal Imputability the three distinct capacities—(1.) to form an Intention, (2.) to Will, and (3.) to Act, must all be present, in however slight a degree one or other of them may be manifested. In deciding upon the Moral Responsibility of a Person accused of disobeying a Law, the Judge is under the necessity of ascertaining the degree in which these several capacities are present, and of determining whether any facts are disclosed by which these capacities might be impaired. General Facts limiting Moral Responsibility may be classified according as they are the pure expression of simple Physical or Ethical phenomena, or are the creations of Legal and Political institutions to which an artificial influence on Intention is, for purposes of public policy, and under the guidance of average experience, generally imputed by Law.

The Facts properly held to impair or qualify Moral Responsibility may be arranged under the following divisions:—

(1.) Universal Facts, as Infancy, Old Age, and Difference of Sex.
(2.) Occasional Facts, physical or ethical, as Idiocy, Insanity, Intemperance, Bodily disorder or casual Infirmity, Error or Mistake, Compulsion, and Fraud.
(3.) Facts, physical or ethical, to which an artificial imputation is affixed by Law, as Marriage, Agency, Trust, and what is called, in English Law, "Constructive" Fraud.

It is not necessary to examine in detail the Mode in which every one of the Facts here enumerated operate, or are properly held to operate, upon Moral Responsibility through their direct influence on the Intention of the Agent. The precise investigation of the Mode in which a few of them operate will supply the key to the mode of operation of all.

As to the Universal Facts falling under the first division, they are manifestly bound up with the general condition of Humanity, and therefore are taken notice of with greater or less precision and felicity in every System of Law that has at all developed itself. For instance, very young children Will and Act as really as do their seniors, but, from utter inexperience or thoughtlessness as to the immediate consequences of many of their actions, they cannot, with respect to these actions, be said to form an Intention. Thus the habit of regarding young children as being, for legal purposes, Morally Irresponsible acquires fixity and permanence, and each particular Legal System has only to assign, in accordance with the national temperament, race, climate, and traditions, the Age at which this Irresponsibility shall wholly or partially end. The Age may differ for different legal purposes. It may be held that a child obtains a sufficient knowledge of the world in which he lives to guard him against certain Acts at an earlier Age than against others. On this principle, according to English Law, Criminal Liability commences long before Civil Liability; and even at an Age long before Criminal Irresponsibility wholly ceases, the ordinary presumption in favour of that Irresponsibility admits of being rebutted.

Whether Difference of Sex is an essential and universal or only accidental and local ground for imputing differences of Moral Responsibility, is rather a psychological and political than a juridical problem. In attempting a practical solution of it each nation has differed from every other and each age from every previous age. Guidance has been sought rather from the dictates of inexplicable sentiments and firmly rooted institutions than either from facts or reasoning. The present vacillation both of thought and policy in England, in the United States, and in Continental countries with respect to the real nature and operation of Difference of Sex is far too great to admit of this fact being catalogued in a Systematic view of the Science of Jurisprudence as one of the permanent Facts influencing Moral Responsibility.

As to the Occasional Facts mentioned in the second of the above divisions, they impair the faculty of forming an Intention by rendering the vision even of the immediate Future clouded, distorted, or obscured. Different Legal Systems recognise these Facts as operating in different degrees. In England, as with Infancy so with Insanity and Intemperance, a different sort of Presumption is raised in favour of Moral Irresponsibility as affecting some classes of Acts than as affecting other classes. The identical testimony of Insanity which might suffice to upset a Will or relieve the maker of a Bill of Exchange from all Liability upon it might not suffice to save the same person upon a charge of Wilful Murder committed at the moment of signing the Will or making the Bill of Exchange. On the other hand, a Person being supplied with necessaries of life during a fit of Intoxication might be liable upon a Contract made in the same condition of mind in which he is, for some Criminal purposes, held Morally Irresponsible.

The rules providing for the case of an Agent's capacity of forming an Intention being impaired through the presence of *Fraud* or through *Ignorance* or *Inadvertence*, resulting in what is technically called *Error* or *Mistake*, form a prominent part of every Legal System. In all these cases a misapprehension as to the immediate consequences of an Act is brought about in the Agent's mind. In some points of view the Agent may be held to be Morally Responsible for his mind's perverted condition. A small amount, an average amount, or a very great amount, of Care and Diligence may be properly demanded of him, and he has failed to exercise it. This may be a ground for reducing the compensation due to him for his own loss or for increasing the penalty for the loss he has occasioned to others. But whatever his Liability in this respect, the fact that his Moral Responsibility was impaired, through defect in the requisite Intention, cannot be evaded in a just System of Law. The rules relating to *Fraud, Ignorance, Error*, and *Mistake*, have for their purpose to guide the minds of Judges with respect to the limits of allowance and indulgence which a defective Intention in an Agent may legally meet with.

The regulation of the legal consequences of *Fraud* and of the different forms of *Ignorance* is one of the most arduous problems before the Legislator, and the mode of solving it affords a delicate test of the degree of Moral discrimination characterising his age and country. The actual complexities that arise are of the following sort. A single fraudulent Act may give rise to a long line of transactions, all of them strictly honest, and in every one of which the Agents would be grievously injured were the whole line to be held vitiated through the discovery of a flaw affecting one of the earliest links. To meet this possible case were devised and elaborated the doctrines of "*bona fides*" in Roman Law and of "*notice*" in English Law. A Person in the enjoyment of a Right directly issuing from another Right, the creation of which was due to a Fraud, may have been—(1.) cognisant of the Fraud from the first; or (2.) informed of it after the Right it created had become vested, and before his own Right accrued or he had parted with it to another; or (3.) not informed of it till after this last Right had accrued or he had parted with it to another. Thus in the case of the fraudulent negotiation of a Bill of Exchange, a late Indorsee may have known of the original Fraud at the time the Bill was indorsed to himself; or he may not have known at that time, and may, in consequence, have given what is called "value" for it, but may have heard of the Fraud before he indorsed it to another and yet have none the less indorsed it to the other; or, from first to last, he may never have heard of the Fraud at all. In the first of these cases he would in no country be held to be in *bonâ fide*. In the second case he might or might not, according to circumstances or the accidental national policy.

In the third case he must, in every country, be held to be as much in *bona fide* as if the Fraud had never been committed.

It is scarcely necessary to illustrate by familiar instances the modes in which *Ignorance*, whether as to the state of Facts or the state of the Law is, under one form or another, treated by the Law of all countries as affecting Moral Responsibility. It is held in most countries, as in England, to be the most convenient Presumption that everybody is acquainted with the state of the Law. The Presumption, in its strict meaning, implies an impossibility, or rather an absurdity. It is only more convenient than the opposite Presumption, inasmuch as it shuts out peremptorily the interminable excuses which would otherwise be founded on the Ignorance of Law. Even in countries where this Presumption is most severe, it is held capable of being rebutted where, through youth, idiocy, "rusticity," or other special circumstances, acquaintance with the state of the Law is next to impossible.

Moral Responsibility, it has been indicated, may not be only held to be affected by the inexorable facts of Human Life, and the average vicissitudes of Human Nature, but also through the operation of a class of social or almost artificial Facts which are the creations of nothing else than Civil Society and of Law itself.

Thus Marriage, as a legal Relationship, presupposes the existence of Law, in however inchoate and embryonic a form. This Relationship, in the form in which it has been hitherto exhibited in all nations, presents the Wife as being in such a degree, whether greater or less, of subordination to and dependence upon her Husband as obviously to hinder her freedom of action and therefore to limit her Moral Responsibility. The general possibility of such limitation is recognised in most Systems of Law, and it is enforced by national institutions which, for purposes of Ownership, Contract, and even Personal Liberty, place the Female sex at a standing disadvantage in comparison with the Male.

Another Fact, artificially created by Law, which, wherever it exists, is necessarily held to restrict Moral Responsibility, is Agency. It was seen that the three elements essential to constitute Moral Responsibility are—(1.) a capacity to form an Intention; (2.) a capacity to Will; and (3.) a capacity to Act. In the course of Civilisation the convenience of Mankind has introduced the habit of separating, in a multitude of transactions, the Person who Intends and Wills from the Person who Acts,—that is, in the narrowest sense of the word "Acts," where it means simply "puts the necessary muscles in motion so as to produce the desired effect." In this case the whole Moral Responsibility is shared between the two persons engaged, the so-called "Principal" and the "Agent." The distribution of the exact share of Responsibility attributable to each is a matter of considerable moment both to themselves and to third Persons affected by the complete transaction. It is customary in Legal Systems to make certain general rules, suggested by the nature and habits of Mankind, for determining where the Responsibility in such cases is presumed to lie. The Law directs the Judge to presume that Acts of a particular class are, for all purposes of legal Liability, the Agent's own and nobody else's; that other Acts are imputable in the way of legal Liability to somebody else and not to the actual Agent; that other Acts, again, are either imputable to the

Agent or to somebody else, as special circumstances may suggest. The kind of Signs which the Law will look to in order to affix Moral Responsibility will be such as the general or special relation existing between the Parties, the customary course of similar transactions, the knowledge actually or presumptively possessed by a third Person affected of the representative or non-representative character of the Agent. Each Legal System will have its own rules, prescribing the use to be made of these and cognate Signs.

Closely akin to Agency is the equally artificial legal phenomenon of Trust. This phenomenon is eminently a modern one, though the main idea of presuming, for general purposes of public convenience, a Special Confidential Relationship between two or more Persons figured largely in the Prætorian department of Roman Law, and must, indeed, enter more or less into all advanced Systems of Jurisprudence. A Trustee is a Person regarded by Law as competent to form an Intention and to Act, but the region of whose Will is circumscribed by limits of all kinds invented and imposed by Law itself. Thus a Trustee is held responsible in the highest degree for every one of his Acts in the matter of his Trust, but his freedom of action is narrowed to certain very definite directions. It may be said that a Trustee derives his Rights or his capacity of controlling the Acts of others from one class of Laws, and his Duties or his liability to have his own Acts controlled from another. In respect of the former class, he is Morally Responsible to the extent that he is a free agent. In respect of the latter class, that Responsibility is severely limited to the extent that his course of action is restricted to the channels marked out by Law itself. Thus, so far as a Trustee confines his voluntary action to the limits prescribed by Law, his Moral Responsibility will be judicially tested in the same way as it would be were he physically incapable of Willing otherwise. The whole historical origin, meaning, and doctrine of Trusts will come under consideration later on, as one of the divisions of the head " Laws affecting Special Classes of Persons."

Another artificial class of Facts, owing their origin to Law itself, and, by a presumed operation on the Intention of an Agent, held, in many Systems of Law, to qualify the Agent's Moral Responsibility, are those of the nature of what is called in England *Constructive Fraud*. This class of Facts is formed by an inductive process out of a series of observations of average human conduct. It is noticed that in the play of domestic relationships, of commercial transactions, and, more generally, of negotiations implying mutual fidelity, the weak, or the ignorant often come to be placed in a position very disadvantageous compared with that of those with whom they are dealing. There may be no imputations of selfish or unworthy conduct on the part of anyone, and yet the Lawgiver may think it well to determine that exceptional securities for fairness, impartiality, and diligence, ought to be given by the stronger to the weaker. To provide these securities he creates a number of Rules controlling the conduct of the stronger, and raising an irresistible Presumption, in case of their breach, of a privation of Moral Responsibility on the part of the weaker. In such cases it is presumed irresistibly, that the Person in the less favourable situation was prevented, by him in the more favourable, from forming the Intention requisite to carry with it complete Moral

Responsibility. He has, so to speak, been the victim of a *Constructive Fraud*.

8, 9.—ACT AND EVENT.

Corresponding to the distinction between *Person* and *Thing* is the allied distinction between *Act* and *Event*.

An *Event* is an actual change in the relative situation of Persons or Things, or of the composing elements of Things, such change being estimated quite apart from the consideration of any of the causes that may have brought it about.

An *Act* is a muscular motion regarded as following that peculiar kind of Desire (termed *Will* or *Volition*) which in a condition of health, and in the absence of all external restraint, is necessarily and invariably followed by such motion.

The word *Act* is, in truth, often used in a narrower or lower sense than this. Any muscular motion, whether preceded or not by the phenomenon of Will, acquires the name of "Act." Thus, the muscular movements of the sleep-walker, the vibrations of the victim of St. Vitus' Dance, the frantic gestures of the delirious and the insane, are dignified with the same name as the orderly and normal movements of the healthy and rational man. It is indeed one of the hardest problems for the judicial psychologist to distinguish, in some of these cases, between Voluntary and Involuntary motion, and to impute Moral Responsibility accordingly. But because Human Nature is mysterious and obscure in its more morbid and sinuous operations, and therefore Human Justice will frequently be baffled, this is no reason for confounding distinct ideas and their corresponding names.

There are, in fact, many critical changes in the situation of Persons or Things, or in the component elements of Things which admit now of being viewed merely as Events, now as Acts. The death of one Person at the hand of another is regarded as an Event so far as the Testamentary dispositions of the deceased thereupon come into force, the cause of the death being generally for that purpose irrelevant; but it is regarded as an Act when it is attempted by a Judicial process to impute Moral Responsibility to the Person bringing about the death. In the course of the Trial, it may be again sought, in favour of the prisoner, to establish his Insanity, his Passion, or the presence of what is called Chance or Accident, by way of forcing on the conclusion that, in respect to the Person charged, the alleged Crime can only be treated as an Event, and not an Act.

Marriage, again, may be treated for some purposes as an Event, and for others as an Act. It is an Event so far as the sole matter of contemplation is its operation on the capacities of the Married Persons for Ownership and for making Contracts, or upon the Rights and Duties of other Persons in respect of them. It is an Act when looked upon in reference to the competency of Persons to enter upon the Marriage-state, to the solemnities which are held legally necessary to authenticate the fact of such entrance, and to the Moral Duties presumably undertaken by the married Persons, the neglect of which, in some systems of Law, are held to be grounds of legal Divorce.

So *Bankruptcy* may be treated either as an Act or an Event, according as attention is fixed on the Voluntary agency and consequent Moral Responsibility of the Person who has brought himself into such a situation, or on the bare consequences to himself and other Persons, which the fact of his Bankruptcy involves. It is needless to multiply illustrations which reach to every department of the Legal System.

The term *Motive* is often introduced in judicial investigations, though it is never, in England, introduced into strictly legal documents, and scarcely claims a place among the terms proper to the Science of Jurisprudence. In order to ascertain an agent's "Intention" at the time of his doing an Act, it is sometimes essential to notice the attitude of his mind towards the *remoter* consequences of his Act. This attitude is expressed in saying he was determined by such and such a "Motive." The predicate "good" or "bad" is obviously irrelevant, and in fact means nothing more than that the consequences contemplated are thought desirable or the contrary by the speaker.

CHAPTER VIII.

CLASSIFICATION OF LAWS.

THERE are many different Modes of Arrangement which may be adopted for the purpose of exhibiting, in the most convenient and accessible form, the Laws existing in a National Community. These Laws may have arisen from different groups of Historical or Social Events, may be administered in Courts of Justice employing different Modes of Procedure, may affect different classes of Persons in the Community, or may relate to different kinds of Civil transactions or species of Wrong-doing. Each of these grounds of difference may be adopted, and in some one or other actual Institutional treatise or Legal System has, in fact, been adopted, as a basis for the logical distribution of a nation's Laws. Thus differences of Historical Origin and of Procedure have led to the notable divisions in English and in Roman Law into "Equity" and "Common Law," "Prætorian Law" and "Civil Law." In like manner, a recollection of the different Classes of Persons directly affected by different parts of the Law suggested the venerable and still-subsisting separation of the "Law of Persons," meaning thereby the Laws applicable to particular Classes of Persons, by reason of some peculiar moral or legal situation which they occupied in respect of other Persons, and the "Law of Things," meaning thereby the Laws applicable to *all* Persons whatever without distinction. The ground of distribution suggested by the varieties of civil transactions, or of species of wrong-doing, is exemplified in the other two great divisions of the Institutes of Roman Law, the "Law of Obligations," and the "Law of Actions." Similarly in English Law, and in all modern Codes, the Law of Contract, or still more generally Mercantile Law, has always tended to withdraw itself, for the purpose of independent consideration, from the body of Laws concerned with every other topic. The Law of Crimes, again, and so-called "Constitutional Law" form, even in the least artificial Legal Systems, distinct chapters wholly separate from the rest. In no System or Institutional treatise, probably, has any one of these principles of division been rigidly adhered to. The most convenient is perhaps the last, that is the one based upon nothing else than the quality of the Acts which the Laws affect to control. The mode of Arrangement thence resulting has the advantage of being capable of easy adaptation to changes in the Legal System as they are naturally developed. The most primitive and essential laws will thus occupy the earliest place; the more special, accidental, and refined modifications and additions being subsequently introduced from time to time, as fresh national facts give birth to them.

Thus the notion of Government is contemporaneous in its origin with that of Law itself, thereby pointing to the advantage, or rather the necessity, of handling first of all the topic of Constitutional Law, or those Laws directly relating to the Constitution and Administration of the State, which must have a place in the most elementary Legal System belonging to the most embryonic National Society. This body of Law is indeed the last to come into complete consciousness and to attain exactness and precision in its lineaments and proportions. It is also more dependent than any other part of the Law upon casual political Events and even upon fleeting popular sensibilities. Nevertheless its true place is anterior to all the body of Law which constantly presupposes it.

In some Systems it has been habitual to include Constitutional Law, strictly so called, together with the Laws relating to Procedure and Crimes, or to one or the other of these, under a general head of "Public Law" as opposed to all other Laws denominated "Private Law." This arrangement, it is conceived, is dictated by a perverse and fallacious instinct, that somehow the State is more prominently and immediately active in the punishment of Crimes and in the regulation of the machinery of Courts of Justice than in the mere process of creating Rights of Ownership or of determining the Rights and Duties of Persons who have entered into a legal Contract. Of course, the whole value of a Right of Ownership or of a Right under a Contract is due to nothing else than the direct authority and activity of the State. It is at once the effect and the cause of endless confusion to suppose that the Law of Ownership or of Contract, just because the prosecution of claims arising therefrom is usually left to be initiated by private Persons, has anything in it more private or less directly dependent upon the physical energy of the State than any other part of the Law. For all these reasons there is an obvious advantage in treating Constitutional Law, in the strict sense of "Laws directly relating to the Constitution and Administration of the State," apart from the rest of the Legal System, and in treating it first.

The next place is indisputably claimed by Laws of

Ownership. All Civil Society presupposes the existence of the notion and fact of Ownership, in however rude, limited, and precarious a form. Thus distinct Laws of Ownership necessarily make their appearance sooner than any other kind of Laws. The supreme importance of reinforcing with the might of the whole State the weakness of private Families, and afterwards of isolated individual Persons, is the earliest necessity that presses upon the primitive Statesman; and in every antique Code a certain sacredness is seen to attach to Duties in respect of Ownership which puts those Duties quite on a par with religious and moral Duties consecrated by the most binding sanctions. Then, again, Rights of Ownership, being Rights existing in a particular Person or in particular Persons against all other Persons, are the simplest and least complicated of all Rights. They are simpler, for instance, than Rights under a Contract, which cannot be treated without keeping in view at once the Wills and Acts of two Persons at least and all the circumstances by which the Moral Responsibility of either of the persons may be impaired.

For similar reasons, that is, partly in deference to the fact of historical development and partly to that of progressive complexity, Laws of Contract will properly occupy the third place in a complete exhibition of the contents of a Legal System. Roman lawyers, indeed, and modern Jurists who have constructed Codes on the basis of the Institutes of Roman Law, though treating Laws regulating Contract after Laws regulating Ownership, have made the former subordinate to the latter by including Contract among the various ways in which the fact of Ownership may begin. There are many objections to this course. Besides the fact that thereby the true moral situation of a Contractor as contrasted with that of an Owner is liable to be lost sight of or slurred over, there are many other purposes for which Contracts are made besides the acquisition of Rights of Ownership.

Three main classes remain,—Laws affecting Special Classes of Persons, Laws of Civil Injuries and Crimes, and Laws of Procedure. The special situations of particular Persons in the Community relatively to others have attracted the attention of Jurists in all ages to such an extent as to give an almost undue prominence, on the face of most Legal Systems, to the Rights and Duties of such Persons. It was felt that the healthy action of Civil Society depended upon nothing more nearly than upon the proper fulfilment of the mutual Duties implied in the relations of Husband and Wife, and Parent and Child, and in the later and more artificial relations of Guardian and Ward, Attorney and Client, Trustee and Person for whom the Trust is held. The tendency was to place the consideration of the legal Rights and Duties which supported these relations in the fore-front of the whole legal system, under the head "Law of Persons," irrespective of the fact that, however momentous were these Rights and Duties, they were special, exceptional, and narrow in their character, and only affected limited classes of Persons in the whole Community. The same sense of convenience, however, which originally suggested their undue prominence still enforces their separate and distinct treatment. It is well that those classes of Persons who, in their relations with others, are vested with or made liable to assemblages of Rights and Duties together constituting what is called "Status," should know distinctly to what part of the Legal

System to have recourse for information upon what more immediately concerns themselves; and it is also well that what concerns all Persons whatsoever should be treated independently, so as to dispense with the need of constant repetition. Thus the head " Laws affecting Special Classes of Persons" is properly placed in immediate succession to " Laws of Contract."

At this point of the Legal System the principle of arrangement, were it determined by Rights or Duties singly instead of by the quality of the Acts affected to be controlled, would appear to undergo a change. Rights would no longer be pre-eminent, and Duties would take their place in leading the way. Civil Injuries and Crimes are objects of the Lawgiver's anxious care from the very foundation of the State, and Laws relating to them are implied in every other kind of Law. It will be seen hereafter that the arbitrary division between Civil Injuries and Crimes is unknown to early Communities, that it is invariably exposed to the influences of confused moral sentiments, as it has been conspicuously in the history of English Law, with its eccentric division of Misdemeanours and Felonies, and that it is in fact founded on no real and essential difference in the nature of things. There are some Acts which the State holds it to be desirable to prevent at all hazards and by the use of all the machinery of Government disposable for or essential to that purpose. These Acts are strictly *Crimes*, and no others are. Some other Acts it holds it to be desirable to prevent conditionally upon certain Persons co-operating with or specially inviting the instrumentality of the State. These are *Civil Injuries*, or in English Law " *Torts.*" The peculiar and mixed process for prosecuting Crimes in England, has, among other causes, impeded the recognition of this real and sole distinction.

"Laws of Procedure," including "Laws regulating the Admission of Evidence," naturally closes the whole subject. These Laws prescribe the Rights and Duties of all members of the Executive directly concerned in carrying into effect all the Laws of the State by discovering the Persons who disobey those Laws, assigning and inflicting the punishments entailed by disobedience, and, in cases of doubt, determining the application of the general language of Law to the particular cases that present themselves for decision. This class of Laws, again, is addressed not only to Judges, Magistrates, Sheriffs, Policemen, and Gaolers, but also to all Persons in the Community who, in the guise of Witnesses, Jurymen, or Professional or Scientific Counsellors, are invited or compelled to co-operate, from time to time, as occasion arises, with the Executive in the Administration of Justice.

In accordance with the above mode of distributing all the possible Laws which constitute a complete Legal System, both for purposes of Codification and of Scientific instruction, the whole subject will now arrange itself under the following heads, each of which will be treated in succession:—

I. Laws directly relating to the Constitution and Administration of the State. (Constitutional Law.)

II. Laws of Ownership.

III. Laws of Contract.

IV. Laws affecting Special Classes of Persons.

V. Laws relating to Civil Injuries and Crimes.

VI. Laws of Procedure.

CHAPTER IX.

LAWS DIRECTLY RELATING TO THE CONSTITUTION AND ADMINISTRATION OF THE STATE. (CONSTITUTIONAL LAW.)

THE materials of this chapter will naturally and most conveniently distribute themselves into the following departments:—

A. Description of the general nature, province, and limits of this part of the Law.

B. Meaning and scope of the phrase *Supreme Political Authority*.

C. Legal relations to each other, and to all other Persons, of the Persons (if more than one) composing the Supreme Political Authority.

D. Modes in which changes are brought about in the class of Persons composing the Supreme Political Authority, or in the relations of such Persons to each other and to all other Persons.

E. Meaning of the phrase *Executive Authority*,—Legal relations to each other and to all other Persons of the Persons composing that Authority, and Modes in which changes are brought about in those relations.

A.—DESCRIPTION OF THE GENERAL NATURE, PROVINCE, AND LIMITS OF THIS PART OF THE LAW.

If it be true that all Law consists of Commands addressed by a body of Persons in the Community to all the rest, it may well be asked whether this body of Persons themselves are, in their corporate capacity, subject to any Law whatever. It is a fact that in all settled Communities this body is practically coerced on every side. The penalties of unpopularity, of imperfect obedience, or expulsion, are ever hanging over its head. It may make certain Laws, but it will in vain attempt to make others. It may modify its own Constitution, but only within very definite limits. It may amplify or restrict its own numbers, but it cannot commit suicide. The collection of Rules which circumscribe the action of a Supreme Government are only unlike true Laws in that they are neither devised nor can be readily altered by that Government. In some countries, as in the United States, these Rules were once and for ever constituted at the foundation of the National Polity, and it demands a most circuitous process in order to obtain the assent of every State of the Union in order to introduce the minutest change. In other countries, as in England, there is no so-called "Paper" Constitution, but the rules prescribing the general bounds and character of the Government are none the less deeply fixed in the sentiments of the people, and are even reduced to the technical form necessary when employed as a basis for argument in Courts of Law. These Rules, resting as they do on a more adamantine foundation than the passing caprice of the Government of the hour, which, indeed, to them owes its very existence and authority, have been called by some writers " Constitutional Morality," to distinguish them from the other rules directly relating to the Constitution and Administration of the State, which, owing their creation and force to nothing else than the will of the Governing Authority (hereafter called the Supreme Political Authority), are to all intents and purposes properly called Laws. As a matter of ethical or historical research, the use of the word "morality" is here neither inappropriate nor uninteresting, but, just as in the parallel case of International Law, the rules in question are as unlike as possible to moral principles and maxims, and are as like as possible to genuine Laws. They are inextricably implicated with all the other Laws pertaining to this part of the subject, and when once their true qualitative difference has been, as above, fixed and recorded, they may properly, both in a Code and an Institutional treatise, be indistinguishably blended with the general Laws relating to the Constitution and Administration of the State.

The main purpose of these Laws is to mark the classes of Persons who shall be empowered, through the assent of the rest of the Community, to make Laws for the whole; to determine the usages which shall be observed in the processes of making and publishing these laws; and to mark out the class of Persons whose special function it shall be to enforce obedience to Law with a due regard to the protection of every individual citizen against tyrannical abuses.

There is no distinction of more common acceptance than that between what are called the "Legislative" Authority and the "Executive" Authority. The former is said to represent the Persons who devise and enact Laws; the latter those whose province it is to enforce them. It has been doubted by some writers, and notably by Bentham, whether this distinction serves any other purpose than that of the loosest popular classification. The persons who are said to constitute the Executive Authority are necessarily endowed with a very extensive power of subordinate

Legislation. It is they who devise rules for the regulation of the army and navy, for the collection of the revenue, for the accomplishment of postal, locomotive, sanitary, and possibly commercial and moral purposes, and especially for the preservation of peace and the detailed administration of Public Justice. Each subordinate of the Executive, again, in his turn has to make fresh general rules for the carrying out of his special work. The so-called Legislative Authority, on the other hand, in the very process of enacting a Law, must provide by anticipation for every stage in the course of its effectual enforcement.

The true distinction is not between a Legislative and an Executive Authority, but between a Supreme Governing Authority, on the one hand, and all the Persons whose services it employs for the purpose of giving effect to its commands, on the other. A convenient name, indeed, for all this assemblage of functionaries is "the Executive Authority." It stands opposed to the Supreme Authority from whom alone it derives all its powers. The head of the Executive Authority in European countries is invariably the Person who in Feudal times absorbed in himself the whole Governing Authority of the State. He still retains his station as a constituent portion of the Supreme Political Authority. It is the province of the Laws that relate to the Constitution and Administration of the State, after marking the classes of Persons composing the Supreme Political Authority and providing for their change, to determine the classes of Persons who shall constitute the Executive Authority, to assign their several functions, and to protect individual citizens against every form of tyrannical abuse.

B.—Meaning and Scope of the phrase "Supreme Political Authority."

It has been seen, in the course of defining the term *State*, that in the use of that term there is predicated of a nation a certain organised life and essential unity which is independent of the accidental modes of Government which from time to time may prevail, of the mere lapse of Time, of the life and death of successive generations, and of historical vicissitudes of all sorts. At any epoch in the existence of a State there is to be found in it a Person or assemblage of Persons who, for the time being, have the irresponsible and effectual power of controlling the Acts of all Persons in the Community, or at least to whose commands the bulk of the Community exhibit an habitual obedience. It has already been seen that this sovereign, or so-called "Supreme Political," Authority, even in its most absolute and irresponsible form, has its capacity of command ever hedged round by certain indeterminate instincts and sentiments prevalent among the people. Therefore all that can be asserted of any such Authority is that, within these limits, its power is despotic, that these limits are only very obscurely and indefinitely marked, and that in the whole Community there is no Person or number of Persons who can at the moment successfully compete with itself for the actual submission and loyalty of the citizens.

The practical difficulty in giving a precise meaning to the phrase "Supreme Political Authority," as applicable to the facts presented in European States, is mainly due to historical causes. By a certain national courtesy or reverence for venerable traditions, the King, the Queen, the Emperor, is invariably invested with all the dignities and honourable appendages anciently and still familiarly associated with the possession of Absolute Power. In truth, however, there is no State in which the whole Legislative functions any longer centre in the person of the Monarch. Usually these functions in fact, or at any rate in form, are distributed among three Orders of Persons selected out of the Community, and who, therefore, together constitute the true Supreme Political Authority. One Order, whether the most influential, as in some countries, or the least so, as in many, represents the old Feudal Sovereign chosen by reference to an inflexible rule of hereditary succession. Another Order, chosen also by reference to birth in some countries, but also by reference to wealth or even to merit and services in others, constitutes a select and aristocratic Chamber reproducing the Barons of Feudal and the Senators of Roman times. A third Order, again, gradually forcing its way forward and tending to absorb, or even now actually absorbing, all the rest, represents directly the claims, the sentiments, the aspirations, or, it may be, the prejudices and the political incompetence of the general body of the people.

Such is the universal picture presented by almost all States in the Old and even in the New World. For even the most republican nations have, wisely or not, constructed their Constitutions on the model supplied by European facts, and the Constitutions awarded to English Colonies are fashioned after the same identical type. A President or a Lieutenant-Governor may take the place of a King or Queen. The Elect of a State Legislature or a grazier qualified by wealth may stand for a Baron or a Duke. The Elect of the most democratic of Constituencies, holding his precarious seat for a couple of years at the most, may recall the English County Member, with his seven years' tenure. Whatever the particular rules for describing the classes out of which the several Orders shall be constituted, the phenomena are everywhere much the same. The Supreme Political Authority in any country consists of all the Persons forming the aggregate of these Orders. It belongs to this part of the Law to determine the Persons who shall compose these several Orders, and to prescribe the legal relations of the several Orders to each other.

It is sufficient just to allude to one abnormal and erratic form of the Supreme Political Authority which is occasionally presented through a concurrence of historical causes. It is that in which there are two or more independent bodies, each enacting effectual Laws at the same time. This phenomenon was exemplified during nearly the whole period of the Roman Republic, when Assemblies representing severally the Aristocratic, the Popular, the Plutocratic, and the professionally Political forces of the country each made Laws, whether named "*leges*," "*plebiscita*," or "*senatus-consulta*," binding on the other Assemblies and on the whole Community. In truth, one or other of these Assemblies was generally predominant at a particular moment or else took cognisance of a particular class of affairs. Any way, the true Supreme Political Authority included all the Persons making up all these Assemblies, the mode of distributing the Legislative functions among them being matters of further limitation.

The matters falling under this first department of the branch of Law now being dealt with may be compendiously summarised in the following way, which will also serve as a type for the codifier to keep in view.

I. Brief description of what is meant by the expression "Supreme Political Authority" generally.
II. Description of the general Mode in which such Authority is constituted in a given Community, (whether consisting of one or more Persons, sitting in one or more Chambers, with joint or independent Legislative functions.)
III. Precise determination of the Modes in which the Person or all the Persons constituting the Supreme Political Authority are nominated. (Whether, for example, by birth, wealth, popular election, or public services.)

C.—LEGAL RELATIONS TO EACH OTHER AND TO ALL OTHER PERSONS, OF THE PERSONS (IF MORE THAN ONE) COMPOSING THE SUPREME POLITICAL AUTHORITY.

Assuming that this Supreme Political Authority is once constituted and all its component portions accurately described, the Persons of whom it consists are necessarily invested with certain Rights and made liable to certain Duties for the purpose of the more effectual accomplishment of their Legislative functions. Some of these Rights and Duties will be in reference to each other, to the corporate portion of the whole Supreme Political Authority which they help to make up, or to the other corporate portions of the same Authority. Others of these Rights and Duties will be in reference to private members of the general Community. A large part of the branch of Law now under consideration is concerned with determining these two divisions of Rights and Duties. It is true that many of these Rights and Duties will have gradually emerged through a series of accidental historical combinations, will bear the marks of antiquated party feuds and long-forgotten jealousies, and will be sustained rather for their associations with the venerable past than for their intrinsic usefulness in the present or the future. Nevertheless they have all the force and vitality of Rights and Duties dictated by the most novel sense of political expediency, and therefore demand the clearest description and limitation in this part of the Code.

What is called "the Prerogative" of the English Monarch partly consists of Executive functions traditionally entrusted to him, partly of Rights of the nature just described, whether in reference to other component members of the whole Supreme Political Authority or in reference to the general Community. Of those Rights not arising out of strictly Executive functions instances are supplied by the Right of convoking, proroguing, and dissolving Parliament, of withholding assent from any of its Measures (a Right, by the way, severely restricted in the case of the President of the United States), and of being exempt from Civil or Criminal Process in a Court of Law at the suit of any Person whatever in the Community.

Again, what are called "the Privileges" of members of the two Houses of the English Parliament, as well as the joint Rights, which each Assembly enjoys in its corporate capacity against the other and against the Crown, are Rights created by the Laws now under consideration. The familiar "Privileges" of members of the Houses of Parliament are those by which a member of the House of Commons is exempted from liability to arrest on Civil Process during the Session and for a short period before its commencement and after its conclusion; by which a member of the House of Lords is similarly exempted at all times; by which the latter, furthermore, has a right to an interview at all times with the Monarch; in a case of alleged treason, " misprision of treason," or felony, to be tried by his fellow-peers; and in a Court of Justice to depose on his " honour " instead of upon his oath.

As to the Rights of the several corporate Assemblies which together constitute the whole Supreme Political Authority, in respect of each other and of the rest of the Community, conceded to them for the better discharge of their public functions, instances are supplied by the singular functions claimed by the House of Commons with respect to Bills involving taxation at every one of their stages; by the same House with respect to all measures for the reform of its own Constitution; by the House of Lords with respect to questions of pedigree, legitimacy, succession, or to any historical event touching its own members; and, lastly, by the peculiar jurisdiction enjoyed by the English Houses of Parliament over their own members and over all members of the Executive with the exception of the Monarch. Such a jurisdiction is exercised when the Speaker of the House of Commons avails himself of the instrumentality of the Serjeant-at-Arms to compel an absent member to appear in his place, or imprisons a member of the House during the Session for breach of its rules, or, after formal trial at its bar, punishes by a like imprisonment or by fine any member of the Community who has invaded its " Privileges." The process of impeachment of public servants by the Commons at the bar of the Lords is an exercise of a like Right of Jurisdiction. Possibly also the Appellate Jurisdiction of the House of Lords, though now recalling little of its original Constitutional character, ought strictly to be included among the Rights conceded to a portion of the Supreme Political Authority for the purpose of more effectual co-operation in the work of the whole.

This part of the Law would be properly codified in the following form:—

1. Rights of each constituent portion of the Supreme Political Authority as against the rest in its corporate capacity.
2. Rights of each constituent portion in its corporate capacity as against the individual members composing it, and as against all other Persons in the Community.
3. Rights of individual members of each such constituent portion—(1.) against all other members; (2.) against all other Persons in the Community.

D.—MODES IN WHICH CHANGES ARE BROUGHT ABOUT IN THE CLASS OF PERSONS COMPOSING THE SUPREME POLITICAL AUTHORITY, OR IN THE RELATIONS OF SUCH PERSONS TO EACH OTHER AND TO ALL OTHER PERSONS.

There are two leading forms which an attempt at altering the constitution of the Supreme Political Authority may take according as the attempt is originated outside or within the limits of that Authority itself. In the former case the attempt is made by violent insurrection, by forcible substitution of a new set of Governors for the existing ones, or by such a long course of habitual disobedience and disloyalty as renders, sooner or later, the tenure of its office by the existing Political Authority impossible. In the latter case, the change is carried out by the regular operation of general rules providing beforehand that, in certain cases, at certain times, or on the declaration of the will of certain Persons, changes may hereafter be introduced into the constitution of the Supreme Political Authority. Or else it may be carried out by a simple discretional power committed, within certain limits, to the Supreme Political Authority to reconstruct itself when and as occasion shall demand. Between these two Modes of provisional change it is not always easy to draw the line, and it is the less so as in most States both Modes are found to exist side by side, though one may be more prominent here, and another more prominent there. There is a certain nervous apprehension always attending the very idea of modifying the structure of what seems the very pillar of national order and the heart of national life, which, in itself, leads nations rather to leave the introduction of necessary changes to the dictation of pressing emergencies than to provide for them by formal anticipative measures. Of all progressive Communities Great Britain and the United States afford the best instances of reconstructing in an orderly fashion the Supreme Political Authority. Great Britain, indeed, affords a most remarkable specimen of a State ever shrinking from all contemplated change as a possibility, and yet providing, within well-defined limits, the most elastic machinery for promoting every variety of change. The Constitution of the United States distinctly and in terms foresees the need for its own amendment, and describes with punctilious accuracy the Mode in which reference is to be made to the Legislatures of the several States with a view to obtaining the common assent to such an amendment.

There have been hitherto seventeen Amendments made to the Constitution of the United States, and divers English Acts of Parliament have been passed for the Reform of the House of Commons, that is, for marking a new and different class of Persons as admissible to be electors or candidates. Other Acts have been passed for regulating the succession to the Crown, for appointing a Regent, and even, as in the case of some of the clauses of the Bill of Rights and of the Act of Settlement, for seriously restricting (though mainly in its traditional Executive aspects) the Prerogative of the Crown. Were an Act of Parliament passed, as has been already attempted, for the institution of Life-Peerages, such an Act would be another instance of a reconstitution of the Supreme Political Authority through the agency of that Authority itself. Such Laws, when made, are, like all other Laws, addressed to all Persons in the Community, the effect of them being to release those Persons from their legal duty of loyalty and submission to the existing Political Authority, and to substitute an Authority in its place consisting of a set of Persons differently described or having different relations to each other from those constituting the Authority now dethroned.

Such are the more formal modes by which a Supreme Political Authority may have its Constitution changed. But the more effectual and important changes are often brought about by silent causes which wholly elude observation at the time. In England, the competition and idiosyncrasy of eminent individual Persons; the relative weight, incessantly changing, of wealth, birth, and merit; the force of religious enthusiasm, or the vehemence of partisan antipathies; the outward events reacting at every point on Home, Foreign, and Colonial policy; the shock of national calamities and the passing predominance of a philosophical Theory—all these causes, and a thousand still more delicate and hidden, keep playing at every moment on the constitution of all the parts of the Supreme Political Authority, and ever afresh adjusting and readjusting the balance of real influence. It has been now the Upper House, now the Crown, now the Lower House, now the Upper House again, now the Crown again, and finally the Lower House which has in turn drawn to itself the whole practical government of the nation. In the United States, again, no question is more debateable than whether the House of Representatives is a tyrannical Oligarchy or an impotent rabble, and whether the President is a cipher or a despot. No doubt one of these alternatives is true at one time and another at another. It is a weakness in the Political Constitution of a State to afford the possibility of these alternatives too rapidly and constantly following upon each other. It is evident that, though it is important for the Jurist to notice how inaccurate a representation of the real constitution of the Supreme Political Authority is the technical description of it, yet it is with this technical description of it and of the formal Modes of altering it that he must content himself. The following is the form in which this part of the Law will present itself in a classificatory arrangement:—

1. Limits within which the constitution of the Supreme Political Authority admits of change whether in respect of—(1.) the description of the Persons who compose the several parts of it, or (2.) the Rights of the several parts of such Authority in their corporate capacity, as against each other.
2. Description of the formal machinery by which changes within the above limits have to be effected.

E.—MEANING OF THE PHRASE "EXECUTIVE AUTHORITY:" LEGAL RELATIONS TO EACH OTHER, AND TO ALL OTHER PERSONS, OF THE PERSONS COMPOSING THAT AUTHORITY, AND THE MODES IN WHICH CHANGES ARE BROUGHT ABOUT IN THOSE RELATIONS.

It has already been observed that there is no strict opposition between the functions of the Legislative Authority and of the Executive Authority. The Supreme Political Authority, in every Law it makes, foresees from first to last the whole process of its execution, and provides the whole instrumentality necessary for preventing any failure in that execution. It nominates, either directly or indirectly, Ministers of State, Judges, Magistrates, Sheriffs, Police, and invests them severally with the powers needed for the work committed to them. The same Authority, furthermore, calls into being a great hierarchy of other functionaries entrusted with the execution of those special laws which are made for the protection of the national safety and honour against enemies at home and abroad, for the collection of the revenue, for the promotion of easy transit and communication between different parts of the national territory, and for the general furtherance of the sanitary, commercial, moral, and religious welfare of the whole people. The Person or Persons to whom the regulation of this hierarchy is entrusted, who may be called the Head of the Executive, may be either the identical individual Persons who compose the Supreme Political Authority itself, or may be a select number of the Persons composing that Authority, or may be some other Persons outside the body of Persons composing that Authority. The first of these cases, except in the most primitive state of Society, will always be found extremely rare.

Experience is not long in teaching that a different class and number of Persons and different qualifications are needed for the task of determining upon the probable expediency of a suggested Law from what are wanted for the purpose of punishing those who disobey it when once it is made. The recognised value of a Division of Labour drives home the lesson, which, again, derives constant support from actual competitive Institutions growing up side by side with each other, such as a Priesthood, a Military Class, Administrators of the National Exchequer, and Judicial Magnates, all tracing back their independent functions to an obscure antiquity.

The most frequent form, then, in which the Head of the Executive presents itself is that of a Person or Persons detached from the general body of the Supreme Political Authority with which they maintain intimate and incessant communication, from which directly they derive all their Rights, and to which they are responsible for the performance of their Duties. The reality of this situation may, through historical causes, be accidentally disguised, as in the case of the English Monarch. The courteous shelter which is accorded to the English King or Queen against every form of legal responsibility is exactly co-extensive with the personal impotence for Executive purposes which is its necessary correlative. If the King or Queen can do no wrong, neither can he or she do right. The Supreme Political Authority in England delegates, in fact, its Executive functions to certain members of its own body, as from time to time they happen personally to command its confidence. Against them it possesses a formidable machinery for securing diligence and faithfulness in doing their work. The Laws describing and regulating this machinery, by which all members of the Executive are made directly responsible to the

Supreme Political Authority, form one great division of this part of the Law.

Another great division consists of the Laws which ensure to all Persons in the Community, even to the most obscure and the least influential, effectual protection against the ignorance, indolence, corruption, maliciousness, or despotism of every member of the Executive from the highest to the lowest. The elaboration of this part of the Law, its establishment on an immovable basis, and its assiduous defence against everlasting assaults from ever fresh and unsuspected quarters, is the hardest and most critical struggle which a progressive nation has to engage in. To the fact that England has fought this fight well in the Past, her Magna Charta and its successive confirmations; her Trial by Jury; the Habeas Corpus Act, the Petition of Right, the Bill of Rights, the Act of Settlement and the independence of her Judges as against the Crown thereby secured; the effectual resistance to General Warrants; and Fox's Libel Act;—all these monuments bear unmistakable witness. Whether England will fight the battle equally well in the Future against the natural encroachments of every Executive Authority not severely chained may well be a matter of anxious doubt. As the Supreme Political Authority becomes indefinitely popularised, the Executive appears in a more amiable guise, as the natural friend, rather than the natural enemy, of the people. Suspicion is lulled to sleep, Constitutional energy becomes paralysed, and a degree of unlimited jurisdiction is committed to the local magistrate and to the police, with a view to carry out the last scientific conjecture or moral or economical panacea with a fatal facility, at which the founders of English Constitutional Liberty would have flinched and shuddered.

It is said that in the United States the political danger

is at present to be looked for in the opposite direction, and that in many States of the Union, through the direct influence of the people brought to bear at the constantly recurring elections of Judges, Magistrates, Revenue Officers, and others, an amount of wide-spread corruption and abuse prevails, against which no efficacious remedy has yet been propounded. The constant policy of the Union has been to counteract the disintegrating popular forces by strengthening the Executive. The Supreme Court of the United States, independent as the members of it are, both as respects salary and time of service, is always regarded as one of the most precious and healthy Institutions of the country. Whether, however, immediate danger is to be apprehended in any country from a too much relaxed or a too overbearing Executive, among the " Laws directly relating to the Constitution and Administration of the State" will be found two great classes: the one having for its purpose the precise description of the Rights and Duties of every member of the Executive from the highest to the lowest; the other having for its purpose the providing for the individual citizen a peculiar set of guarantees or securities against usurpation of Rights or the neglect of Duties on the part of any of those members.

Under the first head come the Laws prescribing the Modes of appointment of subordinate members of the Executive by the higher. To the same head belong Laws prescribing the functions of Persons belonging to the Army and Navy, as the English Mutiny Act and the Articles of War embodied in it. Under the same head might be included Laws regulating the conduct of Ecclesiastical and Municipal officials, did not this last class of Laws more conveniently fall, as will be hereafter explained, under the title " Laws affecting Special Classes of Persons." Laws of Procedure also might be suitably treated here, were not their claims greater, on the score of convenience, to be placed in a separate compartment by themselves. So far as they are not included in Laws of Procedure, to this place of course belong the Laws fixing the Rights and Duties of Magistrates, Police, Sheriffs, Gaolers, and the like.

Under the second head of "Laws providing for the special Defence of the individual Citizen against illegal acts of the Executive," come the important classes of Laws forbidding the demand of excessive Bail, for securing the speedy trial of accused Persons, for describing and fencing round the right of Trial by Jury, for protecting private residences against unreasonable invasions by public officers, and generally for providing Rights of Action or Rights of putting in motion the summary or extraordinary jurisdiction of a superior Court of Justice for the punishment or reparation of delay, misconduct, or malicious perversion of justice on the part of Persons invested with a judicial or quasi-judicial authority. The following is the form in which this part of the Law would be properly codified:—

1. Precise meaning of the term Executive Authority.
2. Modes in which the Head or the subordinate members of that Authority are properly constituted, suspended, or removed.
3. Rights and Duties of all classes of members of the Executive Authority severally.
4. Special securities accorded to individual Citizens for their protection against the usurpation of Right, the neglect of Duty, or general malversation on the part of any member of the Executive.

CHAPTER X.

LAWS OF OWNERSHIP.

It is scarcely possible to picture a condition of Human Life in which the fact of Ownership is not even dimly and imperfectly recognised. In the most barbarous condition it seems to be essential to the possibility of preserving Human Life that there should be found a prevalent acknowledgment of the claims of individual Persons to enjoy the undisturbed use of the materials they need for their support, of the weapons wanted for defence against beasts of prey, and of the instruments required for providing these materials and weapons. It is true also that this dawning fact of Ownership expresses something more than a mere condition precedent to material progress, though the fact owes its most conspicuous development to the obvious convenience of enforcing and extending proprietary claims in such a way as to encourage Agriculture, by cherishing a habit of reliance on the future fruits of present labour; to favour the Division of Labour; and to promote the practices of self-restraint, of saving, and of continuous accumulation, apart from which Industry and Commerce could never advance beyond an embryonic stage. The fact of Ownership, however, beyond all this has its exact correlative in the dignity and the independence of the Human spirit itself. It represents and enforces, by an objective symbolism in the world without, the true relation in which man ever stands to his fellows. At every moment of his career, he is called upon to abstain from intruding upon the realm of unfettered action within which each one of his fellows moves at large. Each of these, also, is called by an equally peremptory mandate to display the like abstinence in respect of him. The physical objects around, the soil, the streams, the products of the mines, the beasts of the field, and especially all things wrought or changed by Human hands, present the earliest and, at one epoch, the only materials on behalf of which the competitive and endless spiritual struggle ceaselessly rages. It is only at the last climax of Civilisation that the truth begins to be apprehended that the only justification of proprietary claim is a special call to a more devoted and concentrated service on behalf of those who do not share in it. Between this last and the primitive epoch, mankind passes, with respect to the fact of Ownership, through all the vicissitudes of—(1.) simple Occupation; (2.) rude Rivalry; (3.) tolerated Privilege; (4.) selfish Absorption; (5.) sharp legal Distribution; (6.) revolutionary Communism, terminating finally in the last stage of (7.) Appropriation recognised solely as a Trust for Humanity.

In this view of the subject the fact of Ownership, though of transcendent importance as an instrument, is, after all, nothing more than an instrument in perfecting the relations of mankind with one another. It operates through the cultivation of their faculties, through the concentration of their efforts, through the connection of the Past and the Future thereby represented and fostered, and, above all, through the mutual dependence it cherishes of every member of the Society upon the exertions and services of all the rest.

The interesting investigations conducted by such writers as Professor Maine and Sir John Lubbock with respect to certain transitory phases in the history of the fact of Ownership as exhibited in certain special Communities, point to the fact that the actual form that Ownership takes in primitive times admits of endless varieties, according to the habits of the people, whether migratory or stationary, agricultural or predatory; to the nature of the Things accidentally in request; and especially to the peculiar Patriarchal, Tribal, or National Institutions which, from a number of independent causes, may happen to prevail. The last and, for European and other Aryan Societies, the most momentous form of Ownership, which immediately preceded that now universally existing under different modifications, is what Professor Maine has signalised as the Joint Ownership, firstly, of the Family; secondly, of the Village; thirdly, of the Tribe. So far as early Law is concerned, it is needless to go back further than the first of these stages, and it is equally needless to take into account the Communities in which none of these stages have been found to exist at all.

The general *Fact* of Ownership, so far as it is the foundation of and distinguished from a *Law* of Ownership, having now been cursorily described, the true meaning and compass of the whole Fact will gradually discover themselves as progress is made with treating Laws of Ownership under the following divisions:—

    A. General character and purpose of Laws of Ownership.
    B. Things Owned.
    C. Persons who Own.
    D. Rights of Ownership.
    E. Acts or Events which determine the accruing of a Right of Ownership. (Title.)
    F. Modes of protecting Rights of Ownership.

A.—General character and purpose of Laws of Ownership.

The general purpose of a Law of Ownership is to give stability and distinctness to a claim, inherent as it would seem in the very constitution of Social Life, on the part of individual Persons to keep for their own use objects belonging to the material world, to the exclusion of all other Persons. The Law takes the form of a command addressed to all Persons in the Community, forbidding all Persons other than the Owner, who is specifically marked out and distinguished by the terms of the Law, to interfere with the Owner's full enjoyment and use of the object to the extent the terms of the Law permit. Thus every Law of Ownership, when looked at in its entirety, will be found to consist of several parts. It determines, firstly— (1.) that a particular object or class of objects belonging to the material world may be appropriated for the use of some definite Person or number of Persons less than all the Persons in the Community; that, secondly (2.) the Person or Persons so entitled to appropriate the object or class of objects are characterised by such and such authentic signs; that, thirdly (3.) the object or class of objects, on appropriation, must be used only in such and such ways; that, fourthly (4.) the fact of appropriation is determined by the performance or occurrence of such and such Acts or Events; and that, fifthly (5.) on such appropriation within the defined limits being interfered with, such and such protective remedies are available on behalf of the Person interested in having recourse to them.

In constituting Laws of Ownership as a distinct department both of a Code and of an Institutional Treatise, it is impossible not to recur to the position which the same topic has occupied from the most ancient times in similar compositions. The *Jus Rerum* as opposed to the *Jus Personarum* and to the *Jus Actionum*, and more specially the Law regulating *Jura in Rem* or *in Re*, as opposed to the Law regulating *Jura in Personam* in Roman and Mediæval legal systems, and in all the modern Codes that have been based upon them, as well as Blackstone's *Rights of Property* as opposed to so-called *Personal Rights* on the one hand and to so-called *Rights in Private Relations* on the other,—each and all point to an instinctive sense of the necessity of isolating Laws regulating Ownership or Ownership and Contract together from all other parts of a Law, though in no one of these instances has the ground of the distinction been clearly ascertained nor the distinction itself carried out to all its legitimate consequences.

As to the opposition of *Jus Rerum* to *Jus Personarum*, which has been adopted by Sir Matthew Hale, it no doubt proceeded upon an indistinct apprehension that in one large branch of the Law the different qualities, situations, and mutual connections of Human Beings or Persons were the prominent matter of attention, and in the other and far larger branch of Law those of material Things. The mental distortion thereby produced blinded men to the fact that all Laws whatsoever are addressed to Persons, and have for their purpose nothing else than to control the Acts of Persons. Some of these Acts, so affected to be controlled, relate immediately to the objects of the material Universe, and some do not. Of the Acts relating immediately to Things, some are concerned with nothing else than the hypothetical interference of Persons with the appropriation, to some extent or another, by other Persons of definite Things. It is with these Acts alone that, according to the distribution here adopted, Laws of

Ownership have to do. The *Jus Rerum* of the Roman Lawyers and of Sir Matthew Hale extended nearly to every part of the Law which was not concerned with a few definite private or public relations in which men might stand towards each other. The *Jus in Rem*, again, of the Roman and the Mediæval Jurists was a true Right of Ownership, corresponding with a special department of the Law defining and enforcing that class of Rights. But in opposing it exclusively to *Jus in Personam* by explaining that the one Right availed against all Persons generally and the other only against Persons determinately described, a misconception was encouraged to the effect that Rights of Ownership (*Jura in Rem*) were the only Rights availing equally against all Persons whatever. Thus Rights to Reputation, Monopolies, Franchises and Dignities were wholly left out of account. Perhaps Blackstone's Mode of distribution is the most unobjectionable of all, did he not fall into the all but universal error, which will be more fully exposed later on, of treating Laws of Contract under the head of Laws relating to Rights of Property, thereby implying that the sole purpose and meaning of Contract is that of conveying a title to Ownership.

However, as has been already indicated, the above distinctions, Roman, Mediæval, and Modern, inaccurate and imperfect as they are, point to really useful Modes of separating different matters which, when properly understood and guarded against logical and ethical misconceptions, may be made of very considerable use. In the present distribution of all the topics of a Legal System, Laws of Ownership are kept entirely distinct from Laws of Contract on the one hand, and from Laws affecting Special Classes of Persons on the other. There are also grounds, which will hereafter be more fully explained, for treating

Rights of Ownership, the subject of this part of the Law, apart from the protective Remedies accorded by Law to Persons in whom such Rights vest. Furthermore, it is only in connection with these Remedies that the true extent of most Rights of Ownership can be apprehended at all. Thus, while there is on the one hand a convenience, more or less obvious, in treating the topic "Modes of protecting Rights of Ownership" under the special department of "Laws of Civil Injuries and Crimes," on the other hand the mutual relation of the two departments is as close as can well be imagined.

B.—Things Owned.

The kind of physical appropriation of which a Thing is susceptible depends on the constitution and qualities of the Thing itself. Things differ from each other in size, durability, mobility, chemical and mechanical structure, as well as in the amount of demand for them arising from the greater or less quantity of them that is present or from their greater or less serviceableness for the purposes of Human Life. For the Jurist a method of distribution of Things is needed which is neither so grossly practical as to be useless for all finer applications nor so severely logical as not to satisfy the wants suggested by actual Judicial business. Keeping clear, then, both of too loose and vague a division of Things on the one hand and of too exhaustive, subtle, or curious a division on the other, the following different modes of dividing the objects belonging to the material Universe severally need independent consideration as being authorised by the methods pursued in celebrated Codes, by the practice of eminent Jurists, ancient and modern, or by the intrinsic value and expediency of the classification itself:—

1. "Natural" agents as opposed to all other Things.
2. Things set apart for the general purposes of the State, as opposed to all other Things.
3. Things Movable and Immovable.
4. *Res fungibiles* and *non-fungibiles*.
5. Things "Corporeal" and "Incorporeal."
6. *Singulæ Res* and *Universitas Rerum*.
7. Sundry other oppositions, as between Things Divisible and Indivisible, Principal and Accessory, *Existing* and *About-to-exist*.

1.—*"Natural" agents as opposed to all other Things.*

As Ownership implies the use of some Things by one or more Persons to the exclusion of all other Persons, where a Thing habitually exists in such superabundant quantity as to satisfy the utmost possible demands of every Person in the Community, there is, in the case of that Thing, no occasion for Ownership. Thus it is customary to say that air, light, and the water of the sea are generally not capable of being Owned. Particular circumstances, however, may limit the abundance and the unlimited supply of any of these Things, and the dense and struggling life of modern cities or the artificial relations of modern States notoriously impart to everyone of them in some of their forms a capacity of being Owned. For instance, air combined with combustible compounds, taking the form of what is called gas; air and light, regarded as essentials to the complete enjoyment of other Things, and capable of being obstructed by the interposition of other Things; waters of the sea mainly enclosed by the territory of a State, or within a definite distance of the shore bordering such territory,—all give rise to Rights, Duties, and Remedies, of exactly the same nature as do Things indisputably capable of strict legal appropriation. The true mode of distinguishing Things capable of Ownership from all other Things is to ascertain whether or not any benefit can be conferred by Law upon individual Persons employing them for some purpose or other, by protecting them against the interference of other Persons. It is of no consequence to the Jurist what the purpose is, however relevant this may be to the Legislator as a guide to the kind of Laws he shall make. It is of no consequence what are the kinds of Remedies which the Legislator shall invent in order to guard the free and undisturbed employment of these Things. Accident, no doubt, will from time to time, as in the case of certain animals, of mineral products, and of other heterogeneous classes of objects, capriciously determine their capability of appropriation, but the above principle will always reassert itself, and this is the only principle which it is possible here to accept as a permanent and efficacious test.

2.—*Things set apart for the general purposes of the State, as opposed to all other Things.*

In every State there are to be found large masses of Things which are either permanently or temporarily held to be incapable of appropriation on account of what may be called reasons suggested by public policy or based on general expediency. Some classes of these things, as undrained marshes, waste lands, newly colonised or conquered territory, are often for a long period protected by the State against indiscriminate competition for Rights of Ownership in them, and during such periods there is, strictly speaking, no Owner at all. It is only by a popular abuse of language that the State itself can be called an Owner, inasmuch as all legal Rights of Ownership owe their existence to nothing else but the creative and sustaining energy of the State itself. A similar kind of protection is thrown round other large classes of Things, and even provisional and limited Rights of Ownership are conceded to assemblages of Persons for the purpose of enabling them to effect important or sentimentally precious public ends. Such Things are ecclesiastical structures, burial-grounds, the land and buildings appertaining to schools and public Universities, public offices, dockyards, arsenals, lighthouses, fortresses, materials for equipping the Army, Navy, and subordinate functionaries of the Executive, public repositories for the cultivation of Science and Art, the sea-shore, and the banks of navigable rivers. In the case of all these Things, though certain restricted Rights of Ownership are conceded to definite classes of Persons, yet the possibility of Ownership of any of them to the full extent to which they might otherwise be appropriated is wholly and permanently excluded. There can neither be *Dominium* in the Roman, nor a *Fee-simple* Estate in the English sense.

3.—*Things Movable and Immovable.*

The very earliest Things Owned must have been Things that could easily be carried from place to place: such as food, arms, dress, ornaments, and rough implements of husbandry. It would appear, however, that in the chief Communities to which research has hitherto extended, the first existence of true Laws of Ownership is associated with what may be called the systematisation of Family

Life and with the stability of an Agricultural state of Society. It is only at a far later stage that the Individual citizen disengages himself from the Family group and becomes, for the purpose of being invested with and protected in the enjoyment of Rights of Ownership, as well as for other purposes, the immediate object of the attention of the Legislator. Thus in primitive times, however much the restless incidents of a feudal, military, or predatory condition may distract the notion, Ownership and physical immovability are closely bound up with each other. Apart from all consideration of the actual value of the soil, the wells, the pasture-ground, there seems hardly occasion worthy of the Legislator's interference in the case of any other objects but these. Other things come and go, are born and die, change and pass, many times during the life of a single man; but these last through many lives or through the whole life-time of the State itself, and are ceaselessly inviting the Legislator to prevent a distressing struggle for their possession. The very conception of Ownership includes the elements of stability and permanence, and so the most stable and permanent of all Things will rivet that conception the most firmly and will even threaten entirely to absorb it. Such an absorption, however, is practically impossible, and, progressively, all the materials of Agriculture, as well as all the human beings associated with the Father of the Family in his daily toil, are embraced by the dominant conception. The Roman *Pater-familias* in the earliest times held by a complete legal title his land, his slaves, and his cattle, and over them all, as well as over his wife and his children, he exercised the most unrestricted Rights of Ownership, all distinction between these Rights, founded on any difference of quality or constitution in the Things Owned, being entirely lost sight of.

In early England, again, the large mass of the Law is concerned with Rights of Ownership in Land and with injuries to the Person. Thefts of, and damages to, Movable Things seem only to have presented themselves as deserving public attention because of the personal violence with which they were generally accompanied.

But, as a nation progresses (and this is conspicuously illustrated in the history of modern England), two series of phenomena relating to the distribution of Things Owned present themselves. On the one hand, industry, commerce, social and international intercourse, are constantly calling into being new classes of material objects capable of the readiest possible transfer from place to place. It is out of these objects, in their different forms and combinations, that the main elements of national wealth are constructed. Mediums of Exchange are invented, themselves the most plastic and mobile possible, for facilitating negotiations of all sorts. In fine, the prosperity and the economical life of the people turn upon nothing more certainly than upon the rapid multiplication and the commodious transfer of portable Things. This series of phenomena results in Movable Things gradually acquiring an importance wholly unknown in a primitive Age. But, on the other hand, a different series of phenomena keeps imparting to land, houses, and Immovable Things generally, a fresh and hitherto unrecognised value. They are limited in quantity, and become more and more obviously disproportioned to the demands of the whole population. They gather round them a congeries of peculiar sentiments and traditional memories which, linking one generation on to another, cannot be always safely violated by Legislative sacrilege. They are ever furnishing a true though unspoken political education to the whole people by teaching them the debt of gratitude they owe to labourers and to frugal capitalists in the Past, and what is their own weight of moral obligation to the yet unborn inheritors of the national soil. In this way, side by side with the growing dignity of Things Movable, a politically conscious Age is reviving on quite an original foundation the antique supremacy, as a topic of political attention, of Land. What is Immovable is generally less destructible than other Things, and this attribute of indestructibility again calls for special legislation. So, gradually, the notion becomes prevalent that the Things which can never be taken out of the guardianship of the State, which do not admit of annihilation nor of change, and which may be usefully employed for the service of all, may be put into a class of Things regulated by Laws of Ownership different from those regulating all other Things.

The history of the English distinctions between "Real" and "Personal" property may be taken as illustrating, in however zig-zag and amorphous a fashion, an invariable and necessary progress of ideas. In the first stage, "Real Property" or "Realty," which was originally exactly coextensive with the field of Immovable Things, absorbed the main attention of the legal practitioner, the Judge, and the Legislator. In the next stage the class of Immovables, under the title of "Personal Property" or "Personalty," gradually comes into prominence, and while dividing with its venerable competitor the attention of the legal Profession, reacts beneficially on the whole Law of Ownership by suggesting the general use of more expeditious and unceremonious modes of Conveyance and of Testamentary disposition. At this point, however, began a struggle, which is still continuing, between a logical and an historical Mode of distributing Things Owned. The rules found convenient for regulating the Rights of Ownership in what was called "Personal Property" could not be boldly extended to Rights of Ownership in "Real Property" simply on the ground of the expediency of those rules. It was necessary to effect this by the timid device of classing certain Immovable Things, when owned for a period less than the duration of a life-time, as, for all purposes, "Personal Property," and then of subjecting these to all the rules of Conveyance, of Testamentary disposition, and of Inheritance appropriated to Things originally falling under this class. As a kind of counterpoise, the true distinction was further confused by classing certain obviously Movable Things, as Rent, Heirlooms, and what are called "Fixtures," under the head of "Real Property," and making the proper legal consequences follow accordingly. In this way the actually existing distinction between "Real" and "Personal" Property in England, though mostly resting upon, is by no means identical with, that between Immovable and Movable Things. The historical and the logical method have blended with and confused each other.

The Roman Law and the modern Systems founded upon it, have maintained with great precision the distinction between Immovable and Movable Things. Though the antiquarian opposition of *Res mancipi* (including Land in Italy, Cattle, and Slaves), and *Res nec mancipi* was fostered by historical circumstances, yet this distinction operated over a comparatively narrow area, and in no way confused or obliterated the more dominant division of things into Movable and Immovable.

Even if the distinction of things into Movable and Immovable be ever so rigidly adopted, there must be an intermediate class, either created apart or provisionally sorted with one of the others, of Things which are for a time Immovable, but afterwards, with or without change of nature, cease to be so. To this class belong the Things, in modern times becoming of inordinate importance denominated "Fixtures."

Modern inventions and general mechanical and agricultural improvements, as well as the constantly widening extent of manufacturing, mining, and railway enterprises, have raised this class of Things to special importance, and call for special Legislation or legal decisions to determine into which class under different circumstances and for different purposes Fixtures shall be made to fall. Two main questions are involved. One is as to the amount of damage caused to one Thing by the severance from it of another Thing to which it has been long closely attached. This question opens out a minute series of investigations as to the closeness of the juncture between the two Things, the usefulness of either apart from the other, and the amount of destruction effected by the mere process of separation. The other question relates to the legal character of the Persons between whom at any moment the doubt as to Ownership arises. Thus English Law, while for purposes of public policy it is always more favourable to the removal of Fixtures set up for some classes of purposes than for others, nevertheless has different rules according as the claimant of the Fixture is an heir, an executor, or a tenant. It may be said, in fine, that the history of modern Law applicable to this subject is that of continuous limitation of the maxim, "*Quidquid plantatur solo, solo cedit*," such limitation, however, being applied in every class of cases only so far as the natural expectation of Parties, whether based on custom or other circumstances, and public policy allow.

Things may pass from the condition of Immovability to Movability not only, as in the case of Fixtures, without change of nature, but also through what must be taken to be, for legal purposes at least, a change of nature. The incessant operations of Nature supply multiform instances of this passage from stagnation to habitual motion and from habitual motion to stagnation. The Roman lawyers occupied themselves much with determining the "*apices Juris*" applicable to Things either in a state of transition between these two conditions or during a certain interval immediately succeeding that transition. The most obvious instances of such phenomena are the changes brought about in the surface of the earth through the action of the sea or of rivers resulting in alluvial deposits, in the gradual formation of islands, in the excavation of new channels for streams and in the desertion of old ones, and in the alteration of the line of the sea-coast. In these cases land becomes in fact a movable Thing, though only actually changing its place at long intervals of time. In spite, however, of the usually slow gradation of these transitions, it becomes from time to time necessary to determine whether the soil so submerged, elevated, or transferred, is regulated by the rules of Ownership applicable to Movable or to Immovable property. It is said that much of the Roman and the modern Law applicable to alluvial deposits owes its existence to litigation brought about through the disturbance of Rights of Ownership effected by the incalculable vagaries of the Po and the Mississippi. Roman and American law-books devote far more attention to this topic than do those of any other nation.

One more class of Things passing from Mobility to comparative Immobility is instanced by the case of wild and domestic animals. Both Roman and English Law have determined with considerable precision the marks by which certain animals are recognised—(1.) as capable of appropriation at all; (2.) as, for all purposes of Ownership, Immovables, being as it were fused with the land upon which they are found; (3.) as simply Movables, and for all purposes subject to the ordinary Law regulating Things.

It may be interesting, before leaving this topic, to append the passage from the *Code Napoléon* which introduces the subject of Immovable Things: " *Les biens sont immeubles, ou par leur nature, ou par leur destination, ou par l'objet auquel ils s'appliquent.*"

4.—" *Res Fungibiles* " and " *non-Fungibiles.*"

A celebrated division of Things admitting of Ownership is grounded on the fact that some Things admit of being replaced by others in no way and for no purposes distinguished from them, while other Things have an individuality of their own which admits of no substitution. Of the former class of Things it is said, by rather a lax use of language, that they have to be furnished *in genere*; and of the latter that they have to be furnished *in specie*. An instance of the former kind of Things is supplied by such aggregate masses of Things as a bushel of corn, a pipe of wine, a ton of hay, as to which the only point to be insisted upon is that the quality and the value be such as is described, and no attention is directed to the identity of the component elements.

This distinction is, however, far more arbitrary than real; because the nature of the contract may be such that the transfer of the particular bottles of wine indicated, the very grains of corn, the identical particles of hay, be distinctly contemplated and the contract be fulfilled in no other way than by such a transfer being actually carried out. In fact, though undoubtedly some Things are more usually treated as constituting a mere mass and others more usually described individually, " whether a Thing is due *in genere* or *in specie* depends, in each case, on the will of the transacting parties; so that Things of the same description must in one case be furnished *in genere* and in another *in specie*." If a picture of Raphael is to be delivered, a defendant cannot discharge himself by furnishing a picture by another Master. If one picture by Raphael have to be delivered, it will not suffice to deliver another. If a bottle of wine of the vintage of 1834, now standing in my cellar, has to be delivered, it will not be enough to deliver a bottle of the same vintage standing elsewhere.

The expression of this division of Things, as *Res Fungibiles* and *Res non-Fungibiles*, is founded on the language of the Digest when speaking of Things which " *in genere suo magis recipiunt functionem per solutionem quam specie.*"

5.—*Things Corporeal and (so-called) Incorporeal.*

The very essence of a Thing, for legal purposes, is that it belongs to the material Universe, that is, that it has a body, or is corporeal. Hence, strictly speaking, an Incorporeal Thing is a contradiction in terms. Nevertheless it has come about, in the course of the evolution of juridical ideas, that certain Rights in Things have acquired the name, pomp, and circumstance of Things themselves. The Romans, indeed, not only included among incorporeal Things "*servitutes*," "*hæreditas*," and "*obligationes*," but (according to the best authorities) Rights and Duties of whatever description, and even Acts and Events. Among "*incorporalia*" are included "*omnia quæ in jure consistunt.*" The English Law has been more parsimonious and precise in its use of the word Incorporeal. Among Incorporeal Things are mainly included certain narrow classes of Rights in Things closely bound up with fixed National institutions, and the enjoyment of which Rights is made the subject-matter of a fresh class of Rights accompanied with all the incidents of ordinary Rights of Ownership whether in Real or Personal property. Such Incorporeal Things are Advowsons, Tithes, Commons, Offices, Dignities, Franchises, Annuities, and Rent-Charges. The Rights to these Rights are, for all purposes, the same as Rights of Ownership in Real-estate. They admit of the same modes of transfer ; they descend in the same way on the death of each Owner ; they admit of being parcelled out into the same kinds of limited and partial Rights.

To the Class of Incorporeal Things giving rise to Rights of Ownership attended with all the legal incidents of Rights of Ownership in personal property, belong those peculiar and indeterminate advantages which are the subject-matter of what are called "Copy-right" and "Patent-Right." The truth is, that in this last case, as in some of the instances given in the last paragraph, there are no actual Things which are the bases of Ownership at all. Nothing is gained by speaking of "property in ideas" any more than by supposing that a Franchise or a

Dignity has any direct or necessary relation to Land. It is convenient, for purposes of public policy, to make certain classes of Rights follow in all respects the analogy of certain classes of Rights of Ownership. In order to satisfy the popular demand for logical consistency, the supposition is favoured that some Thing or other Owned must be at the bottom of both classes of Rights. The Thing Owned not being visible, tangible, audible, or apprehensible by any of the senses, that is, not existing at all, is by a sort of humorous honesty denominated an Incorporeal Thing. If the word Thing is to be of any real service either in Legal education or in the construction of a Legal System, the use of it must be severely limited to objects belonging to the material universe, capable of being apprehended by the senses, and every other sentimental, analogical, or metaphorical abuse of the term must be rigidly excluded.

It is well just to note that the peculiar Rights designated as "Copy-right" and "Patent-right," need not be treated as Rights of Ownership at all. They may be treated as merely personal Rights conceded by Law on grounds of public policy, having corresponding Duties, which are imposed upon Persons in the Community generally. These duties are such as to abstain within a limited time from publishing copies of a literary work, from making and selling certain manufactured articles, from using certain trade-marks, and the like. The truest analogy to these Rights is to be found in Rights to Personal Security, and to Personal Reputation, though the object of the Right be rather the enjoyment of wealth than of a secure and undisturbed existence. On this account there would be good reason for treating such Rights rather under the head of Laws relating to Civil

Injuries and Crimes than under the present head. It happens, however, that the Modes in which these Rights are created, are transferred, descend, and are protected according to most systems of Law, bring them so close to Rights of Ownership, properly so called, that they are universally treated side by side with these. The nearest analogy to them is that supplied by the sort of Right styled a "Monopoly."

6.—"*Singulæ Res*" and "*Universitas Rerum.*"

It sometimes happens that certain agglomerate masses of really distinct Things are so constantly regarded as indivisible wholes, that for all legal purposes they are treated severally as single Things and not as many. This habitual agglomeration may be either the result of natural facts or of artificial institutions. To the former class of cases belong a flock of sheep, a draught of fishes, a swarm of bees, a ship, a bale of goods. To the latter class of cases belong the multitudinous articles which, under the name "*hæreditas*," passed by Roman Law to the heir on the death of his ancestor; the imperial privy-purse, or "*fiscus*," which in another aspect was also regarded as a "*persona*;" a "Real estate" in Land according to English Law, with all the appurtenances in the way of forests, streams, buildings, game, and minerals, which in the generality of cases accompany its legal vicissitudes, in block.

In fine, the distinction between "*Singulæ Res*" and "*Universitas Rerum*" is only worthy of notice on the grounds of the occasional abbreviation in expression which it provides, and of the actual political Institutions, past or present, which it records or substantiates.

7.—*Sundry other oppositions, as between Things Divisible and Indivisible; Principal and Accessory; Existing and About-to-exist.*

The above have been historically, and are practically, the most notable Modes of classifying Things Owned. The process might be continued indefinitely; but no greater advantage would be reaped than that of gratifying an overstrained logical instinct or a curious ingenuity. Suffice it to say, that in treating of Things,—that is, of fragments of the material Universe,—the invariable order of that Universe is everywhere presupposed. The facts of time, space, and matter imply sequence, division, or possible separation. Hence Jurists have gone on to create great bifurcate Divisions between " Things Existing " and " Things likely to exist shortly ; " between " Things admitting of Division without Change of Nature and Things not so admitting ; " between Things Principal and Things Accessory. It often happens that, for particular purposes and in certain departments of a Legal system, such Modes of distribution must be kept carefully in mind; but they are at once too vague and too precise, too sweeping and too microscopic, to be the basis of leading divisions of Things Owned.

C.—Persons Who Own.

A Person in a modern State has already been explained to be a Human Being looked upon as capable of being invested with Rights, or made liable to the performance of Duties. The facts of Human Nature, however, and the circumstances, natural or artificial, of Civil Society introduce a graduated scale of qualifications in the Persons, who are members of the State, for the discharge of the moral functions which such legal Rights or Duties involve. Infancy, Puberty, Idiocy, Insanity, Marriage, and such more artificial incidents as Bankruptcy, operate generally, and some of them universally, upon the capacity to Will, to Act, and to form an Intention. The partial incapacity thereby brought about excites the anxious solicitude of the Legislator, and, guarding against introducing a general sense of insecurity in Ownership, he betakes himself to protecting the infirm or the imbecile Owner against the consequences of his own ill-advised acts, and all other Persons against them likewise. This process of protection is effected in two ways: firstly, by not allowing the incapacitated Person to be invested with a Right; and, secondly, by forcibly restricting his power of exercising it though he is invested with it.

Strictly speaking, according to the definition of a Right which has here been given, it is not possible to distinguish between a Right and the exercise of it. A Right was defined as a "measure of control over the Acts of Persons." Where the possibility of this control is not present there is no Right at all. However, it has become such a fixed habit with Jurists to make the distinction in question that it is useless to attempt to discard it. Hence instead of saying, as would be rigidly correct, that a Minor or a Lunatic has, in a large class of cases, no Rights of Ownership at all, it is customary to say that the Rights of Ownership are in no way impaired by the facts of Minority and Lunacy, though the exercise of those Rights is hemmed in on every side. The true meaning of this is that whereas the Rights of Ownership proper to a healthy adult are, to a certain extent, annulled in the case of a

Minor or a Lunatic, yet they are kept, as it were, in suspense, ready from moment to moment to revive in full force as soon as ever the invalidating facts of Minority or Lunacy cease to be present.

During this period, for which the Right is partially withdrawn, or (to use the popular language) its exercise is restricted, it is customary in all States to interpose some competent adult for the purpose of being invested with the Right to its fullest extent, which Right he is called upon to exercise solely for the benefit of the incompetent Person whose place he fills. In this way Roman Law provided for the interests of "Infants," Minors, Lunatics, and reckless Spendthrifts by the institution of the "Patria Auctoritas" supported as it was by those of the "Tutela" and the "Curatela." English Law similarly guards the interests of "Infants," Orphans, and Lunatics, by the general recognition of the principles of Trusts and Trustees, and of the special form of Trust designated "Guardianship," as well as by the peculiar protective jurisdiction vested in the Lord Chancellor. The principles of Trusteeship will come on for consideration under the subsequent head of Laws affecting Special Classes of Persons. It may here, however, be noted that the conflicting views taken by an English Court of Common Law and by an English Court of Equity with respect to the question as to where the true Right of Ownership lies in the case of a Trust, exactly represent the distinction above dwelt upon between the view that a Right can be distinguished from the capacity of exercising it, and the opposed view that a dormant or suspended Right is no Right at all.

The situation of a Married Woman in the Roman and

in almost all modern Systems of Law, and that of a Person adjudged guilty of Felony or proclaimed an Outlaw, present almost unique instances (with the exception, perhaps, of the consequences of a *diminutio capitis* in Roman Law) of an entire incapacity of Owning brought about by causes wholly personal to the particular Owner. The legal position of a Married Woman will come on for particular consideration under the subsequent head just alluded to of Laws affecting Special Classes of Persons. The topic affords an instance of the difficulty of treating any part of a Legal System independently of every other part. Marriage cannot be handled completely apart from Ownership, nor Ownership apart from Marriage. And one of these topics must, from the nature of the case, be treated before the other. In a Code the most convenient method to adopt would be in this place briefly to summarise the Laws regulating the Rights of Ownership of Married Women, and under the later head, treating of Married Persons generally, to develope these Laws in full.

It is necessary to notice that in Roman Law, and in many modern Systems of Law, Women are through their whole life treated as being in a state of perpetual Minority. This cannot be looked upon as other than a temporary though very protracted phenomenon. Aliens, again, and Persons only admitted to incomplete Rights of Citizenship are, in most States, subjected, for purposes of public policy, to special incapacities with respect to Ownership; as, for instance, in the matter of shipping, land, factories, buildings in towns, and various other things. Speaking generally, the classes of Persons whose capacity of Owning is either temporarily or permanently annulled or restricted by the policy of modern States are the following:—

1. Infants and Minors.
2. Idiots and Lunatics.
3. Felons and Outlaws.
4. Aliens.
5. Married Women.

To this list there might be added the class of what are called "Fictitious Persons" or Corporations, but the whole Law relating to them is so peculiar that it is more conveniently treated, without anticipation, in its entirety under the subsequent head of Laws affecting special Classes of Persons.

D.—Rights of Ownership.

A Right of Ownership is a measure of control delegated by the State, having for its purpose the exclusion of all Persons other than the Person invested with the Right from interfering with his use of a definite Thing in certain definite or in a number of indefinite ways. The largest Right of Ownership is where the Thing Owned is movable and destructible. Such a Right, by involving the power of destroying the Thing (*facultas abutendi*), carries with it the power of excluding all possible Persons other than the present Owner from ever using it in any way whatever. In the case of an immovable and therefore, for the most part, an indestructible Thing, the largest Right of Ownership is that which implies the liberty of using the Thing in the greatest number of Modes, for the longest duration of Time, and with the greatest possible facilities for Alienation either during the life-time or upon the death of the Owner. The policy of every known civilised State has always led to the restriction, in certain directions, of even the largest Rights of Ownership. Such a restriction has been dictated by regard to the interests of future Owners, to general economical or political views in respect of the cultivation and proprietorship of land, or to the urgency of State necessities in the way of locomotion, commerce, national health, and defence. Hence, as Mr. Austin has explained, the largest Right of Ownership in land known to Roman Law, *Dominium*, and its English equivalent in a *Fee-simple Estate*, are rather marked off from every lesser Right of Ownership by their indefiniteness in respect of limitation than by their actual freedom from all limitation. Negative terms suit the definition of such Rights better than positive ones. " The idea of absolute property," says Mr. Austin, " is a Right indefinite in point of User, unlimited in extent of Duration, and alienable by the actual Owner from every successor who, in default of alienation by him, might take the Subject of it." This definition points at once to the natural mode of classifying all lesser Rights of Ownership. These may owe their inferiority of value to—

(1.) The Mode of User being definitely described.
(2.) The Time during which they last being strictly limited.
(3.) Restrictions imposed upon the actual Owner in the matter of Alienation.

Now it will generally happen that any Right of Ownership inferior to the highest will exhibit that inferiority in all these points at once ; and in fact, this follows almost as of course, inasmuch as the identical policy which dictates that an Owner should be severely hemmed in with respect to the kind of uses to which he may turn the Thing Owned, also suggests that the time during which his Right lasts should be sharply limited, and that in the matter of alienation the interests of the Public, present and future, should be watched with quite as much anxiety as the interests of the existing Owner himself.

Hence arise two great leading divisions of Rights of Ownership, which, between them, comprehend all conceivable Rights of Ownership.

I. *Dominium*, or Absolute Ownership, in which the Mode of User, Duration of the Right, and facilities of Alienation are unlimited or indefinite.

II. All lesser Rights, including Estates for Life, for years, or upon condition; Copyhold Estates, and Estates Tail in English Law; *Emphyteusis*, *Métayer*-tenancies, and Usufructuary Estates generally; Servitudes or Easements, and generally all *Jura in Re* according to the largest intent of the classical Jurists, including the Rights of Carriers, of Depositaries, of Pledgees, and of the merest " Possessors."

All the Rights belonging to the second class are strictly limited on many sides; and a classification of them may rest upon the differences in the Mode of User allowed, in the Duration of the Right, or in the facilities for its transmission from hand to hand. It is necessary, in fact, to combine the different bases of classification, and first to make one lead the way and then the other. In the following arrangement the first three classes are determined by reference to Time of enjoyment, the other three by circumstances in the Mode of User.

Classification of Rights of Ownership less than the most unrestricted ones.

1. Rights of Ownership for a period determinate though uncertain, as a Life Estate, an Estate liable to come to an end on the performance of a condition or on the

happening of an event which must be performed or must happen at some time or other, or on the non-performance of a continuing condition as the Roman Estate called *Emphyteusis* and an English Copyhold Estate.

2. Rights of Ownership enjoyable for a period determinate and certain, as for years or for a period less than a year. This class includes the briefest tenancy, as from week to week, it being noted that the briefer the tenancy the more severely limited is the Mode of User. For the protection of future tenants it is customary, especially in agricultural leases, to introduce, either by judicial Interpretation or by special Covenants, particular restrictions on the Owner's powers as the time during which the Right lasts draws to a close. Local and general customs, recognised in Courts of Law, define in these cases the Mode of User, respect being had not only to the interest of the immediate incoming tenant, but to that of all future Owners, as well as to the concern of the whole Community in the productiveness of the ground and in the progress of Agriculture.

3. Rights of Ownership enjoyable for a period indeterminate and uncertain, as Estates at Will and Estates held upon a Condition which may never be performed.

4. Rights of Ownership enjoyable for a period longer or shorter, determinate or indeterminate, certain or uncertain, and which are distinguished by the narrow and simple Modifications of Use which they suppose. Such are Easements or Servitudes, which may be regarded as limited and special Rights parsimoniously carved out of indefinite and general ones. Such are the more familiar Rights of Way and of Common, Rights to Tithes, to Light, to Air, to Running Water, to the benefit of a supporting

Wall; the less familiar Rights, in Roman Law, of *Stillicidium*, or the Right of leading off the water from one's own house to the house or ground of one's neighbour, and *Fumi immittendi*, or the Right of leading off heavy smoke or other unpleasant vapour through the chimney or over the ground of one's neighbour. In addition to such Rights, the term *Servitus* in Roman Law occasionally included other classes of Rights, or *Personal* as opposed to *Real* or *Prædial* Servitudes. Such were *usus, usufructus, habitatio*, the peculiarities of which need not be here described. To the same head also belong the Rights of working a mine or a quarry, of fishing in a stream, of hunting or shooting over land. All these Rights have this in common, that they deprive him who has the *Dominium*, or complete Ownership, of some but not of all the practical advantages he was able to draw from it. On the other hand, a Letting (*locatio, conductio*), or a Pledge accompanied with Possession (*pignus*), deprived for a time the *Dominus* of all practical advantages he was able to draw from the Thing let or pledged. Rights of this class imply indefinite degrees of variation according to—(1.) the Mode of User and of responsibility for abuse; (2.) the Time during which they last; (3) the facility of transmission by Deed, Will or a mere Event, such as change of habitation and the like.

- 5. The transitory Rights of Ownership coming under the English head of *Bailments*, such as the Rights of Carriers, Mandatories (in the Roman sense), Depositaries (in the same sense), Mortgagees in possession in English Equity, and Pawnbrokers or Pledgees generally. It is manifest that Rights of this class, though importing the unfettered use of Things for certain purposes, are strictly limited as to the Mode of that use, as to the Time during which it is permitted, and as to the degree of facility with which the so-called "special" Owner can part with his Right to another. Thus by English and by most systems of European Law a ship-master is entitled, "when the whole adventure is in jeopardy," to levy a contribution from the cargo for the purpose of lightening the ship. Railway Companies receiving live animals for the purpose of conveying them from place to place are required to give them proper food and to bestow upon them sufficient care, and, in the event of their not being claimed, are entitled to sell them for the purpose of paying the expense of their keep. So a gratuitous Depositary is universally held liable for "*crassa negligentia*," that is, an extravagant amount of negligence, and for that only; in other words, only a very small degree of diligence is demanded of him. The Rights and Duties of the Pledgee or Mortgagee in possession are described with great exactitude in every System of Law, and will come under more particular consideration when the subject is specifically handled under the subsequent division of "Laws of Contract." In this place it is sufficient to note that the Pledgee or Mortgagee in possession has conceded to him by Law special opportunities for making his security valid without impairing the just claims of the true Owner. Such opportunities with their attendant precautions are provided by at once extending and defining his Power of Sale, by ensuring the payment of his Interest out of the rent or the employment of the Thing pledged, and by guarding against illegitimate abuse of the confidence reposed in him through an unwarrantable parting with the possession of the Thing to another. It is only by a technical and antiquarian distinction that English Common Law treats the Mortgagee as the true Owner, and English Equity the

Mortgagor. In both Systems the Mortgagee and Mortgagor are true Owners for certain purposes though their Rights of Ownership are different in nature and extent.

6. The last class of Rights of Ownership is the most evanescent and ephemeral of all. It includes all the Rights which arise from nothing else than from the mere fact of Possession. In all systems of Law, for the sake of the public peace, the mere fact of a Person's exercising Rights of Ownership, that is, acting as a true Owner in respect of using the Thing Owned, has been held to impart to such Person provisionally some of the legal capacities of the true Owner. The Person actually personating, as it were, the Owner may be in the several situations of the Thief, the Finder, or the Person whose legal claims to Ownership are incomplete, but whose moral claims are greater than those of anybody else. In English Law, according to a celebrated case, the finder of a jewel is entitled to bring an action for detainer of it against everybody but the true Owner. In Roman Law the Possessory Interdicts of the Prætor had the greatest possible validity for all purposes of guarding even the most transitory and casual claims of an actual Possessor, and, under certain circumstances, of enabling such claims to ripen into substantial Rights of Ownership. There was the *naturalis possessio*, which implied mere Physical contact with a Thing apart from all attempted exercise of Rights with respect to it. Such a Possession indeed carried no Rights of any kind with it. But where such Physical contact was accompanied with the fact of Intentional and conscious exercise of Rights of Ownership (juridical Possession, *possessio ad interdicta*), there the Interdict of the Prætor was available to reinstate the Possessor provisionally even if ousted by the true Owner. Where such a Possession as this

last was further accompanied by a *bonâ fide* belief in the validity of the Possessor's claims and by the presence of some legally recognised Mode in which the Thing came into the Possessor's hands (*justa causa*), after the lapse of a certain definitely fixed period of time, such merely Possessory claim (*possessio civilis, possessio ad usucapionem*) ripened into the fullest right of Ownership above described as *Dominium*. The legal aspects of Possession in Roman Law are so characteristic of the System, and so illustrative of the meaning of a Right of Ownership in its most incipient and embryonic form, as well as of its transitional stages from that of a mere protected claim to retain from moment to moment, through that of a Right against all Persons except one, up to that of a Right against all Persons whatever, that it has been thought worth while to exhibit briefly the Roman doctrine of Possession with more particularity than is usually required by the abstract mode of treatment here pursued.

E.—FACTS (ACTS OR EVENTS) WHICH DETERMINE THE ACCRUING OF A RIGHT OF OWNERSHIP.

In according Rights of Ownership to Persons in a Community, it is not only necessary that the Nature, Extent, and Duration of the Right accorded in each particular case should be described by the terms of the Law, but that the Persons who are to enjoy the Right should be marked out by determinate and unmistakable Signs. This may be accomplished in several ways; as— (1.) by mentioning individually by name the Persons to be made Owners; (2.) by describing them generically as belonging to certain well-known classes (as members of Corporate Bodies, for instance, or as born in a particular locality, or as professing a particular religious creed, or as holding certain public offices); or (3.) by selecting certain general and familiar Facts, whether Acts of Persons or Events, which may serve as convenient marks of the Persons to whom Rights of Ownership are to be accorded.

Of the first of these Modes of attributing Rights of Ownership specimens are presented in the Monopolies conceded to their favourites by the Tudor Princes, and in the estates, pensions, or heirlooms still granted from time to time to distinguished citizens by special Acts of Parliament. Of the second Mode (that by generic description) instances are at hand in the Roman Law of Intestacy, where the *sui heredes*, the *heredes sui et necessarii*, the *agnati*, the *cognati*, and the *gentiles*, were severally large classes of Persons, the individual members of which in turn, according to the Law of Succession prevailing at different periods of the Republic or of the Empire, were called to inherit the Rights of deceased Owners. So, in English Law, the Endowments of ecclesiastical, educational, charitable, and municipal Institutions are successively owned by a series of Persons marked out as time goes on, as satisfying the requirements essential to bring them under the class of Persons intended to be benefited by the Founder, or under such a similar class of Persons as the State may, at its discretion, and for purposes of its own, from time to time substitute for the class originally contemplated. The Fact upon which the accruing of the Right of Ownership in these last cases is made by Law to depend is the complex assemblage of all simple facts which together result in a Person's becoming a member of the class indicated. Thus the enjoyment of a Right of Ownership in respect of the income attached to a College Fellowship in an English University depends upon the combination of all the single circumstances which go to make an individual Person a Fellow of his College. These are such facts as Matriculation, the passing certain University Examinations, Election by the existing Fellows of the College, and (it may be) an oath or declaration of political opinion or of religious belief. These facts having all met in the case of any given Person, a Right of Ownership in respect to a certain proportion of the income of the College vests at fixed intervals of time in such Person absolutely in such a way as to impart to him a Right of Action against all Persons attempting to interfere with the full fruition of his Right. It is a like assemblage of simple facts which vests in an inhabitant of a particular Parish a Right of Common, a Right of Way to Church, a Right of Fishing, or other Rights exclusively confined to the inhabitants of that Parish,—or vests in the residents of a particular Town exclusive Rights to share in the contingent privileges of a School Foundation or of a University Scholarship.

Far the most ordinary Facts, however, upon the occurrence of which the State determines the accruing of Rights of Ownership are first introduced by the spontaneous habits of mankind and then stamped and authorised by the State on grounds of political expediency. The mere prevention of disputes by choosing some Person as Owner rather than leaving the question of Ownership a matter of incessant contention, the encouragement of industry and Agriculture, the facilitation of Commerce, the satisfaction of humane, benevolent, and affectionate sentiments, the satisfaction of fairly-grounded expectations, are a series of causes which, in their different degrees, have first suggested and then controlled the action of the State in the process of selecting the Facts which shall determine the accruing of Rights of Ownership.

The familiar forms in which these Facts have classed themselves in the best organised systems of Law are the following:—

1. Occupancy.
2. Specification.
3. Accession.
4. Invention.
5. Prescription.
6. Alienation in Life.
7. Alienation on Death.
8. Adjudication.
9. Forfeiture.

This arrangement is very arbitrary in its character, and, indeed, perhaps, under any arrangement, the several groups of Facts do not admit of being kept quite distinct. Some of these distinctions, indeed, may seem to rest upon too refined considerations to be fitted for the somewhat coarse Procedure of a Court of Justice. Nor in fact do any two Jurists or Systems of Law present exactly the same list. The above list, however, has been compounded rather with a view of neglecting no one of the principles upon which such Facts have been classified than with that of dogmatically overriding Modes of classification in use elsewhere. For the purpose of insisting on the true reasons for adopting these leading Facts as the criteria for the accruing of Rights of Ownership, they must each be submitted to a more particular examination.

1.—OCCUPANCY.

The Fact of being the first Finder, Discoverer, or Possessor of a Thing has invariably enforced in favour of such a Person the claim, in the sentiments of mankind, to actual proprietorship. This claim rests on a multitude of considerations, distinct and indistinct, important and worthless. Among these are that, historically speaking, all Rights of Ownership must have grown up in this way, the first Possessor being the first Owner; that no Person has a better claim; and that every Thing ought to have some Owner; that he who finds a Thing will have his expectation disappointed by non-acknowledgment of his claim, while no one's expectation is disappointed by acknowledgment of it; that it is to the advantage of the State to recognise rather than to disturb actual Possession; and that it is a further advantage to the State to stimulate the activity of all Persons in reducing Things not hitherto Owned into a condition serviceable to mankind.

Whatever be the grounds for recognising Occupancy as one of the Facts serving as the occasion for the accruing of Rights of Ownership, in all Systems of Law it is recognised as such to some extent, and in no System of Law to an unlimited extent. Thus in Roman Law the claims of a Finder of treasure were limited by reference to the place of finding and to the intentional or accidental nature of the discovery. In English Law the Finder of buried gold and silver, even in his own land, has no Rights whatever against the Crown. The English Game Laws, again, severely restrict the Rights which might otherwise be held likely to arise from the first occupancy of animals without an Owner. The Roman Lawyers drew fine distinctions in the case of Bees or animals *feræ naturæ* capable of being tamed, and determined what sort of Occupancy did, and what did not, impart Rights of Ownership.

2.—Specification.

When one Person works up the materials belonging to another into something which must be taken to be a new substance, which is the fact to which the Romans gave the name of *Specificatio*, the Legislator may be called upon to settle the rival claims of the Owner of the materials and the manufacturer of the new substance. The Roman Lawyers defined with well-known precision the respective claims of the two Persons in different cases. The grounds for apportioning Rights of Ownership to one or the other are such as—(1.) The *bona* or *mala fides* of one or the other person concerned, or more generally the Intention of the parties; (2.) the impossibility or difficulty of undoing the work and rescuing the materials in their original form; (3.) the amount of labour bestowed and the proportionate value of the work as compared with that of the materials; and (4.) lastly, the interest of the State in encouraging manufactures, in rewarding the manufacturer, and in preserving the fabric unmutilated.

3.—Accession.

A good deal of argument has arisen in modern times as respects the mode in which the fact of what is called Accession results in the accruing of Rights of Ownership. The *Accessio* of Roman Law was the Thing which, either through some silent and subtle operation of Nature, or through the almost involuntary or at least unintentional action of Man, became attached to a Thing already owned. This sort of annexation is illustrated in the product of fruit-trees and of corn-fields, in the birth of animals, in alluvial deposits, in the formation of islands, in the mixture (*commixtio*) of solid substances and of fluids (*confusio*), and in the attachment of beams or other movable Things to immovables (*adjunctio*).

The main source of controversy as to the way in which the Owner of one Thing acquires, through the mere fact of Accession, a Right of Ownership in another Thing turns upon whether this fact of Accession brings about the Right through the primary Occupation which it supposes, or whether it has some novel operation peculiar to itself. The truth is, that the ground upon which Accession is universally recognised as one of the Facts giving rise to Rights of Ownership is the same as that upon which Occupation itself and the other Facts in the same catalogue are so recognised. The ordinary habits and expectations of mankind are first respected and deferred to by the Lawgiver. The resulting rules are either gradually extended or restricted according as public policy undeviatingly points in one or the other direction. Thus in the case of Accession the industry and attention of the Husbandman is most stimulated by enforcing his claims to the products of his labour. The claims of rival Proprietors on the banks of a stream, in the case of the emerging of an island or of the deposit of an alluvial bed, will need to be adjusted with reference to their own natural and gradually *formed* expectations and to the inconvenience of encouraging universal competition from without. The well-known instance of the painter decorating the canvas of another with a priceless picture calls to mind the interest that the State may have in enforcing claims founded on nothing but Accession rather than risk the destruction of an object which can never be made good again. The policy which regulates the modern Law of

Fixtures, and which was dwelt upon above, presents the State in its most dignified attitude of doing as little violence as possible to the common practices and familiar expectations of its individual citizens, while for the public interests of Art, Agriculture, and Manufacturing enterprise, it does not hesitate to repudiate Accession as one of the Facts on the occurrence of which Rights of Ownership accrue.

4.—INVENTION.

For the encouragement of artistic or manufacturing ingenuity, it is the policy of most modern States to give certain Rights of the nature of Rights of Ownership to the Inventors of new processes for the fabrication of Things useful to the Community. The same sort of favour, and for the same reasons, is habitually shown to the Writers of literary Works. These Rights, in either case, are so peculiar in their kind that it is doubtful whether their consideration more properly falls under the present head or under that of Laws relating to Civil Injuries and Crimes. The peculiarity of the Rights accruing upon the Fact of Invention or of first Publication is, that there are no specific *Things* to which the Right has reference. It is a *Jus in Rem* in the largest sense, that is, a Right against all Persons whatever; but, instead of these Persons being forbidden to interfere with the free use of a Thing Owned, they are simply forbidden to sell duplicates or copies of a Thing. The beneficial result to the Inventor or the first Publisher is similar to that attached to a strict Right of Ownership, inasmuch as the market value of the process, the fabric, or the Work, is indefinitely enhanced through the Monopoly.

5.—Prescription.

Under the general term *Prescription* are gathered together all those Facts which result in Rights of Ownership being accorded simply on the ground that they have, during a certain space of time, been actually exercised. The way in which the complex Fact "Prescription" is made to operate is different in different States and at different epochs. The most complete and efficient mode of operation is presented in the Judicial or Statutory rules regulating *usucapio* in Roman Law, and the Acquisition of Easements in English Law. In these cases it is the actual exercise of Rights of Ownership during a period of Time strictly defined, coupled with more or fewer other circumstances with respect to *bona fides* and to the Mode in which Possession began, which serves to impart an indefeasible Right of Ownership as against the true Owner and against every other Person. Another form in which the same Fact of Prescription is made to operate to a more partial extent is by simply denying Rights of Action to those who have forborne to exercise their Right during a certain space of time. The Right of Ownership acquired in this last case may for many purposes be as large as one acquired in the more positive way just described, but it sometimes happens that a Person, who Owns simply because nobody can legally dispute his Right, has only imperfect powers of positively protecting his Right as against thieves, trespassers, and fraudulent or malevolent detainers.

The period and general conditions of acquiring a Right of Ownership by Prescription must naturally vary from State to State and in respect of different sorts of

Things. The actual habits of mankind and the probabilities which these habits raise will cause a very different Presumption to be made as to the true Owner of certain Things at one epoch, and as to that of the same Things or of other Things at a different epoch. Nothing could be more opposed than the habits, social condition, tastes, industrial occupations, propensities to travel and to general absence from home at the era of the Twelve Tables and at that of Justinian,—except perhaps the same characteristics at the era of Justinian, and in England during the reign of William IV.

The general policy of attaching Rights of Ownership to the actual exercise of such Rights during a definite time rests upon several considerations. Among these are—(1.) the expediency of encouraging Owners to protect their own interests by due personal vigilance rather than by litigation; (2.) the practical difficulty of ascertaining the true Owner when the actual Rights of Ownership have been long and uninterruptedly exercised by one whose claims are only at the last moment brought into dispute; and lastly (3.) the political convenience of treating the Person actually in possession as the responsible and beneficial Owner for all purposes whatsoever.

6.—ALIENATION IN LIFE.

Under the Modes of Acquisition described generally as Alienation, are properly included every kind of Intentional Transfer of Rights of Ownership by one Person to another, which is duly authenticated by the conspicuous Acts which the State insists upon as sufficient and necessary Signs of such Transfer. The actual grounds or occasions of such Transfer are the social, industrial, and mercantile operations of common life, such as gift, exchange, sale, pledge, loan, carriage, "mandate" in the Roman sense, deposit, and the like. The kinds of conspicuous Acts which in different nations, at different periods, and for different purposes, have been selected as authentic Signs of Transfer are,—*tradition*, that is, the actual handing over of a Movable Thing; symbolic forms of the same, as the *mancipatio* at Rome and a deposit of title-deeds, or a *feoffment*, in England; simple writing, or formal writing certified by witnesses and accompanied by technical marks and solemn words or gestures, as in the English Deed; or the entry of the transaction in some public Register, as in the case of mortgaging land in Scotland, or conveying a Copyhold Estate in England. The policy of insisting on such definite Acts as Signs of the intentional Transfer of Rights is determined with a view, partly, to the facilitation of Procedure through the presentation of clear, notorious Evidence; partly, to the protection of third Parties whose Rights might otherwise be tampered with, as in the case of successive Mortgages of the same thing by the Owner; partly to vindicating the concern the State has in knowing who is the true Owner of Things, especially Immovable ones, for the enforcement of its own Constitutional claims in the way of Taxation, and of general guardianship of all Things and Persons in the Community.

Most of the Acts above exemplified, and the kinds of Intentional Transfer they represent, follow upon previous mutual promises and arrangements between the old and the new Owner. This has led to an erroneous notion which has deeply coloured the history of Roman Law in the Middle Ages, and which reappears in most European Codes, to the effect that all Rights of Ownership whatever are of necessity preceded by a Contract, or at least an "Obligation" arising out of a Contract or a *delict*, and that a Contract has for its main, if not its only, purpose the bringing about the Acquisition of Rights of Ownership. The falsity and mischievousness of this notion has been exhibited in great detail and with much assiduity by Mr. Austin. It is sufficient here to summarise the argument by noticing—(1.) that where a legally effectual Transfer of Rights of Ownership is brought about by Gift, Prescription, Inheritance, or Occupancy of Things having no known Owner, no Contract or *Jus ad Rem* precedes the Act signifying the Transfer; and further (2.) that some of the most important of all Contracts have no reference whatever to any prospective Transfer of Rights of Ownership, but simply contemplate the control of the Promissor's future Acts, as in the case of Contracts of Apprenticeship, Contracts for Marriage, Contracts "in partial restraint of Trade," and generally the large class of Contracts falling under the head "*Facio ut facias.*" The consequence of this erroneous notion has been that in all European Codes the artificial and accidental divisions of the Institutes of Gaius and Justinian have been servilely reproduced, and the large topic of Contract, of course far less prominent in Roman than in modern times, has been simply treated under the general head of " Modes of Acquiring Property." It is fair to say, that the New York Code, which is not exempt from special vices of its own, treats Contracts, or rather " Obligations," as a distinct head co-ordinate with those of Persons and Property.

It will have been seen from the above analysis, that by " Mode of Acquisition " is here meant nothing else than the notorious Act which the State insists upon as a necessary and sufficient Sign of an Intentional Transfer of Rights of Ownership. There are cases, however, in which the same Act may operate as a Contract as well as a Conveyance. An ordinary English "Deed of Grant," a Mortgage, or even the common Act of Pledging, and every Lease, written or unwritten, has this effect. Over and above the Transfer of Rights of Ownership, a Court of Justice attaches by implication to every such Act certain promises about the future, such as, to give all assurance which may be required to make the Transfer effectual, to indemnify against previous charges subsequently discovered, to repair, to ensure, or possibly to reconvey the premises. Thus the same Act gives rise to two classes of consequences, the one being the Transfer of a *Jus in Rem* or Right of Ownership, the other the creation of more or fewer *Jura in Personam* or Personal Obligations.

7.—ALIENATION ON DEATH.

It has already been noticed, that, among prevalent methods of generically designating Persons who shall be invested with Rights of Ownership, that of selecting certain members of a present Owner's Family, whether naturally or artificially composed, has always been and still is the most conspicuous. The rules in early Roman Law, by which the *Agnati*, the *Cognati*, and the *Gentiles*, in a different order at different epochs, were called to enter upon a vacant inheritance, form one of the most illustrious and significant branches of the Roman System. The parallel phenomena in England attending the distribution of Real and Personal Property, either under the general rules of the Common Law or by force of special Statutes, are further illustrations of the generical mode of describing Persons in whom shall vest Rights of Ownership on the death of an Owner. In all these cases the policy of the State is to prevent disputes, to satisfy natural expectations, to carry out the probable wishes of the deceased Owner, to favour as far as possible a spirit of accumulation and frugality, or, more specially, to effect distinct national objects connected with the distribution of the national soil as in Modern France and Republican Rome, and, to a growing extent, even in England.

But a far more momentous and interesting method of determining the Persons in whom shall vest Rights of Ownership on the death of an Owner is that of giving validity to the expressed wishes of the deceased Owner. This method combines the advantages of being historically and morally natural, and politically expedient. It has exhibited itself from the earliest rise of civilised nations in a variety of forms. The public sale in the life-time of the Owner in early Roman times; the *donatio mortis causâ*, or gift in prospect of death, made only available in case of death, in Roman and English Law; the nuncupatory Wills of soldiers or sailors, recognised both in ancient and in most modern Systems of Law as conveying Rights of Ownership on death by no more formal method than a mere verbal declaration; the strict and formal written Testaments in Rome and England, from which none of the essential solemnities could safely be absent; the *fidei commissa* and *codicilli*, invented by way of equitable relaxation in early Imperial Rome;—these and all the more eccentric and possible varieties of Testamentary disposition which exist in Eastern Countries, such as public registration, superstitious ceremonies, and the like, are all nothing more than diverse fruits of the general principle that the deceased Owner has a more or less limited claim to dictate who shall succeed to his Rights of Ownership, but that the State has a counter-claim to dictate the Method and Form by which he shall make known his determination.

As confidence in the stability of Political Institutions has increased, and the Things capable of indefinite variations of Ownership have multiplied,—as, for instance, money secured by Life-Assurances, shares in Joint-Stock-Companies, money secured by Mortgages of every sort, the proceeds due to a Copy-right or a Patent-right, the damages payable under modern Legislation for injuries to life, limb, and property,—the desire of Owners to enforce their claims after their deaths becomes inordinate on the one hand, and, on the other, the public necessity of making the Process by which these claims are to be enforced as stringent and definite as possible. Hence follows such Legislation as that which in England prescribes an inexorable Mode of Making and Authenticating a Will, whether dealing with Real or Personal Property. The directions these essential formalities take, of which part have to be observed by the Testators and part by the Survivors, are in— (1.) the expressions by which their Authentication is to be signified, and the Mode of noting the connection of the Testator with the transaction, as by Signing, Sealing, and the like; (2.) the Number, Age, and Competency of Witnesses; (3.) the Deposit of the document in a public office; and (4.) the Acceptance and final Registration of the document by the proper officer. To these formalities may be added, as a *sine quâ non* of the efficacy of the document, the payment of such Taxes in the way of "legacy," "probate," or "succession duty," as the State may think fit to impose.

Over and above what may be called the general and essential formalities which a State imposes for the protection against abuse of so momentous a Right as that of Testamentary disposition, a number of subordinate, though important, restrictions are invariably applied for the same general purpose. These restrictions have reference to the Age, Mental Capacity, or possibly the legal Situation of the would-be Testator; to the use of special Terms to which Courts of Justice are bound to attach a technical Interpretation; and to the Time from which the operation of the Will is to date, whether from the moment at which it is made, from the moment of death, or from some later moment.

8.—ADJUDICATION.

The mode of acquisition styled "Adjudication" consists of the assemblage of Events or of Acts of Persons of which the outward expression is a formal sentence of a competent Court of Justice. The ancient Roman Conveyance by the fictitious process of a *cessio in jure*, and the corresponding devices in English Law of "Fines" and "Recoveries," are instances of Modes for vesting Rights of Ownership which are likely to characterise the less self-conscious and less resolute eras of every Legal System. In more modern times Bankruptcy, followed by the definite appointment of Assignees; actual Execution, following upon a Judgment and Verdict for Damages; a Distress for Rent followed by Sale of the articles distrained upon; the payment of a public Fine judicially imposed, or the liquidation of the penalty incurred by "estreated" recognisances,—are further instances of the most familiar and modern description of the Mode in which Adjudication, actual or presumed, operates as a Mode of Transferring Rights of Ownership.

9.—Forfeiture.

The operation of Forfeiture, that is, of some Act or Event arbitrarily selected by the State as a mark of the surrender of Rights of Ownership by one Person to another, is rather of political and historical than of juridical interest. It is purely a creation of Positive Law, inasmuch as its existence in particular Legal Systems has been far more due to what is peculiar in the circumstances of each Community than to those common exigencies and conditions of Humanity which prescribe the adoption of the other Modes of Acquisition hitherto passed in review. Under the term Forfeiture is included every Act or Event on the occurrence of which the State determines that some or all of a certain Person's Rights of Ownership shall summarily pass over to another Person strictly defined; such Act or Event not falling under any of the Classes above described generally as Alienation. Instances of the recognition of Forfeiture are supplied by certain consequences of the *diminutio capitis* in Roman Law, whether as affecting Liberty, Citizenship, or Family Relationship; by the Feudal doctrine of "*Escheat*" to the Lord of the Feud, for want of heirs, or for the attempted creation by the tenant of an "Estate larger than his own;" by the deprivation, in favour of the Crown, of Rights of Ownership in Goods, and even to some extent in Land, following, according to English Law, on "conviction" and "attainder" for a Felony; and by the legal effects of the antiquated process of Outlawry.

Some discussion has arisen among Jurists about the

propriety of giving the name "Title" to such Acts or Events as have been above enumerated as marks adopted by the State of the effectual acquisition of a Right of Ownership. The word "Title" has the disadvantage that at least three classes of meanings are attached to it. There is—(1.) the strict use of the word in Roman Law, according to which it signifies a definite portion of the whole formal process necessary for the effectual Transfer of Rights of Ownership, and in this sense was contradistinguished especially to the other portion of the same process denominated " *modus acquirendi* ;" (2.) the loose popular meaning prevalent among English Lawyers and in most English Text-books, according to which the word signifies not a specific Act or Event upon which a Right of Ownership is held by Law to accrue, but, sometimes, nothing else than the Documentary Proofs of such an Act having been performed or of such an Event having happened; at other times, the legal attitude of a Person invested with Rights of Ownership as a consequence of some such Act or Event, as in the loose expressions "Title by Contract," "by Gift," "by Invention," "by Prescription," "by Forfeiture" and the like; there is lastly (3.) the severe meaning which Mr. Austin aspires to attach to the word, according to which, in audacious violation of popular habits of speech, he would speak of a Title to Duties as well as to Rights, thereby using the word "Title" as expressing every Act or Event upon which Rights or Duties arise or terminate owing to Legislative provision, but as distinguishable from the Law itself. Mr. Bentham's "Investitive" and "Divestitive" Facts are useful expressions, and might be brought into legal circulation with advantage.

In view of this diversity of nomenclature, the purpose of the scientific Jurist must be to avoid all risk of ambiguity without attempting any too rash innovation. This purpose may be secured by designating all the complex Facts, whether Acts or Events, upon which Rights of Ownership accrue, as Titles. In this sense a Title is an arbitrary and visible Sign selected by the State, partly in deference to the general habits of mankind, partly with a view to political expediency, for the purpose of ascertaining the Persons in whom Rights of Ownership shall vest. The Mode of attributing Rights of Ownership through the use of Titles is then readily co-ordinated with the other Modes of attaining the same end, namely, that of describing the Person who shall Own individually by name, or that of describing him generically as belonging to some existing Class of Persons in the Community.

A few remarks must be made, lastly, on the expression " *Vested* and *Contingent* Rights." It has been seen that the Acquisition of a Right of Ownership is legally marked in one of three different kinds of fashions : either the new Owner is individually described by name ; or he is pointed out generically by describing the Class of Persons to which he belongs and the place he holds in that Class; or certain complex Facts are selected as definite tokens that Rights of Ownership have passed over from one Person to another. In all these cases a number of separate and distinct conditions have to combine in order to vest a Right of Ownership in a particular Person. Some of these conditions may be fulfilled at one time, and the essential complementary ones may not be fulfilled till a later time, or may never be fulfilled at all. So soon as a sufficient number of the conditions are fulfilled to ensure that a particular Person or his Representatives or Assigns shall succeed to a Right of Ownership either immediately or at some future time, the Right is said to be a *Vested* one. Nothing is wanting to the complete Acquisition of the Right by the Owner but the happening of certain Events which are certain to happen, or the lapse of a certain space of Time definitely fixed. But after some of the conditions for the complete Acquisition of a Right of Ownership have been fulfilled as above, it may be that it is uncertain whether the remaining indispensable conditions ever will be fulfilled. The Persons described by the Testator or Settlor may never come into being; the Persons whose existing Rights of Ownership it is purported to deal with, on their surrender of them by death or otherwise, may not have surrendered them at the Time contemplated; the Things to which the Rights have reference may perish or undergo a substantial change; certain other Persons may do or not do Acts with respect to which no certain provision can be made by the Person affecting to direct the succession to the Rights of Ownership. In all these cases, inasmuch as from one point of view it is a matter of mere chance whether an effectual Right of Ownership is really transferred to the Person indicated, the Right has been called a *Contingent* Right.

The expressions *Vested* and *Contingent* are, as Mr. Austin has pointed out, when applied to Rights, awkward and misleading. In either case the Right transferred may be identical in all respects, and the only difference is as to the time or the chance of the Right being acquired. It becomes a question in particular countries whether this sort of claim or expectation, which is founded on the prospect, more or less certain or definite, of a future Right of Ownership, is itself a sort of Right capable of being dealt with by transmission like any other Right; the decision is one of mere positive Institution, and different principles as respects the conveyance of what is called a "possibility" have been held at different periods of English Law.

F.—Modes of protecting Rights of Ownership.

As a mere question of Classification it may be doubted whether the topic of the legal expedients for making Rights of Ownership effectual properly belongs to the general head of Laws of Ownership or to that of Laws of Procedure. It belongs in truth to both heads: to the former, so far as the general classes of expedients available for protecting the Rights here concerned admit of being broadly distinguished; to the latter, so far as the detailed Processes by which these expedients are made operative by Courts of Justice have to be precisely investigated.

The general Modes by which the State gives security to Owners may be arranged as follows:—

    1. A Process of the most Summary description, of the nature of the Roman Interdict and of the English Injunction, by which an immediate Remedy is granted upon a *primâ facie* allegation of the actual or probable disturbance of the Owner in the actual exercise of his Right in its fullest comprehension. This Interdict, Injunction, or Summary Process may have in view either the forcible Expulsion of an Intruder and the Restitution of the Owner, or the Restoration, in kind, of Things wrongfully removed or detained, or the Arrest of the alleged wrong-doer in his conduct, either peremptorily,

or subject to the conflicting Rights of the Parties being hereafter formally ascertained in a Judicial Proceeding.
2. An ordinary Action or Suit having in view the Compensation of an Owner for Injuries received of the nature of wrongful removal or detainer of his goods; as for Trespass in the largest sense of this large term, and for interference of every sort with the freest and fullest enjoyment by the Owner of his Rights.
3. An Action or Suit, having in view not Compensation so much as actual Restoration and Restitution.
4. A Criminal Proceeding, by which the invader of a Right of Ownership is treated as a public enemy, is prosecuted at the public cost, and is punished in a definite Mode, over the quality, extent, duration, and necessity of which the Owner immediately injured has no manner of control.

The Injury punished may be either a Direct Injury, taking such forms as those of Theft, Robbery, Embezzlement, Receipt of Stolen Goods, or Malicious Injuries to Property (as in the quasi Criminal proceedings under the *Lex Aquilia*), or an Indirect Injury, as " Slander of Title " and the Injuries implied in the invasion of Rights essentially appendant to Rights of Ownership, such as Rights to Transfer those Rights. Under this last head come Forgery, the Suppression and Mutilation of Wills and of other Documents of like import, and certain Frauds by Trustees and by Bankrupts, or committed upon Public Securities.

CHAPTER XI.

LAWS OF CONTRACT.

The possibility of a prevalent national habit of relying upon Promises depends on the presence of several classes of Facts which, in spite of numerous celebrated but now exploded Theories to the contrary, are in early times in a very rudimentary state of development. Such a habit implies—(1.) an imaginative and dominant Conception of a Future Time as likely to become Present; (2.) a Belief in the probability of perfecting in the Future a plan of action sketched out in the Present; and (3.) such a knowledge of and confidence in Mankind as to be a ground for the Belief that another can and will control his own actions in the Future in the way he engages to do in the Present. To all these conditions must be added the one of the occurrence of a sufficient number of occasions in daily life for cultivating and maturing the Conceptions and Beliefs implied. According as these conditions present themselves more and more frequently and decisively, owing to the increase of social intercourse, of co-operative industrial effort, and of acquaintance with the constitution of Nature and of Man,—the whole intensified, it may be, by a progressive apprehension on the part of all Men of their real destination as Social Beings,—the fact of what is called Contract becomes a conspicuous element in National Life. Professor Maine has pointed out with what difficulty the idea is at first elaborated; how cumbrous the detailed ceremonial with which every compact between Family and Family is associated, and how slowly the mental elements of a mutual Promise disengage themselves from all that is formal, material, or merely evidentiary. The phenomenon of Contract as a social characteristic implies that men have found out that they can rely not only on their own conduct in the future, but on that of each other, and that they can safely guide their present conduct, under the assurance that others will do or not do hereafter certain acts specifically described.

In this way, as the German Jurists say, man's empire is extended over the wills of other Persons by Contract as it was extended over the natural world by Ownership, and over his own will by the primitive recognition of social order and liberty. He who relies on the Promise of another as respects the conduct of that other in the future has reduced so much of the fluctuating and incalculable chaos, constituting the realm of chance and accident, within the confines of what is clear, definite, and reliable. It is this habitual and growing human confidence which is even supposed in the very fact of Ownership itself and appears in new and larger manifestations as (according to the hypothesis of Professor Maine) the *mancipium* becomes severed from the *nexum*, and the *nexum* becomes the *obligatio*. Formal Exchange and Sale,—a Sale in which the purchase-money remains unpaid,—and a Sale in which neither is the purchase-money paid nor delivery made at the time,—is doubtless a true historical series of epochs in the development of Contract as a social Fact; though with economical occasions like these there would be keeping a constantly accelerated pace the more domestic transactions of hiring for service, carriage of goods, and the general employment of labour in the simplest pastoral, agricultural, or even predatory and military pursuits.

It is upon the prevalent tendency to make Contracts that a Law of Contract is grounded. Like all other Laws, this class of Laws arises out of the constitution of Society and reacts back upon that constitution by way of defining and maintaining it. These Laws have for their purpose the guiding of those who on the whole desire to submit themselves to such direction, and the punishing of the few refractory Persons who, being out of harmony with the current disposition of the whole Society, would otherwise hamper the progressive movement of the whole. The more special end of Laws of Contract is to facilitate the working of the social forces of the nation in respect of that mode of co-operative action by which the wills of two or more Persons are economically disposed towards certain harmonious courses of action. Where these courses of action are not of a kind that the State holds to be obviously prejudicial to the general life of the nation, and where the Persons interested have, by some unmistakable Act, signified their desire of controlling their own future actions severally, the State is ready to stand by on behalf of each as against the other, and threatens to punish the one who disappoints the expectations that have been formed.

Such is the general purpose and policy of what are called Laws of Contract, and it will be manifest that where a State thus specially intervenes in the private negotiations of its citizens, there is needed a special amount of determinateness as to the occasions upon which it will take upon itself so to interfere, and the most anxious solicitude to prevent its hampering the easy play or degrading the free spirit of that very life which it affects to quicken and regulate. Thus the consideration of Laws of Contract involves a careful scrutiny into all the parts of which every such Law is necessarily composed, as well as into the unbending natural facts, or common artificial precautions which control the operation of all such Laws. Such a scrutiny will best be performed by treating the subject in accordance with the following arrangement:—

- A. Explanation of the legal term *Contract*.
- B. Persons who make Contracts.
- C. Authentic Signs by which the making or dissolving of a Contract is notified.
- D. Rights accruing through the making of a Contract.
- E. Classification of Contracts.

A.—Explanation of the legal term *Contract*.

In attempting a definition of the legal term *Contract*, the modern Jurist is at once met by the difficulty he has to encounter at every point arising from the fact that the use of juridical terms has undergone an indefinite amount of vacillation according as they have been employed by the Roman and Middle-Age Jurists, by modern speculative theorists, or by the authors of practical treatises on branches of Positive Law. In view of the perplexity so arising, the best he can do is to find a definition which shall cover the most numerous and important uses of the term to be defined, and shall do as little violence as possible to popular usage. In order to frame such a definition of the word *Contract*, it must be recognised that the essential notion of a legal Contract contains the following ingredients:—

1. There is a complete and Joint Act of two or more Persons, from which Act Rights and Duties take their rise.

2. Some of the Duties so arising relate to the *future* (and not the *present*) Acts of one, some, or all of the Parties to the said Joint Act.

3. The said Joint Act may either be held by the State as alone sufficient Evidence of such Act itself having been performed, or else other and different Acts may be required to be performed by way of providing Evidence of the due performance of the Joint Act, and from which Joint Act the evidentiary Acts are more or less clearly distinguishable.

The recognition of these principles justifies the following definition of a *Contract*:—

A Contract is such a Joint Act of two or more Persons as is held sufficient in Law to determine the present and future Rights and present and future Duties of one, or some, or all of such Persons; of which Act specific Evidence is required by Law.

It might be said that the last part of this definition is only descriptive, and therefore superfluous. It is, however, important, on every occasion of using the term *Contract*, to distinguish clearly between the Act of efficient consent between the Parties and the Evidence of the Act required by Law. This Evidence, indeed, may be of the most varied and even artificial kind. It may be, on the other hand, only the accumulation of circumstances or Events, or subsequent Acts of the Parties, or the Acts of other Persons which tend to render it probable that the Act of efficient Consent was really performed.

In the above definition, the word *future* has been carefully introduced. This serves to distinguish the present definition from the celebrated one given by Savigny, which, from its extreme comprehensiveness, becomes almost valueless. His definition of a *Contract* is "an Union of two or more Persons resulting in an Accordant Declaration of Will, whereby their Legal Relations are determined." The omission of the word *future* here results in the inclusion of a number of Joint or accordant Acts which no known Legal System and no popular dialect have ever associated with the notion of a Contract. He admits, indeed, that the kinds of Contract which give rise to Obligations are the most important and frequent, but that simple Tradition or delivery of a Thing is a true Contract. It is here asserted, on the contrary, that Tradition, like Exchange or a Sale for ready money, are nothing more than simple Acts by which, with or without other surrounding circumstances, rights of Ownership are acquired. The essence of a Contract is the reliance on the Promise of another as to his Acts in the future; and it is in recognising the growing disposition on the part of its citizens to entertain such reliance that the State evolves the strict legal notion of a Contract, and constructs a Law of Contract.

B.—PERSONS WHO MAKE CONTRACTS.

While every legal Person, that is, in modern States, every member of the Community, is presumed to be possessed of a certain degree of Moral Responsibility, in default of evidence to the contrary, for some purposes a higher degree or different kind of Moral Responsibility is demanded than for other purposes. Thus in respect of the ordinary Duties attaching to every citizen as such, (in view of which he is compelled to abstain from troubling the general peace of the Community, from plotting against its Government, or from violently invading the simplest private Rights of personal Security and of Ownership,) the presumption, not rebutted, of some degree—however minute—of Moral Responsibility, will render an offender liable to Punishment. In other words, it is held, with good reason, in all Systems of Law, that even a very infirm capacity of voluntary action and a peculiarly restricted experience of the ordinary consequences of Acts and of sequences of Events will suffice to enable any citizen to do his negative part as an inoffensive member of the Community, even if they do not entitle him, with due regard to the safety of himself and others, to engage in the more complex and artificial sort of intercourse which is implied (for instance) in making a Will, in endorsing a Bill of Exchange, in bringing an Action at Law, and, more generally, in co-operating with others in the more complicated negotiations of commercial life.

Thus it comes about that, though the general marks or signs of a legal Person have been already described under the head of the *Explanation of Legal Terms*, yet in the treatment of each department successively of a complete System of Law, the matter comes on afresh for consideration, according as the Rights and Duties assigned under that department, and the Acts from which those Rights and Duties take their rise, necessarily presuppose varying measures of capacity, and varying amounts of knowledge, in the Persons to whom the Law is immediately addressed. The explanation given above of the notion expressed by the term *Contract* suggests at once that, for the purpose of engaging in the Joint Act described, a superior degree of capacity of voluntary action and an amount of knowledge reaching to a point beyond the immediate consequences of Acts is imperatively required. In order for Persons honourably and discreetly to undertake such Duties in the future as they do when, with the sanction of Law, they recognise Rights in another as controlling their own future Acts, they must be able in some measure to anticipate future Time, and to foresee how far they can themselves rely upon their own actual performance of what they Promise. The moral aspects, as well as the commercial expediency, of the engagement will depend upon the accuracy of this prevision, though it would be vain for Law in its formal shape, or through the process of its Administration, to attempt to secure a completely honest moral attitude in all Persons making Contracts. Nevertheless, Legislators in all countries ever show an increasing tendency to favour by their support most of all, if not exclusively, the classes of Promises in which the foresight and wisdom of the Promisors are most conspicuously present, and to abstain altogether from countenancing Promises as to which it may reasonably be inferred that the Promisors had not the capacity of knowing what was the nature of the future Duties to the performance of which they were binding themselves.

But furthermore,—inasmuch as the Law always demands certain strict Evidence of the fact of a Contract having been made, whether that Evidence be the mere Act of consenting itself, or it be some Supplementary Act, or it be implied from certain surrounding circumstances, —the Evidentiary Act, (where one is required) being of a strictly formal and solemn, even if not generally now of a cumbrous nature, demands a peculiar amount of capacity for voluntary action. It has been pointed out by Professor Maine, how the formal part of a Contract is at first the only essential part, and the part upon which public attention is exclusively concentrated. In the Roman Contract by *Stipulatio* a capacity of articulating the formal words in the proper language or languages and sequence was, at all periods, held essential to the validity of the Engagement. So even in modern times, where, as under the Statute of Frauds, the only admissible Evidence of certain Contracts is a Deed, the entire amount of capacity necessary for executing a Deed is presupposed. These considerations, whether grounded on the nature of a Contract in itself or of the Evidence of it insisted upon by Law, are sufficient to explain why, in all countries, all or some of the following Classes of Persons are, for some purposes or other, under special disabilities in the matter of making Contracts:—

1. Infants.
2. Lunatics and the like, including Drunkards.
3. Persons under Duress of all kinds, physical, moral, or legal.
4. Married Women.
5. Agents.
6. Outlaws, if such exist.
7. Aliens.

1.—INFANTS.

Infancy, or that condition of mind and body in which the faculties have not obtained the average pitch of development which characterises the most important years of Human Life, must necessarily be recognised in all

Systems of Law except the most immature, and in every department of each Legal System. It is not necessary here to distinguish between the popular and the legal use of the term *Infancy*, nor to note that the Roman use of the term *Infans* rather corresponded with the popular English use, while the English law-term *Infant* rather corresponds with the Roman term *impubes*. A very slight experience of worldly affairs may be supposed to teach a young man, after he has passed the years of childhood, the purposes of and the liabilities attached to some of the simpler classes of Contracts,—as those of Sale, Loan, Hiring, and Carriage. There are, however, other classes of Contracts which, concerned as they are with the most complex transactions of mercantile life, demand a very considerable experience of those transactions in order to enable anyone fairly and discreetly to enter upon them. Of this latter class are those which result from "stating an account," accepting or indorsing a Bill of Exchange, trading generally, insuring goods, engaging in a Partnership, and referring a disputed claim to Arbitration. It is the anxious endeavour of all advanced Legal Systems to protect Minors and the Community generally against the pernicious consequences likely to arise from the premature handling of such matters as these by those whose youth raises an irresistible Presumption of inexperience. In Roman Law the whole Institution of the *Patria auctoritas* and the *tutela*, as well as special Legislation such as the *Senatus-consultum Macedonianum* for the protection of Heirs against the exactions of Usurers, were ever ready for the deliverance of the young from the consequences of inexperience in the matter of Contracting. The Law of England is equally solicitous in pursuit of the same ends, though by a less circuitous path. By this Law no action for Breach of Contract can be sustained except for what has been called and interpreted to be the " necessaries of life," if the Defendant was below the Age of twenty-one years at the time of making the Contract, and has not confirmed the Contract after attaining that Age. By the doctrine of a " natural obligation" the Roman lawyers contrived to parry, to a certain extent, the practical injustice and even Fraud which might occasionally result from the severe application of their own protective Rules.

The precise Age, of course, at which the capacity for Contracting is attained, and the kind of Contracts, if any, permissible even under that Age, will differ from country to country. The leading idea which underlies the prevalent exclusion of the young from the power of Contracting is contained in the following assumptions :—(1.) That the Law generally protects, by anticipation, its citizens against probable fraudulent Acts on the part of one another and against the possible consequences of inexpedient Acts of their own to the performance of which they were induced by inevitable causes, such as, in this case, the deficient understanding incident to Youth: (2.) That in undertaking any Duties in the future a larger amount of knowledge and self-possession is needed than in doing present Acts of which the consequences are at once apparent: (3.) That a special knowledge of mankind is needed to enable a Contractor to ascertain the integrity and general competency of the other Persons joining in the Act in which the Contract results.

2.—Lunatics and the like, including Drunkards.

Another class of Persons whose ability to make a Contract is restricted in all mature Systems of Law consists of those who, through congenital malformation or accidental affliction, temporary or permanent, or even as the consequence of voluntary action, are under a special incapacity either to Act freely or to understand the consequences of their Acts. The habit of Contracting is so far artificial and is a result of such subtle grounds of mutual confidence between man and man, that a very small degree of mental aberration is universally held to suffice for the purpose of disabling a would-be Contractor. In constructing the rules for the regulation of this class of disabilities there are certain competing considerations which cannot be left out of sight. In the first place, the same difficulty is encountered here as in all other matters relating to purely mental conditions, which is due to the practical impossibility of discriminating precisely between the different degrees of Moral Responsibility. In the second place, the very attempt to apply refined distinctions in matters of this nature must lead to the aggravation of the protective characteristics of this part of the Law, must promote an excessive interference in the ordinary industrial concerns of Mankind, and indeed must tend to generate the very evil it is designed to prevent, that is, the multiplication of Frauds. But again, in the third place, if the doctrine as to the complete inability to Contract in the cases now under contemplation were pressed to its full logical extent, all Persons labouring even under trivial forms of mental disease might experience a difficulty in procuring the necessaries of life, or even the proper services of others, and the requisite medical attention.

The different considerations here alluded to have led to proportionate modifications in the most celebrated Systems of Law with respect to the Contractual disabilities of Persons in the position of Lunatics. The Roman Institution of the *curatela*, and the corresponding English institution of Guardianship in Lunacy; the cautiously applied Rule of English Law that where a reasonable Contract has been made by a Lunatic with a Person not aware of the patient's condition, and the Contract has been so far performed that the Parties cannot be restored to their original position, the Contract will be held valid; the equally beneficial rule, that a Contract made by a Lunatic during a lucid interval, (where no advantage has been taken of the patient,) and also one made at any time for necessaries, will also be held valid; and the inverse rule, that a Contract made during a fit of drunkenness, and instantly repudiated on the return of sobriety, will not be supported,—these Institutions and Rules are instances at once of the general incapacity of those in the position of Lunatics to Contract, and of the special methods in use for the correction and qualification of this incapacity.

3.—PERSONS UNDER DURESS OF ALL KINDS, PHYSICAL, MORAL, OR LEGAL.

The ground of incapacity resulting from what is called Duress,—that is, a condition of real or apprehended physical restraint,—is of a twofold nature. In the first place, the would-be Contractor who is under Duress is assumed to be, to a greater or less extent, unable to perform the formal and material Acts, whether Constitutive or Evidentiary, implied in a Contract, with that absolute freedom from impediment from without which a true *act* presupposes. In the second place, it is assumed that to a Person under Duress certain inducements are likely to be presented which render him to a greater or less extent incapable of estimating properly his own true interests. Thus, a Contract made with him under such circumstances is, for the other Party, tainted with Fraud. Some Systems of Law, as the English, go even to the extent in some cases of not allowing this Presumption to be rebutted, even where the term Duress is extended to that sort of legitimate influence which is exercisable by Trustees, Guardians, and professional legal advisers. The English doctrine of "Constructive Fraud," as applied by Courts of Equity to large classes of Contracts, however honestly made in fact, between Persons in the relation of confidence to each other, over whom the Law assumes a special protectorate, is in fact nothing more than an extension of the principle of disability now under consideration.

The position of convicted Criminals suffering legal punishment is so exceptional and peculiar that it throws little light on the general doctrine of Contractual disability. What has been said as to the reasons for disability found in ordinary Duress is applicable in a far higher degree to that limited class of Persons to whom the smallest amount of freedom of action is permitted, and whose inducements to barter for insignificant present objects their own future welfare and that of their Families are likely to be in many cases inordinate. It is an anomaly in the Law of England, that felons are liable upon the Contracts made by them while under sentence, though incapable of ever taking advantage of them. This is, in fact, a circuitous and irrational mode of merely increasing the punishment.

4.—MARRIED WOMEN.

The remaining classes of Persons whose incapacity of Contracting is generally announced by Law are in a different position from most of those hitherto mentioned, inasmuch as here the Incapacity is not due to natural facts or misfortunes with which the Law endeavours to grapple, but to Institutions owing their birth and existence to Law itself. Thus it is nothing more than mere arbitrary Legislation (whether wise or unwise) which, in all countries, ancient and modern, has placed and still places a Married Woman in such a state of physical and civil subordination to her Husband that her Rights of Ownership are severely restricted on all sides and even her rights of Personal Security restricted as against her own Husband. This artificial state in which a Married Woman is placed naturally carries with it for many purposes the Presumption of incapacity for voluntary action, and also of a want of such an acquaintance with the affairs of the world as is needed for prudently engaging in the more complicated transactions of life. In such a case the main conditions for making a valid Contract are presumed to be absent or in abeyance, and the legal conclusion is expressed in the general incapacity on the part of Married Women to Contract, as recognised by all known Systems of Law. This incapacity extended under the Roman Law to all Women whatever, who accordingly, under that Law, were throughout their lives in a like condition of pupilage and Civil dependence as are Married Women in modern Europe. The successive invasions that have been made by the system of "*Communauté*" abroad, and by the doctrine of the "Wife's Separate Estate" in English Equity, upon the general legal relationships of Married Persons, have carried with them proportionate modifications in the Rules applicable to the Contracts of Married Women. The older exceptions introduced by the Law of England for the case of a Woman trading under the "Custom of London," and of a Woman whose Husband is, through a sentence of transportation Civilly dead, recognise and illustrate the general principles on which the ordinary Rule is founded.

5.—AGENTS.

The fact of Agency may be treated from two distinct points of view, according as it is regarded as furnishing the basis for a distinct and peculiar kind of Contract or as qualifying the capacity of Persons in the course of making other Contracts. For purposes of convenient reference, which is the main object in the construction of a Code, all the aspects of Agency will best be treated together under one head. In a logical exhibition of the contents of a Legal System, on the other hand, the disabling effects of Agency should be treated apart from the general description of the Contract of Agency in order to lay those effects side by side with the effects of similar disabling conditions.

Suffice it, then, in this place, to notice that for the convenience of practical, and especially of commercial, life, the complete series of Personal qualities essential to characterise a Contractor are, under the doctrine of Agency, regarded as being distributed between two Persons, called the *Principal* and the *Agent*, sometimes in one proportion and sometimes in another. The Principal is in all cases the Person who,—supposing a Contract with third Persons to have been effectually made,—is treated by Law as one of the Persons who joined to make it. It may happen that, through absence, through special ignorance of certain facts, or through indisposition personally to interfere, the Principal may prefer, in conformity with legal permission, to delegate to another Person, called his Agent, his own proper functions, whether of engaging in the Joint Act or of merely or also performing the Supplemental and Evidentiary Act, if such there be, which is required by Law. Of course, for the other Persons engaging in the Contract, it becomes a matter of the greatest importance, and one upon which it is often very difficult to obtain satisfactory Evidence, how many and which of his own appropriate functions an absent Principal has delegated to the Person who actually interposes in the transaction. Two distinct questions here present themselves: the one, as to the validity of the Contract, supposing the Agent to have been acting in excess of or without authority; the other, as to the distribution of liability between the Principal and the alleged Agent, supposing the Contract to be valid. The answer to these two questions involves an enquiry, first, into the private dealings between the Principal and the Agent; and, secondly, into the public dealings between the Agent and the other Contractors. As to the private dealings between the Principal and the Agent, the doctrine of Ratification, by which the Principal is able to adopt his Agent's conduct and to incur as much responsibility for it as if he had authorised it, often tends to supersede an investigation which must in many cases be hopeless. Apart from a publicly announced Authorisation of an Agent, from the Ratification just alluded to, and from the operation of certain fixed Presumptions based on the general course of trade or on the nature of official or domestic relationships.

the Law can only resort, in order to ensure the safety of Contractors, to certain arbitrary and loose Presumptions having the effect of fixing with liability the Agent, the Principal, or neither of them, according to the peculiar facts of the special case.

It has been necessary here, in introducing the topic of Agents for the first time, to anticipate a general description of the matters which, in a Systematic exhibition of a body of Law, like a Code, will only be explained and worked out in detail under the head "Agency" as a department of a classified enumeration of the different kinds of Contracts.

With respect to the distribution of personal capacity between the Principal and the Agent, it is important to notice, that where an Agent has only to perform a supplemental Evidentiary Act, only so much knowledge and capacity of voluntary action may be required from him as is needed for that. Thus, in Roman Law, a Slave or a "Pupil" could perform all the essential ceremonies of a *stipulatio*, though the *dominus* or the *tutor*, representing the "pupil's" estate and general interests, would be the Principal on behalf of whom the Contract was made. In English Law it is laid down broadly by Sir E. Coke, that "Infants, Married Women, Persons attainted, outlawed, or excommunicated, and other Persons labouring under disabilities, may be Agents." This language would seem large enough to cover all functions of Agents whatsoever.

6.—The topic of Outlaws is covered by the observations in the last paragraph.

7.—ALIENS.

An Alien, or citizen of a Foreign State residing in the

country, suffers, under most Systems of Law, from special disabilities in respect of Contracting, which differ according as their own State is or is not at war with that within the Territory of which they are resident. It is not necessary here to detail the character of these disabilities. They are not brought about as of necessity by any of those widely prevalent facts of which Jurisprudence must take notice. They are only relics of past jealousies and a spirit of national isolation. In a later chapter on Private International Law, it will be seen that the more advanced States of modern Europe have almost vied with each other in counteracting this selfish propensity to confine the benefits of a Law of Contract to their own citizens.

C.—Acts by which the Making of a Contract is signified.

A Contract has been above called an *Act*. The mere simultaneous acquiescence of two Persons' minds with a view to one or the other independently undertaking a future liability is of itself never invested by Law with the character of a Contract, that is, it never is held sufficient to determine future legal Rights and Duties. This mental acquiescence or assent on the part of each Person professing to make a Contract must be accompanied by a communication of the fact of the existence of such a mental state to each of the others, whether the communication be effected, directly, by speech, writing, gestures, or signs having in view nothing else than, or nothing beyond, the fact of the negotiation in question, or, indirectly, by like methods having directly in view some other or ulterior purposes. It is at least essential that at the precise moment at which the Contract is professedly made the mental state of each of the Contractors, as implying assent to the whole arrangement in contemplation, should either be then and there communicated to all the rest, or be already known to all the rest owing to some previous Act of communication.

From what has been already said as to the true nature of a legal Contract, it is obvious that the critical Joint Act which really constitutes it may be analysed into certain Mental and Physical elements which may be described in the following way:—

1. A Mental State, on the part of each of the Persons professing to Contract, implying acquiescence in one and the same contemplated course of action as indicated by the purpose or object of the Contract; such course of action to be pursued either solely by one of the Contractors, or, partly, by one and, partly, by the other or others.
2. An Actual and Physical Communication, having reference to the above-mentioned Mental State, through the only possible *media* for communicating a knowledge of states of mind. Such Communication may either be made at the same instant by all the Contractors or at different intervals of Time, in which last case the whole Act is not complete till, and is complete when, the last Person communicating has made his Communication.

Such, then, is the generic nature of the Joint Act denominated a Contract, and the conditions of its validity just explained must be invariably present. It happens, however, that experience of the ways of mankind has enforced the expediency of adding to these conditions certain other arbitrary and artificial ones, partly in order to secure due deliberation of mind in Persons wishing to Contract, partly to obviate Frauds, partly to provide satisfactory Evidence of the essential conditions of the Contract being fulfilled. Thus in every Contract a distinction has to be made between the necessary and universal conditions of its validity and what may be called the variable and artificial ones introduced from time to time by different Legal Systems. The history of the Law of Contract is that of the gradual adaptation, in the most expedient modes, of the latter set of conditions to the former; in other words, it is a history of the struggle of the human mind to reconcile the Moral notion of Contract with such a Legal one as admits of being immediately applied to the rough and multifarious intercourse of daily life. If, on the one hand, the Mental and Moral elements were subjected to an over-keen analytical scrutiny on every occasion of a disputed Engagement, the dealings of the market and of the Exchange would become impeded and clogged, as well as a large opening afforded to hypocrisy and Fraud not discoverable by the rude instruments of Judicial Procedure. If, on the other hand, the Formal and Physical elements were lifted into undue prominence, practical justice must constantly be denied, a large mass of business, for the rapid discharge and easy flow of which there is neither time nor disposition to provide incessant formal solemnities, must be excluded from the cognisance of Law, and the feelings of mankind must undergo a constant succession of shocks through the public enforcement of claims against Persons who never really intended to subject themselves thereto.

Professor Maine has portrayed the historical phases of

this struggle as it accidentally evolved itself in Ancient Law, and the story is much the same for Modern Law, except so far as the issue of the struggle has been decided by a more self-conscious spirit animating those on whom the scientific development of Law has depended, and by a more precise knowledge abroad of the true ends of Legislation. In some respects it may be said that in modern times a reaction has set in in the direction of insisting upon the formal elements in a Contract. The policy of the English Statute of Frauds and Lord Tenterden's Act, requiring certain Contracts to be evidenced by Writing accompanied with the Signature of the "Parties to be charged therewith" and other Contracts to be evidenced by Deed, as well as the general Commercial policy of Europe in respect of the essential and sufficient forms of a Bill of Exchange, afford specimens of a novel view of Contracts, differing at once from the superstitious reverence paid to the outward solemnities of a *stipulatio*, and from the loosely liberal policy which was constantly multiplying the kinds of binding Contracts classed under the general head of *consensu*.

The following may be summarily stated as the main grounds upon which a supplemental Act may be specially insisted upon by Law over and above the performance of the Joint Act in which the Contract essentially consists:—

1. The check that is supposed to be thereby provided upon inconsiderate engagements likely to be entered upon at a momentary exigency, and affording a perilous scope to the assiduity of Fraudulent speculators.
2. Provision for the facility of the Administration of the Law by procuring, as by anticipation, clear

and satisfactory Evidence belonging to a class of a fixed character, and the treatment of which is regulated by well-known and determinate Rules.

3. Aid to the natural infirmities of memory experienced in the course of conducting multiform transactions extending over a great length of Time.

4. The general prevention of Frauds in cases not coming under the previous heads.

Over and above these supplementary legal Rules by which the whole character of modern Contract Law is largely qualified, many other practical modifications have been gradually brought about even in applying the most widely-recognised and necessary principles. Thus all Legal Systems have gradually recognised that the Acts of communicating mutual assent must in some cases be presumed to have been performed where any other hypothesis, or the making of no hypothesis at all, would apparently lead to gross practical injustice. In some cases even this Presumption is made where not only the Act of communication, but even the assent itself, is, from the nature of the case, impossible.

Thus, when one Person lends a Thing to another, the ordinary habits and constitution of Mankind justify the Presumption that at the time of making the loan they both knew well the Rights and Duties in the future which thereupon took their rise. So the conduct of Persons engaging side by side in a series of transactions with others may reasonably afford ground for presuming a Contract of Partnership even where, in fact, no such Contract was ever made. Again, the fact of professing to do Acts in another Person's name, and of subsequent adoption by that other of the Acts done, may fairly be taken as a Presumption that a Contract of Agency was really made.

It is obvious that Presumptions of this class rest rather on grounds of general utility than upon any conjectural estimate of what were the facts actually present. The case of Contracts *quasi ex contractu*, and, in England, of money had and received for a Person's use, is an anomalous extension of this class of Presumptions. In these cases not only is the assent and mutual notification of assent presumed, but no such assent and notification can, by the very hypothesis, have existed. Strictly speaking, the topics placed under this branch of the Law ought to fall under the division of Laws relating to Civil Injuries, and, in that branch, under the special title of Injuries to Rights of Ownership. The Law here interferes to redress some disturbance in Rights of Ownership brought about not through the force, Fraud, or inadvertence of the Defendant, but through the one-sided voluntary action of the Plaintiff, moved solely, it may be, by benevolent, or at any rate by perfectly harmless, impulses. He pays to the Defendant what was not due to him, or more than was due to him; or he incurs expenses to which the Defendant is properly liable; or he makes a payment under a legal compulsion as Security for the Defendant; or, in the absence of the Defendant, he manages his affairs on his behalf; or as his Guardian he pays money out of his own pocket for the education and maintenance of the Defendant as his Ward. The liability to repayment on the part of the Defendant is often, in English Law, said, in these cases, to arise upon an "Implied Contract." There is an ambiguity in the use of this phrase, because there is here in very truth no Contract at all; only it is convenient for purposes of general expediency to estimate the Rights and Duties of the Parties by the same modes and measures *as if* a true Contract had preceded. Another use of the phrase "Implied Contract" is where, to all intents and purposes, a true Contract was made, though the Evidence for the Constitutive Act was to be gathered from the surrounding circumstances, and not from the Act itself, nor from any one supplemental Act required by Law.

It was in Roman Law an interesting recognition of the purely Moral aspects of a Contract, and one which still survives for some purposes in the Law of England, that certain Contracts which were legally defective, through the absence of the solemnities required by Law, or through the Incapacity of the Parties, were yet available for defence by way of plea. In such cases what was called a "Natural," though not a "Civil," "Obligation" was said to arise, though the occasions for such a construction were strictly defined, and the legal consequences precisely ascertained and restricted. Among these consequences were that money paid in pursuance of a Natural Obligation,—as, in English Law, money paid in discharge of a debt barred by a Statute of Limitations,—could not be recovered back. Similarly, a Natural Obligation might serve as a ground of "Set-off," and as a legal basis for the personal Security given by a third Person, or for a valid Pledge or Mortgage. This doctrine of a Natural Obligation well illustrates the distinction between the Formal and the Material sides of a true Contract, as well as the fixity with which the Law clings to the notion of a Moral Engagement, even when most decisively impairing its general validity.

D.—Rights accruing through the Making of a Contract.

When once a Contract has been made, one or more Parties to it have become liable to the performance of Duties, and have become invested with Rights. A consideration of all the Rights possibly accruing will involve the consideration of the corresponding Duties. In fact, the Rights can only be expressed in the terms of those Duties.

The possible Rights accruing through the making of a Contract may be arranged under the following heads:—

1. Rights to Performance of all the Acts promised to be performed, and in the Mode, Measure, and Time promised.
2. Rights, in the event of a Non-performance of the Acts promised seeming at any time probable, to do such Acts as may minimise loss.
3. Rights to Compel Performance, by process of Law, or to obtain Compensation for losses sustained through the Non-performance, of the Acts promised. [These Rights might also come under another head.]
4. Rights to a Dissolution of the Contract on clearly ascertained conditions.

Each of these heads demands a particular examination.

1. Rights to a Performance of all the Acts promised to be performed, and in the Mode, Measure, and Time promised.

As to the first class of Rights, a main difficulty is due to the want of explicitness, which is the peculiar characteristic of the most familiar Contracts of daily life. Such are Contracts of Hiring, Carriage, Loan, Pledge, Agency, Guaranty, and even of Sale and of Exchange. The facile intercourse of civilised Mankind depends upon mutual engagements of this nature being readily undertaken without too frequently pausing to ascertain their precise extent, or to preserve elaborate Evidence of their details. Hence, in all such Contracts the ordinary usages, expectations, and faculties of Mankind come into direct consideration so often as the question arises as to the limitation of the Duties undertaken by the Contractor. A great burden is thus laid upon the Judicial Administrator of the Law, and (apart from distinct Legislative provisions) he must depend upon the Jurist to tell him what the essential nature of any particular kind of Contract is, and what sort of Mental elements are required for a due fulfilment of it, and upon the experienced man of the world to tell him what amount of those Mental elements would probably have been contemplated by the Parties at the time of making the Contract.

The Contract of Bailment in English Law affords a good instance of the general mode of ascertaining the Rights arising under one of the most familiar, and therefore indeterminate or loosely constructed, Engagements. The Contract of Bailment is one, according to Sir William Jones, where " a delivery of goods takes place on a condition, expressed or implied, that they shall be restored by the Bailee to the Bailor, or according to his directions, as soon as the purpose for which they were Bailed shall be answered." Thus a Contract of Bailment is admitted to have been as effectually made when one Person does no more than move the casks of another from cellar to cellar, as when a Railway Company carries goods for hundreds of miles. On the necessity arising for determining the precise mode of Performance to which the Bailee has bound himself under such a Contract, the services of the Jurist are invoked to declare the general nature of the Contract, and to point out that the Person moving the casks, or the Railway Company carrying the goods, will be held liable to display different degrees of Diligence according to what may be considered to be the reasonable expectations of the Parties at the time of making the Contract. At this point the man of the world steps in and says that, where nothing is paid for the work, only a very small amount of Diligence could have been expected to be given by the Person doing the work, though some small amount of Diligence must have been looked for or the goods would never have been entrusted to the hands of such Person. If, again, a reasonable compensation has been agreed upon for the labour to be performed with respect to the goods entrusted, a considerable amount of Diligence and Care in protecting them from injury is reasonably looked for. If, lastly, the goods are committed to the hands of the Bailee solely at his request and for his benefit, rather than for that of the Bailor, the largest amount of Diligence and Care in their guardianship is part of the natural price to be paid for so receiving them.

It has been endeavoured in the most celebrated Systems of Law to reduce to a theoretical mould the varying shades of liability in the matter of Diligence according to the subject-matter of the Contract. According to one form of this mould, a sharp distinction is made between *culpa lata*, or the want of such Diligence as even a Bailee receiving goods wholly for his own benefit ought to show, the *culpa levis*, or the want of that Diligence which a Bailee under a Contract equally beneficial to both Parties ought to show, and the *culpa levissima*, or the want of that amount of Diligence which a gratuitous Depositary, receiving goods wholly for the benefit of the Person depositing them, ought to show. Another, and the most approved, form of this theoretic mould is that of distinguishing between (1.) Fraud, (2.) Negligence *in abstracto*, (3.) Negligence *in concreto*. Negligence *in abstracto* is said to be the want of that amount of Diligence which an average householder ordinarily bestows upon his private affairs. Negligence *in concreto* is the want of that amount of Diligence which the Person whose liability is under consideration himself habitually bestows on his private affairs.

These distinctions are so celebrated, and are made so much account of by the most authoritative juridical writers, that it has been necessary to explain them in this place. They are, however, in themselves, nothing more than serviceable generalisations from the current habits and expectations of Mankind. Their real value, either in the construction of a Code or in deciding on a case of disputed liability, can only be very small. For in a matter such as that of Contract, where everything turns upon the moral attitude of the Parties to each other, and upon the expectations arising out of that attitude, the slightest variation in the circumstances will introduce a proportionate modification in the definition of Negligence for the purposes of the case in hand. Negligence, in fact, is always the absence of that amount of alacrity or advertence of mind which a Person's Legal Duty in the special circumstances demands.

One more instance of the sort of indefiniteness in the Rights accruing from one of the most familiar forms of Contract may be taken from the circumstances attending the Hiring of a horse for a limited time. The question often arises as to what is the kind and measure of the responsibility attaching to the hirer in the event of the horse being damaged when not in the course of being used in the exact way and for the exact purpose contracted for. Here again the solution is to be sought by estimating the probable expectations of both Parties at the time of Hiring; consideration being given to the habits of the class of Persons concerned, the custom of the country, the previous dealings of the Parties, and the special circumstances surrounding the fact of Hiring.

In endeavouring to ascertain the true expectation of the Parties with respect to the Rights and Duties involved, a difficulty may arise through one Party having attached one meaning to his words or gestures, and the other Party having attached a different meaning to the same. It has been said by Paley that the true sense is to be taken to be the one in which the Promisor believed that the Promisee accepted the Promise. Mr. Austin substitutes for this, "the sense in which it is to be inferred from the words used, or from the transaction or from both, that the one Party gave, and that the other Party received, the Promise," in other words, "the understanding of both Parties." This does not wholly clear up the difficulty; because where there is no writing, and even no words pass, the only mode left for conjecturing what was that to which both Parties really assented may be by falling back on the ordinary usages of mankind, on the general moral requirements of the case, or on the accidental circumstances of the Parties. The true explanation of the dilemma is that when, in some points of view, the transaction was in a high degree precise and explicit, the obvious fact of a real misapprehension, in other points, by one or other of the Parties lets in, by way of Presumption, a mode of arbitrarily interpreting the extent and nature of the Promise, as understood by both Parties alike, founded on an entirely new class of considerations, such as the common usages of Mankind or Public Policy.

Even in the case of Mercantile Contracts and Contracts usually made with the greatest amount of explicitness and precision, it is impossible to get rid altogether of indefiniteness in the points now under consideration. For instance, in the case of a Contract founded on a Bill of Exchange, upon its being dishonoured by the Acceptor, the Indorsee is required by Law, in order to enforce his Rights under the Contract, to give Immediate Notice to the Maker, and to all the Indorsers of the Bill whom he intends to sue. The question arises as to what is Immediate Notice, and whether the delay of a single day's post will relieve a Defendant who would otherwise be liable, or whether inevitable accident will be held sufficient to excuse the Plaintiff for a day's delay. The topic, indeed, more properly belongs to the Law of Procedure than to the Law of Contract. But it is convenient to allude to it here as affording an apposite illustration of the mode in which the reasonable expectation of Parties is inferred by Courts of Justice from a number of general circumstances and fixed rules of universal application elaborated and adhered to. Other instances might be taken from Contracts of Insurance; as Marine Insurance, where multifarious grounds of exemption from liability are included in the terms of the written Contract; or Life Insurance, where a number of implied conditions are held to be included as to the non-concealment of facts impairing the value of the Insurer's life, and the non-exposure of the Insurer's life to exceptional risks as by travelling far from home; or Fire Insurance, where fine questions come up as to the liability of a Company in consequence of a fire brought about by the Insurer's own Negligence, even where such Negligence lays him under no suspicion of intentionally seeking to defraud the Company.

Other questions as to the nature and extent of the Rights accruing upon the making of a Contract are presented when (1.) the Acts promised are, in their nature, or become through other circumstances, immoral, illegal, grossly unreasonable, or impossible; (2.) in the case of money to be paid or services to be rendered, at a given date, or at a series of given dates, if the Promisor is behindhand in paying the money or rendering the service, whether the Contract is to be looked upon as simply broken, or, the Contract still subsisting, an accession of liability is incurred by way of Penalty, such as to pay simple or compound Interest, to be charged with increased responsibility for loss or damage, or to pay a liquidated compensation. In all such cases Courts of Justice will have general rules at hand, founded on the current practices and expectations of mankind, but admitting of the most plastic adaptation to the special circumstances in each particular case.

2. Rights, in the event of a non-performance of the Acts promised seeming probable, to do such Acts as may minimise loss.

The Rights falling under this head are of a strictly positive character, though they are found, in some form or other, to be recognised by all mature Systems of Law. Taking the English Law as a specimen of such Systems, these Rights may be classified under the heads of the processes by which they are enforced: as, Lien, Stoppage *in transitu*, Bankruptcy, and the Writ of *Ne exeat regno*. Each of these processes supposes that a Person who has promised to do an Act under a Contract will probably not do it, and, in consequence, the other Party to the Contract has a Right to minimise his loss at once without waiting till the time at which the Contract ought to be performed shall have elapsed.

This description, on the face of it, discloses the indefiniteness of the conditions upon which the processes are available. They cannot be available before a certain moment, and this moment is only fixed by an apparent Improbability of a Person being able to do something he has promised to do. In order to determine the question of improbability, the Law may either throw the responsibility on the Judge, who is called upon to decide upon the validity of the process, or may assist him by furnishing him with fixed rules of Presumption based on the ordinary habits of Mankind.

The case of Lien is peculiar inasmuch as, in those cases in which the Right of Lien is conceded (in English Law a very limited class), a Creditor has in his own hands, from the very first, the means of minimising his loss, and it is generally only by actually paying the debt or by obtaining Possession of the goods that a Debtor can establish the probability of his keeping his Contract for the purpose of defeating the Creditor's Right.

The question of Improbability is most difficult to answer in cases arising in the course of applying the doctrine of Stoppage *in transitu*. The Right of Stoppage *in transitu* is that of arresting the delivery of goods in the course of their transit, upon receiving information of the *probable* insolvency of the Contractor to whom they are being arried.

The line is drawn with far greater precision in the case

of Bankrupt Laws, in which a number of unmistakable Acts are usually named as creating an irresistible Presumption that a Debtor will be unable to satisfy the claims of all his Creditors. Such Acts, in English Bankrupt Laws, are " departing the realm," " departing from his dwellinghouse, or otherwise absenting himself," "beginning to keep his house," " suffering himself to be arrested or taken in Execution for any debt not due," " making Fraudulent grants," and the like. Upon the performance of any such Acts, the whole process of Bankruptcy is permitted to operate in favour of the Creditors so as to secure an impartial distribution of the existing assets, and in favour of the Debtor so as to provide to a greater or less extent for the protection of his person, for his maintenance, and, possibly, against a revival of his Creditors' claims as against subsequently acquired property.

It is necessary, in speaking of Bankruptcy, to notice that, like many other complex juridical facts, it has several aspects, bringing it under different departments of a Legal System. It is eminently, as here, a mode of protecting Creditors against an exaggeration of loss, that is, it is one of the Rights conferred, in certain events, in order to minimise loss. It is, again, an important Mode of acquiring Rights of Ownership, falling under the general head of Adjudication. It involves, lastly, a peculiar and technical Procedure, by which Persons having Rights are enabled to make them available; this brings it under the general division of Laws of Procedure.

3. Rights to compel Performance by process of Law, or, similarly, to obtain Compensation for losses sustained through Non-performance of Acts promised.

The Rights falling under this head are, of course, implied in the existence of the Rights already mentioned under the first head. If a Person has a Right to have an Act performed in a Mode, Measure, and Time, promised, he must, by the very meaning of a *Right*, have Auxiliary— or, as they have been called, Secondary—Rights accorded to him, by which, on Breach of the Contract, he may obtain Compensation. This Compensation may take the form of a compulsory power, lent by the State, to exact a precise Performance of the Acts promised, though such a Mode of Compensation can only be applicable to certain classes of Contracts; as, to convey Land, to transfer Stock, or do some other definite Act which, under the circumstances, still admits of being done. The course implied in this doctrine of "Specific Performance" is obviously inapplicable where the subject-matter of the Contract has perished, or where peculiar Moral Relationships, as those of Agency, Partnership, or Marriage, are at stake.

Again, the Compensation may be obtained, as is usually the case, through the payment of a sum of money, supposed to be an equivalent for the advantage the Plaintiff would have obtained had the Contract been fulfilled. Interesting questions here arise as to whether the loss is to be estimated by the current prices at the time and place of making the Contract, or by those at the time and place for performing the Contract, or at some higher price which may make up for the inconvenience caused through the disappointment in the Plaintiff's engagements. These questions, like other similar ones, must be referred to the principle of satisfying the expectations of the Parties, while, in cases of doubt, interpreting those expectations in the light of the common course of business and in that of the particular circumstances of the Parties. The question of Interest here again is introduced, the payment or non-payment of it being determined in some cases by express Legislation, in others by mercantile Usage adopted as Law by Courts of Justice, in others by distinct stipulation of the Parties through a kind of supplementary Contract.

Lastly, the Compensation for Breach of Contract may be considerably in excess of the real loss incurred, that is, it may be of the nature of what is called a Penalty. This Penalty may be either agreed upon by the Parties beforehand, or may be assigned by operation of Law. An instance of this latter course is supplied by the kind of Penalty which the Law of England permits Juries to affix for Breach of a Contract to Marry, in the shape of what are called " Vindictive Damages." The case of the operation of a Bond in English Common Law, as contrasted with its operation in Equity, is an instance of a liquidated sum, far in excess of what would represent the money loss incurred, being agreed upon beforehand by the Parties as Compensation for that loss.

4. Rights to a Dissolution of the Contract on clearly ascertained conditions.

It has generally been customary in theoretical and practical works on Law to make a distinct division with reference to the Modes in which Contracts are dissolved. It is conceived that such a distribution of the subject is misleading, inasmuch as if the Rights under a Contract are thoroughly understood and exhausted, there is no place left for the topic in question.

A Contract can only be dissolved because, at a certain moment, no one of the Parties to it has any longer a claim to control the Acts of any of the others. Obviously this is brought about either through the original Rights of all having come to their natural close, or through some new or additional Rights having come in to supersede the former ones. These new or additional Rights may either be created by the Parties or may be conceded by Law independently of any Act of theirs. In the former case the new Rights may have been created at the time of making the Contract, to come into operation conditionally upon certain Events subsequently happening; such as, the Non-performance or imperfect Performance of the Contract, the Deaths of any of the Parties, the attainment of Majority by other Persons, or the mere accident of change of mind by the Parties. Or, again, these new Rights may be created, at any time subsequently to the making of the Contract, through a fresh Contract, the purport of which may be the simple Dissolution of the old Contract, or the substitution of a new one for it (*novatio*), or mere modification of some of its terms.

The case of the Law introducing new Rights modifying or annulling the Rights of Parties under a Contract is illustrated by the Mode in which it arbitrarily determines what Rights and Duties shall descend on the Death of one of the Parties to what are called his Successors or Legal Representatives. Different rules are laid down in these cases for different sorts of Contracts and the expressed Intention of the original Parties is not always allowed to conflict with their operation. This is the meaning of the expression that certain Contracts are presumed to " run with the land;" that is, the liability upon them passes, as of necessity, to every Person who, by Succession or by one or more Assignments, stands in the position, solely with respect to the subject-matter of the Contract, of an original Contractor.

A familiar instance, from Roman Law, of an arbitrary legal interference with the consequences of an existing Contract is supplied by the *restitutio in integrum*, by which a Person under the age of twenty-five could, in certain cases, where it was otherwise possible, be relieved from the disastrous effects of an unwise Contract by the restoration of the Parties to their original position. Similarly in English Equity, by an inverse process, a Contract, otherwise informal and therefore invalid, is, in certain cases, made efficient if it has been partially performed, and the Parties cannot be restored to their original position.

Thus, if it be borne in mind that every Contract is dissolved because the Rights created by it have reached their natural term and no longer exist ; or, because some conditions have been fulfilled whereupon new Rights, previously created, come into force and override the old ones; or because a new Contract is made, having the effect of annulling the old one ; or because the Law arbitrarily interferes and destroys an existing Contract by substituting new Contracting Parties for the old ones, or by other methods; there is no further place for treating the subject of the Modes of Dissolving Contracts.

E.—CLASSIFICATION OF CONTRACTS.

The number of kinds of Contracts that are daily being made in all civil Communities being coextensive with the needs of Social, Industrial, and Commercial intercourse, and having developed themselves in each Community as those needs gradually discovered themselves, there are more bases than one for a Classification of all the possible forms of Legal Contract to be looked for in a highly organised

Community. There is (1.) the Historical basis, which was the one mainly adopted by the Roman lawyers and their modern followers. The nature of this basis has been fully expounded by Professor Maine, and is well-known to consist in the gradual evolution of the Mental and Moral aspects of Contract from the Formal and Mechanical elements which, in the earliest times, essentially characterised it. There is (2.) the basis indicated by the varieties of the Formal Acts by which the making of a Contract may be legally authenticated. This is the Mode which has been most popular among English text-book writers, who usually start their investigations into the Law of Contract by distributing all Contracts into "Contracts under Seal" and "Contracts not under Seal." There is (3.) the basis furnished by the Material Contents of the Contract, that is, by the Social or other purpose which the Contract has to serve.

It is obvious that an arrangement of all possible Contracts upon any one of these bases is very likely to coincide, for a large part of it, with an arrangement upon any other basis. Historical progress implies a constantly increasing quantity and variety of social co-operation, and it is the necessities incident to this co-operation which dictate the characteristic Acts selected as Legal Evidence that Contracts of different sorts have been made. Probably the best mode of division can only be determined by reference to the general purpose of the division. Thus it may be different for a Code, for a Scientific Treatise, and for an educational Text-book.

For the purposes of the present Work, which in some way aims at all these objects at once, it will be expedient to combine the first and the third of the above-mentioned bases in such a way as to present at one glance the historical and scientific harmony which actually prevails in this part of the Law. The following Mode of distributing the leading Classes of Contracts for an advanced Modern State is suggested as an universal framework, though the lines separating the leading compartments are necessarily drawn after rather an arbitrary fashion.

I. Contracts in aid of the Essential Relationships of Society: as

1. Contracts having in view future Marriage.
2. Contracts made either at the time of the Marriage or afterwards, for the purpose of modifying the legal Status of Married Persons towards each other.
3. Contracts made before, at, or after Marriage, for the purpose of modifying the Rights of Ownership of Married Persons as existing by the ordinary Law.
4. Contracts made before, at, or after Marriage, having reference to the conflicting Rights of the Married Persons in respect to Children of the Marriage.

II. Contracts in aid of Co-operation for Social and Industrial purposes:—

1. Sale, including Exchange.
2. Letting and Hiring.
3. Bailments, including all that comes under that head in English Law.
4. Loan and Deposit.
5. Pledge, including Mortgage Securities of all sorts.
6. Agency.
7. Apprenticeship.

III. Contracts in aid of Co-operation for more or less artificial and complicated Commercial purposes:—
1. Partnership.
2. Assurance (of all kinds).
3. Guaranty.
4. Affreightment.
5. Negotiable Securities.
6. Indemnity.

In this enumeration of all the more important Classes of Contracts there are some general observations to be made on the different groups, as wholes, and some particular observations on the several Classes of Contracts comprised in these groups.

As to the first (I.) group, it is conspicuous that all the Classes of Contracts composing the group revolve round the Institution of Marriage. It is customary in English Law-books to treat Marriage as constituting a Contract itself, on the hypothesis that the Rights and Duties of the Husband and Wife with respect to each other are of exactly the same kind and flow from exactly the same Source as those created by, (say), a Contract of Mercantile Partnership. This view is at once juridically misleading and morally false. Marriage, when once properly constituted by such ascertained consent of the Parties as the Legislator shall require, carries with it its own peculiar Legal Rights and Duties, which can be modified only to the very slightest extent by the Will of the Parties, and which, unlike all Rights and Duties created by Contract, can neither be suspended nor annulled by the operation of that Will. Even under the most amply conceived Law of Divorce that ever suggested itself to the brain of the political speculator, some consideration at least for the interests of the State—if only for the purpose of securing publicity, and of guarding the Vested Rights of third Persons—has invariably been insisted on.

Marriage, in truth, when once the Act of Marriage is complete, is a Natural and Moral Relationship out of which spring a vast and indefinite assortment of moral Rights and Duties. Just as the State imparts definiteness and fixedness to the Moral Relations existing between the People and the Supreme Political Authority, and to the Moral Relations existing between a Parent and Child: so does the State select some of the Moral Rights and Duties by which Married Persons are related to each other, gives them formal shape and definiteness, and in fact converts them into true Legal Rights and Duties. In some Systems of Law, indeed, the determination of the extent of these Rights and Duties may, within very narrow limits, be left to the Will of the Parties, as was the case in early Rome under the doctrine by which a Wife might or might not, according to private arrangements, come under the *patria auctoritas* of her Husband. Contracts modifying in this way the ordinary Rights and Duties of Husbands and Wives are placed in the second rank of the group now under consideration.

The above remarks in no way conflict with the fact that Contracts can be made, as those of the first rank in the present group, having direct reference to the Act of Marriage—that is, the Act of entering upon the Marriage-state—just as a Contract may be made for the Performance of any other Act.

From the nature of the present group, the Contracts belonging to it can only be very few. The essential Relationships of Society which afford the basis of the group little need the support of voluntary Promises to give them reality or permanence. Did they need such support, Society would be far advanced in the direction of decay. It is thus, perhaps, by a genuine instinct, though by a juridical accident, that the Institutes of Gaius and Justinian commence with an elaborate account of the essential Relationships of Society, or of those which seemed essential to the Roman world. This part of their work, which, in the present treatise, is represented by the department entitled Laws affecting Special Classes of Persons, was, in Roman times, through the simplicity of Commerce and the depression of Industry, of paramount, and almost of absorbing, interest—to the Jurist as much as to the Moralist and the Politician. In modern Europe Family Life and Relationships are more and more escaping the interference and introspection of the Lawgiver; while Ownership, and that sphere of voluntary or spontaneous Legislation called Contract, are gradually covering almost the whole field of Law.

Thus it comes about that the only Contracts properly belonging to this group are those having for their objects the Act of Marriage; certain minute variations in the fixed Rights and Duties of the Married Persons towards each other in respect of liberty of action; their respective Rights of Ownership, under existing or hypothetical circumstances, in Things belonging to either of them at the time of the Marriage, or to be acquired by them at any future time, as in the Marriage Settlements customary in England, and in the Contracts of *communauté* on the Continent; or their respective Rights of Control over the Education of Children, and, in case of their living apart, their respective Rights to retain the Children in their several households, and their respective Duties to contribute severally to the Children's Maintenance.

Passing on to the second (II.) group, it is necessary again

to avoid a confusion similar to that which has pervaded the treatment of the Legal aspects of Marriage, through a prevalent want of clearness in distinguishing between the Contract and the situation of the Parties brought about by a Contract when it is fulfilled or even partially fulfilled.

The first class of Contracts in this group, those having for their object a Sale, is illustrative in many points of view, and especially in that of the confusion here noticed. A complete Sale may include a number of Acts jointly resulting in the Transfer of Rights of Ownership. Generally a Contract precedes these Acts or rather constitutes one of them. Professor Maine has given a more than plausible theory to the effect that, historically speaking, Contract-Law owed its first establishment to the gradually-formed habit of not paying for things purchased at the moment of the purchase. Thus the *nexum*, which was originally nothing more than the *mancipium* or formal Conveyance, became specialised to mean "an incomplete Conveyance," and finally a true Contract. Now if all purchases were for ready money, as they seem to have been at the first, there would be a Sale, but there would be no Contract. A Contract of Sale is made at the moment one Person binds himself to deliver to another, at some future time, Possession of a certain Thing or of certain Things, the other Person either transferring at the time a Right of Ownership in something else, or binding himself to make such a transfer at a future time. The confusion arises from the fact that, with respect to many Things which are the subject of Sale, Rights of Ownership are effectually transferred without Possession being given, or, as it is called, "without Delivery being made." Hence a kind of misty notion prevails that, because something yet remains to be done after the true Sale is complete, therefore the whole transaction, from first to last, is a Contract and nothing more. In many cases, indeed, it is true that Possession of the Thing sold is retained by the Vendor for a certain time in consequence of an implied or express subsidiary Contract to that effect. In other cases, however, Possession is retained for a certain time in obedience to local or Commercial usage, or even in reliance on the distinct provisions of Positive Law. In some cases, indeed, Possession may be retained, as has already been explained under a former head, by way of Lien, or in pursuance of an entirely fresh Contract of Deposit, Loan, or Agency.

In watching the execution of every Contract having for its object a Sale, the moments at which the Rights of Ownership are severally transferred by the two Parties have to be marked with especial care. From those moments, respectively, the Transferees are Owners and no longer Contractors. If they accidentally retain Possession, they are liable, like some other Possessors, to a greater or less extent, for injury to the Things in their Possession, or to render account of Profits and Fruits which may have accrued to it by way of Accession.

The true nature of Sale, and of the Contract having for its object a Sale, has thus been clearly expounded. But another difficult question is here presented, to which different Systems of Law may give very different answers: What are the Acts which indicate that the Sale is complete—that is, that the Rights of Ownership on both sides, or even on one side, have been effectually transferred? According to some Legal Systems, as the French, a Contract for the Sale of an Immovable operates, itself, as a Conveyance; the Agreement to Sell is registered; and the Rights of Ownership at once pass to the Purchaser. The same principle is recognised in English Equity. In English Common Law, on the other hand, and in Roman Law the Sale is not complete—that is, the Rights of Ownership are not transferred till Delivery is made or a formal Conveyance executed. In the former case—that is, when the same Act is said to operate as a Contract and a Conveyance—the only object of the Contract is the Delivery or the Possession of the Thing or subject-matter of the Contract. Thus in countries where Registration is sufficient to complete a Sale, there is either an implied Subsidiary Contract or a positive rule of Law, operating in default of an express Contract to the contrary, that Possession shall be conceded at a certain Time or under certain Conditions. It is of the greatest importance to distinguish clearly between (1.) the Contract having for its object a future Sale; (2.) the Sale itself; and (3.) Subsidiary Contracts, express, implied, or, under certain circumstances, imputed by Law with reference to the surrender of Possession.

It is scarcely necessary to do more than allude to the other Subsidiary Contracts which often attend a Contract of Sale. Such are Contracts having in view the Indemnification of a Purchaser in case he be evicted through some Person having a Right superior to that of the Vendor; Contracts of Warranty; Contracts to Indemnify the Purchaser in case the subject-matter of the Contract has been previously burdened with Mortgages; Contracts to give " Further Assurance,"—that is, to do all such future Acts as may be found necessary completely to vest the Rights of Ownership in the Purchaser. Such Contracts may be either express or implied by the special circumstances of the case or by the conduct of the Parties, or may arise, as it is said, by " Implication of Law."

Passing on to the other Contracts in the second (II.) group, it is obvious that the notion of Sale underlies most or all of them. The subject-matter, indeed, of the transaction contemplated by the Contract is no longer the Transfer of Rights of Ownership (at least of the most unrestricted sort), but either Services to be Conditionally rendered, or restricted, Rights of Ownership to be Conditionally transferred. The Conditional and Restricted character of the objects of such Contracts as those of Letting and Hiring, Bailment (including Carriage), Loan, and Pledge, leave, for their determination, a field for the operation of the mere arbitrary will of the Contractors which is wholly wanting in the case of a true Sale. In the case of a Sale the Contract, if there is one, is finally performed by the completion of all the essential Acts,—the *jura ad rem* become converted into *jura in rem*, and the Law of Ownership, and not the Law of Contract, henceforth determines the Rights and Duties of the Parties.

But in the case of the Contracts now under consideration, they are continuously being performed and, up to a definite point of time, they have yet to be performed. The exact nature and amount of the Services to be rendered in pursuance of the several Contracts; the Times of rendering them; the Conditions under which Performance of the Contract may be suspended or dispensed with, —may, according to circumstances, be dependent entirely on the terms agreed upon by the Parties or be qualified by the general Legal Rules applicable to each particular class of Contracts. Furthermore, the general grounds of excuse for Non-performance or for Imperfect Performance, and the general kind of responsibility imposed by Law as to Diligence, as to the avoidance of Delays, and as to Good Faith, are subject to the operation of the still more general Legal Rules indicated under the previous title of Rights accruing through the making of a Contract.

The Contract of Pledge is especially assimilated to that having in view a Sale. Indeed, it is sometimes represented as a Sale under Conditions, and the usages of some Legal Systems, as that of the English Common Law, favours this view. But the accidents of Legal History must not confound the distinctions drawn by Juridical Science. In all the forms of the Contract of Pledge, whether the Possession of the Thing pledged be retained by the Borrower or parted with conditionally to the Lender, or whether (as in some cases of Mortgage of Immovables) these Modes are compounded, the Borrower retaining Possession and the Lender receiving the rents,—the Contract, by its very nature, has in view the concession of Restricted and Conditional Rights and not the Unrestricted Rights resulting from a Sale. The consent of the Parties as to a right of Sale under certain Conditions forms, indeed, an implied or expressed Subsidiary Contract which almost universally attends the main Contract of Pledge.

The remaining Contracts of the second (II.) group, Agency and Apprenticeship, are placed in this group because of their appearance at a very early and simple stage of Social Life. Otherwise, from the enhanced delicacy of the services contemplated by those Contracts, and their increased remoteness from the Contract having in view a simple Sale, they are more conveniently considered, as they will be here, side by side with the Contracts falling under the third (III.) group.

As to Contracts under this last (III.) group as well as Agency and Apprenticeship, it is to be noticed that the very possibility of their existence depends on the presence of a high degree of Social and Commercial Credit, and an advanced range of Economical enterprise. The notion of Agency, especially of the most extended kind, implies a habit of reliance by one man on the Good Faith of another with respect, it may be, to the most serious and critical transactions of Human Life. The results of a Contract of Agency, or of an allegation of a Contract of Agency, on the Contractual capacity of the alleged Agent in relation to third Persons has already been considered under the head of "Persons who make Contracts." The Contract of Agency itself, as made between the Principal and the Agent, properly belongs to this place.

The elementary conception of the Contract of Agency, as one the object of which is certain Services to be rendered by way of Impersonation, within more or less strictly defined limits, of the Principal, is in itself simple and intelligible enough. A practical difficulty, however, in determining liability under this Contract arises from two causes: (1.) the extreme variety of the transactions to which the Contract is applicable, which may reach from paying a simple and ascertained Debt on the part of another to engaging in a complicated Process for the purpose of settling a Lawsuit before an Arbitrator: (2.) the fineness and the variety of the grounds upon which the Contract in question may arise by implication. The Roman lawyers elaborated the doctrine of *mandatum* with great care and acuteness, and deduced the Rights and Duties of the Agent according to the varying circumstances—allowed to qualify even an express Contract— of the direct purpose of the Contract being the advantage of the Principal alone, of the Principal and the Agent together, of a third Person alone, of the Principal and a third Person, of the Agent and a third Person.

It is more than doubtful here, as in other cases previously alluded to, whether, in the practical Administration of Law, such sharp distinctions are of much service. However, they are of use by way of enforcing general principles which may guide the Judge. Obviously it is the interest of the State, in its work of protecting all its citizens, to control the power of Impersonation so far as is consistent with the real necessities of industrial and commercial life and with the general claims to liberty of Contract. On this account there exist in all Systems, certain arbitrary rules of Law regulating the formal Mode of appointing Agents for some purposes and also sharply defining the limits within which an Agent can act as such. Of the last kind of rules the maxim *Delegatus non potest delegare* is a specimen.

The principles underlying the Doctrine of Agency are of the greatest importance in consequence of the fact that some Systems of Law, as the English, base their Modes of Interpreting the Rights and Duties arising under other leading classes of Contracts upon analogies drawn from this doctrine. Thus in matters affecting Rights of Ownership, Husband and Wife are in England generally presumed to be Agents for each other in dealings with third Persons, the Presumption, however, admitting of being rebutted through the presence of special circumstances. In interpreting the Rights and Duties arising from a Contract of Partnership, again, it is said that each Partner is an Agent of all the rest.

The Contract of Apprenticeship is, perhaps, peculiar, in the amount of what may be called Moral services, which form its subject matter. It is this indefiniteness which necessarily clings to the Legal Rights and Duties which are based on the Moral ones, and in fact here are almost coextensive with them, which is the infirm side of this species of Contract, and in practice is known in some Countries to afford an opening to a plausible method of furtively reintroducing Slavery.

The Contract of Partnership already alluded to, though referable for some purposes to that of Agency, nevertheless has a distinct standing-ground of its own. The complexity, magnitude, and obscurity of many of the transactions for which Contracts of Partnership are capable of being made demand at the hands of the State a peculiar exercise of supervision and vigilance in order to protect the interests of third Persons, and even of each of the Partners themselves against the Fraud or Culpable Negligence of the rest. For these purposes Positive Law usually determines (1.) the class of matters which may form the object of a Partnership-contract; (2.) the Modes in which the existence of such a Contract shall be Publicly Authenticated; (3.) the extent of the mutual Liability of the Partners towards each other, and of the Responsibility of each of them for dealings of any of the others with third Persons; (4.) the Mode of Authenticating the fact that the Partnership no longer exists.

The Contracts of Assurance, of Guaranty, and of Indemnity, though resting on complicated economical conditions, and being, for that reason, of an extremely artificial sort, present, on these very accounts, fewer purely juridical difficulties. The perplexity rather is in applying the Law than in ascertaining it. The application of the Law demands a knowledge of two complex sets of circumstances,—the one, the Rights and Duties actually contemplated by the Parties to the Contract, which, in these classes of Contracts, are generally of the most multiform description and are beset with innumerable Conditions; the other, the actual concrete Facts as to an alleged Breach of the Contract upon which a judicial decision is sought to be obtained. The general principles already examined under the head " Rights accruing from the making of a Contract," taken with the prescriptions of Positive Law in relation to these Contracts, are sufficient to render tolerably simple and straightforward all questions of pure Law.

The same remarks are applicable to the case of the two last remaining classes of Contracts, the importance of which, for modern States, can hardly be over-estimated; that is, Affreightment and Negotiable Securities. The Law with respect to these topics is no doubt in all countries, by the necessity of the case, voluminous, involved, and artificial, or even capricious. But for this very reason the Jurist is relieved of much of his toil. The less there is left to mere Logic, to pure Morality, and to such universal assumptions as are gathered up in the term Common-sense, the less space or need there is for his characteristic work.

With respect to Bills of Exchange, it is to be remembered that the question in all cases is on what Conditions and by the use of what Formalities a Creditor shall be entitled by Law to transfer to another his own existing or future Rights of Action against his Debtor. The whole Law of Negotiable Securities turns on the possibility of this being accomplished, with due regard to the protection of innocent Persons, through the machinery of simply handing over a piece of written paper properly signed. The Formalities that have to be gone through in order to the new Creditor enforcing his Rights against the Debtor or against the old Creditor belong more properly to the Law of Procedure than to the Law of Contracts.

In classifying Contracts in the manner above adopted, it is to be remembered that a State may recognise the Contracts of its citizens by the assumption of two different principles. It may either Presume that every object for which its citizens may make a Contract is a justifiable one, and may only except a few distinct classes of objects expressly named, on the ground of their immorality, their uncertainty, or their supposed inconsistency with the well-being of the State. It is on this principle that modern States mostly proceed, and that the Law of England attaches varying degrees of Invalidity to Contracts made in contemplation of a future Breach of Conjugal Duty, of a Breach of the Criminal Law, or of Fraudulent Evasion of other parts of the Law; of perplexing or perverting the process of Administering the Law; of the uncertain issue, as by way of Assurance, of certain Sports and Games of skill; of the fluctuations of the Stock Exchange; and all the class of Contracts said to be "in Restraint of Trade."

The other principle, which is more prevalent in primitive Law,—as in that of Rome in earlier times,—is that by which the State only recognises certain distinct objects as justifiable bases for Contracts. Such objects are those only which present themselves in the simplest stage of Social Life, and which a wide experience proves to be compatible, as matters of Contract, with the general interest of all members of the State. The transition from this principle to the one previously mentioned is marked in Roman Law by the growing favour shown to merely Consensual Contracts, and to the indefinite multiplication of classes of true Legal Contracts under the title "Innominate." The increasing honour shown to mere Pacts, under the Prætorian jurisdiction, was a tendency in the same direction.

On concluding the topic of Laws of Contract, it may be noticed that no division has been introduced formally corresponding with the head entitled "Modes of Protecting Rights of Ownership" in the treatment of Laws of Ownership. The truth is that the Rights and Duties arising upon even a probable Breach of a Contract are (as has been already seen) so important, so various, and so closely allied to all the other Rights and Duties arising out of a Contract, that it has been here held to be more convenient to treat the Rights directly connected with the Judicial Enforcement of a Contract under the general head of "Rights accruing through the Making of a Contract."

CHAPTER XII.

LAWS AFFECTING SPECIAL CLASSES OF PERSONS.

A DISPLACEMENT of the ancient title "Law of Persons" from its prominent situation on the very threshold of an Institutional Treatise or a Code is an innovation so bold and startling that nothing but the most cogent considerations of Logic and expediency could justify it. Such considerations, however, both are in themselves of the most obvious character, and derive weight from the authority of one and another leading modern Jurist, though no modern Codifiers, it is believed, have yet had the resolution to adopt the conclusion in practice. It has been pointed out, for instance, by Savigny, that it was by a mere accident, as it may be called, that Gaius led the way in commencing the Systematic treatment of a body of Laws with the title "Law of Persons." In one work of his, the "Res Quotidianæ," he seems to have adopted a different mode of distribution. Other Jurists, again,—and pre-eminently Mr. Austin,—have pointed out that the expression "Law of Persons" is in every way misleading, while its usual position offends against the cardinal rule of all correct Classification—that the General should precede the Special.

All Law is addressed to Persons, and is solely concerned with the Acts of Persons. This is quite as true with respect to Laws of Ownership and of Contract as to those of Marriage and of Guardianship. The Laws which have been usually treated under the head "Law of Persons" are, on the other hand, addressed more particularly to certain exceptional Classes of Person who, because of a peculiar Moral Relationship in which they stand towards others, or because of the peculiar Functions they discharge in the Public Economy of the State, are invested with special Rights and made liable to special Duties over and above the general Rights and Duties they share equally with all other members of the Community. Such special Rights and Duties, when contemplated in a mass as distinguishing the Person to whom they belong, constitute (according to Mr. Austin's acute and exhaustive analysis) that Person's *Status*. Some such term as this is highly convenient, though the use of this particular term has by no means been steady and uniform. In fact, a kind of imaginative colouring has floated round the word *status* so that the actual Rights and Duties alone really signified have either been lost sight of or mixed up with idealistic images which have nothing to do with them.

In the last Chapter it was intimated that an excuse is afforded to Roman Lawyers for the prominence they gave to what may be called Domestic Law by the fact of the practical subordination in Rome, as compared with modern Europe, of the facts of Industrial, Commercial, and Political Enterprise to the facts attending the complex relationships of Private Life. A further and not wholly dissimilar excuse is to be discovered in the strictly Educational character of the Commentaries of Gaius and of the Institutes of Justinian. For the instruction of the youthful Student the conception of a State as such, and of the elements of a State as supplied by the primary Relationships of Family Life, is essential as an introduction to the study of Law. It was pre-eminently so at Rome, where the innumerable legal ties of the Paterfamilias to the Wife, to the Children,—Natural, Adopted, and Emancipated,—to the Slaves, to the Freedmen, and to kindred Families, so markedly qualified the actual Prescriptions and the practical operation of every other part of the Law. Even in the Middle Ages,—when Slavery as a Legal Institution had become obsolete, and the Father's Power existed rather in name than in fact,—the secondary influences of Roman Law, conjoined with the direct influences of the Canon Law framed after the model of the older Imperial System, still had the effect of favouring a constitution of Society in which Family or Ecclesiastical Relationships obscured, throughout the whole field of Law, the notion of the simpler Relationship between the Individual Person and the State. Here, then, again, the position of the Law of Persons truly expressed its preponderant importance. The actual result survives in every modern Continental Code.

For a variety of reasons, English Law has pursued a more independent course, and in that System the clear idea of the Rights and Duties of every individual Citizen in respect of every other has been less hampered than elsewhere by considerations of Family or Ecclesiastical ties. Feudal ties, indeed, struggled vigorously for Legal recognition in the earlier days of English History, and, in respect to the Ownership of Land at least, not unsuccessfully. But a host of other influences, social, political, and religious, told in a directly opposite way. The result was, in respect of the Ownership of Land, a severe circumscription of Feudal Rights and Duties, followed by their eventual Commutation for mere pecuniary liabilities; in respect of Contract, the entire abandonment of any conception conflicting with the widest possible latitude of action for every individual citizen in his relations with others. From this time any attempt to preface the treatment of the aggregate body of English or of Abstract Law with an investigation of the Special Relationships of particular Persons in the Community becomes in the highest degree misleading and embarrassing. It is true that the existence of certain of these Relationships,—as that of Marriage,—must be assumed in treating most other Branches of the Law. But such *præcognoscenda* will be found existing under every possible Method of Distribution. All that can be done is to choose the Method which shall make such *præcognoscenda* as few and as immaterial as possible, and to avoid, as far as it can be done, the treatment of the same matter more than once.

Assuming then that in Modern Systems of Law the treatment of Laws regulating Status,—in other words Laws affecting Special Classes of Persons,—ought to follow and not to precede that of the main bulk of the Law, the question arises as to what is its true place, keeping in view both general Convenience and a Natural Order of Classification. Some writers (as Mr. Austin) have proposed to treat under the Law of Persons the whole body of Constitutional Law, taking successively the several Persons who are directly the Objects of that Law, or who are concerned in Administering it. This might be logically justified by an appropriate extension of the signification of *Status*; but there are two potent objections to any such extension. First, the proposed extension wars against common language and sentiment. Secondly, the arrangement proposed to be based upon such extension is practically inconvenient and confusing in the highest degree. The conception of *Status*, whatever other vacillations have attended the use of the term, has always circled round the Rights and Duties arising out of either purely Moral Relationships or out of such Voluntary Connections as, for public purposes, are specially countenanced by the State. The conception has never been extended to the Rights and Duties of Persons essentially concerned in the Administration of the State,—that is *as* so concerned, —nor to Persons who, apart from all voluntary Acts of their own, are simply invested with Rights or made liable to Duties for the sake of carrying on subordinate Functions of Government. Thus the proposed extension of the meaning of the term *Status* involves a change in a universally popular conception, of such a violent nature as could only be properly purchased at a highly remunerative price.

But the extension itself is worthless, even if purchased at so great a price. The convenience of discussing and arranging apart by themselves all the Laws directly relating to the Constitution and Administration of the State (which is the method employed in this Treatise) is transparent. Because it happens that the Duties of a Father to his Child and of a Custom House Officer to the Chancellor of the Exchequer are equally unlike the Duties of a Tenant to his Landlord and of a Railway Company to a Traveller on its line, there is no sufficient reason why the Duties of a Father and of a Custom House Officer should be classed together, to the endless embarrassment of students, practising lawyers, Judges, Legislators, and the general Public. The following conclusions may be stated to be the result of the above criticisms, or may be independently established.

1. In every body of Law Systematically arranged, Laws affecting Special Classes of Persons, often called " Laws regulating *Status*," ought to be distinctly separated from Laws directly relating to the Constitution and Administration of the State, and may usefully be also separated, in order to prevent repetition and to facilitate reference, from the rest of the body of Laws.

2. If such separation be made, the true place of the department of the Laws in question is after, and not before, the rest of the body of Laws; and, more particularly, must find its place between Laws of Contract and Laws of Civil Injuries and Crimes.

3. The several Assemblages of Rights and Duties falling under the present head owe their existence to one or the other of the following complex Facts; either (1.) original Moral or quasi-moral Relationship, as Marriage, Parentage, Adoption, Guardianship, and the like; or (2.), the formation of certain classes of Voluntary Connections specially countenanced by the State as conducive to the furtherance of important Public ends.

Thus the main divisions of this department for a modern State will be as follows:—

- A. Husband and Wife; Father and Child.
- B. Guardian and Ward.
- C. Trustees, Executors, and Administrators.
- D. Barristers, Advocates, Solicitors, Attorneys, Proctors, Writers to the Signet, Notaries Public, and the like.

E. Public Corporations, whether existing for Municipal, Educational, Ecclesiastical, or certain other purposes.

A. Husband and Wife: Parent and Child.

The Juridical aspects of the Law relating to this topic will most conveniently be considered under the following heads :—

I. General description of the Moral and Legal Relationship.
II. Authentic Signs that the Legal Relationship has been Created.
III. Rights and Duties accruing (1.) as between the Parties, (2.) as between the Parties on the one hand and each of them and the Children of the Marriage on the other, (3.) as between the Parties and all other Persons.
IV. Authentic Signs that the Legal Relationship has been Terminated.

I. General description of the Moral and Legal Relationship.

The Relationship of Husband and Wife is on one side a Moral and on the other side a Legal one,—that is, the Rights and Duties to which that Relationship gives rise and in which it really consists are some of them Moral and some Legal, the two kinds co-existing together. The Moral Rights and Duties flowing from the fact of Marriage might be conceived of as existing previously to and independently of the formation of a State; though, in fact, such a conception is false and misleading because (such is the reciprocal reaction of Positive Law and of Moral Sentiment upon one another) it is only through the presence of Law that the idea of Marriage acquires reality and fixity; while, on the other hand, it is only through the Institution of the Family, resting as that does on Marriage, that the State developes its own true and proper life. Nevertheless it is possible to distinguish clearly the Rights and Duties which the Legislator may take, and in fact does take, under his protection from those other innumerable and commanding Moral claims which lay a far stronger hold on the innermost Conscience of the Parties, and which are directed to emotions and to infinitesimal minutiæ of daily conduct of which no Court of Justice could ever take cognisance.

The essential ingredients of the Moral relationship are (1.) a peculiar and life-long Association of one Man with one Woman originating in a Joint Voluntary Act, (2.) the contemplation of the Birth, Nurture, and Education of Children, (3.) the exercise of mutual affections and the tendering of mutual offices of Sympathy, Companionship and Solace reaching to the supremest needs and the loftiest aspirations of Human Life. This description may be taken as a type of the true Moral relationship denominated Marriage. It may take many ages in any country for this type to be approximately even so much as conceived. In different Countries and different Ages all kinds of variations from this type have been manifested or experimentally attempted. Such eccentric variations are Polygamous Marriage; " Temporary Marriage," or Concubinage; " Spiritual Marriage," where the Birth of Children is essentially absent from the conditions contemplated; and all Marriages which profess to rest upon any other basis than the satisfaction of the characteristic instincts of Humanity to which deference is paid in Marriage according to the true type.

Now though Legislators have at all times erred both in excess and defect in respect of enforcing the true Moral aims of Marriage by direct Legislation, the importance of legally ascertaining the epoch at which a new Family takes its rise, and of protecting the Personal Rights and the Rights of Ownership accruing to both the present and future members of the Family, at once casts upon the Legislator the responsibility of taking public cognisance of the Fact of Marriage, even were the integrity of Family Life not in itself, so far as it can be guarded by Law, of the most intimate concern to the Statesman and the Lawgiver.

But the importance of accurately fixing the Fact of Marriage in a mode cognisable by a Judicial Tribunal is in nowise limited to such elementary considerations as these. The necessity is presented at every turn of determining the Family which is responsible for the Maintenance and Guardianship of Children; of distributing on just principles Things left by a deceased and Intestate Owner among those for whom he is morally bound to provide, or of carrying out a Testamentary Disposition; of discovering the Persons on whom Taxation for special purposes properly falls; and, lastly, of solving the problems presented by the Doctrine of "Domicile," and by that of "Settlement" for the purpose of administering a Poor-law.

In order, then, for the above reasons, to give the greatest possible precision to the Fact of Marriage so far as it is one of direct interest to the Legislator, a certain class of Laws is demanded having this special object in view. By these Laws are defined the Competency of the Persons entering into the Marriage-state, the Authentic

Signs which shall notify,—for legal purposes,—that a Marriage has taken place (or, in cases in which such a course is permitted, where it has been Dissolved during the life-time of the Parties); and the Legal Rights and Duties of the Married Persons in respect of each other, of the Children, and of other Persons.

The Competency of the Persons is eminently a matter of purely Positive Prescription, and will differ for every country according to local Usages generally prevalent, to Religious beliefs or traditions, to the prejudices of Race, to the exigencies of Climate, and to accidental Political convenience. The most peculiar class of difficulties which this part of the Law opens up are those connected with Marriages of Affinity or Consanguinity. But it is not necessary here to linger over these difficulties, as they appertain rather to the Statesman and to the Moralist than to the Jurist, the practical Lawyer, or the Judge.

II. *Authentic Signs that the Legal Relationship has been Created.*

It has already been noted that the Moral side of Marriage far exceeds in importance and interest the Legal side, and the recognition of this fact is conveyed in the notorious circumstance that in all Communities, and eminently in Primitive ones, Marriage is bound up with the Religious Life of the People, and all that concerns it is draped in the garments of a ceremonious Ritual. Thus it often comes about that the Authorities whose special charge it is to guard and cultivate the direct Moral life of the people widely differ from the State Authorities as to the Modes of regulating the formal Conditions of Marriage. The one set of Authorities will demand one kind of Authentic Signs of Marriage, the other another kind; the one will recognise and provide for Divorce, the other will discountenance and reject it, or,—both allowing it,—one will allow it on one class of grounds, and the other set only on another; one set, again, will regard certain Persons as Competent to marry, the other will regard the same as Incompetent. The amount of divergencies of this kind will be different at different epochs, and, of course, in different countries. The true principle undoubtedly is that, inasmuch as the State, on its Legal side, affects only to interfere in the matter of Marriage for certain very definite purposes, and is wholly unqualified to engage in such processes of Moral discrimination as an omniscient Spiritual Authority could alone properly conduct,—the State, in making its Law of Marriage, must restrict itself severely to carrying out such objects of simple Expediency and Justice as the rude machinery in its hands enables it to compass.

This principle will dictate that, in fixing the Authentic Signs of a Marriage, the Signs selected be notorious, simple, non-inquisitorial, and such as may fully suffice to ascertain that the Persons marrying are within the class of Persons held by the State not Incompetent to marry either by reason of Age or of Consanguinity, and that no Fraud is being practised, by the Persons marrying, upon each other or upon other Persons. The State, in order to secure these ends, may either invent Authentic Signs of its own by appointing special Officers to Register Marriages, and by declaring the Solemnities or Forms to be observed by the Parties; or else may adopt the Authentic Signs already in use among any particular Religious body or bodies; or may allow an alternative use of one class of Signs or the other.

Under this head of Law, in accordance with the above considerations, will be subdivided the following topics:—

1. Persons who are or who are not competent to marry by reason of Age; of Consent or want of Consent of Parents, Relations, Guardians, or other Persons; of peculiar conditions of Citizenship; of Affinity; of mental and physical health; or of other circumstances.
2. Rights and Duties of Officials and other Persons entitled by Law to witness or assist in performing the Act of Marriage.
3. Forms and Solemnities to be observed by the Persons marrying, or by other Persons, before and at the time of Marriage.
4. Subsidiary or accessory Solemnities with a view to Registration, Publication, and the like.

1. As to questions of Competency, it is obvious that some of the causes of legal disqualification to marry are based on purely Physical conditions, whether temporary or permanent, and whether affecting the body or the mind. Such are physical immaturity, malformation, or even special disease, as Lunacy, or complaints producing mental imbecility. Others are based on supposed Moral considerations, as the general protection of Family Life in its integrity and immaculate simplicity, or the prevention of fraudulent intrigues: such is the absence of the Consent, formally expressed, or else implied, of certain Persons—generally the nearest relatives. The tendency of modern Legislation is to dispense with the necessity for such Consent, except in the case of Minors. Other causes of the same nature are those implied in blood-relationship

and in the more artificial relationships growing out of Marriage itself, that is, in "Consanguinity" and "Affinity." The former of these may be held to be connected with purely Physical reasons; but the defence of the moral and inviolate unity of the Family is a sufficient, and probably a main inspiring, ground of this class of Legislation. Again, other causes of legal disqualification are based on purely Political considerations. To this class belong the ancient obstacles at Rome to Marriages between Plebeians and Patricians, or between Roman Citizens and *Latini* or *Peregrini*; the later obstacles in Imperial Rome to Marriages with Heretics; and the modern legal obstacles, existing to so large an extent in Switzerland, for the prevention of intermarriages between Persons belonging to different Cantons.

2, 3, 4. As to the Rights and Duties of Officials concerned in the celebration of a Marriage, and the forms and solemnities legally prescribed as essential to its due celebration, the following various predicaments are presented:—

(1.) Either a due performance of the Duties imposed on the Officials is essential to the validity of the Marriage, or it is not.

(2.) A neglect of such due performance may either impair the validity of the Marriage, and thereby may or may not entail Penal consequences to the delinquent Official; or, without impairing the validity of the Marriage, may entail such consequences.

(3.) The due observance of all or of some of the Forms and Ceremonies prescribed by Law either may be an essential ingredient in the validity of the Marriage, or the omission of them may simply afford ground for obstruction and postponement to be encountered at the hands of anyone who chooses to take advantage of it.

Over and above the protection afforded to the integrity of Family Life, and the security provided against fraudulent impositions, by Legislative precautions in the matter of "Consanguinity" and in that of publicity and regularity in the celebration of Marriage, it is not infrequent to seek to attain the same ends by an adaptation of the Criminal Law. From this policy flow such Laws as those forbidding, under severe Penal Sanctions, the offences of Abduction, Bigamy, and Incest.

III. Rights and Duties accruing : 1. *As between the Parties ;* 2. *As between the Parties on the one hand, and each of them, and the Children of the Marriage on the other ;* 3. *As between the Parties and all other Persons.*

In respect of the first of these divisions, that comprehending the Rights and Duties of Married Persons towards each other, the main question is as to the actual degree in which the Laws of civilised States do in fact attempt to reinforce Moral Duties by rendering the Husband and Wife severally amenable to Courts of Justice for Breach of any of these Duties. It is notorious that the largest possible diversity of practice exists, and has always existed, with respect to Legislation in this matter. In some States, especially in primitive ones, the Legal and the Moral Rights and Duties are co-extensive with, and, indeed, scarcely distinguishable from each other. In others the Legal Rights and Duties are reduced to the smallest possible amount; while in others again—as in most European States, including England—the Legal Rights and Duties affect to cover a large portion of the same ground as the Moral, but of course not the whole, nor even the more important part, of that ground. The Jurist, then, has to discover a Mode of Classification, which, by the use of the most general *formulæ*, will adapt itself to all these different cases.

The Rights and Duties of Husband and Wife with respect to each other are either

(1.) In respect of the *person* of each other, or
(2.) In respect of Things owned by one or the other.

(1.) Under the first of these heads will be included all the Laws regulating the Claims of one of the Parties to the Society of the other (so far as the Law affects to guarantee it); to physical Submission (so long as Law continues in the barbarous condition in which it attempts to enforce or promote such submission); and to Maintenance and Support of either of the Parties at the hands of the other. The exact amount and kind of Society, Submission, and Maintenance which the Law attempts to secure will be described in this place, and will be expressed under the form of Reciprocal Rights and Duties. The Modes of enforcing the several Duties may be by destroying or qualifying the Marriage Relationship, by providing Pecuniary Compensation to be paid to the injured Party, or by enforcing, through any available means, the actual performance *in specie* of the Duties imposed. It is important to notice that some of the Laws belonging to this head have respect to what may be called purely negative Duties; that is, Duties to abstain from forming connections of a well-defined kind with other Persons.

(2.) Under the second head will be included the Laws regulating the changes effected in the Rights of Ownership of the Parties severally by the Act of Marriage, and the Laws determining the claims of the Parties severally in respect of Things acquired by either of them during the continuance of the Marriage. This part of the Law might either come in this place or, under the head of Laws of Ownership, among the "Modes of acquiring Rights of Ownership." It happens, however, that the Laws of Ownership affecting Married Persons have generally formed so conspicuous and compact a System by themselves, that they more conveniently fall under the present head than under the former one.

There are three distinct methods which Laws regulating the Rights of Ownership of Married Persons in respect to each other may pursue.

(1.) The Married Persons may, after the Marriage, retain for all purposes the same Rights of Ownership and the same capacities for acquiring Rights of Ownership, whether in respect of each other or of other Persons, which they had before, their several Duties in respect of contributing, both during life and afterwards, to the expenses of the household and to the Children's maintenance being legally assigned on some broadly recognised principle. This seems to be the method to which the best European Legislation is gradually tending, and which has nearly been completely developed in some of the States of America.

(2.) According to a second method some artificial Relationship between the Husband and Wife with respect to their Rights of Ownership is instantly created by the Marriage. This Relationship, in the countries where it exists, has been based upon largely prevalent traditional maxims or beliefs, though it owes its actual shape to certain precise legal assumptions or moral theories as to some immutable attitude of Husbands and Wives to each other. The best and readiest instance of Legislation, proceeding by the method now under consideration, is supplied by the English Common-Law doctrine by which, with respect to all available Rights of Ownership, a Woman's personality, by the very act of Marriage, instantly merges in that of her Husband. The injurious and often the cruel consequences of Laws of this species have been often pointed out, and, indeed, have been recently confessed by the English Legislature, which has already taken a timid and furtive step in the opposite direction. In criticising Laws regulating the Rights of Ownership of Husband and Wife in respect of each other, it is too frequently forgotten that the value of all such Laws is only tested when the moral Duties of the Parties to one another, or of one to the other, begin to fail. So long as they are keenly felt and adequately discharged, Laws of all sorts for this purpose are of equal value or valuelessness. But it is when inconsiderateness, with all its attendant and growing spectres of selfishness, cruelty, and tyranny, disturbs the home, that the goodness of a Law is tested for the protection of the barest moral claims of each, and especially of the one who is physically (and perhaps, through a crowd of social influences, even mentally) the least capable of resistance.

It is impossible to stigmatise in too severe terms a Law which, worthless in moments of tranquillity and confidence, so soon as these are broken instantly starts forward and sides in every possible case with the man against the woman. The iniquity is all the more flagrant in a country where all the resources of judicial machinery have been strained to the uttermost to wrench the Law in the direction of justice to Women in any class of Society which is able to pay for this protection.

(3.) A third method of legislating with respect to the Rights of Ownership of Married Persons is, strictly speaking, a combination of the two other methods. It starts with presuming a certain artificial legal Relationship as to Ownership to be created by the Marriage, but leaves to the Parties themselves a considerable latitude of discretion for the purpose of qualifying the nature of this Relationship. The English rules as applied by the Court of Chancery, recognising a Wife's "Separate Estate," and an almost unlimited power of pre-nuptial Settlement; the various systems of the "*Régime dotal,*" and of "*Communauté,*" prevailing on the Continent, are sufficient illustrations of this last method.

2. As to the Rights and Duties of the Married Persons as respects their Children, they concern :
   (1.) The Guardianship of the Children's *persons.*
   (2.) The Maintenance, Nurture, and Education of the Children.
   (3.) The Rights of Ownership of the Children.

(1.) The Rights of Guardianship over the *persons* of Children as held by one of the Parents correspond with Duties imposed on the other Parent, on the

Children themselves, or on third Persons. The only case in which competing Rights of this sort can come into question as between the Parents themselves is upon the Parents living apart from each other without dissolution of the Marriage, and in the absence of special regulations decreed by a competent Court of Justice. The modifications introduced may depend upon the Age or the Sex of the Children, or—after a certain Age—upon the will of the Children themselves, or even upon special terms of the arrangement entered into between the Husband and Wife.

Laws, again, regulate in many countries the amount of castigation which the Parent in charge of the Child is justified in inflicting upon the Child who resists what is regarded as his legitimate authority.

As respects the Duties of third Persons, Remedies either Criminal or Civil are usually provided for the use of the Parent in order either to rescue a Child wrongfully detained, to obtain Compensation for injuries done to the Child, or to inflict Penalties on offenders in these respects, in order to deter others from the commission of like offences.

(2.) As to the Maintenance, Nurture, and Education of Children, much will be made to depend during the lifetime of the Parents on the fact of Guardianship. Nevertheless the pecuniary responsibility of providing for the expenses of the Maintenance, Nurture, and Education of Children may be made to fall upon one Parent, while the Guardianship or even the choice of the method of Nurture and Education may be left to the other. The Law regulating the pecuniary responsibility of the Married Persons severally will of course be qualified by the general Law of Ownership as peculiarly affecting Married Persons.

With respect to the other circumstances, the possibly different Religious Faith of the two Parents introduces a difficult and almost insoluble problem. This problem may be roughly solved for practical purposes, either by (under the circumstances presupposed) making an irresistible legal Presumption in favour of some specified Faith, as, for example, that generally upheld by the State Authorities; or by conclusively determining in favour either of the Father or of the Mother or of the actual Guardian of the Child, if the Parents are living apart; or by one or other of these methods for the first few years of Infancy, the Child being allowed, so soon as these years have expired, to elect for itself. Obviously this problem presents the greatest difficulty when one of the Parents is dead, and the responsibility is cast on the Court of determining the Duties to which the surviving Parent is liable. In such a case the Court can only act by very general rules, and it seems almost impossible to avoid the perpetration, even under the best considered rules, of frequent injustice and cruelty.

There is a class of Laws which might with almost equal propriety be placed here or under either of the heads of Laws relating to the Constitution and Administration of the State, or of Laws of Civil Injuries and Crimes. These are the Laws which impose special Duties on Parents with respect to their Children for the sake of comprehensive public ends as well as of the private advantage of the Children. Such are Laws commanding, under assigned Penalties, the Vaccination of infant Children, and the Education, according to certain approved methods, of all Children up to a certain Age. Such also are Laws of the nature of the Factory Acts, and like Laws regulating the employment of Children. Such again are Laws introduced, in connection with a general System of Poor-Laws, for the punishment of Parents deserting their Children and so casting the responsibility of maintaining them upon the State.

(3.) As to the legal relations of Parents to their Children in respect of Ownership, the ordinary modern Law, in the event of Children acquiring Rights of Ownership otherwise than through their Parents, treats the Parents as mere Guardians or Trustees on behalf of their Children till they become of Age. In Roman Law, where the *Patria auctoritas* drove its roots so deeply into the whole Legal System, it was only under very special Legislation that a Child of any Age could have any Rights of Ownership as against its Father. The constant inroads made on this doctrine by the *castrense peculium* and the *quasi castrense peculium* are known to all students of Roman Law. On the other hand, the necessity under which a Father lay to provide for his Children at his death is testified to by the equally well-known *querela de inofficioso testamento*. In modern France the relics of this last Institution survive in the restrictions in favour of a man's Family imposed on his power of Testamentary disposition.

In Ancient Rome, in Scotland, and in many countries on the continent of Europe, there is permitted what is called a *legitimatio per subsequens matrimonium*, or the possibility of rendering Illegitimate Children Legitimate by the Marriage of their Parents subsequent to their birth. The main objection to a Law having this effect exists in the case of there being Legitimate Children (that is, Children born after the Marriage), as well as the others. In this case it is alleged with reason that Rights of Ownership as acquired through the Will of the Parents or by Intestate Succession from them may often be indefinitely in suspense, it being always open to the chance that Children alleged to have been born before the Marriage, or the descendants of such Children, may appear to put in their rival claims even at a period of time indefinitely remote. Possibly by providing for due publication of the Marriage and by fixing a limit of Time within which such Children must appear, the claims of humanity and morality might be reconciled with those of practical justice.

3. As to the Rights and Duties of the Married Persons in respect of Other Persons, they concern :

    (1.) Personal Injuries inflicted by third Persons on one of the Parties to the Marriage.

    (2.) Liability of either of the Parties for Contracts made with or Injuries inflicted upon third Persons by the other Party either before or during the Marriage.

    (3.) Certain peculiar Legal results of the assumed intimacy of the association between the Parties, as exemplified in the English rules regulating the Admission of the Evidence of Married Persons for or against each other and the amount of Responsibility incurred by one of the Parties committing a Crime in the presence of the other.

The first of these divisions covers the whole subject of Compensation in the way of Pecuniary Damages for adultery, abduction, detention, defamation of character, and assaults of all sorts proceeding from third Persons.

The second division is concerned with the effect of the Contracts made and the Civil Injuries committed by either Party; with the doctrines, familiar to English Law, of the Wife's presumed Agency on behalf of her Husband, and of the possible liability of her Separate Estate to answer for her Husband's partnership or other debts; with some of the consequences of the French *séparation des biens*; and with the consequences of the Wife's being or not being *in manu viri* in Roman Law. The doctrine of the Roman *dos*, in some of its aspects, and of the English "paraphernalia" and "pin-money" will also find a place here.

The third division in its terms speaks for itself, and, unless relegated to the department dealing with Laws of Procedure, will take its place here, solely for convenience of reference. It will probably be characterised by more that is irrational and accidental than other branches of this part of the Law, and will contain very different matter in different countries and at different epochs.

IV. *Authentic Signs that the Legal Relationship has been Terminated.*

In the description of the Marriage Relationship it was said to be essentially life-long,—that is, enduring for the joint life-time of the Parties. Looked at from the moral standing-point, any contemplated termination of the Relationship to be brought about by Acts or Events less inevitable or momentous than the close of Human Life would wholly alter the character of Marriage in respect of the total self-surrender which it demands as well as of the reality, the strength, and the unchangeableness of the bonds which it presupposes. Thus, in treating of Marriage even from the juridical point of view which can only be based on the moral one, the sole authentic Sign which, in a typical constitution of Society, can be selected as indicating the termination of the Marriage Relationship is the Death of either of the Parties.

It happens, however, that the actual problem proposed to Legislators, so far from being of this simple nature, is one of the highest degree of complexity, and has led to the greatest possible variety of handling in Ancient and in Modern States. Owing to the imperfect development of general Human Nature hitherto; to the distorted and abortive products of individual growth; to the vicious educational and political systems which have everywhere prevailed; to the unhappy historical antecedents which have damped the energies of even the most aspiring nations; and to a number of other more indefinite causes, it is only very rarely, both in national habits and in individual instances, that the Marriage Relationship attains to a standard at all resembling that of its typical perfection. Short of attaining this standard, it admits of exhibiting an indefinite number of gradations down to a vanishing-point, at which it can be said to exist in no sense whatever, except in name. At some points on the scale of progressive degradation it retains a considerable semblance to, or reminiscence of, the true type. A limited number of the affections and of the intellectual faculties are called into play, and a tolerably sincere, though by no means complete and unreserved, self-surrender (especially on the physically weaker side) is accomplished. The fruits reaped are those of a more or less agreeable partnership, mutual solace of a more or less serviceable kind, and in the average of cases a courteous compromise of individual and opposed claims. Far removed as such a state of things is from the true Marriage, in which every particular and most characteristic emotion, faculty, and function of either Party has its own individuality intensified to the uttermost through baptism in the font of self-sacrifice, still it is not incompatible with domestic repose, and with a life neither unhappy nor unprofitable. Unfortunately, however, the outward form and legal incidents of the Marriage Relationship are not seldom present when even this imperfect amount of union is discovered to be wanting. The sad story of such cases need not be told here. The actual legal bond is found to be too fragile to resist the strain of temptation, or the attraction of what is only too readily accepted as a possibly higher and fuller life. The old tie is rudely severed, and new ones of every shade of moral value are entered upon with more or less of rashness or awe-stricken hesitation. The result is the creation of a number of newly-competing blood-relationships preferring claims of different kinds to the solicitude of Parents, to the protection of Laws, and to the indulgence of Society.

The question, then, before the Lawgiver is as to whether in any case whatever he shall recognise, and, as it were, condescend to this imperfect and lamentable state of things. So far as he does, he may undoubtedly be said to incline to the support of it, and—to that extent—to debase the ideal conception of Marriage. If he do not, he allows misery and confusion to be the lot of a number of innocent Persons, who thus become destitute of many just claims as against the Society which has given them birth, and more especially as against their natural Parents who are jointly responsible for all that befalls them.

It is not necessary to do more here than thus briefly to

indicate the nature of the problem which lies before the Lawgiver. It has been practically solved in all countries, both of the ancient and of the modern world (subject to certain temporary exceptions due to the supremacy, in the field of Law, of the Ecclesiastical Authority), by the creation of Laws of Divorce. The general effect of such Laws is to recognise certain facts, other than the death of either of the Parties, on the occurrence of which,—as properly established before a Judicial Authority,—the Marriage Relationship is legally terminated. The selection of such facts, and of the kind of Evidence necessary to establish them, are matters at once of the highest importance and of the greatest difficulty. The infidelity of one of the Parties would of itself be an obvious ground for the release of the other; but the application of this test demands the most keen judicial acumen, inasmuch as a wide opportunity is opened for the promotion of conspiracies between the Husband and Wife, of a nature fatal to the public support of the Institution of Marriage. Furthermore, questions of Conjugal Infidelity are dangerously favourable to the propagation of a system of espionage subversive of the best tendencies and habits of domestic life, and generally detrimental to Social confidence.

Whatever facts are selected as grounds of Divorce, it is indispensable to the support of Marriage in its essential moral integrity that the tests should be equally applicable in all possible respects to both Sexes without distinction.

There are, indeed, two distinct, and in some measure opposed, grounds upon which Divorce may be granted, according as the purpose is to afford relief to either Party suffering from the Infidelity of the other, or to afford a general relief to both Parties on the ground that the Marriage is proved to be infelicitous, and its continuance detrimental to the interests of the Parties themselves or of Society at large. If Legislators generally hesitate to apply, otherwise than on the most cautious principles and after the strictest investigation, the Remedy of Divorce on the first of these grounds, it is with still greater reluctance that (if at all) they apply the same Remedy on the latter class of grounds. Indeed it is customary in most modern States to stop short of applying the full Remedy in any case other than where one of the Parties, being transparently innocent, has been grossly injured by the other Party in a matter inseparably bound up with the bare existence of the Marriage Relationship in its moral aspects. In cases not falling under this head, as in those involving cruelty, recklessness, negligence, desertion, and what may be called moral tyranny, modern Laws usually supply (but in this case with a parsimony and a timidity which is much to be deprecated) the sort of Remedy which is implied, not in dissolving the Marriage, but in modifying and restricting certain of its general Rights and Duties. Some Systems of Law, indeed, favour Modifications of this sort when brought about by common consent. The English Judicial Separation and the French *séparation des biens* are notable instances of Special Legislation, introduced in order to carry out, in different ways, the last class of objects.

Assuming that it has been determined by a competent Court of Justice that either the Legal Relations of Marriage shall be dissolved, or its ordinary Rights and Duties qualified, a difficult problem is yet presented as to the consequent alterations in the Rights and Duties of a variety of Persons whom the change of circumstances affects. The Persons whose interests are most nearly at stake are necessarily the Children of the Marriage. Special provision will have to be made by the Court, subject to general Rules of Law, as to (1.) the Guardianship of the Children; (2.) the expenses of their Maintenance and Education, and the character of the latter; (3.) as to opportunities of more or less frequent intercourse with the Children on the part of the Parent who is not recognised as their Guardian. It is obvious that the Rights of Ownership of the two Parents severally will have to be judicially readjusted in accordance with the novel state of circumstances. In some cases, also, a Law of Divorce may provide for Pecuniary Compensation being obtained from a third Person, through whose Acts the occasion of the Divorce has been brought about.

In the above general review of Laws regulating the peculiar Rights and Duties of Husbands and Wives, and of Parents and Children, it has been necessary to assume provisionally either that a true Marriage exists, or that it does not exist, and to take no account of the unhappy, though too frequent, cases in which, even in highly advanced countries, the relation of Parent and Child is a reality, but that of Husband and Wife—in any legal sense at least—is not. Many of the same considerations which may be urged for supporting, through the medium of Law, the Institution of Marriage might also be urged for giving some passing validity, even to those fleeting and insecure Connections which at least have this momentous result in common with Marriage,—that from them Children derive their birth.

s

No doubt in cases of this sort the Legislator is surrounded with perplexity. He will hesitate to recognise various grades of Marriage, and thereby incidentally to promote their formation; and he will equally hesitate to deny the moral claims which Children have upon their natural Parents, and which each Parent has upon the other to contribution for the proper Maintenance, Nurture, and Education of Children. For Juridical purposes it is sufficient to notice the nature of the problem in order to explain the Legal theory of Marriage, and to point out how far some of the Rights and Duties involved in it may not be confined to it, but may, under a just System of Law, be attached to Connections upon which the Statesman and the Moralist properly frown. The details of the part of the Law here alluded to will probably fall under Laws relating to the Relief of the Poor, and thereby under the general head of Laws relating to the Constitution and Administration of the State.

B. Guardian and Ward.

It has been customary in most organised Systems of Law and Institutional Treatises to handle under a separate heading of its own the topic of Parent and Child. This topic has here been included under the general heading of Husband and Wife, or rather the two topics have been treated as scarcely distinguishable from each other. The grounds for this redistribution will be easily apprehended by those who recognise that the best system of classification is that which is at once most natural and most convenient. Now it is impossible to treat of the relation of Husband and Wife without adverting to their joint, or, it may be, their conflicting, Rights and Duties with respect to their Children, far more decisively than to their Rights and Duties with respect to any other Persons. It is, then, better to treat in one and the same place the class of Rights and Duties of Parents in relation to their Children, and that of the two Parents in relation to each other. Indeed it cannot but lead either to much repetition or to needless confusion to endeavour to break up the subject into two parts.

No such reasoning applies to the heading of Guardian and Ward. It is a purely artificial and independent Relationship, created by nothing else than Positive Law, though in compliance, like most other legal creations, with the demands of sentiments having a purely moral origin. The obvious possibility of both Parents dying before the Child or Children of the Marriage shall have attained to an Age at which they may be presumed competent to avail themselves of the Rights or to perform the Duties cast upon them suggests the necessity of substituting, for these purposes, some Person or Persons in the place of the natural protectors of whom they are bereft. A like necessity may be held to arise when accidental Events, other than the Death of both Parents, seem likely to prejudice the legal interests of the Children themselves, or of other Persons liable to be affected by their legal Incompetency. Such Events are the Death of one of the Parents, coupled with the Insanity, Imprisonment, Absence, or re-Marriage of the other, or the happening of any one of these Events to one of the Parents and of some other of them to the other, or,—when possible,—of the same Event to both. In such cases all civilised States have provided for the appointment of competent Persons to watch over the interests of Children, to maintain their

Rights, and to perform, as far as may be, the Duties to which the Children might, otherwise, be held liable.

It is, indeed, not only in cases of Infancy that Guardians for the above general purposes are needed. The Roman *Curator* was appointed to guard the interests of the Young in the matter of Ownership after the true Guardianship of the *Tutor* had ceased, and yet it was not held expedient to trust the Minor,—owing to his presumed inexperience of the world,—under the Age of twenty-five entirely to himself. Similarly the condition of the Lunatic presents, for many purposes, the same claims upon the protective care of the State as does that of the Infant. The main differences between the regulations as to Guardianship in the two cases are introduced by the universality, certainty, and definiteness of the physical and mental circumstances of Infants, as contrasted with the numberless vicissitudes and individual idiosyncracies which characterise a condition of Lunacy. The possible suspension of that state during what is called a lucid interval demands, again, fresh modifications. The policy of protecting dissolute or profligate Persons against the consequences of their own acts, as recognised by the Roman Institution of the *curatela prodigi*, is one that commends itself little to modern States, though, where the direct legal interests of other Persons are involved, Courts of Justice, such as the English Court of Chancery, will sometimes interfere by the momentary assumption of the Duties of a Guardian, and will protect the Rights at stake.

The Mode of Appointment of a Guardian for any of the above or other purposes is naturally a matter of great anxiety to the Legislator or the Judge, and admits of the application of different or divergent rules for different states of Society according as the moral claims or particular interests of the Person protected, of the Persons related to and connected with such Person, and of the State itself, are held to be of paramount consideration. The modern tendency is to recognise as far as possible the usual dictates of natural feeling or National custom without sacrificing the claims of certainty, or of efficiency, and without disregarding the proper responsibility of all Parties concerned. In the case of the Guardianship of Infants, it is an obvious course to permit to Parents the greatest latitude in the way of appointing Guardians to their Children by Will, and the Law must declare whether the Will of the Father or that of the Mother is to prevail, in the case of discrepancy between them ; whether the surviving Parent can be excluded from being a Guardian, or can be associated with another Guardian, by the Will of the deceased Parent ; and what rule shall prevail in the case of one or both Parents dying Intestate or making no provision for the case. Under the last-mentioned circumstances, and also in cases of Lunacy and the like, the Law may either provide for certain Persons, generically described, being nominated as Guardians, in default, perhaps, of objections formally established, or else it may provide that every case be considered by itself and brought under the jurisdiction of a special set of officers, as—for instance—of the Prætor at Rome or of the Chancellor or of the Commissioners in Lunacy in England. The duration of Guardianship, the mode of investigating and redressing Injuries committed by Guardians, the mode of changing or of supplementing Guardians, and the Rights and Duties of Wards in respect of their Guardians, will form the topics of other parts of this branch of a complete Code.

Thus the whole scheme of this head of the subject will be as follows:—

I. General description of the Legal Relationship of Guardian and Ward.

II. Events of different sorts on the happening of which the Relationship is demanded.

III. Mode of Appointment of Guardians for different purposes.

IV. Rights and Duties of Guardians and Wards respectively:

1. In respect of the Personal Rights of the Wards,— that is, of Maintenance, Nurture, Education, Protection, and Good Fame.
2. In respect of the Rights of Ownership, or of the Rights under a Contract, of Wards.
3. In respect of Duties to be performed by Wards.
4. In respect of Rights and Duties of Guardian and Ward reciprocally.

V. Duration of Guardianship and Modes of changing and supplementing Guardians.

VI. Modes of investigating and redressing Injuries committed by Guardians.

C. Trustees, Executors, and Administrators.

There are at least two distinct Modes in which the notion of a legal "Trust" may be regarded. It may be regarded from an historical point of view, as a device spontaneously invented by the Administrators of Law for the purpose of redressing the moral unfairness which accidentally becomes prevalent through the rigid stiffness of antiquated Law. Or the notion of a Trust may be regarded as bound up with the very existence of every Legal System, however refined and developed, and as likely to become more and more prominent with every forward step in Civilisation. Both of these conceptions are in fact at once true. The early notion of a Legal Trust was undoubtedly due to the conflicting claims of a reverence for the formal side of Existing Laws, and for the demands of Moral Justice or of Social Expediency. On the other hand, so soon as ever the notion of a Legal Trust was adequately evolved, the possibility of creating, under the name of Trusts, enormous classes of novel Rights and Duties, needed by the expansion of National life, progressively discovered itself. The history of *Fideicommissa* at Rome and of many of the leading Equitable doctrines of the Courts of Chancery in England, are only specimens of a natural process which might reproduce itself any number of times. Whatever may be the case on the first budding of the conception, it is to be remembered that the creation or recognition of a legal Trust does not in itself imply any attempt to make coextensive the provinces of Legal and of Moral Right and Duty. All it implies is the attempt to mark out with a fresh subtlety of description and of limitation a newly introduced class of strictly Legal Rights and Duties, and so far to innovate upon all existing Rules of Interpretation and of Procedure as is needed in order to make those Rights and Duties effective. Thus the leading elements in the conception of a Trust are: (1) a special description and limitation of a newly introduced class of Rights and Duties, the general characteristic of such class being that of an increased plasticity, exactness, and adaptability to special circumstances, as compared with the Rights and Duties under the older

Law; (2) a suspension or abrogation of all existing Legal Rules, to the extent necessary to give complete effect to the supplementary or substituted Rights and Duties thus newly introduced; and (3) a special System of Procedure for the purpose of supporting such Rights and enforcing such Duties.

But a radical element in every Trust has not yet been stated. It is true, on one side of it, that a Trust implies nothing more than the recognition of certain novel Rights and Duties over and above those recognised by the general body of the existing Legal System. On the other side, a Trust is at once the effect and the cause of a real increase of moral sensitiveness in a Nation. It becomes more and more cogently felt that in spite of the rigorous universality of Legal Rules and of the general expediency of respect being paid to that universality, nevertheless it is too great an outrage on public feeling to permit persons to use the very machinery of Justice as a means of doing unjust Acts; to become, through the help of the Law, enriched by their own wrong-doing; and to countenance Persons in a Court of Justice in not being open, honest, fair, and even-handed in all their dealings. Such sentiments become more and more incorporated in the very structure of Legal Systems. The doctrine of *bona fides*, as entertained by the Roman Prætor, and that of " Conscience " or " Equity " in the English Court of Chancery, are illustrious instances of such Juridical progress. Still more interesting is the growing extension of Equitable Procedure to English Common Law Courts, and the recent " fusion " of Common Law and Equity in the Legal Systems of some of the American States. In this way, where conscientious action is clearly absent, Courts of

Law not only resent the strain of all Legal Rules, transmuting, as in the crucible of the Alchemist, a Right in respect of one Person into a Duty in respect of another, but, furthermore, they encourage the multiplication of transactions between Persons where the only basis of reliance is the Good Faith of the Parties. In this way a larger incubus of responsibility is thrown upon the Judicial Authority, and it may be open to doubt whether the interference of Law in such fine matters of Moral conscientiousness is, in the long run, favourable or otherwise to National Morality. However this may be, the department of Law which deals with Trusteeship, which defines its nature, which describes the Rights and Duties implied in it, and which determines the Modes in which it takes its rise, is one of the most momentous sections of modern Legal Systems. It is here coupled with the part of the Law which deals with Executors and Administrators, inasmuch as these latter are only Trustees of a particular sort, though from their importance they deserve to be especially named.

It is obvious that Trustees eminently fulfil the conditions required to be satisfied by the Special Classes of Persons forming the subject-matter of the present chapter. In one aspect, their Rights and Duties have solely reference to the interests of Private Persons within the narrow circle of Domestic or of limited Social Life. In another aspect, they are State Officials, whose conduct is a matter of incessant concern to the Authorities of the State, and whose Acts are controlled, supervised, and directed from first to last by a Court of competent jurisdiction.

One large class of Duties appertaining to Trustees is that of doing Acts on behalf of Persons invested with Rights or made liable to the performance of Duties, who by reason of special Incapacities of body, mind, or situation, whether permanent, temporary, or occasional, are unable themselves to do the Acts those Rights and Duties presuppose in order that the benefits of the one may be reaped, and the liabilities of the other be discharged.

Another class of Duties appertaining to Trustees presupposes no Incapacity in any other Person, but is imposed either by the mere will of Private Persons, as enforced by the State, with or without the consent of the Trustee,—as in the case of *fideicommissa* at Rome, and of all that large class of things which, under the technical System of English Law, are capable of being left by Will or of being conveyed to one Person "to the use of," as it is said, or "in Trust for" another.

A third class of Duties appertaining to Trustees is imposed upon them by the State, wholly independently of their own will, and, possibly, of the intention of other Persons, solely for the purpose of preventing Frauds, of satisfying natural expectations, and of carrying out ends generally recognised as of public importance. To this class belong many of the Duties arising out of what are called in England "Constructive Trusts." Thus where a Person employs another Person's property in any trade or speculation there is, under certain circumstances, a "Constructive Trust" as to the property so acquired or the profits so made for the benefit of the Principal, Owner, or other Person whose property has been involved in the transaction.

The following may be taken as a sketch of the natural method according to which this part of the Law may be distributed :—

LAWS AFFECTING SPECIAL CLASSES OF PERSONS. 267

    I. Description of the general Legal Relations implied in the fact of Trusteeship.
    II. Modes in which the Relationship takes its rise.
        1. Existing Legal or Moral Relationships giving rise, under special circumstances, to a legal Presumption of Trusteeship.
        2. Acts of Private Persons.
        3. Acts of Judicial Officers.
        4. Acts of Persons who become Trustees.
    III. Rights and Duties of Trustees.
    IV. Modes of enforcing the Duties of Trustees.

I. Description of the general Legal Relations implied in the fact of Trusteeship.

Where two or more Persons are so related to each other that, independently of the operation of the general Law of Ownership, of Contract, of Civil Injuries, or of Crimes, one of those Persons is held liable by the State to the performance of certain Duties in respect of the other or others on the ground of a presumed Moral Confidence existing between them, the Person so held liable is said to be a Trustee for the other or others. In England the Person, on behalf of whom the Duty, or the so-called "Trust," is to be discharged, is called, from the Norman-French, the *cestui-que trust*. In Rome he was called the *fidei-commissarius*, and the Trustee the *fiduciarius*. The object of the Trust may be the Personal Security, the Moral Welfare,—(as the Education),—or the general Maintenance of the Person on behalf of whom the Trust is held; or it may be the exercise of Rights of Ownership, or the performance of Duties arising either out of Ownership or out of Contract, or it may be the bringing or defending Actions at Law.

II. Modes in which the Relationship takes its rise.

1. The most ordinary cause, historically, of the development of the idea of Trusteeship has been a tendency on the part of Law to convert a widely recognised Moral Relationship into a Relationship strictly Legal. This may be done either by transforming a purely Moral Duty into a Legal one, or by expanding the confines of a Legal Duty and increasing its stringency. The early history of the Jurisdiction of the English Court of Chancery in the matter of Lands, settled on Persons generally capable by the ordinary Law of holding them but so settled with the Intention, more or less avowed, of benefiting Religious Corporations, or of benefiting a variety of more or less deserving Persons incapable, by the same Law, of holding the Lands,—or at least of taking them under the circumstances of the case,—affords an instance of the Mode in which a Court may attempt to create Trusts in the face of the letter of the Law, simply for the purpose of satisfying expectations grounded on a sort of Moral Relationship. In the instance here selected it is true that two kinds of policy,—that of discouraging "Gifts in Mortmain" (or gifts of land to a certain class of permanent Corporations), and that of carrying out the Intentions of Donors or Settlors,—came into conflict with one another, the Courts of Chancery and the Legislature severally personating the rival political conceptions. Nevertheless, in all matters in which the Mortmain Laws have not been involved, the principles of the Court of Chancery have triumphed, and the largest branch of its Jurisdiction is that of supporting Rights of

Ownership growing out of the expressed words or the implied Intention of Settlors, which Rights are not only wholly ignored in Courts of Common Law, but are there held to be wholly superseded by Rights existing in the Trustee which these Courts recognise as efficient for every possible purpose.

Another instance supplied by English Law may be taken from the case of an ordinary Sale of Land, where the Purchase is partially completed. A Court of Common Law, representing the severity of the ancient doctrine, can do no more than decide by the roughest and most materialistic of tests whether the Vendor or the Purchaser is, at a given moment, the technical Owner of the Land. In such a case the Court of Chancery will usefully interfere and determine, after investigating all the minute facts of the case, whether the Vendor is Trustee of the Land for the Purchaser, or the Purchaser Trustee of the Purchase-money for the Vendor.

So in the case of part of the Things Owned by a deceased Person descending to the legal "heir," and part to other Persons, either by Will or by Intestate Succession, and of a claim being enforced against the whole Estate by third Persons, the Court will determine how far the Persons exempted from contribution in a Court of Common Law shall, nevertheless, be held liable to it in Equity,—that is, how far they shall be treated as Trustees of what by Common Law they owned, for the Persons actually compelled to contribute.

The respective claims of Mortgagor and Mortgagee in Courts of Common Law and of Equity afford one notable instance of the rise of a Trust through the mere existence of another Legal Relationship. In a Court of Common Law, a Mortgage is an ordinary Conveyance following upon a Contract for a Sale or for a Lease. The Mortgagee takes the place of the Mortgagor as Owner of the Land, and the Mortgagor that of the Mortgagee as Owner of the Money borrowed, the subsequent repayment of the Money and reconveyance of the Land being regulated by what is in fact nothing else than a Subsidiary Contract. In a Court of Equity, the Mortgagee is recognised as having nothing more than the sort of Security for his debt which is provided by a conditional Power of Sale, and, whether he be in possession of the Land or not, is treated as the mere Trustee of the Land for the benefit of the Mortgagor and his Heir. The Money lent descends, on the death of either of the Parties, as a debt due from the one, or his Executors, to the other, or his Executors.

2. Instances of the Relation of Trusteeship created by the Acts of Private Persons are those of Executors, of Trustees of Marriage Settlements, of a *fiduciarius* in Roman Law (created by such words as "*fideicommitto, peto, volo dari*" and the like), of the unpaid Treasurers of private Societies, and of Guardians of all sorts appointed by Private Persons and not by Public Authority.

When Persons have been appointed Trustees in this way, and where they have, by the due method prescribed, assented to such Appointment (as at Rome by accepting the Inheritance charged with a *fideicommissum*, in England by taking out Probate of a Will or by acting in a Trust created by a Marriage Settlement), the condition of Trusteeship, with all the Rights and Duties appertaining to it, is as completely created as when created by the direct operation of Law in the cases already considered.

3. A Trust may, again, be created by the arbitrary interposition of a Court of Justice. According to a well-

known maxim of English Equity, a Trust is never allowed to fail for want of a Trustee. Thus when the Public advantage needs the performance of Duties in respect of Private Persons, and no Person is generically determined by Law as liable to perform those Duties, the Court will sometimes appoint an Officer of its own to undertake the responsibility,—as for instance by vesting the Funds of Suitors in the Accountant-General, or by appointing temporary Guardians of Children, of Lunatics, or of others under the special protection of the Court.

Again, when Private Persons have, by their express language, or by the implied meaning of their Settlements or Wills, intimated a wish to create a Trust, but have omitted to designate Trustees, or the Trustees designated have failed through Death, through refusal to Act, or through Personal Incapacity, the Court of Chancery,—and in some cases the Court of Probate,—will step in and nominate some Person, either individually or generically determined, to act as Trustee with or without the concurrence of third Persons. The most signal instance of this Mode of Appointing Trustees is supplied by the practice of the English Court of Probate, (inheriting the functions of the Ecclesiastical Courts), with respect to the appointment of Administrators for the management of the Estate, for the performance of the Duties, and for the enforcement of the Rights, appertaining to the Legal Successors of a Person dying without having made a Will.

4. A Person is generally recognised as constituting himself a Trustee by his own Act in the case of his trading with Funds of other Persons, accidentally in his hands; of his assuming, without authority, the Duties of Guardian to an Infant or other Incapacitated Person; of his

interfering with the Estate of a Deceased Person without being appointed Executor or Administrator; and generally of his inducing other Persons, whether fraudulently or not, to believe that he is a Trustee and that he is not acting for his own advantage. In all these cases it is a matter of public policy to interpret the Duties of Persons in circumstances of peculiar temptation, and peculiarly exposed to suspicion, according to the most exact and severe standard.

III. *Rights and Duties of Trustees.*

The Rights conceded to Trustees have one of two objects in view; either the Security and Indemnification of the Trustee in the discharge of his proper functions,—that is, the direct benefit of the Trustee himself; or the enlargement of his Capacity, for the sole purpose of his doing Acts in the discharge of the Trust. To the former class of Rights belong the generally recognised claims of Trustees to be reimbursed all necessary expenses incurred by them in the matter of the Trust, as for purposes of Travel, of reasonable Litigation, of conducting protracted Negotiations by correspondence, and, in some cases, of advancing needful Funds. In estimating the limit of these Rights, rigid accuracy and particularity in matters of Account will be insisted upon throughout, and *bona fides* of the highest possible order will be demanded as a condition precedent to the effectual support of any such claims.

The other class of Rights,—those conceded in order to facilitate the discharge of the Trust,—are Rights to do Acts the due performance of which implies: (1.) a capacity to acquire or to exercise Rights of Ownership vested in other Persons (that is, in those on behalf of whom the

Trust is held); (2.) a Capacity to make effectual and binding Contracts on behalf of such Persons; (3.) a Capacity to stand in the place of such Persons for the purpose of bringing Actions at Law or of defending Actions brought by others on behalf of those who are objects of the Trust. These Rights, being of the highest importance, are, of course, strictly limited by the purposes of the Trust; by the situation of the Persons on behalf of whom it is held; and,—if there be an express Instrument creating the Trust,—by the terms of that Instrument strictly interpreted. In doing all the Acts comprehended in the Rights now under consideration, the English Court of Chancery exacts from a Trustee a far higher degree of circumspection, diligence, and prudence than an ordinary man would be expected to show about his own private affairs.

As to the Duties imposed upon Trustees, their direct objects are, either (1.) the efficient performance of the purposes of the Trust, or (2.) the general protection of the Public against the possibly injurious or fraudulent results of the divided responsibility which the fact of Trusteeship implies. In pursuance of the first object, the Rights to do all the Acts above described as possible to be performed by a Trustee are converted into legal Duties to perform them. A Trustee is thus legally compellable to acquire or to exercise Rights of Ownership, to make Contracts, to bring or to defend Actions; for which purposes the Law imparts to him a peculiar and idiosyncratic competency. The Law furthermore defines with the utmost possible precision the Mode, the Time, the latitude of Discretion, the quality of the Diligence, appertaining to the Duties incident to each particular kind

T

of Trust, according to its general nature or to the special circumstances of its creation. It is also customary to invent a class of Rules, founded on the teachings of experience, for the more minute direction of Trustees, and for the general protection of the Public. These Rules, being of a more or less arbitrary character, embrace the second general object to which the Duties imposed upon Trustees point, though in truth the two objects,—that is, the interests of the Persons for whom the Trust is held, and the interests of the Public,—are, for the most part, forwarded by identical means. It is in view of both classes of objects that the English Court of Chancery exercises a most jealous watchfulness over the habits of Trustees in the matter of their mixing up the Trust-funds in their hands with their own Private funds, and, generally, of their confounding their characters as Trustees and as Persons interested on their own behalf. So, likewise, the Court views with suspicion all dealings, not Judicially authorised, in the way of Sales, Mortgages, Guaranties, and the like, of which the subject-matter is Trust-funds. The adequacy of the price, the sufficiency of the "notice," the commercial value of a fresh investment, and the conspicuous honesty of the whole transaction are regarded, in negotiations of this sort, as elements of the most serious concern. Sometimes these elements have a still higher adventitious interest imparted to them by the existing Moral Relations (as by Guardianship, or by confidence between Lawyer and Client) between the Parties. It is by way of applying the severest possible test to transactions which, from their very nature, lay the way open to deceit, to overreaching, or, at the least, to unfair pressure, that the English Court of Chancery has developed the large branch of its Jurisdiction previously alluded to, which is implied in the doctrine of "Constructive Fraud." The Roman Lawyers, in their ample and plastic use of the doctrine of *Bona Fides*, recognised an equally wide and beneficial Jurisdiction in their Courts, though in many respects the English doctrine has been generally expressed in a more artificial and stringently limited guise.

As with Rights under a Contract, so, in the present case, it is not necessary to have a separate heading for the Modes in which Trusteeship comes to an end. The full description of the Rights and Duties of a Trustee carries with it that of their Modes of Limitation through the efflux of Time, through the happening of Conditional Events, or through the Acts of Persons. Of some of these Modes of Limitation instances are supplied by the Deaths of either of the Parties; by a repudiation of the Trust sanctioned by the Court; by a formal Release executed by the Parties on the purposes of the Trust being satisfied; and by a revocation or qualification of the Trust through the direct action of the proper Court. In the case of one of two or more Trustees dying, special Rules will be needed as to the responsibility of the Survivor or Survivors in the matter of continuing the Trust.

IV.—*Modes of enforcing the Duties of Trustees.*

The Duties of Trustees may be enforced directly, by a compulsory process issuing from a Court of Justice, commanding the Trustees who shall have omitted to perform the Duties imposed upon them, then and there to proceed to their Performance. Thus they may be compelled under threat of special Penalties,—as of Imprisonment,—to pay over or to invest Trust funds in their hands, to sign or "execute" Deeds or solemn Documents of public significance, to surrender the Possession of Things under their control, and to prosecute or to defend Actions at Law. Or these Duties may be enforced indirectly, by expelling from the Trust Trustees found to have omitted or negligently performed their Duties, and by substituting fresh Trustees; or, again, by exacting Compensation for the consequences of the omission from the delinquent Trustee, or by punishing him for his default or Fraud by proper Proceedings in a Criminal Court. Recent Acts of the English Legislature have facilitated the last-mentioned resource, while, under the Roman Law, the punishment of *Infamia*, carrying with it the loss of certain Political Rights, and following (among other causes) upon a condemnation in an Action *Bonæ Fidei*, is a notable example of the same Mode of enforcing this class of Duties.

D. BARRISTERS, ADVOCATES, SOLICITORS, ATTORNEYS, PROCTORS, WRITERS TO THE SIGNET, NOTARIES PUBLIC, AND THE LIKE.

Among the Special Classes of Persons whose Rights and Duties are most conveniently considered and tabulated in a department by themselves, the class of Professional Lawyers has many peculiar claims to be included. In any highly-organised Community the study of the Law always has a tendency to become an absorbing pursuit, demanding the devotion of a lifetime, and taxing the energies and zeal of the student to an extent which leaves only a small amount of leisure for other occupations. On the other hand, the generally recognised claims of the private Litigant to protection against Fraud and Culpable Negligence in the conduct of his Suit, as well as the necessity of expediting the course of public business, have led to the universal recognition of a class of Persons officially authorised to assist Suitors in prosecuting their Rights. This assistance is conferred either by acquainting suitors, on consultation, with the nature and extent of their Rights and of the Mode of Remedy provided, or by actually helping them in the conduct of portions of the Judicial Process, and even by advocating their claims before the Judicial Tribunal. The capacity to do this work implies a tolerably minute and exact knowledge of the contents of the existing Legal System, and a special familiarity with the processes of Courts of Justice, that is, with the part of the Law which falls under the head of Laws of Procedure. In nominating a class of Persons of the sort now indicated, the State will generally take, or profess to take, suitable means to ensure the presence of a sufficiency of this kind of knowledge.

It is an important feature in the history of Social Life, both Ancient and Modern, that the whole class of Professional Students of Law has generally undergone a bifurcation into two divisions, of which the one is concerned more especially with the study of the general Legal System, and with giving, or learning how to give, in somewhat of an abstract form, opinions on particular questions submitted to their consideration; the other professes or learns to instruct the private Litigant in the formal Mode of prosecuting a subsisting Legal Claim, and to represent and personate the Litigant at every stage of the Proceeding within and without the walls of a Court of Justice. Other peculiar Functions have, in course of time, and in accordance with special National customs, gathered round and modified the tasks of these opposed classes of Professional

Lawyers severally. The former class has in England, for instance, largely encroached, even to the extent of entire usurpation, on the proper Executive work of the latter, especially in the matters of Public Advocacy, of what is called "Pleading" (or the preparation of systematically regulated counter-statements made outside the Court by the opposed Parties), and of "Conveyancing" (or the Drawing of some of the more solemn Written Instruments known to the Law). The latter class, again, have shared largely with the former in giving "Responses" or general or special advice on the Rights, Duties, and Remedies appertaining to particular states of circumstances. Nevertheless in England, at least, there is one main Sign which distinguishes the two classes of Professional Lawyers one from another. Of the one class,—that of Barristers or Advocates,—the Rights and Duties are held, for the most part, if not wholly, (as is generally alleged) to be of a Moral nature, and so far not capable of enforcement for any purpose whatever in a Court of Justice. Of the other large and important class,—comprehending all the various Functionaries known as Solicitors, Attorneys, Proctors, Writers to the Signet, Notaries Public, and the like,—the Rights and Duties are not only Moral, but are universally recognised as strictly Legal. In this last aspect they find their appropriate place under the present Section.

This is not the place to discuss the expediency of this division of labour and variety of Legal Responsibility, nor to examine the degree in which a number of Social causes seem to be tending in this country, as in the United States, to bring about radical changes in the organisation of the Legal Profession. It seems scarcely deniable, on the one hand, that there are true and lasting differences between the distinct functions of (1) conducting personal intercourse with Clients for the purpose of ascertaining, out of a vast assemblage of complicated Facts in their possession, what are those essential to the Judicial Process impending; of (2) mastering the general body of the Legal System to the extent needed in order to give a reliable Opinion on the Rights and Duties involved in any Case presented; and of (3) presenting to a Tribunal, more or less skilled and qualified, the actual Facts of the Case and the Principles of Law applicable to them, in such a way as best to ensure a true and logical conclusion being inevitably reached. In spite, however, of these varieties of function, it may be very inexpedient for the State to place any impediments in the way of Persons, otherwise competent, exercising more than one or all of the functions at once. It must be still more detrimental to the interests of Clients, and of the general Public, to prevent the passage from the professed exercise of one set of functions to another set being as facile as possible. It is worse than detrimental,—it is destructive, —to the morality and to the honest aspirations of a great Profession, for the State to apportion a different meed of Social dignity and appreciation to Functionaries of one class from what it apportions to those of another.

The following is the general form under which the Laws creating and regulating the Rights and Duties now under consideration will be represented :—

I. Complete and generally descriptive list of the Classes of Persons specially authorised to assist Private Persons in the following respects :—

   1. Informing them as to the exact nature and extent of their Legal Rights and Duties, or of the nature and

Mode of using the Remedial Processes provided by Law for their enforcement.

2. In case of impending Litigation, preparing the Subject-matter of dispute for Judicial investigation (as by searching out and examining Witnesses, by conducting the formal and Judicial correspondence essential to bring into relief the real question at issue, and generally by saving the Litigant the labour, time, and mistakes his inexperience would cost him).

3. Representing Litigants in a Court of Justice.

4. Performing Public and Solemn Acts demanded either by the Practice of Courts of Justice in the course of Litigation, or by Mercantile or other Customs Judicially recognised (as by receiving the "Protest" of Bills of Exchange, witnessing Oaths, Signatures, and the like).

II. Qualifications and Modes of Appointment through which Persons become members of the Classes now under consideration.

III. Rights and Duties of such Classes of Persons severally in respect of each of the kinds of functions enumerated under the first (I.) head.

IV. Modes of enforcing such Rights and Duties, whether by the ordinary or extraordinary Processes of a Court of Justice.

V. Special and arbitrary provisions in contemplation of the possible Events of sudden Change, Removal, Incapacity, or Death of such Persons in the midst of performing their appropriate Functions.

E. Corporate Bodies, whether instituted for Municipal, Ecclesiastical, Educational, or Eleemosynary Purposes.

Corporations of the character here described might appear rather to be claimed by the chapter dealing with Laws directly relating to the Constitution and Administration of the State, if not by that dealing with Laws of Contract. The Corporate Bodies, however, here under contemplation differ at once from purely Governmental Institutions and from Industrial or Mercantile Associations. They combine, in a manner peculiar to themselves, a Public and a Private character. They may have originated in special Historical circumstances, or even in the more or less eccentric exercise of Individual wills. But, starting from these beginnings, they have progressively allied themselves with the general objects of National Policy. The Persons who administer them are treated as Public Officials rather than as Private Trustees; they are oftentimes directly appointed, changed, and controlled by the Executive Authority, while their Rights and Duties are interpreted and enforced far rather in view of the general interests of the whole Community than of any particular body of Persons, however immediately concerned. It is, of course, not possible to predicate all this as being exactly true of any particular body belonging to the class. The actual variations from this type, brought about by long ages of corruption, selfishnesss, and illiberality, which great Public Institutions often notoriously present, afford one of the largest and most useful fields for the modern Political Reformer. Nevertheless, for purposes of Classification, the type remains distinct enough to determine the Class to which the Corporation belongs, and the Place it occupies in an organised System of Law.

The Systematic arrangement of this part of the Law may be represented in the following manner:—

I. General description of Public and Corporate Bodies properly falling under the present head, with a discrimination of their several Objects.

II. Particular description of each Class of such Bodies in succession.

III. Enumeration, for each such Body in succession, of:—

    1. Its Officers.
    2. Modes of their Appointment.
    3. Their Rights and Duties.
    4. Modes in which their Functions terminate, or in which their Rights and Duties may be suspended or qualified.
    5. Modes of Enforcing such Rights and Duties.

IV. Rights and Duties of each class of Corporate Bodies in their Corporate Capacity, with the Formalities indispensable to a proper performance of the Acts implied in such Rights and Duties.

V. Modes of enforcing such Rights and Duties or of qualifying or suspending the same.

VI. Modes of suppressing or modifying each Class of such Corporate Bodies, as provided by anticipation.

CHAPTER XIII.

LAWS OF CIVIL INJURIES AND CRIMES.

INASMUCH as the full description of a Right involves, of necessity, an equally full description of the corresponding Duty, it might seem to be in the highest degree arbitrary and unsymmetrical to discuss the topic of Rights in one part of a Legal Treatise and that of Duties in another. A latent sense of the inharmoniousness of this method, and yet withal a clinging desire to conform to Schemes largely recognised have led Jurists to adopt various logical devices by way of disembarrassing themselves of the difficulty. Sir W. Blackstone seems to have taken shelter under the ambiguity lurking in the word "Right," and, as the basis of his Classification, to have opposed "Rights" to "Wrongs," treating under the latter head not only Laws of Civil Injuries and Crimes, but also Laws of Civil and Criminal Procedure. Mr. Bentham opposed "Substantive Law," as distributed into Civil and Penal, to "Adjective Law," or Laws of Procedure, including the Administration of Justice generally. Mr. Austin, again, insisting on building up his Classification of the topics of a Legal System on the severe conception of Rights only, distinguishes between "Primary Rights" and "Secondary, or Sanctioning, Rights"—the latter phrase implying those Rights which are conceded by the State solely for the purpose of reinforcing the former after these shall have been invaded.

Mr. Mill has pointed out that this division is valuable, as far as it goes, but that it fails altogether to include "Absolute Duties," or Duties corresponding with no "Primary Rights" at all. Mr. Mill himself suggests, as a principle of division, the main and immediate Purpose of the Law, according as that Purpose is the Creation or Extension of a Right,—that is, the Benefit of a Private Person,—or the achievement of some Public end through the imposition of a Duty implying the immediate Disadvantage of a Private Person. These two classes of Laws, and the Rights and Duties to which they give rise, may be, Mr. Mill submits, treated apart from each other with logical correctness and without doing unnecessary violence to current habits of Classification. The method pursued by the Roman Lawyers in treating the *Jus Privatum* was to relegate to the one general head of "*actiones*," all the matter that became of interest upon any actual or apprehended Breach of the Law,—that is, most of the matter here arranged under the several heads of Laws of Civil Injuries and Crimes, and of Laws of Procedure.

There is, no doubt, a real difficulty in the way, which accounts for these numerous and heroic attempts at a solution. The familiar oppositions in English Law between a "Tort" and a Breach of Contract, and between a Civil Injury,— whether arising through "Tort" or through Breach of Contract,—and a Crime, will afford some key to the way in which the difficulty has been brought about. These two series of oppositions are really due, partly, to Historical differences of Procedure, and, partly, to a want of clear perception that a "Tort," a Breach of Contract, and a Crime, all (with a very few exceptions) suppose that a Right of some sort, if only a

Moral one, has been invaded, and that a strictly Legal Duty has been omitted or wrongly performed. Owing, however, to the fact that the popular imagination has a more firm and ready hold on some classes of Rights than on others, as, for instance, on Rights to Personal Security and to Good Fame than on Rights of Ownership, and on Rights of Ownership than on Rights arising under a Contract, invasions of the one class of Rights are popularly treated as due to greater viciousness and perverseness in the Offenders, and as deserving of more stringent repression than invasions of the other. Hence, with respect to Rights under Contracts and Rights of Ownership, attention has been more steadily fixed on the Nature and Limits of the complicated advantages enjoyed by the Persons invested with the Rights than upon the probability, or the conceivable Modes, of infringing those Rights. With respect to the other classes of Rights, their Nature and Limits have been taken as a matter of course, and attention has been mainly arrested by the Modes of their Infringement, and by the Penalty such Infringement ought to bring with it.

Perhaps the only safe, though courageous, solution of the difficulties attending this part of the subject is to be found in first denominating a Violation of any Right whatsoever as either a Civil Injury or a Crime, or as both; and, secondly, in recognising it to be possible, as all past experience proves it to be commodious, to give superior prominence in one part of the Legal System to Rights as contrasted with Violations of Rights, and in another part to give superior prominence to Violations of Rights as contrasted with Rights. Thus the natural Mode of Distributing the topic of Laws of Civil Injuries and Crimes is already provided by anticipation through the distribution of the previous topics of this Work.

This is the place to insist on a clear conception being attained of what is meant by a Legal *Crime*. The word has been so much used and abused in the dialect of the people, and so heterogeneously combined with Moral and Religious sentiments, that it is especially hard to rescue it for the purpose of purely Juridical employment. In the face of these obstacles, however, a Crime may be provisionally defined to be " an Act which the State absolutely Prohibits, or a Forbearance from an Act which the State absolutely Commands to be done, the State making use of such a kind and measure of Punishment as may seem needed to render such Prohibition or Command effectual." Thus it is not of the essence of a Legal Crime that it should be peculiarly abominable in the eyes of all men. The non-repair of a Public highway or of a bridge is often treated by English Law for all purposes as a Crime. On the other hand, many flagitious acts of Fraud and of Violation to Rights of Ownership may be treated as no more than Civil Injuries, the application of the Remedy being practically left to the discretion of the injured Person. Theft and Frauds of the grossest sorts were treated by Roman Law as Civil Injuries rather than as Crimes.

Again, the form of Procedure in Criminal Actions may perchance closely resemble that in Civil ones, and a varying degree of discretion may be left in the hands of private Prosecutors. Wherever this exists it points to a certain indistinctness of view and antiquarian retentiveness of the familiar and the past, but in no way confounds the radical distinction between the two classes of Acts. As to the Breach of the Law in the one case, the State actively interferes to prevent or to punish it by the use of all the resources within its control. As to that in the other, it simply engages to co-operate with Private Persons who are interested in preventing or punishing it.

Again, a Crime may be committed where a Civil Injury could not be, inasmuch as a Civil Injury always presupposes the Infringement of a Legal Right, and a Crime, only the Non-compliance with a Legal Duty which may be "absolute" and corresponding with no Legal Rights in others. Thus Treason, Coining, Breaches of the Revenue Laws and of many Police regulations, are absolutely prohibited, and yet there may be no Person, single or corporate, whose legal Rights are immediately abridged or threatened by the Acts forbidden.

On all these grounds, and on others which have scarcely been alluded to, it will be expedient to adhere to the generally recognised practice of treating Laws relating to Crimes apart from, though in close connection with, Laws relating to Civil Injuries.

Laws relating to Civil Injuries.

It has been seen that many of the Rights, the violation of which is a Civil Injury or a Crime, or both, have already come under review, whether under the heads of Rights of Ownership, of Rights under a Contract, or of Rights appertaining to Special Classes of Persons. There are, however, other Rights, the violation of which is a Civil Injury, or a Crime, but which only come under notice for the first time in this place. The Rights of this class are so universally diffused, so simple and distinct in the advantages they confer, that it is only through the violent rupture of them by mischievous members of the

Community that they attract attention to themselves. Such Rights are those to Personal Security, to General Freedom of action and of locomotion, to the enjoyment of the necessary Conditions of Health, and to what is called a Good Reputation. These Rights are in themselves of a vague and indeterminate kind, and, unlike most Rights of Ownership and all Rights under Contracts, they only become defined in the progress of time through repeated and multifarious Violations of them. In this way it comes about that it is under the head of Laws of Civil Injuries and Crimes that such Rights are heard of for the first time. It is necessary to make this explanation, because loose notions prevail to the effect either that no such Rights exist, or that, if they do, some mysterious and incommunicable character belongs to them which, separating them from all other classes of Rights, makes them peculiarly the subjects of this part of the Law.

If, then, it be definitely determined that the Modes of Injury to Rights ought to follow the method of Classification pursued in arranging the Rights themselves, subject to the fact just mentioned that certain Rights appear in this place for the first time, the following will be the natural order in which the present part of the subject will be generally presented :—

- A. Injuries to Rights to (1) Personal Security ; (2) Free Locomotion ; (3) Conditions of Health ; (4) Reputation.
- B. Injuries to Rights of Ownership.
- C. Injuries to Rights under Contracts.
- D. Injuries to Rights appertaining to Special Classes of Persons.

The secondary and subordinate Mode of Distribution will be determined in any particular System of Law by the most familiar and accidental forms of violating recognised Rights. The conception of a Right is a very abstract one, and only gradually grows up among the people or even in the minds of Lawyers, out of a long series of concrete manifestations of particular mischievous Acts. It is historically true that Actions at Law are conceded by Courts of Justice for the Remedy or for the Punishment of injurious Acts long before a scientific grasp is obtained of the real nature and extent of the Right invaded by those Acts. Hence, the specific Legal Remedy obtainable is seldom quite co-extensive with the Right practically enjoyed, though, as time goes on and changes in the Law are less dreaded, the Remedy is constantly in the way of being made more comprehensive, immediate, and efficacious. An illustration of this progress may be found in the gradual expansion of the ancient Action of Trespass in English Law to meet the Violation of a variety of Rights of Ownership and of Personal Security not originally comprehended in it. The distinct steps in this progress are marked by the introduction of the Action on the "Case,"— applicable to circumstances where the damage inflicted is only circuitous and indirect,—and of the more recently admitted option of Suing either "in Tort," or "in Contract," without naming the form of the Action. In Roman Law a parallel line of advance is exhibited in the gradual substitution, for the "formulary" process, of that denoted by the *extraordinariæ actiones*, whereby the Suitor was relieved from the burden of formulating his Facts in view of an anticipated Remedy, and a single Magistrate was entitled to take cognisance of the whole matter from first to last, in respect to questions both of Law and of Fact.

Keeping in view, then, the necessity,—for purposes of Classification,—of accepting, (at any particular epoch in the development of a Legal System,) as the sole available index to the Civil Injuries recognised, the Judicial Actions practically allowed, and adopting the convenient expression "Secondary Rights," to denominate Rights arising out of the Breach of other, or "Primary," Rights,—the Law of Civil Injuries may be compendiously presented in the following summary form; the English Law, as it is at the present day, being taken as a readily available type of all particular Systems of Law :—

Primary Rights.	Secondary Rights.
I.—Rights to—	Rights of Action for—
1. Personal Security.	Assault, Battery, and Trespass to the *Person*; Death caused by Negligence (Action brought by surviving Relatives); Nuisances or Injuries to Health and Comfort; False Imprisonment; Malicious Arrest and Prosecution; Slander and Libel.
2. Free Locomotion.	
3. Conditions of Health.	
4. Reputation.	
II.—Rights of Ownership.	Rights of Action for— Trespass; Malicious Injury to Property (*Lex Aquilia*); Detinue; Conversion or Trover; Nuisance (by way of Obstruction or otherwise); Waste;

	Piracy of Copyright; Infringement of Patent-right; Slander of Title.
III.—Rights under a Contract.	Rights of Action for—Breach or Approximate Breach of Contract.
IV.—Rights of Special Classes of Persons.	Rights of Action for Injuries to Husband or Wife; to Child or Ward; to Servants or Apprentices.
	Rights of Action for Injuries committed by—Trustees; Executors; Solicitors; Municipal and Ecclesiastical Authorities.

There is one anomalous class of Civil Injuries, omitted from the above list, which in some respects are allied to Crimes, inasmuch as they imply absolute Duties without reference to corresponding Rights; and yet, as a matter of Procedure, they are treated rather in accordance with the analogy supplied by ordinary Civil Injuries. This Class of Civil Injuries is that implied in the Rights of Action vested in certain Executive Functionaries for unpaid Customs or Taxes, or for Public Indemnities, Guarantees, Bail-bonds, and the like.

It has been seen that a Civil Injury is always the Violation of a Right, and is therefore naturally measured by the extent of the Right, though, through historical accidents, the Right itself may be practically larger than the Remedy actually provided. In estimating, then, the quality and extent of a Civil Injury, the Limits of a Right must be clearly ascertained. The Right implies that some Act or other has to be done or to be refrained from by some Person or Persons other than the Person vested with the Right. It is obvious from the nature of an Act (which always implies a willing Agent), that no Person is responsible for that which he has involuntarily done or omitted. The apparent Act or Omission is nothing more than an Event for which nobody is responsible; though, by a special form of Contract, by way of Insurance, the sufferer may be absolutely indemnified against loss.

Nevertheless, in Judicially applying the test of *voluntariness*, Courts of Justice are in this matter obliged to resort to large and general Presumptions. These Presumptions must be based upon the records of experience as deduced from a wide observation of Human Nature. They will vary with the quality of the matter in respect of which they are resorted to; according as, for instance, the Person, whose conduct is the subject of enquiry, is accused of a grave Moral delinquency, (such as are most Crimes;) of a Breach of Mercantile and Social Confidence; or of a mere wayward Neglect of the general Mora. Claims of all Persons whatsoever.

In casting the eye over the list of Civil Injuries above enumerated, it will be seen that very different Mental states must, from the nature of the case, go to constitute the essential element of Culpability. In some instances,— as in Trespass, in Nuisance, in Detinue, and in Breaches of Contract,—the bare Consciousness, which is just sufficient to indicate the presence of Will, is all that is needed to create Liability. In other cases,—as in Libel, in False Imprisonment, in Injuries to Children or to Apprentices,— Intention, (that is, a special attitude of the mind towards the immediate Consequences of the Act,) is often made an indispensable ingredient. This Intention may take all the forms, positive and negative, of Cruelty, Negligence, Recklessness, Heedlessness, and Fraud. Lastly, with respect to some of the Civil Injuries above denoted,—such as Malicious Arrest and Prosecution, Slander, and Malicious Injuries to Property,—an aggravated kind of Intention, implying either a vehement Desire or a peculiarly clear apprehension of a particular and probable Consequence, is often held essential to constitute the imputed Liability.

From the extreme vagueness or rather indefiniteness and variability of many of the Primary Rights the Violation of which constitutes a Civil Injury, it happens that the function of the Judge in any given case is quite as arduous with respect to determining what is the precise Duty of the alleged Offender as with respect to investigating whether, in fact, he committed the alleged Offence. Instances are supplied by the case of Injuries to Reputation and to Personal Security. A notoriously bad man has not a legal Right to be as respectfully described, in speech or in writing, as a good man has. A man doing an important Public Act or addressing a literary Treatise to his fellow-countrymen has no Right entitling him to shut the mouths even of harsh and severe critics, even though their general Intention be unkindly but not accompanied by that vehement Desire or distinct Consciousness of doing evil which alone the Law denounces. For general Public reasons it may be that no man has a Right entitling him to close the mouths of even the severest critics of his conduct in the course of the Administration of Public Justice; in that of the Deliberations of the Legislative Assembly; or in certain other more private circumstances, as in the course of tendering confidential advice with respect to trustworthiness for important employments.

This topic of so-called "Privilege" may be approached from two sides, according as it is looked upon as limiting the Right of a Plaintiff, or as extending the Right of a Defendant. It is more coherent with the universal doctrine, that everyone has certain Rights to Reputation, to make these Rights,—as has been done above,—the starting point, and to take into consideration, in each particular Class of Cases, what is the exact nature and comprehensiveness of the Right. A parallel set of questions is suggested in the case of many alleged Injuries to Personal Security. In all cases the exact measure of the Right has to be estimated in view of all the surrounding circumstances. Thus it may be that the Young, the Sick, the Aged, and those who are taking an ordinary amount of care to protect themselves have a Right to a greater immunity from peril at the hands of others,—that is, in fact, to a larger amount of such Care and Diligence as may prevent the peril,—than those who, from whatever circumstances, are thoroughly competent, and who do not use all available means, to protect themselves. Again, assuming the Rights to Personal Security to be the same, the Duty as to the amount of Diligence and Care may be different in a country lane from what it is in a crowded thoroughfare. The former Class of Cases may involve questions of what is called "Contributory Negligence;" the latter, the investigation into the requirements and into the actual presence of fine shades of Diligence and Care.

Inasmuch as a Civil Injury is in all cases an Act or a conscious Abstinence from an Act, the ordinary Personal Incapacities which restrict the faculty of Acting must, by converting Acts into Events, to a greater or less extent relieve certain Classes of Persons from Culpability. Such

Persons are Infants, Idiots, Lunatics, Drunkards, and Persons under special Duress. The order of Civil Society is so deeply concerned in Civil Injuries being as infrequent as possible that even these Classes of Persons must be severally laid under the strictest amount of Responsibility which is compatible with Moral Justice. The exact amount of Responsibility must vary (1.) with the quality of the Duty, whether implying or not implying a considerable amount of worldly discretion, as in the case of many Contracts and of certain kinds of Fraud; (2.) with the general nature of the Incompetence in question, being different in the case of a Child, of a young man nearly approaching the age of Manhood, of a Lunatic during a partially lucid interval, and of a Drunkard who has consciously brought himself into a condition of Incapacity; (3.) with the actual and special circumstances of the individual case. The rules applicable in these cases will be supplied partly by the general Law, partly by ordinary Legal Presumptions more or less capable of being rebutted, and partly by special conclusions drawn by the Judge in the exercise of such discretionary power as may be vested in him.

It is, perhaps, scarcely necessary to notice the ancient class of *quasi-delicts* which Mr. Austin and others have clearly shown either to have no resemblance to the opposed class of Civil Injuries denominated *delicts*, or else in no way to differ from them. A *Paterfamilias* was thus held liable, as on a *quasi-delict*, for a damage sustained through Things being thrown out of a window of his house by somebody else. So the Innkeeper or the Ship-owner was liable for Thefts committed in an inn or on board a ship by a Servant or Sailor. These cases are simple cases of Civil Injuries, the culpability being due to a general want of Diligence in taking due precautions,—as by providing fit Servants,—to prevent the mischief. Another case of *quasi-delict*,—that of a Judge giving a Judgment contrary to Law, from Corruption or from Ignorance,—has this peculiarity, indeed, that he neglects a Public Duty and in consequence is liable to a Private Action. The same principle is recognised in English Law, and is certainly anomalous even though it be beneficial.

The Modes of obtaining Compensation for Civil Injuries belong partly to this place and partly to that of Laws of Procedure. They belong to this place so far as the Method of estimating the Compensation and the Form of that Compensation is concerned. They belong to the other, so far as the actual Mode of setting the necessary machinery to work, in order to secure that the Compensation be made, is concerned.

The object of the Compensation is the complete Restoration of the Person Injured to the favourable position he would have occupied but for the Injury, together with such additional satisfaction as may be needed, both amply to make up for the inconvenience and pain he may have been subjected to and indirectly to operate as a check on the recurrence of such interruptions to Public Order. The last-mentioned purpose was especially aimed at in many celebrated Roman Laws for the prevention of Civil Injuries, but is generally discountenanced in Modern Law, as confusing the realms of Civil and of Criminal Jurisdiction.

The actual Form the Compensation takes must generally be Money, as being the only universal,—though, of course, often an absurdly disproportionate, or irrelevant,—measure of loss. In some cases,—as in that of the Breach of certain Contracts,—the measure of the loss admits of being calculated with considerable precision, the circumstances and prospects of the Parties, the state and fluctuations of Trade between the Time of making the Contract and that at which it ought to have been fulfilled, being taken into account. In some few cases, indeed, the loss admits of Compensation in kind by the return of a Thing detained, or by a public Apology for a Slander or Libel. The Roman *noxalis actio*, by which a Theft or Outrage, committed by a Son or by a Slave, might be compensated for on the part of the Father or the Master by surrendering the Delinquent to the injured Person, affords an instance of a Mode of Compensation at once erratic and unparallelled.

Laws relating to Crimes.

Like Laws relating to Civil Injuries, Laws relating to Crimes are concerned directly with Duties rather than with Rights. Indeed the notion of Private Rights, though presupposed in the vast majority of Crimes, is subordinated entirely to considerations of Public Order, of Economy, or of Security. It has already been seen, under the last head, what is the strict nature of a Legal Crime. The essence of it has been described to be that the State, endeavouring to operate on the fears of Mankind, organises a Method of absolutely repressing or of absolutely commanding certain classes of Acts. In order to make such a device successful, many conditions must be combined. There must be devised and adjusted a wise Scheme of Punishments. There must be an effective

Police, and a well-regulated Reformatory System. There must be, lastly, a skilful Classification of Crimes, and well-constructed and ably administered Judicial Institutions. Some of these requisites depend upon nothing else than the genius and activity of the Executive Authority. Others depend on Laws of Procedure, which form the subject of the following chapter. The only requisites that belong to this place are those implied in the Classification of Crimes and in a Scheme of Punishments.

In order to attain to such a Classification of Crimes, with the Punishments appertaining to them, as may carry out the object in view, the Essential ingredients of a Crime must be first more precisely investigated.

A Criminal Act, like any other Act, has two aspects, a Mental and a Physical one. Also, like other Acts, it has Consequences, some of them Direct or immediate, and others of them Indirect and subsequent. The distinctive Criminal character of an Act, or that element which bears culpability in its very bosom, is the attitude of the Agent's mind, at the time of doing the Act, towards its immediate Consequences,—in other words his *Intention*. This Intention may take a variety of forms, some Positive, some Negative. It may be nothing more than the barest Consciousness. It may be (negatively) the Absence of a Thought which ought to have been there. It may be the Knowledge of Evil, with or without the Desire of it. It may be the intensest Desire of Evil, either for its own sake, or as an intermediate means to some ulterior end.

But there are other more prominent and more easily decipherable elements of a Crime than Intention. There is the Act, including the joint elements of Will and Muscular

Motion. To constitute Criminality, the Will must be present and normally active, and the proper Muscular Motions must obsequiously comply with its dictates. If, either through disease or through external impediment, either the Will or the proper Muscular Motions are impaired in their harmonious activity, there is no true Act and there can be no Crime.

These considerations introduce the following Systematic View of a Scheme of Criminal Law.

  A. General Description of a Crime.
  B. Essential constituent Elements of a Crime.
    I. The *Act* (including Will and Muscular Motion).
    II. The *Intention*, under forms of 1. Negligence; 2. Knowledge of Consequences; 3. Desire of Consequences.
    III. Grounds of *Exculpation*, (general or special).
      As to I. (*Act.*) Disease; Chance; Physical Restraint or Constraint.
      As to II. (*Intention.*) Ignorance, Infancy, Insanity, Drunkenness; Strong Moral Pressure or Physical Alarm; that the Act was done in pursuance of Legal Duty [Arrest of Criminal, Execution of a Sentence]; that the Act was done in pursuance of Legal Right [Self-defence or Defence of Family].
      Special Personal Exemptions, as in case of King, Ambassadors, Foreigners.
    IV. Distinction between *Consummate* Crimes and Crimes consisting in *Attempts* to commit Crimes; [Where the Crime admits of being analysed into a continuous series or a complex assemblage of distinct Acts, the Performance

of any one of them, accompanied by an Intention to perform the whole of them, is an *Attempt*.]

V. Principals and Accessories, (Indian Penal Code, Ch. 5. "Of Abetment.")

VI. Classification of Crimes.
1. Acts Directly menacing the Constitution and Administration of the State, as:

(1.) Acts Directly Injurious to the Supreme Political Authority as a Corporate Whole, or to one or another of the Persons constituting it, in his or their character as constituting it; [Treason, Constructive Treason and Misprision of Treason.] (2.) Acts Directly Injurious to the Head or to the Subordinate Officers of the Executive; [Treason and Contempt of the Lawful Authority of Public Servants.] (3.) Acts Indirectly Injurious to the whole Community, though possibly not Directly Injurious to some Persons more than to others; [Perjury and Offences against Public Justice, Blasphemy, Indecent Libels, Coining, and Suicide.] (4.) Acts Indirectly Injurious to the whole Community, though Directly Injurious to some Persons more than to others; [Public Nuisances, Adulteration of Drugs and of Food, Frauds by False Weights and Measures.]

2. Acts Directly Violating the Rights of Private Persons, as:

(1.) Acts Violating general Rights of all Persons in respect of Personal Security, of the necessary Conditions of Health, of

Freedom of Locomotion, and of Reputation; [Murder, Manslaughter, Kidnapping, Rape, Injuries to Unborn Children, Assaults, Nuisance, Malicious Libels.] (2.) Acts Violating Rights of Ownership; [Burglary, Robbery, Theft, Extortion, Forgery, Fraudulent Bankruptcy, and Offences relating to Trade or Property-marks.]

3. Acts Violating Rights of Special Classes of Persons, as:

(1.) Offences relating to Marriage; [Bigamy, Incest, certain forms of Adultery, Fraudulent Evasion of Marriage Laws.] (2.) Offences committed by or against Trustees, Executors, Guardians, and Solicitors; [Suppression or Mutilation of Wills or other Documents.]

VII. Enumeration and Classification of *Punishments*.

1. Enumeration of possible Punishments, reference having been made to them severally by anticipation, in the description of each class of Crimes, under head III.

2. Rules for the Application of Punishment, with respect to Quantity of Punishment or to Accumulation of two or more kinds of Punishment, according to the special circumstances,—as for instance a Repeated Conviction for the same Offence,—or in the case of Concurrent Crimes.

3. Grounds of Extinction of Liability to Punishment, as by Previous Acquittal, by Limitation of Time, or by Public Pardon.

The Classification of Crimes is likely to proceed, in all

countries in which Systematic Codification has not been yet attempted, after a more arbitrary and capricious fashion than that of any other part of the Law. An instance near at hand is supplied by the notorious English distinction between "Felonies" and "Misdemeanors," which has played such a curious part in the Judicial, and even in the Political History of this country. The prominence of this celebrated distinction at once affords a signal proof of the immature conceptions, at a certain stage of Society, of the limits marking the appropriate regions of Law and of Morality, and is a standing tribute to the value of the Science of Jurisprudence in clearing up this dangerous confusion. In modern English Legislation any affected demarcation of Crimes by the sort of Moral or Social Significance anciently implied in a Felony as contrasted with a Misdemeanor is practically abandoned, though a memory of the distinction is preserved in certain Judicial Forms. The tendency of all modern Legislation is to arrange Crimes on no more logical or abstruse principle than that based upon either the gravity of the Punishment with which they are visited, or the dignity and constitution of the Courts of Justice in which they are investigated. It is likely that these two grounds of arrangement will generally concur, the lighter classes of Offences being brought before Courts more simply constructed, and possessed of a more facile and elastic action, the more ponderous Cases being reserved for Courts furnished with a higher order of skill, of erudition, and of capacity for leisurely search. The French division of Penal Offences into *Contraventions*, *Délits*, and *Crimes*, though professedly founded on differences in the Penalties, in Practice coincides with the principle of distinguishing Crimes by the Courts in which they are severally adjudicated upon.

It is to be noticed that there is a tendency in England at the present day to multiply indefinitely the classes of Crimes which at once entail the lowest order of Punishment and require for their investigation the lowest rank of Judicial Tribunals. A reckless multiplication of Crimes of this class, while it affords a constant temptation to a Legislature importuned on every side by every species of Fanatics and of Political and Scientific Empirics, is probably one of the most disastrous forms in which Public Liberty is silently undermined. The immediate ends in view are often plausible enough; the immediate Offenders contemplated by the Law may command little or no Moral Sympathy; the Police charged with executing the Law may, in average cases, be fairly honest and fairly discreet; the Tribunal having cognisance of the Crime may be generally conscientious and occasionally competent. But it is never to be forgotten that loss of Political Liberty is not to be estimated by the Quantity of the loss nor by the Quality of the immediate Sufferers. It is an evil hour for any State when, in order to compass present ends however attractive, it parts, even for a day, with those Securities of Public Liberty which are implied in limiting to the utmost the list of Crimes and in ensuring to all Offenders, however miserable their circumstances or however minute their Crimes, an order of Tribunals unimpeachable alike for integrity, for laboriousness, and for Judicial accomplishments. The institution of such Courts, publicly exhibiting the amplest guarantees for the protection of the Liberty of the humblest, the weakest, and the vilest, is in no way incompatible with their possessing a ready and inartificial Procedure such as may befit the investigation of frequently recurring Offences neither subtly defined, nor, in themselves, of wide-reaching importance to the well-being of the Community.

The question of *Intention* (falling under head II. of division B. in the above Classification), and that of certain grounds of *Exculpation* having relation to it, (as *Infancy* and *Insanity*,) assumes an importance in Criminal Cases,— both in view of the terrible issues frequently at stake for the Life and Liberty of Private Persons, and of the inherent difficulty of the investigation into complex states of mind as exhibited under the strangest conditions of Human Life,—which can scarcely be said to belong to it in any other part of the Law.

The occasional difficulty of determining the past attitude of mind of an Accused Person in respect of the immediate consequence of the Act or alleged Crime, the investigation of which is being proceeded with, is so great as to drive the Legislator, or else the Judge, to the use of special Presumptions, which either may or may not be capable of being rebutted. Such Presumptions are, for instance, that every Person "intends" the natural or ordinary consequences of his own Acts; that every Person who causes the Death of another desired the Death of that other Person, either as an end in itself or as a means to some other end; that Children below a certain fixed Age (*seven* years, in English Law) are incapable of forming any Intention whatever for the purposes of Criminal Law; that Children below another, and a higher, fixed Age are, indeed, *capable* of forming such an Intention, but that, in default of distinct Evidence to the contrary, they do not *in fact* form one. The part that the vague term

Malice has played, and still plays, in the Administration of English Criminal Law is known to all students of that Law. Here, again, it is due at once to the difficulty and to the necessity of arriving at a decision as to the complex state of mind of an Accused Person that this word has been tortured into all the Protean phases represented by *Actual Malice, Legal Malice, Implied Malice, Malice in Fact* and *in Law,* and *Malice Aforethought.*

This vacillation and hankering after a joint Legal and Moral Term is a curious illustration of the Ethical element which must enter even into the strictest Judicial enquiry. In the use of the word *Malice,* in all cases, there is undoubtedly always a lurking reference to some sort of Moral Depravity, though perhaps only of a temporary sort. But the intangible nature of such an element compels the Legislator and the Judge to select certain determinate Signs as essential characteristics of this depravity. Such Signs are the definite and familiar states of mind described as "Knowledge" and "Desire." Either of these states may be (1.) implied from surrounding circumstances; or (2.) presumed for purposes of Judicial convenience in default of satisfactory Evidence to the contrary; or (3.) presumed peremptorily, in the absence of certain definite and limited kinds of Evidence to the contrary. The ordinary Law of Murder in modern States, and especially in England, in India, and in the United States, affords a sufficient illustration of the last-mentioned variety of Presumed Malice. The mere Act of Killing a Person carries with it a Presumption of Malice which can only be rebutted in a few distinctly determined ways, such as those implied in the grounds of Exculpation afforded by Self-defence, by grave and sudden Provocation, or by

x

"exceeding Legal powers" in the course of discharging a Duty as a Public Servant. That the elements of Desire or of Knowledge are only matters of inquisition as denoting what may be called Moral Mischievousness is intimated in the universal practice of holding Persons to be guilty of Murder, though the Person actually killed be not the Person against whom the Intention was directed. A curious illustration of the same point may be found in the old English Rule of the strictly Murderous character of a Death incidentally caused in the course of committing even the most trivial Felony, and, still more, in the more rational Rule of attaching the same character to the Death of a Policeman violently, though accidentally, brought about in a fray arising out of the Execution of his Duty.

Closely connected with the topic of Malice, as an element in Culpability, is that of *Insanity*, in the largest sense of the term, as a ground of Exculpation. This topic, which in many Criminal cases excites an interest oftentimes of the most strained and afflicting sort, is one surrounded with peculiar difficulties of its own, due to the complexity and variety of the Facts which it brings into consideration. These Facts are partly Physical, or belonging to that indistinctly marked region which lies between Physical and Psychological Science; partly Ethical, or dependent on a given Person's apprehensions of Right and Wrong under abnormal and exceptional conditions; partly Legal or Political, or dependent upon the amount of Legal Responsibility attributable to varying degrees of Mental Health, in view of the protection claimed by individual Persons, and of a due regard to the general safety of the whole Community.

It is probably rather in the first of these regions,—that

is, the Physical, or Psychological one,—that the main practical difficulty is experienced. It is generally admitted in all Systems of Law that sufficient and satisfactory grounds for Exculpation are found in an actual Mental Incapacity, whether fixed or transient, of knowing at the moment of doing an Act, that it is forbidden by Law, or at any rate that it is Morally Reprehensible according to some Moral notions in the Agent's own mind; or in a Physical Incapacity to abstain from doing the Act. The difficulty is presented at the moment at which it is attempted to establish the fact of either of these sorts of Incapacity, and it is greatly exaggerated in cases where a Legal System, instead of exculpating all Insane Persons as a Class, affects to attach different degrees of Punishment to different measures of presumed Moral Responsibility. The ordinary Modes in which Evidence is produced as to the state of mind of an Accused Person, in the above respects, at the time of doing an Act, are by testifying to his general antecedents, Mental and Moral, possibly reaching many years back, from which an inference is suggested as to the probabilities of the case under consideration; or by drawing attention to the surrounding facts at the time and place of the Act, from which a like inference is suggested, without resorting for help to any circumstances in the Past; or, lastly, by tendering the recorded results of a strange and anomalous experience as to special manifestations of Mental Derangement, accompanied by Acts resembling that under consideration.

The records of Criminal Trials are full of an almost endless diversity of conditions of Mental Aberration, and, indeed, of an equal diversity of Medical and Moral Theories to account for them. The confusion thus arising is aggravated by the necessarily unscientific education of the popular Tribunals which, in modern times, are wisely entrusted with the Jurisdiction in Criminal Cases. It requires no ordinary training in special Medical Science to appreciate the true bearing of the Evidence of an accomplished Expert, or even to be cognisant of the amount of authority properly attributable to his opinions. This is all the more so as Ignorance often enough seeks to hide itself in emphasis, and true Knowledge, through the amount of accumulated material and the absence of rash generalisations, perplexes and wearies the attention. It is also matter of common experience that so-called "Specialists," or Persons who have given a disproportionate amount of attention to a special branch of a subject, are either less likely than others to arrive at a wholly truthful conclusion in a complex case, or are, at least, likely to produce an impression upon an unskilled Tribunal of having an authority which does not belong to them.

The question of the value of Medical Evidence in Cases of Lunacy is connected with the larger question of the general treatment of the Evidence of *Experts*. It has been advocated in some quarters that Government should in all cases undertake the task of supplying a competent staff of accomplished Technical Witnesses,—especially in cases involving Medical enquiries,—and that the decision of these Officials should in all cases be final. A practical difficulty is here encountered on the ground that, in the most perplexing instances both of Injuries to the *person* (as of Infanticide and Poisoning) and of Insanity, a large mass of Evidence which can never be excluded must, from the necessity of the case, have been provided long before a Criminal investigation is thought of. It may be, indeed, that a highly trained body of Medical Jurists, properly authorised by Government, or organised on some system which shall prevent them from becoming a narrow and exclusive clique, might advantageously be called in to assist the Tribunal in the course of the Trial, or even might render valuable service as Assessors to a Court of Appeal. But in no case could any Evidence supplied by ordinary Medical Attendants, by Hospital Surgeons or even by accidental Medical Visitors, be properly excluded from consideration. The only hope of arriving at a theory of Insanity which shall supply a series of serviceable Presumptions to the Judge lies in the mature perfection at once of Physical and of Ethical Science.

The topic of *Punishments* has been placed in the last head of the above classified arrangement of all the topics forming the materials of a Criminal Code. For purposes of Judicial and of Popular convenience, it will probably be necessary to distribute this topic over the whole Code in such a way as to assign to every Crime, when and where completely described, its appropriate Punishment or range of Punishments. Nevertheless, there will remain a quantity of general matter, respecting the strictly Juridical aspects of Punishments, which will most properly be treated in a department by itself. It is perhaps needless to notice that the theory of Punishment, looked at as a whole, belongs as much to Ethics and to Politics as it does to Jurisprudence. Indeed, it only belongs to the last-mentioned Science to the extent that it qualifies the formal Construction and Administration of Law. For instance, it has already been noted that, in some countries, Crimes themselves have been classsified solely with reference to the kind and measure of Punishment apportioned to them. In all Legal Systems, again, a marked distinction is drawn between a mere Compensation to a Sufferer and a Penalty inflicted for the general Political purpose of effectually discouraging a special Class of Offences. So, again, the Punishment attached to a Crime may be fixed imperatively and definitely by the Legislator, no discretionary power of modifying it being left to the Judge; or, again, it may be fixed within definite Limits by the Legislator, or alternative Punishments may be propounded by him, and no more discretionary power may be left to the Judge than is needed to enable him to choose within those Limits or between those alternatives. It is obvious that the selection of one or other of these courses by the Legislator not only qualifies the Formal Structure of Criminal Law but affects the mechanism of its Administration. To this extent, then, the topic of Punishments strictly belongs to the Science of Jurisprudence. The relative Political value of the several courses above suggested belongs, as already said, to other closely-related Sciences.

Apart, however, from a consideration of the amount of Discretionary Power, if any, left to the Judge in the application of Punishment, there are certain generally-recognised Modifications in Punishments with which the Jurist is intimately concerned. It may be, for instance, that owing to the very restricted number of kinds of Punishment, which, in a modern State, are possible, there may be a great chasm between the Punishments applied to two sorts of Crime closely resembling each other, and there may be no chasm at all between the Punishments for Crimes of the greatest variety of Moral complexion. This, no doubt, is to some degree unavoidable, inasmuch as the purpose of Punishment is now generally recognised to be, not an effective and dramatic retaliation, but such a rough mode of securing obedience to Law as is compatible with a regard to the claims of Humanity, and even, to the utmost extent possible, to the permanent welfare of the Criminal.

In spite of the inevitableness of these incongruities, their operation on the Administration of Law must not be allowed to escape notice. In England there are many Crimes, which are punished with some of the severest Punishments known to the Law, an Attempt to commit which is visited only with a Penalty comparatively light. The consequence is that there is a prevalent tendency in a popular Tribunal to fall back, in case of conflicting Evidence, on the lazy expedient of finding the Prisoner guilty of an Attempt to commit a Crime, where all the Evidence,—if it is good for anything,—goes to prove that the complete Crime was committed.

The question now under consideration,—namely that of the necessary disproportion between gradations of Crime and gradations of Punishment,—is brought to the most perplexing issue in the case of the Punishment of Death. This Punishment has the following characteristics as distinguished from all others. It admits, in itself, of no gradation; it is irrevocable; and it is more different in kind from all other Punishments than they are from each other. In the use and application of this Punishment, two opposite instincts or sentiments have, especially in Modern Society, competed with each other. On the one hand it has been demanded that inasmuch as Murder, —the offence to which the Punishment of Death is now almost universally restricted,—differs from every other

Crime, in quality if not in atrocity, so its Punishment should be equally *sui generis*, and should differ from every other Punishment in its Quality and in its Exemplary character as well as in its Amount. No doubt other more indistinct feelings, and even Religious associations, go far to reinforce these sentiments; while the same Political considerations in reference to the Punishment of Death, as being presumably the only available means of rendering infrequent the most disastrous of all Crimes, are present as in appreciating the general utility of any other form of Punishment. An opposite class of sentiments takes note, first, of the infinite number of variations in Moral Culpability necessarily included in any Legal description of such a complex offence as Murder; secondly, of the impropriety, on the one hand, of always affixing the severest Punishment to every variety of Offence falling under the general Legal Class; or, on the other hand, of leaving a Judge — or, still worse, a Popular Tribunal — to determine when this Punishment shall fall, and when not. Other considerations, —based on Humanitarian views, more or less enlightened; on the actual or presumed reluctance of Tribunals to convict Prisoners of an Offence followed by a Punishment so signal and irrevocable; on the ascertained variability of the Punishment according to the Mental and Physical circumstances of the Culprit; as well as on more broad and general Political considerations as to the inexpediency of all violent and excessive Punishments,—add their force to the purely Juridical arguments, and probably, for the generality of Persons whose thoughts tend in favour of this latter view, are a substitute for them. It will have been noticed that, in thus arraying the arguments for and against the Punishment of Death, only those considerations have been brought into relief which are based on distinctly Juridical grounds. The topic is, of course, capable of being viewed, and in fact is generally and properly viewed, rather on its numerous Ethical and Political sides than in its narrower aspect as an instrument for giving the greatest possible efficiency to certain Classes of Laws. On those other sides the question as to the general expediency of retaining the Punishment of Death may have to be resolved differently in different countries and at different epochs.

An interesting and often a perplexing problem, both in the estimation of Criminal Culpability and in the Adjudication of Punishment, is presented in the case of resorting to Evidence of what is called *Character*. This class of Evidence may be resorted to for the purpose of suggesting an inference of improbability either as to the alleged commission of an Act or as to the alleged Intention with which it was committed. Or, again, recourse may be had to such Evidence solely for the purpose of estimating the probability of the offender repeating the Act,—a possible contingency which is properly taken into account in measuring the amount of Punishment, assuming that Discretionary Power for such a purpose is left in the hands of the Judge.

In view of the close association between the Moral and Logical faculties, especially in untrained Persons, great care is often exercised to prevent the unfavourable antecedents of a Prisoner,—such as his previous Conviction for the same or for a different offence,—coming to the knowledge of the Popular Tribunal which is charged with the duty of investigating the Facts of a particular Case. The justification of this practice must be found in the fact that Evidence of general Character, unless it be given by

Persons peculiarly competent, from their special situation, to form an opinion (as in the case of Employers, Fellow-Labourers, Fellow-Clerks, Superior Officers, Trade-Associates, and Ministers of Religion), is generally of the most loose and flimsy description, being based on the most unchallenged Hearsay, and often dictated by nothing else than a weakly Humanitarian sympathy. Evidence, on the other hand, of previous Convictions weighs down the probabilities of present guilt with almost too crushing a force, even if those Convictions were just, and if they were accidentally unjust the Prisoner's prospects can hardly fail to be seriously compromised.

Nevertheless there is a certain artificial insincerity in excluding the sort of grounds for forming an opinion which are most familiarly relied upon in the ordinary intercourse of life; the more so when that exclusion reaches to the most solemnly authenticated Judicial Facts. The histrionic insincerity is all the more glaring when, as in England, one portion of the Tribunal,—that is the presiding Judge,—is, all through the Trial, in possession of Facts of the most damaging nature, from any use or knowledge of which the other part of the Tribunal is carefully shut out. The practical solution is to be found,—as in all cases where an over-anxiety to provide fallacious securities has led to the exclusion of Evidence,— in welcoming and freely handling all Evidence fairly pertinent to the Case (the question of pertinency being left, as elsewhere, to the general discretion of the Prosecutor and of the Accused), due precautions being taken by the presiding Judge to inform the Jury of the special infirmities attaching to the sort of Evidence now under consideration, and of the consequent deductions to be made from its apparent value.

In the case of referring to Evidence of Character for the purpose of apportioning Punishment, the Judge is necessarily less hampered in the choice of his Witnesses and in the class of Personal Antecedents with respect to which he may require Evidence to be produced. There are some Technical Offences as to which this sort of Evidence, bearing as it does on the probability of the recurrence of the Crime, may be of the utmost importance. For instance where three Persons are equally found Guilty of maliciously setting fire to stacks or houses, it may be established before the Judge, on his proceeding to pass Sentence, that one of the Prisoners is a young man of generally unblemished Character, who, on the solitary occasion in question, was, after a convivial meeting, engaged with others in a riotous brawl, his comrades and Accomplices in guilt having escaped the hands of Justice; another of the three convicted Prisoners is, as frequently happens in this class of Crimes, a mere reckless, idle vagabond, who has done the Act from a sort of silliness approaching to Imbecility, or, as is sometimes said, "just to get up a blaze;" the third convicted Prisoner is a Farmer whose general Character is bad, who has been dismissed from his Tenancy, and who is known to have vowed vengeance against the new Tenant whose stacks he is proved to have destroyed. It is obvious that, in each of these cases, Evidence of general or of special Character is of the greatest moment, both in order to estimate how far the Offender is incorrigible, and how far there is a probability of a repetition of the same specific Offence. The Crime of Manslaughter, again, which presents every variety of shade of Moral qualities, demands, in nearly every case, for apportioning the Punishment due to it, a most anxious introspection of the Mental and Moral antecedents of the convicted Prisoner. It is needless to add that all Offences in which the Moral element is essentially predominant, as in those against Reputation and in defiance of Sexual Relationships, eminently need, on the conviction of an Offender, a scrutiny into Motives, Dispositions, and modes of Life, without which the Punishment may chance to be wholly ineffective or intolerably and unnecessarily severe.

CHAPTER XIV.

LAWS OF PROCEDURE.

It is well known that, in one sense, Laws of Procedure, of a very elementary sort, are the earliest of all Laws. In fact it seems indisputable that the first form in which Law, as a body of inflexible Rules proceeding from a competent Authority, obtains a practical ascendancy over the minds of a Primitive People, is in that of the actual application of such Rules to real controversies between one man and another. No doubt Professor Maine's use of the Homeric representation of the Arbitrator determining a disputed Case by reference, now to a rough-and-ready standard of Moral justice, and now to Traditional Maxims known to and cherished by the bystanders, is justified by the actual phenomena of all early Societies. Even at a much later stage it is in the actual scenes presented by the conduct of a Court of Justice that the Citizen finds most vividly mirrored the stern realities and meaning of Law. It is on this account that changes in Procedure are the most difficult of all changes in Law to bring about. Inveterate usage, and all the potent influences of sight, hearing, and touch, render the average citizen exquisitely sensitive to the minutest modification of the accustomed solemn order ; and it is only by quickening effete forms with a new meaning, without invading the forms themselves,—a result which is accomplished by the device of Legal Fiction,—that, at some ages of Legal Development, necessary Reforms can be introduced at all.

A *Right* always means the kind of control exercised by one man over another which is delegated by the State itself to the Person vested with the Right. Thus the control implied in the Right is indirectly exercised by the State; and the only meaning of a Right is that the State has both the will and the power to make it real and effectual. At the primitive period just alluded to, this fact would be unmistakeably clear, inasmuch as a Right would only be known to be such because the chosen Officers of the State declared it to have been Violated, and then and there reprimanded, punished, or exacted compensation from, the Violators of it.

The purpose of Laws of Procedure is to give reality and efficiency to Rights, and to secure the performance of Duties. In order to carry out this purpose, a Hierarchy of Official Persons has to be constantly employed; a number of Persons, chosen from time to time by various methods out of the general body of Citizens, have to be invited or compelled to co-operate; " Courts of Justice," or formal Assemblies of Suitors, Judges, Witnesses, and Officers, convoked at fixed Times and Places, have to be instituted; inflexible Rules for the statement of grievances and of the reply, for the conduct of argument and for the production of Evidence, have to be devised and observed; provision for correcting the accidents, the irregularities, and the mistakes likely to occur in every lengthened and complex transaction has to be made, as by New Trials, Delays, and Appeals; and, lastly, machinery has to be provided for actually Punishing a proved Offender, for making him actually Compensate the Person he is proved to have injured, or for forcibly Confiscating the Things the Offender owns, if he be unwilling otherwise to make the satisfaction which the Judicial Sentence commands.

Thus the general matters with which Laws of Procedure have to deal may be distributed under the following heads :—

A.—The establishment of Courts of Justice, Inferior, Superior, Civil, Criminal, Commercial, Original and of Appeal, and for Local matters.

B.—The Formal Mode of Investigation of alleged Breaches of Law : by

1. Preliminary Process for the purpose of ascertaining the real matters in controversy.
2. Trial of Issue of *Fact*. (Evidence.)
3. Trial of Issue of *Law*.

C.—Sentence, Assignment of Punishment, or of Measure and Mode of Compensation, and Execution of Sentence.

D.—Extraordinary Remedies, as by Interdict, Injunction, *Mandamus*, special Process of " Commercial Tribunals," Bankruptcy, *Distress*.

E.—Limitation of Actions.

F.—Parties to Actions.

A.—The Establishment of Courts of Justice.

A Court of Justice is *a concrete Assemblage of Persons and Things organised and regulated by the State for the purpose of formally investigating the Truth as to alleged*

Breaches of Law. The actual Courts of Justice, existing at any moment, usually owe their origin, in a large measure, to Political accidents or to mere Social vicissitudes. An unconscious sense of expediency, and even an audacious spirit of innovation, will no doubt have introduced important changes in the Traditional System; but the general traces of the Past will linger here longer than elsewhere, the result often being a multitude of Courts existing side by side, with more or less parallel functions and with equal dignity.

The phenomenon of two sets of Courts continuing side by side with each other for generations,—interfering with and controlling each other's free movements; recognising different Legal Principles, even to the extent of one set of Courts supporting Rights wholly ignored by the other, and yet being all the while equal in dignity and authority,—has been witnessed in one country alone, that is, in England. It is not true that the Prætor's Jurisdiction at Rome presents an exact parallel to the incongruous anomaly exhibited for so many centuries by the antipathetic attitude of English Law and Equity. There was at Rome one Judge, one Court, one Trial, however multiform the Principles, the Rights, and the Remedies recognised as available through the Prætorian Jurisdiction.

Nevertheless, as has been said, the air and habits of Antiquity cling to the institution of Courts of Justice, as it were, with peculiar fondness. For this reason, the nature of the Courts existing at any particular time in any country can hardly be explained or even described without constant reference to the facts of their Historical evolution. For the purposes of general Jurisprudence, the bare ground-plan laid down as common to all Systems of Law must here be more than usually skeleton-like and lifeless. Bearing in mind these considerations, the following is the Judicial substratum which gives rise to the leading differences distinguishing Courts of Justice from one another. Courts of Justice differ according as their purpose is :—

1. To investigate Breaches of the Law of less or greater importance or magnitude (Superior and Inferior Courts, Courts of Petty Sessions, County Courts, Courts of Quarter Sessions).

2. To investigate those Breaches of Law which are termed *Civil Injuries*, or those which are termed *Crimes*.

3. To conduct an Investigation into an alleged Breach of Law as a whole, that is, to pursue it from its commencement to its close; or to conduct it partially, leaving another Court or other Courts to do the rest (*Cours de première instance*, Courts of Petty Sessions).

4. To conduct a Primary Investigation into an alleged Breach of Law, or to conduct a Secondary one by way of reviewing, on Appeal, the Decision of another Court of Justice which has already conducted such Primary Investigation.

5. To conduct Investigations into Breaches of Law having reference to peculiar Classes of Facts, or into matters bringing into consideration peculiar and recondite branches of Law.

This last named principle gives rise to such distinctions as those between Courts of Common Law, Courts of Probate and Divorce, Courts of Admiralty, Ecclesiastical Courts, and the like. It may be noticed that the Court of Probate, like those of Chancery, of the Exchequer, and of Queen's Bench (to some small extent), affords an instance of the purely Executive authority attached for some purposes to the Judge or Judges presiding in a Court of Justice. The jurisdiction of the Judge of a Court of Probate with respect to granting Probate in a doubtful case, like that of the English Chancellor in matters of Lunacy, and in making or approving Schemes for the reconstruction of Endowments under the Charitable Trusts Act of 1853, is of a purely Executive character. It is not an alleged Breach of the Law which is in question, and the Judge only represents the Executive Authority of the State.

The constitution of a Court of Justice implies not only the appointment of a Judge or body of Judges but also regulations as to the days and hours and places at which they shall sit. It furthermore implies the appointment of a number of subordinate Officials for the purpose of summoning Witnesses, registering Proceedings, keeping order in Court, and generally co-operating with the Judge or Judges in the details of their work. Again, a body of smaller regulations is needed as to the proper Mode of conducting Proceedings in Court, some of which regulations may be made directly by the Supreme Political Authority, while some are made directly by the Judges themselves subject to the control of that Authority, and others are merely time-honoured Rules which by long Judicial recognition have acquired the character of true Laws.

In many of the Investigations conducted by Courts of Justice, it occurs that the Facts cannot be ascertained without an enquiry into a long and often complex train of Accounts, presenting no difficulty on the ground of conflicting Evidence and no Legal problem of any sort;

or into a number of disputed statements by two Parties, in which each seems desirous of stating and knowing the truth, but through a number of circumstances they have been led to different conclusions as to their Rights in respect to each other. In the first class of Cases it is often expedient to provide, for the use of a Court of Justice likely to have such matters brought before it, some supplementary machinery in the form of a staff of special Officials whose sole function it shall be to investigate cases of Account; and it may be made to rest in the discretion of the Court to determine in what circumstances Parties shall be forced to have recourse to the Officials in question.

In the second class of Cases it is a very ancient custom, dating even from the earliest period of Roman Law, to refer the Parties, either with or without their assent, to an Arbitrator, who may be chosen either by the Parties or by the Court, and whose Award may either be made compulsorily binding or be made so binding subject to confirmation by the Court or by some other Court. The Terms in which the question may be put before the Arbitrator and the latitude of his discretion are matters of great importance, and may be specially controlled by the will of the Parties or, subject or not to such special control, generally controlled by universal Legal Rules.

It is, of course, of considerable moment that, on a Case coming before a Court of Justice, there should be no doubt or ambiguity as to what the Court has to try. It may depend upon the subject-matter whether the issue can be reduced to the simple affirmative or negative of a particular Fact, or whether the decision must be addressed to a large body of more or less mutually involved

Facts. In the matters of the simpler Crimes and of the more elementary Modes of Civil Injury, the former may be the case; in matters arising out of complicated commercial transactions or Fiduciary responsibilities, the latter is more likely to be so. Any way, the Court is interested that the question for trial be divested of all that is irrelevant and only accidentally adhering to it, and, especially, that the points as to which the Litigants differ be clearly distinguished from those in which they agree. The preparatory simplification of a Case forming the subject-matter of a dispute in a Court of Justice, for the greater convenience and expedition of the Court, forms an important branch of the second head of this part of the Law.

B. The Formal Mode of Investigation of Alleged Breaches of Law.

1. Preliminary Process for the purposes of ascertaining the real matters in controversy.
2. Trial of issue of *Fact*.
3. Trial of issue of *Law*.

1. *Preliminary Process.*

The obviousness and the palpable convenience of providing for a large portion of a judicial inquiry being conducted outside the Court has impressed itself on the most primitive Systems of Law. In the old *Legis Actiones* of Roman Law, part of the Proceedings,—that is the part needing the presence of a Person cognisant of the essential Forms to be observed, and competent to insist on their observance, was performed before the Judge, and the other part either on the spot where the Things disputed about lay, or on some other spot. In the "Formulary" system the Parties were obliged to make the Form of their Demand and of their Plea fit into certain rough and familiar moulds, and when this was done, the Prætor had then to ascertain the true matter in dispute, and furthermore to decide what Rule of Law was applicable to it. Thereupon he sent the matter of Fact down to a Judge, or body of Judges, that they might investigate the truth about it. The history of Pleading in English Law is well known. Till within very recent times its technicality and tortuous prolixity, coupled with the narrowmindedness of too many of the Judges who had to pronounce on its validity, rendered it one of the grossest of the many abuses of English law.

There may be, and indeed are, existing in England at the present day, three distinct Modes or species of what is called Pleading.

There may be (1.) that kind which consists in nothing more or less than an elaborate and almost colloquial Statement of all the circumstances out of which a Breach of Law is alleged to have taken place, or in which it is alleged to consist. This is followed by a simple denial; or by an admission of the alleged Facts, attended with the allegation of new Facts giving a different complexion to the admitted ones; or by an admission of the Facts, coupled with the allegation that no Breach of the Law is disclosed or has taken place (*Demurrer*). A reply from the Plaintiff may be made to a similar effect. This is the typical structure of all Pleading, though the unqualified form of it here described has perhaps no better example than in English Equity Procedure.

Another species is that more resembling the one practised under the Formulary System at Rome, namely, that of obliging the Plaintiff to make the Form of his statement square with, or resemble as much as may be, some one of a number of customary, familiar, and alone judicially recognised Forms. It is well known what part this artificial limiting of an injured Person's opportunities of obtaining relief has played in the historical development of English Laws of Procedure. It first gave rise to the interference of the Chancellor for the purpose of providing a Remedy in Cases for which the existing Modes of recognised Process made no provision, and thereby founded the general Jurisdiction of the Court of Chancery. It subsequently introduced an arbitrary tyranny of outward Form, as already noticed, which at one period threatened to bury Public Justice and Common-sense with all the pageantry of a solemn and ceremonious funeral. It has, however, under recent Reforms, especially those effected by the Common Law Procedure Acts, again revived, with a number of modifications in the direction of simplicity, brevity, and general rationality, which, if the theory of procuring a distinct Issue before Trial be preserved at all, will save it from any more pandering to Professional astuteness at the expense of Moral truth and Public Justice.

The abolition, gradual at first, of the Formulary system at Rome, and the introduction of that known as *Extra-ordinaria*, marks the same progress of ideas. In fact, the very same complaints were made at Rome of the artificiality and technicality that gradually adhered to the older System which, a generation ago, were so familiar in the mouths of Law Reformers in England.

The obvious truth is that this System of Pleading errs through throwing too much responsibility on the Plaintiff and his Advisers, and too little on the Court before which the Trial takes place. A Person may have a Right seriously invaded without any knowledge of the formal Class of Remedies to which the Remedy he ought to seek belongs, and, indeed, it may be an extremely fine question of logical Classification to determine to what Class it does belong. Surely the State ought, by its Functionaries, to undertake the task of answering this question, if the Rights it gives are to be actual and not visionary, or to be only conditional on making a happy guess as to the appropriate Remedy. The progressive recognition of what are called "Equitable Pleas," the permission to join several Pleas together in answer to one Count, the concession of ample powers of Amendment, and the abolition of useless and antiquated distinctions between different kinds of Actions, are steps of Reform which may enable the System of Pleading now under consideration to be retained without serious danger or inconvenience.

A third System of Pleading is that of which a type is supplied by the existing practice in the English Court of Probate and Divorce, though the limitation of the subject-matter in that Court prevents the example being so serviceable as it might otherwise be. According to this System, a simple but not a detailed statement is required from the Plaintiff, and the fewest possible technical Rules as to the form, the order, the words, and the description of the Rights involved, are prescribed. Indeed, lengthy or detailed statements are in every way discouraged. Bare Facts and Dates and a mention of the general Remedy sought are all that is necessary. The convenience of this Mode of Pleading for a Court in which all the Rights or Remedies fall under a very few definite heads, and in which the Judge may, at the direction of either of the Parties, himself try all the Issues, both of Law and of Fact, is conspicuous. The propriety of retaining, in any Case, a more artificial system of Pleading, such as those previously described, in their most improved and least objectionable forms, turns partly on the nature of the questions involved, and partly on the constitution of the Tribunal which tries questions of Fact. Under the Jury system, in view of the general inexperience of unprofessional men, it may be essential to restrict the length of the Proceedings, and to evolve the true and sole matter of contention by preliminary Pleading of a more or less strict sort. This is especially the case when the transactions are long and complex, and conflicting Rights exist (as by way of "Set-off" or by way of what is called "Contributory Negligence") in both the parties, and a balance has to be struck between them. When the Jury are accomplished commercial men, as is often the case in the most important English trials, the matter is one of comparative indifference, as they may be assisted rather than confounded by hearing even extraneous, irrelevant, and generally admitted Facts. But, in the majority of Cases, which must needs be tried under less favourable circumstances, a simplification of the Issue by a system of technical Pleading would seem to be indispensable.

This last observation is especially true in relation to Criminal Pleading, as to which it is of extreme importance that the Crime alleged to have been committed should be narrowly limited before Trial, so that the Prisoner may know to what matter to address his Defence. The habit of calling into question a man's whole life, as exhibited in the materials of the French *Acte d'accusation*, however favourable to the procuring of Convictions, certainly is not favourable to Public Liberty.

2. *Trial of Issue of Fact.*

The general purpose of a Judicial Investigation is twofold. It is alleged that a Person duly described has violated some Duty, either positive or negative, imposed by Law. In other words, it is alleged that the Person described has done one of a Class of Acts, or has abstained from doing one of a Class of Acts, which the Law commanded him either to do or not to do, as the case might be. Two matters of Investigation are thereupon presented: the one as to what is the Class of Acts which the Law commands or forbids; the other as to whether the Person indicated has done or omitted an Act which falls under that Class. Thus it comes about that two separate enquiries have to be made, the one as to the state of the Law, that is, the quality of the Acts of the kind in question which its language comprehends, and the other as to what has actually been done or omitted by the Person indicated. The latter enquiry again is often broken up into two parts according as it is the Act committed or omitted which is a matter of uncertainty or as it is the identity of the Agent which is a matter of uncertainty. But the latter enquiry, (as a whole, and comprehending these two subordinate branches,) however complex in some Cases, is clearly distinguishable from the former one, and some Legal Systems recognise the distinction so clearly that they appoint one set of Judges to determine the state of the Law,—that is to conduct the former enquiry,—and a different set to determine the state of what are called "the Facts,"—that is to conduct the latter enquiry. This distinction between the Tribunals severally for questions of Law and of Fact was known even to the Romans during the "Formulary period," when the Prætor named a Judge or body of Judges and directed them as to the state of the Law applicable to the Facts they should find. The habit of drawing a sharp line between questions of Law and of Fact has been highly artificialised in English law, where the method of Trial by Jury, cherished as a great Constitutional bulwark, has given an almost excessive importance to a clear definition of the provinces of the Judge and the Jury respectively.

Assuming then that questions of Fact,—that is of the contested Identity of Persons and of the contested Reality of Acts or Omissions,—admit of Logical separation, for the purposes of Judicial Investigation, from questions as to the state of the Law, the problem is presented as to what Rules shall be observed in bringing before the proper Tribunal Evidence material to the Facts in dispute. In a controverted Case there are, by the hypothesis, two sets of Facts, or two aspects of the same set of Facts. It is in the Public interest that the Time of the Parties and of the Tribunal be economised as much as possible, that is, as much as is compatible with attaining to a knowledge of the Truth. This necessity introduces the expediency of what are called "Laws of Evidence," that is a Code of Rules having their source either in "Statutory" or "Judicial" Legislation, and regulating the Classes of personal Witnessess or of alleged Events or Acts which alone it is competent for those interested to bring before the Tribunal. The ground

of these Rules is often said to be something different from
this, and, no doubt, a certain Legislative distrust of all
Tribunals has led to an arbitrary Exclusion of Evidence
or to absurd and needless restrictions upon its production.
The true principle upon which alone the Exclusion of
Evidence can be justified is that, inasmuch as a very wide
Induction proves such or such a Class of Evidence to be
generally worthless, and the admission of it conducive to
Fraud, it economises the Time and energies of the Court
to spare it the labour of invalidating it once again, or else
of running the risk of being, through accidental inadvertence, deceived by it.

An important question in Criminal Cases is the expediency of allowing the Accused to be publicly examined
in open Court. The objections to this course are that it
is too hard and cruel a test to enforce on an innocent
Person, and that it favours the fraudulent devices of the
guilty. It is probable, however, that the Tribunal would
be awake to distinguish between a genuine explanation
and a clever imposture. Anyhow it seems the height of
injustice to close the mouth of a Prisoner when a tissue of
plausible charges and Facts is alleged against him and he
is the only Person who is competent to give the connecting
link which may change their whole complexion. A
severe cross-examination of an Accused Person is undoubtedly, on many grounds, not to be encouraged.

Apart from all consideration of artificial Rules imposed
by the Legislature or gradually introduced by Courts of
Justice themselves for the Admission or for the treatment
of Evidence of different sorts or produced from varying
quarters, there is one celebrated and, to a certain extent,
real Classification of Evidence which demands particular

attention. This Classification is that giving rise to the distribution of Evidence into the two contrasted varieties of "Direct" and "Circumstantial." The full investigation of the true import of this distribution will afford a most instructive lesson on the general relation of purely Physical and Psychological Enquiries to the Administration of Law, and on the true grounds upon which alone confidence in any kind of Evidence is universally placed.

All a Person knows with respect to any matter is derived from one of three sources or complex conditions of Fact. First, (1.) he may have seen or heard or come into Personal contact with the matter himself. Secondly, (2.) it may be that another Person, who has generally been known to speak the truth, and who has a sound head, good eyes, good ears, and good general health, alleges that he has seen, heard, or come into Personal contact with some Thing or other, or some Fact or other. It has been found that, so often as this man was trusted before about other Things as to which he made similar assertions, those Things proved to be actually situated just in the way he said, and on this ground he is believed in the present case. In either of these two sets of circumstances there is what is called "Direct Evidence" of the Thing or Fact in question, and the value of the Evidence depends on the state of the Investigator's own senses or else on the state of the senses of somebody else, on his opportunities for observation, and on the likelihood of his not being fraudulently deceived, and not telling a lie.

Suppose, however, thirdly, (3.) that neither the Investigator nor anyone else can either see, hear, or come near the Thing or Matter as to which information is required. An Event may have occurred far from any human eye, ear, or dwelling-place, in the darkness of the night, in the solitudes of the forest or of the ocean, under the dark shroud of artful concealment, or in the misty recesses of the impenetrable Past. From whatever cause, the Fact in question cannot be itself approached; but the surrounding Facts, past, contemporaneous, or succeeding, may have been seen, heard, or felt, either by the Investigator or by somebody else more or less likely to speak the truth about them. "Circumstantial Evidence" is, then, that sort of Evidence to a Fact taking place which is supplied not by anybody's having observed it take place, but by a number of other Facts or circumstances having been observed which are held to furnish a legitimate ground for an inference from them to the Fact in question. Hence the whole value and use of this sort of Evidence depends upon the twofold condition of all Facts whatever being bound together by a close and invariable association, and of the Investigator's having acquired some reliable experience of the actual order in which they thus invariably succeed each other or concur. Bentham has named the Fact which is the Subject-matter of inquiry the "Principal" Fact, and the circumstances from which the presence of the "Principal" Fact is inferred, the "Evidentiary" Facts.

There are certain fallacies respecting the true nature of Circumstantial Evidence to which the incessant controversies on the subject in Courts of Justice have given rise, and which have much tended to obscure it. One fallacy is that all Evidence is in some sense Circumstantial, inasmuch as there is required in all cases an inference from the report of the Investigator's own senses or of those of others to the truth of the Facts reported. This fallacy is founded on a mere arbitrary distortion of the common meaning of words. It has been, in fact, conventionally agreed to denominate that as Circumstantial Evidence which demands two Logical inferences instead of one,—that is, one from the sensational Perception of the Evidentiary Facts to the actual and objective existence of those Facts, and another from the existence of those Evidentiary Facts to the existence of the Principal Facts in question. It is agreed to call all other evidence "Direct," and protests against this mode of distinctive expression are simply frivolous.

Another fallacy on this subject is that Circumstantial Evidence is intrinsically and essentially of far higher positive value than Direct Evidence. It has been a commonplace proposition in Courts of Justice that "Facts cannot lie." It is manifest, however, that the only accessible knowledge even of the Evidentiary Facts which constitute Circumstantial Evidence having to be reached through the reports of the Investigator's own senses or of those of others, and each of these sources of information being vitiated by their appropriate possibilities of error,—such as delusion, or deception, or both,—this kind of Evidence is exposed at least to just as many chances of being falsely reported as the class of Evidence called Direct. But, furthermore, in addition to this equal chance of the Facts "lying," there are let in all the innumerable and characteristic possibilities of drawing irrational and erroneous inferences from those Facts even when true. The fallacy here described is, no doubt, founded on the admitted truth that, among a large number of Witnesses to isolated Facts, of which Facts the Witnesses themselves may not appreciate the relevancy and import, there is less likelihood of Conspiracy and Perjury than where a small number of Witnesses come prepared to tell an identical Story about a limited number of Facts obviously of the highest significance.

There is, lastly, the fallacy of assuming Circumstantial Evidence to be radically weaker than Direct. This is a topic much dwelt upon in Criminal Defences, and is about as far removed from the truth as the allegation generally preferred on the other side. The fact is that no general and abstract comparison can be made between the relative values of the two species of Evidence. Some indirect Modes of Proving the offences of Poisoning and of Forgery have been far more convincing than the Direct Evidence tendered, in other cases, in order to establish the truth of an allegation of Slander or of picking a pocket. It is well said that a chain cannot be stronger than its weakest link; but it is also true that several chains together, some of them even having weak links, are rightly treated as stronger than any one single chain many or all of whose links are of uncertain validity.

A case for Criminal Inquiry arises when a certain Fact or a number of assembled Facts are brought to the notice of the Authorities, which Fact or Facts have, in common experience, been generally or sometimes found to originate in a Breach of the Criminal Law on the part of some Person or other. In instituting a Judicial Inquiry with a view to complete the whole history of the isolated Facts alone brought as yet to light, a series of provisional hypotheses are made about them, in the verification of which consist all the ulterior proceedings.

The prominent Fact, for instance, which is the most

conspicuous one in the Case, and which is the first to excite suspicion, is that of some external detriment incurred either by Persons or by Things. The first hypothesis is that this detriment is caused through the *Act* of some Person or Persons unknown. The proof or verification of this is sometimes called inexactly "the establishment of the *corpus delicti*." The Mode of Proceeding is, of course, that applicable to all Cases where the Evidence is Circumstantial. The Evidentiary Facts are first enumerated, such as the loss of the money, the broken desk, the smashed windows, the empty plate-chest, the smoking stacks, the bleeding and bruised body, the arsenic found in the tissues. Thereupon the obvious significance of these indications is determined by a precise or unconscious reference to general experience. Certain suppositions which Bentham has called "Infirmative," and the effect of which is to rebut the more ordinary Presumptions, are then carefully weighed, and the possibility of the actual presence of the Facts they would imply rigidly investigated. Such Facts are Carelessness, Fraudulent fabrications of Evidence, Death from Natural Causes, erroneous Scientific conclusions, Suicide, and Accident. The result of this latter Process is then laid side by side with that of the former, and the general balance of Evidence, either for or against the hypothesis of Criminality, is cautiously struck.

The second hypothesis, made in every Criminal Trial, after the Fact of some Crime having been committed (or the *corpus delicti*) has been established, is that the Criminal Act was that of some assigned *Person* or *Persons*. This hypothesis will be formed in some such way as follows :—The Act was done at a certain place and at or within a certain Time. Again, the Crime was committed by some one possessed of the requisite Opportunity, and therefore not by anyone out of the country, nor a hundred miles off at the Time of the Crime. Thus access at the given Time to the Person Deceased; knowledge of, and proximity to a house broken into; official duty in reference to Bank-books, and the like,—are obvious grounds, on the score of Opportunity, for implicating certain Persons in the preliminary hypothesis of Guilt. Furthermore, the Crime was committed by some one operated upon by such a Motive (or peculiar attitude of mind towards ulterior consequences) as would be sufficient, in the given case, to overcome the ordinary "tutelary" Motives,—Political, Social, Moral, and Religious,—which generally operate as dissuasives from Crime. The actual force of a given Motive, depending as it does on the idiosyncracy and the circumstances of the man upon whom it operates, cannot be measured; and therefore the *smallest* Motive, provided it is proved to have been really present, is ground for Suspicion, as it is very frequently held to be sufficient, when accompanied by other Evidence, to justify Conviction. Lastly, it is probable that the Person who did the Act will have conducted himself in one or more of certain recognised Modes habitual among Persons committing Crimes. Symptoms of Criminality supplied in this way are Sudden Flight, Possession of Things Stolen within a limited Time after the Theft, Purchase or Possession of Poison, Threats or Professions of Hostility, Confessions, and such Dealings with Rights of Ownership as apparently have reference to the results or proceeds of the Crime. To frame and verify hypotheses on such indications as these is the work of the subordinate officers of the Police. The English and

z

French Methods are here notoriously at variance. The English Official proceeds slowly and cautiously, and scarcely ventures to frame a hypothesis till he has congregated together such a number of Evidentiary Facts as shall justify at the least a Magisterial Investigation. He adheres throughout to his hypothesis, when framed, till, by the result of this Investigation, or at the final Trial, it is found baseless, or else is in a greater or less degree substantiated. The French Official grasps at every straw of Evidence ; makes a numberless variety of hypotheses and deserts them as rapidly as made; examines privately any number of Persons whom he suspects, calling upon them to account for every hour of a given period of Time, and even for much of their past life; and ransacks to any amount, without a warrant, every square inch of the most private chambers or sacred repositories, from which Evidence, however seemingly irrelevant, may, with any likelihood, be extracted.

Now, experience has shown, in accordance with the above anticipations, that the typical history of a Crime from first to last includes some or all of the following phenomena and no others. The Criminal is (1.) possessed of an ascertainable *Disposition* or *Character*, belongs to a certain *Station* in life, and is actuated to commit the Crime by the desire of some pleasure or the apprehension of some pain, which desire or apprehension constitute his *Motive*. He has recourse to (2.) certain *Preparations* for doing the Act, and sometimes makes *Declarations* to others relating to it, or uses *Threats* to the Person to whom it will be prejudicial. Next he avails himself of a given (3.) *Opportunity*, and frequently brings with him certain (4.) *Instrument* to assist him in doing the Act. He commits the Act by Violating (5.) some *Material Object*, whether a Thing strictly so called or the *body* of a Person, thereby superinducing a determinate change in its previous and normal condition. In many cases he reaps and carries off with him (6.) certain *Fruits* of the Crime. In nearly all cases he resorts to devices for the purpose of (7.) *Concealing* the Crime. On being charged with the Crime he generally shows unmistakeable symptoms (8.) of *Fear*, and in some rare cases (9.) he *Confesses* the Crime.

It is, of course, by no means true that this is the fixed and invariable history of every Crime. It is only of the nature of a general Formula, filled up with more or less completeness in each particular case. It is scarcely possible, however, to picture any case where, in conformity with general experience, a number of these several circumstances are not present, nor where any other phenomenon, not included under any of these heads, can be present. It is in the skilful Logical use of such of the circumstances of the above several Classes as are supplied by the Evidentiary Facts of any given Case that the successful result, in a vast number of Judicial inquiries, of the part of a Trial which is concerned with Issues of Fact will depend.

Apart, however, from considerations of Legal restrictions imposed on the production of Evidence, and of the Logical value and use of such Evidence as is capable of being produced, certain questions may have to be decided, or general Rules to be laid down, as to the Order in which the Proceedings shall be conducted, and as to the rival claims of the Suitors or of the Prosecutor and the Prisoner, in respect of what is called the " Cross-examination " of each other's Witnesses. In some Systems of Law, the process of Examination and Cross-examination of Witnesses is allowed to go on outside the Court, by a species of searching and

Formal Correspondence, conducted, possibly, under the sanction of Oaths. This Process generally has especial reference to the more private or personal matters within the exclusive knowledge of one of the Suitors. It takes place under the direct Compulsory authority of the Court, and before the Cause comes into Court, that is, while the stage preliminary to the Trial is being proceeded with.

When strict Rules of Evidence exist they must be abided by, or,—in the case of Evidence not allowed by these Rules being admitted, or of proper Evidence being refused,—a Remedy may be obtained on application to another Court, and the whole Proceedings have to commence afresh. It is obvious that the question as to the nature of the Rules of Evidence, and whether a particular Class of Evidence is or is not excluded by those Rules, is (under the above definition) a question of *Law* and not of *Fact*.

3.—*Trial of Issue of Law.*

When once a question of Law is entirely severed from one of Fact, it is merely a matter of Logical argument for the competent Tribunal to determine its merits. It is a general principle to allow Appeals on questions of Law with far greater facility than on questions of Fact. In order to try a question of Fact at all, it may be necessary to make a hasty assumption as to the state of the Law which is in point when any one complains that a Right of his is invaded. The Judge possibly acquiesces provisionally in this assumption if it be not too violent, reserving the question as to its actual value, if necessary, for more calm and mature consideration, when he can have the help of other competent Authorities; or, it may be, he gives a first decision, relying on the ready power of Appeal to some higher Tribunal which he knows is at hand. In England there is a Court of Appeal in Criminal Cases for disputed matters of Law, but none for matters of Fact. Similarly, the *Cour de Cassation* in France only takes notice in Criminal and Civil Cases of questions of Law.

C.—SENTENCE, ASSIGNMENT OF PUNISHMENT OR MEASURE AND MODE OF COMPENSATION, AND EXECUTION OF SENTENCE.

After the question of Law is resolved,—the question of Fact being also decided,—a conclusion is come to that a given Person, either Prisoner or Defendant, has either done or not done some Act belonging to a Class of Acts commanded or forbidden by Law. If he has done an Act forbidden or if he has not done an Act commanded, there remains but to assign the legal Punishment or the Measure and Mode of Compensation which he is to make to the injured Person. It may be, however, that the Members of the Tribunal are undecided, or differ widely in opinion. The question of requiring Unanimity will be considered later on in its bearing, especially, on Criminal Cases. But it may be possible for a Court to accept an intermediate Verdict, as " Not Proven " in Scotland, or "with Extenuating Circumstances " in France. It has even been suggested that the Crime of Murder should be distributed into Classes, and that the Jury should find to which Class the Act in question belonged, the worst Class alone carrying with it the Penalty of Death. The value of these practices or recommendations will also be considered lower down.

The last stage of Judicial Procedure is the Execution of

the Sentence, but this rather belongs to the Duties of the Executive generally, and therefore to the part of the Law which deals with those Duties.

D.—Extraordinary Remedies.

Besides the general Remedies provided as above, and following upon a laborious Trial of questions of Fact and an erudite Investigation into questions of Law, there are in most Legal Systems certain more expeditious and simple Modes of obtaining Relief from threatened or actual Injuries than by thus bringing a formal Action. The method of *Interdict* or *Injunction*, by which a Judge, on a one-sided application of one Party, makes a provisional Order upon the other Party, commanding him to do or to abstain from certain definite Acts on peril of instant Punishment, is a familiar instance of this Class of Remedies. So is the remedy of *Mandamus* in the Court of Queen's Bench in England, by which local Authorities are positively commanded to do certain Acts in the way of making Official Appointments, which they have neglected or hesitated to do.

A curious and, at the present day in England, extremely interesting Class of exceptional Remedies is that provided abroad by *Commercial Tribunals*, a topic which might be appropriately considered either under the general head of the Establishment of Courts of Justice, or in the present place. The grounds for providing the peculiar kind of expeditious and Summary Remedies which the notion of a Commercial Tribunal implies are (1.) that men practically engaged in Commercial affairs are likely to be more competent than other men, and as much so as trained Lawyers, to pronounce upon the Legal Rights and Duties arising out of a strictly Mercantile transaction; (2.) that the regular process of investigating the Facts before an ordinary Tribunal employed in matters not strictly Commercial involves delays, technicalities, and antiquated Solemnities, which, if productive of much or little inconvenience in those cases, are, in Commercial matters, disastrous in the extreme, and provocative of the most ruinous Frauds; (3.) that it is proved by experience in France and in other countries that the institution of such Tribunals tends to render Litigation simpler, cheaper, and more easily and beneficially resorted to, especially in matters of small pecuniary amount; (4.) that the convenience of Foreign Suitors who may not understand the Procedure of the General Courts, but may easily learn that of a Commercial Tribunal, deserves consideration.

The objections to the institution of such Tribunals are that the arguments drawn from the delay, technicalities, and costliness of the other Courts are quite as much arguments for improving these as for introducing new Courts free from these blemishes; while the general habit of multiplying Courts and Modes of Procedure, according to the varying Subject-matter of transactions, produces a serious want of harmony in the Judicial System, and leads to popular confusion and misapprehension as to the grounds of the distinction. Again, it is urged that the use of these Tribunals in France, where they act as a natural and necessary Supplement to the Jury System, as there existing, is no argument in favour of their use in this country, where a Special Jury of Merchants, as almost invariably summoned in important Commercial Cases, has all the efficiency of the best elected Commercial Tribunal in France.

In spite, however, of the force of these objections, the

Special Jury System in England only touches the more momentous Cases, and a large class of these (such as those connected with Partnership and Joint Stock Company liabilities) are adjudicated upon by a single Judge in a Court of Equity. It is for the vast number of trifling Cases, demanding despatch at a few hours' notice at the hands of the most accomplished and honourable traders, that Commercial Tribunals are invoked; though, perhaps, there is reason to be found in the first-mentioned objection, to the effect that the institution of these Tribunals is most conveniently proceeded with at the time of a general re-organisation of the whole Judicial System.

The topic of *Bankruptcy* has already come on for consideration under the head of "Laws of Ownership," where it was treated as a Mode of Acquiring Rights of Ownership by Adjudication, and again under the head of "Laws of Contract," where it was treated as a Remedy provided by Law in order to minimise loss in the expectation of a Contract being broken. The topic also belongs to the present place, inasmuch as it is the function of Laws of Procedure to institute and regulate the Judicial Machinery needed to give effect to the Remedies implied in Bankruptcy. Either a Special Court may be established for the purpose, or the Functions of conducting Proceedings in Bankruptcy may be added to the Functions of some other Court, as they are in France to those of the Tribunals of Commerce; or the two Systems may be combined, as in England, where the whole Administration of Bankruptcy Law is shared between the Court of Bankruptcy, the Court of Chancery, County Courts, and, to a slight extent, the Courts of Criminal Law. The Proceedings are partly Inquisitorial and partly Executive.

The first part of the Proceedings is concerned with (1.) determining, in accordance with Law, whether the Debtor in question has committed what is declared to be one of a Class of Acts termed "Acts of Bankruptcy;" (2.) ascertaining who the Creditors are, and to what amount, and what are the Assets, if any, available for part Payment. The second part of the Proceedings is concerned with (1.) the Appointment of Persons, either nominated by the Creditors, or Officially designated, to be Assignees of the Assets under the responsibility of distributing them in the Order prescribed by the Court, and in obedience to the general Rules of Law; (2.) passing a Sentence on the Debtor, generally based on a review of his Moral conduct in reference to his business transactions, and carrying with it some Penalty or the opposite, in the shape, perhaps, of a greater or less Relief from the claims of his Creditors, (even from those against his after-acquired Rights of Ownership,) and of the exemption of his *person* from the operation of existing Writs of Execution. Provision is generally also made in the part of the Law dealing with the Administration of Proceedings in Bankruptcy for giving Legal Validity to Voluntary Compositions with Creditors, Formally made and authenticated and in no wise tainted with Fraud.

A remarkable specimen of an exceptional Remedy provided by Law is supplied by the Law of *Distress* as existing in England, and which, becoming more and more unpopular, is likely to fall into gradual disuse. By the Law of Distress the direct application of the Remedy for the Breach of a Duty is put into the hands of the Person aggrieved, and it is not necessary for anyone else, other than the very subordinate Public Official known as the

"Bailiff," to interpose at all. The inconveniences of the Law are that (1.) it is executed by the Party interested, and irrecoverable loss may be inflicted on the alleged Debtor before the existence of the Debt, or the non-payment of it, has been ascertained in a Court of Justice; (2.) the Remedy is of such a rough kind that it gives a vast opening to abuse and cruelty on the part of unscrupulous Persons,—a result always to be avoided by Law. The only defence of the practice is that, inasmuch as the Poor have often no other Assets than their few material goods, Landlords would require a higher Rent if they had a less readily available Security than the Law of Distress gives them. A simplification and a reduction in the costliness of Courts of Justice would go far to take away the foundation of this defence of the Law of Distress.

E.—Limitation of Actions.

The Policy of imposing some arbitrary Limit to the Time within which an Action can be brought is recommended by such obvious considerations that they need only to be stated in order to be thoroughly apprehended. Such considerations are (1.) the difficulty of procuring satisfactory Evidence after a long lapse of Time; (2.) the expediency of not disturbing the existing state of things, in view of Public Expectation being based on their continuance and not on their disturbance; (3.) the general importance of restricting Litigation to the Limits imposed by the necessity of encouraging Public Confidence in the readiness of the State to maintain Rights once conceded. This necessity is the less the more apathetic and careless has been the Person in whom the Rights vest,—on the rational principle *vigilantibus, non dormientibus, subvenit lex.*

The effect of a Law for the Limitation of Actions is obviously much the same as one of Prescription,—that is, a Law which allows Rights to be acquired through their actual Exercise for a length of Time, more or less determinate, and with more or fewer other Conditions annexed. According to the details, however, of the special Legal System, the operation of the two classes of Law may, in practice, be different. A Right may not be wholly valueless because a direct Action cannot be brought upon it. It may avail by way of Defence against an Action brought by somebody else. For instance, money paid by a Debtor in recognition of his Debt may, in some Systems of Law, be not allowed to be recovered back, though the payment could not be enforced by an Action.

In all Systems of Law in which Laws for the Limitation of Actions prevail, it may be a matter of much importance to fix the exact Epoch at which an Action begins to be brought, because the period of Limitation dates back *from* that. Of equal importance is it to mark the Moment at which the Right of Action accrued, because the period dates back *to* that. It is customary to provide for the cases of Persons who could be Plaintiffs having been abroad, or not having attained Majority, or otherwise being under Disability to sue, and to except the period of Disability from the period of Limitation as counted for the particular case. In England it is said that no period of Limitation ever runs against the Sovereign, and the same was said in the Middle Ages of the Roman Catholic Church. It is not generally held advisable to have

Statutes of Limitation for Crimes, though much practical injustice and much perplexity is often occasioned by the want of some such provision.

F.—Parties to Actions.

The Modes of practically enforcing Laws, as prescribed in Laws of Procedure, have been hitherto treated on the assumption that every one who has a Right has an equal Capacity to enforce it. This Method has been adopted in order not to distract attention from the topic of Modifications in the application of the Remedies themselves. It is true that whoever has a Right is able to have it enforced. But in some cases he can do so directly in person; in others he can do it, or can only do it, by employing some Representative; in others, again,—as under some Criminal Systems,—the Person interested can do no more than give notice to some Public Official of a Right having been Violated, and it becomes then the Duty of the Public Official to secure that the Offender is punished. Again, two or more Parties having in common a Right Violated may be allowed to sue singly or only together, or to be sued singly or only together. Again, after an Action has commenced, if one of the Parties dies or marries, the Action may either terminate, or it may go on between the Parties who survive, or whose Condition remains unchanged, or it may go on with the Persons Legally substituted for the original Parties.

This part of the Law, which practically is of extreme importance, may be represented under the following general Forms:—

 (*a.*) Those who must sue or be sued in the name of some Person either generically described by Law, or so described subject to the Discretion of the Court (Infants, Lunatics, Married Women, Bankrupts, and the like).

(*b.*) Those who may sue or be sued in the name of a Person chosen by themselves, subject or not to the Discretion of the Court.

(*c.*) Those who can only sue or be sued when joined with other Persons peculiarly Related to them in point of Interest, or assumed by Law to be so Related.

(*d.*) Those who on the Death or Change of Condition of any of the Parties to an Action, after its commencement, can only proceed with the Action on such Terms being complied with, or on such Persons being substituted as Parties, as the Law or the Court may direct.

(*e.*) Those who can only be sued (as on Criminal Charges or in Revenue Cases) by the Executive Authority of the State.

G.—CONFLICTING THEORIES OF CRIMINAL PROCEDURE.

Before closing this chapter on Laws of Procedure it is essential to notice some of the leading Questions in reference to Criminal Procedure and, incidentally, to Procedure generally, on which opinion both in this country and on the Continent is so much distracted. The first set of questions is as to the superior value of what has been called the " Litigious" system, of which the English is held to be a type, and of the "Inquisitorial," of which the Continental systems are held to be equally types. A second set of questions (already alluded to) is as to the propriety of Cross-examining and the Modes of Prosecuting a Prisoner. The third set of questions embraces the "Prerogative of Pardon," "Definitions of Murder," and the "Unanimity of Juries."

With respect to the leading differences indicated by the words "Litigious" and "Inquisitorial," they are based on *degrees* of State interference rather than on any supposed possible absence of such interference in the Administration of Criminal Law. The fact is that Criminal Law by its very nature implies the interference of the State from first to last, though it may happen in some countries, as in England, that, in conformity to traditional usage, the injured Person has a conspicuous part to play, and the Executive Authority is, till properly roused, very inert. It is a real evil if, for the purpose of searching out Crimes, the liberty of innocent Persons be recklessly sacrificed through inordinate powers given to the Police. Nevertheless, as has been already indicated, it is an absurdity to shut out Evidence by closing the mouth of the Prisoner, who is likely to know most about the matter, whether he be innocent or guilty. These remarks tend to recommend the adoption of the Continental Procedure, so far as the management of a Criminal Prosecution by State Officials, with the amplest opportunities of legal Defence invariably accorded to the Accused, is concerned; but the retention of the general English principle of not allowing the Prisoner to be cross-examined in Court, nor a series of innocent Persons to have their character and their comfort brought into jeopardy through the sort of unlimited power accorded to the French Police in preparing a *procès-verbal*. The actual amount of Evidence allowed to be produced as to the Prisoner's antecedents is in itself a gain rather than otherwise, if the pressure of Public business admit of the Time of the Court being occupied with its consideration.

The topic just handled is closely related to one which has of late excited great interest in this country,—that of the expediency of appointing a Public Official of the nature of a Minister of Justice or Public Prosecutor. The advisability of taking this step is not necessarily bound up with the adoption of the Inquisitorial Theory of Criminal Procedure just commented upon; nor does the suggested measure interfere, of necessity, with the Rights of Private Prosecutors as at present recognised. The arguments in favour of the measure are that there are not sufficient inducements to Private Persons injured by the commission of Crimes to bestir themselves in order to track out and secure the Punishment of Offenders. On the contrary, in the generality of cases, the time, trouble, and expense involved in such a Proceeding form the greatest inducements to abstain from taking any step at all, in the somewhat faltering hope that the general chances are against the same Person being a second time a victim of a like offence. Furthermore, a genuine instinct prevails, that Crimes are, by their nature, far more the concern of the State itself than of Private Persons, and that it is a mockery to have an elaborate System of Criminal Law and to leave the Execution of that Law to the chance, leisure, caprice, or wealth of the Private Persons who happen from time to time to be victims to the imperfections of the Authority of the Law. The ground of the existing practice and of its being still affectionately cherished in many quarters is, no doubt, a lurking reminiscence of a primitive, (not to say barbaric,) sentiment that an injured Person has a private and incommunicable Right of Revenge of which no State machinery ought to rob him. A more reasonable argument is discoverable in the general Political principle that it is alway through maintaining a firm grasp on the Execution of the Criminal Law that Governments become despotic and intolerable. It is probable that the claims of Convenience and of Public Justice might be reconciled with what is most rational in the claims of Public Liberty by leaving all existing powers of Private Prosecution as they are, but supplementing them by imposing upon a Branch of the Executive directly responsible to the House of Commons the Duty of securing that no alleged Crime fails to be thoroughly investigated.

The question of appointing a Public Prosecutor or a Minister of Justice opens out a still more difficult and embarrassing question which is often treated in connection with it. This is the question as to the expediency of organising afresh the Department of Government which is responsible for determining the occasions on which the Prerogative of Pardon shall be exercised. It is in connection especially with the Punishment of Death, which in its nature is irrevocable, that the importance of this question is most anxiously felt; but the principle on which the possibility of Pardon, after Trial and Sentence, is secured cannot depend on the quality and effects of the Sentence itself. The main objections alleged against the existing System in England are partly directed against any reconsideration whatever of the propriety of the Sentence when once it is passed, and partly against the special machinery which is in fact at present employed in conducting such a reconsideration. It is said that much of the majesty and popular impressiveness of a Public Trial is divested of its essential significance if the Proceedings are not absolutely final; that an habitual Reconsideration of Verdicts or Sentences after a Public

Trial tends to foster a habit of reserving all the weaker Evidence which cannot stand the light of day, as represented by a searching Cross-examination, for production before a Government Official (in some cases of doubtful competency), and in all cases possessed of a very indefinite amount of Responsibility; that, lastly, the period intervening between the passing of the Sentence and its Execution is a peculiarly favourable one for the exercise of undue pressure on the part of well-meaning Persons, influenced indeed by humanitarian and benevolent views, but wholly inattentive to the value of the Evidence actually produced, and ignorantly indifferent to the Political necessities of the case.

These arguments are directed against a reserved faculty of Pardon however exercised. The special arguments directed against the peculiar Mode of exercising that faculty in England at the present day are still more cogent. In addition to a mass of work extending over nearly the whole field of Law and Politics, the Secretary for Home Affairs in England has cast upon him the possible duty of reconsidering the propriety of every Criminal Sentence passed in the country every day, whether following upon the most insignificant Conviction by Magistrates at Petty Sessions, or upon the most laborious and lengthened Investigation by a Judge of Assize. For this purpose he is not assisted by any competent staff of Officials subject to Public Responsibility, but is wholly left to rely on such casual assistance as he may think it prudent to call to his aid in view of parrying a perplexing Question in the House of Commons. The mass of Cases that might by possibility call for Review at his hands is so enormous, and the want of adequate organisation for the purpose of conducting such a Review is so conspicuous that a two-fold result is, of necessity, brought about: first, only a very small number of the whole mass are in fact ever made the subjects of Review at all; and secondly, the selection of these favoured Cases depends on nothing else than a series of the most adventitious accidents. Such accidents, for instance, are the interference of Local Journals, the Political Questions accidentally involved (as in offences against the Game Laws), the alarming and shocking characteristics of the Crime, or even the interest by chance attaching to the astute method of discovering the perpetrator; to these may be added such more wide-reaching influences as the Age, Sex, Rank of the prisoner, or the prevalence of particular Theories of Punishment among more or less important Classes of Society or in particular Places.

Nevertheless, in spite of all the general objections to any system whatever of Revising Criminal Sentences, and in spite of the special objections to the system which exist in this country, there are certain considerations the other way the quality and weight of which cannot be neglected. In the first place, it is from something more than a mere instinct of Loyalty, traditionally handed down from a primitive Age, that what is called the Prerogative of Pardon is at present, in all States whatever, an inalienable attribute of the Supreme Political Authority as personated by the Executive Authority. The Administration of Criminal Justice must be, at the best, a feeble and imperfect Machinery for determining what are, not unfrequently, questions of the utmost Psychological difficulty and even Moral perplexity. Even with the best Evidence that can be produced, the proper conclusions from that Evidence, especially when it is conflicting, are not always easy to draw. The Evidence, however, is often far from the best, in consequence, it may be, of the Absence of essential Witnesses in distant Countries or under circumstances in which they could have had no notice of the Trial; or of a casual Infirmity,—through ill-health or other causes,—of a Witness's Memory, under conditions in which it was not possible to postpone the Trial; or, lastly, of Facts being discovered subsequently to the Trial, such as the finding of written Documents, or of buried Clothes or Weapons, or such as assertions made in the way of Confessions. Some of these latter Facts may open out entirely new veins of Evidence either with respect to the Identity of the Criminal or to the nature of his Intention.

Admitting, then, that it is in the highest degree expedient, on a variety of grounds which have been already indicated, to force the production of all possible Evidence at the time of the Trial, and to discountenance the desultory tendering of it afterwards, it is obvious that so long as a Sentence is not yet completely executed, in the event of a strong persuasion of its injustice taking possession of the Public Mind, a persistence in its execution will hardly be tolerated. For such a case, which ought to be regarded as of the most rare and exceptional sort, the only conceivable Remedy must be found in the direct interference of the Law-making Power, that is the Supreme Political Authority. The Prerogative of Pardon is nothing more than a phrase, to indicate the outlet through which the Remedy needed may, as occasion demands, be applied in a somewhat organised fashion. The special faults of the English Method of applying this Remedy are that, instead of being regarded as exceptional, it is treated as an invariable concomitant of all Criminal Trials which appeal in any way to the romantic sensibilities of the People; and, instead of proceeding on any distinct and intelligible principle, the only understood ground of it is that, after a series of consultations or communications between the Secretary for Home Affairs, the Judge who presided at the Trial, and possibly some more or less indeterminate Medical Authorities, the whole anterior Proceedings of the Public Trial,—often extending over many days and conducted with all the Formalities believed likely to ensure an almost infallible Verdict,—are discredited and rendered good for nothing. The anomaly here described is naturally presented more frequently in respect of Crimes involving the Punishment of Death than in others, inasmuch as the whole problem included in the notion of Pardon must be perplexing in proportion to the finality and irrevocability of the Sentence.

There do not seem to be any insuperable objections to the institution of a permanent Court of General Criminal Appeal, presided over by a Government Official assisted by Judicial Assessors. In this Court the ordinary Rules of Procedure might be at once more simple and elastic than elsewhere, while the special Rules controlling the Admission of Evidence might be of the broadest possible kind. The Court might or might not sit in public, but a printed and easily accessible Report of all the Proceedings should be invariably published without delay. In order to restrict the business of the Court and to prevent it being deluged with Cases needing no second Investigation, it might be convenient to require a *primâ facie* Case for such Investigation, to be made out on Affidavits before competent representatives of the whole Court.

The responsibility of attaching the severest Penalty known to the Law,—especially where that Penalty is Death,—to an Act legally defined as a Crime, and which Act may yet coexist with an infinite variety of circumstances which alone give it its Moral character, has been felt of late years, both in this country and on the Continent, with constantly increasing force. In the case of Homicide there is familiarly experienced a special Logical and Moral difficulty in constructing a verbal description of the Offence to be Punished with Death which shall be precise and definite enough to correspond with the peculiar and startling definiteness of a Punishment separated by so wide a gap from all others. Different devices have been suggested or practised for the purpose either of limiting the range of this Responsibility or of shifting it to the shoulders of a Popular Tribunal supposed for this purpose to be exempt from the pressure of Legal Technicalities. The " Capital Punishment Commission " of 1866 suggested two expedients for limiting the range of the above Responsibility. The one was to confine the Definition of Murder to Felonious Homicides of great enormity, and to leave all those which are of a less heinous description in the category of Manslaughter. The other expedient was to leave the Definition of Murder and the distinction between that Crime and Manslaughter untouched; but to " divide the Crime of Murder into two Classes or Degrees, solely with the view of confining the Punishment of Death to the first or higher Degree." They recommended that the last method, which they said had been extensively acted upon in the United States of America, should be adopted. The main characteristic of their special Recommendation was that the Punishment of Death be retained for all Murders "deliberately committed with express Malice Aforethought, such Malice to be found as a Fact by the Jury," and for all "Murders committed in, or with a view to, the perpetration, or escape after the perpetration or attempt at perpetration of any of the following Felonies: Murder, Arson, Rape, Burglary, Robbery, or Piracy."

Before the same Commission some highly interesting Evidence was taken with respect to the history and operation in France of what is called the Verdict of *Extenuating Circumstances*. This power of finding the Verdict of Extenuating Circumstances was first given in the year 1832. In the words of one of the Witnesses, " the words themselves, *Extenuating Circumstances*, were a very unhappy phrase, because the idea which is inferred is not correct. It is not Extenuating Circumstances for the Crime itself, but it is Circumstances Extenuating for the Person." The Evidence goes on to state that if the Jury, in their Verdict, declare that there are Extenuating Circumstances in favour of the Accused, the Court is obliged to lower the Penalty by one degree at least; and it may, if it considers it necessary, lower it two degrees. The Jury freely admit Extenuating Circumstances; the benefit of which Verdict may be extended to all classes of Criminals. Extenuation affects more than seven-eighths of the Cases of Capital convictions. The Law forbids the rendering an account of the private deliberations of the Jury, and in general the Motives which have caused the admission of Extenuating Circumstances ought not to be known. One of the Witnesses gave, as an instance, the case of a Parricide tried by the Court of Assizes of the Department of the Haut Rhin, sitting at Colmar. The Crime had, it was evident, been accompanied by the most aggravating circumstances, and it was proved. The only Defence that could be pleaded was the Illegitimacy of the Accused and the uselessness of the Punishment of Death. The question was met on this point by the Procureur-Général, who had personally undertaken the Accusation. After earnest contradictory pleadings, the Jury delivered a Verdict of Extenuating Circumstances.

It has been thought well to describe in some detail the nature and operation of this notorious peculiarity in the French Criminal Procedure. It is the best specimen that could be selected of the sort of Legal chaos or anarchy that results from leaving to a Popular Tribunal the formation of a Criminal Code for themselves, and one which practically has to be reconstructed afresh for every new Case. Through this Verdict every idle Sentiment, every freak of Popular caprice, every misdirected Social impulse, is permitted to play directly upon the Administration of Criminal Law. The utter uncertainty both in the Legal Character of Crimes and in the Degree of their Punishment cannot but tend, as far as it goes, to impair the value of Punishment altogether. The only possible account of the Verdict is the historical one, that it formed for the Government "a *mezzo-termine*, dispensing them from taking a decisive step about Capital Punishment in itself."

Similar objections must be raised against the Commissioners' proposition to leave to the Jury the determination of such impalpable, variable, not to say fearfully dramatic elements as are gathered up in "deliberately committing a Murder with express Malice Aforethought." The result of such a course would be that of simply asking the Jury whether, in view of all the circumstances of the case and with all the susceptibilties roused to which the Counsel on both sides had appealed, they would, on the whole, prefer the Prisoner being executed or not.

The true solution is, of course, to be found in defining *Murder* afresh, a method which the Commissioners have alluded to, but have slightingly passed over on the characteristic plea that such a change would " involve disturbance of the present distinction between Murder and Manslaughter, making it necessary to remodel the Statutes relating to Attempt to Murder, and interfering with the operation of those treaties with Foreign Powers which provide for the Extradition of Fugitives Accused of that Crime." These last considerations no doubt have their value, as importing certain inconvenient changes in the Technical Structure of Legal Systems, but they cannot be allowed for an instant to weigh in the scale against a new Definition of the Crime of Murder if it be recognised that that is one important avenue towards carrying out the momentous ends of Political Safety and Moral Justice.

There is one perplexing Class of Cases in which a combination of Crimes seems to qualify the character of each or of one of them. To this Class belong what are called Political Crimes. These are Crimes in which the general Motive, instead of being the satisfaction of some narrower Personal feeling, is rather the carrying out of some design connected more or less directly with Changes in the Constitution or in the Administration of the State. In all Systems of Law one important Class of Crimes has reference to Acts the Intention of which is the bringing about of such Changes. Such Crimes are Treason, Seditious Conspiracies, Seditious Libels, and the like. It may, however, happen that in the course of committing these Crimes, and with a view to facilitating the commission of them, other Acts are done which, in everything but the accompanying Motive, are not distinguishable from ordinary Crimes. A question, then, may be presented whether these Acts ought to be treated as (1.) ordinary Crimes, and no more nor less, regard being had only to the Intention and not to the Motive; or (2.) as mere incidents to or aggravations of the Political Offence, regard being had to the Motive and not to the Intention; or (3.) as Acts qualified by reference both to the Intention and to the Motive, and so, as *sui generis*, being punishable on principles founded on special views of Political expediency.

In one way it is generally felt that Offences based upon nothing else than desires, more or less enlightened, for Constitutional Changes, are even more noxious than other Offences, because their influence radiates to a far wider circle and their consequences may possibly be far more disastrous. On the other hand, it is felt with equal force that it is, as often as not, the most generous, humane, and valuable Citizens who commit Offences of this Class; that when a momentary and special National crisis has been tided over there may be no probability of the Offences ever being repeated; and that a conspicuously lenient treatment is generally the wisest Policy for a Government to adopt in order to establish itself on the most secure foundations. Amidst these conflicting considerations, the Law must usually be constructed and administered in view of what, upon the whole, seem to be the special or frequently recurrent exigencies of the particular State. For the case of ordinary Crimes, such as Murder, Burglary, and Theft, committed in the course of prosecuting such a Political Enterprise, it cannot be expected that the State should entertain the indulgent view just adverted to, to the benefit of which only those Persons, if any, who are actuated by the purest and most humane Motives, can conceivably lay claim.

The marked distinction between what are denominated purely Political Offences and all others is most obvious in applying the Doctrine of Extradition. There is no point more contested in International Law than whether States have, independently of Treaty, any Rights as against each other to the Surrender of Fugitive Persons who, having committed a Crime in the Territory of one State, have betaken themselves for safety to the Territory of another. The general question is one which properly belongs to International Law, but the discussion of it affords the best illustration of the distinction between so-called Political and other Crimes. The main ground for resisting the Extradition of Fugitive Criminals is the fear that a Foreign Government may dishonestly endeavour to procure the Surrender of its Political Foes by making fictitious charges of Ordinary Crimes having been committed by them. In order to meet this, the modern Policy which regulates Extradition Treaties not only excludes all Political Offences from the category of Crimes to which the Extradition is to extend, but takes the most anxiously pondered precautions to counteract the lurking possibility of a Political or other sinister purpose being the real ground of a demand for Surrender.

There is one more point around which much conflict of opinion has gathered both in this country and on the Continent of Europe; that is, the expediency of requiring that Juries should be *Unanimous*. The question belongs both to Criminal and to Civil Procedure, though, on many grounds, its importance is greater in the former than in the latter.

As to Criminal Trials, the arguments in favour of Unanimity are (1.) that the Presumption ought to be in favour of Innocence, and therefore, unless every one of the Jury is convinced of the Prisoner's Guilt, after an interval has elapsed sufficient to enable each to assist the rest in recalling the Facts of the Evidence, the Prisoner ought to be acquitted by all,—not because all believe him Innocent, but because there is sufficient uncertainty to make *one or more* believe him to be so. Again (2.) it is urged that, but for the pressure incident to the Necessity for Unanimity, Juries might be indolent, neither attending to the Evidence, nor looking for guidance from the Judge towards a truthful Verdict, nor debating the matter with sufficient seriousness and concentration of mind among themselves. It is supposed that the wish to agree will be a most effectual stimulus towards real and sincere agreement. Inasmuch as one account of the Facts alone can be the True one, it is supposed that the readiest mode of coming to a common conclusion will appear to be found in an effort to reach it.

No doubt the actual practice in England of requiring Juries to be Unanimous has not been supported by such rational considerations as these. The cruel and monstrous devices sanctioned by English Law, for precipitating the intellectual action of Persons called to perform the most solemn task to which man is competent, could only rest either upon a superstitious belief that recalcitrant Jurymen were voluntarily resisting a mysterious communication of the Truth, or else upon the stupid adherence to the relics of a barbaric and ignorant Age through which every Institution in the country has been, of necessity, more or less dwarfed and crippled.

All the valid arguments in favour of Unanimity fall under one or other of the above-mentioned heads. It is obvious that both the classes of arguments have a certain, though not an equal, amount of force in favour of the necessary agreement of some large number of Jurors, short of the whole. It is true, however, that where, in the case of each particular Juror, it is open to him to persist without difficulty in his opinion to the last, the Personal Responsibility of each is, to that extent, felt to be less cogent, and the tendency towards Unanimity is less decided.

Nevertheless the following arguments against requiring Unanimity are very forcible, or even irresistible. On the hypothesis of Unanimity being exacted, there is (1.) no opening afforded for the very probable case that in every dozen or so of men, chosen more or less at random, one at least will have less than the average amount of Logical faculty and of Moral Discrimination, or more than the average amount of Self-conceit, Stupidity, and dogged Obstinacy. On this ground alone a single man may, by his habitual Perverseness or Incompetency, over and over again imperil the interests of Public Justice. But again, (2.) in every body of men, chosen more or less at random, the personal Influence, the habit of Self-assertion, the abnormal Experience, the gift of Rhetorical Expression of one or more, are always likely to overawe and to subdue some, at least, of the rest. The necessity of Unanimity converts what would otherwise thus be a real, and possibly precious, force, into practical despotism. Lastly, (3.) the mere desire to get rid of the Proceedings, if it prevents indolence and needless hesitation, also tends to precipitate Verdicts and to stand in the way of all consultation which is likely to lead to embarrassment. The zeal to get at *some* Verdict is only too likely to be stronger than that to get at the right one.

Thus in Criminal Cases the true solution of the problem seems to be found in requiring the agreement of some large number of the Jury, short of the whole. The actual number is matter of detail, and almost of indifference, but some number must be fixed on for the sake of precision and definiteness.

In Civil Suits, over and above the mere question of Liability and Non-Liability, there is presented that of the Quantitative Amount of Liability. For the former part of the enquiry the same arguments on either side apply as in Criminal Cases. For the latter part the amendment above suggested, of being content with the decision of a large Majority, has still more to be said for it. Degrees of Liability admit of an almost indefinite number of shades of opinion; and in assessing merely Pecuniary Damages the pitch of interest and of felt Responsibility can seldom rise high enough to secure greater deliberation through greater delay and pressure. Thus it may be expected that the well-considered opinion of three-fourths or of four-fifths of the Jurymen will generally be at least as satisfactory as any opinion extorted by an irrational process of physical compulsion.

CHAPTER XV.

PRIVATE INTERNATIONAL LAW.

There are two Modes of Extension which the Science of Jurisprudence in Modern times, as contrasted with Ancient, undergoes without a thorough investigation of which any professedly Systematic exhibition of the Science must be seriously incomplete. Indeed it is not saying too much to insist that in the occupation and cultivation of the field of what are called (when opposed to each other) " Private" and " Public" International Law, the Science of Jurisprudence attains or discovers its main practical value. Were there only one State in the world as (for the purposes of any illustrations to be drawn from Roman Law) there was in early Republican, and, indeed, in the later Imperial Rome, the topics of Law hitherto investigated would be the only ones ever brought into controversy or made matter of Judicial Investigation. But at a very early period of Roman History the problem involved in the fact of Rome not standing alone as a civilised State forced itself upon the Government, and in many ways needed practical recognition. As she extended her conquests first to Italy, and then to the Provinces, she was again and again faced by the fact that there competed with her own Institutions certain indomitable Systems of Law and pertinacious Usages which she might wisely incorporate but could not extinguish.

The best she could do, both in the earlier stage of the problem and in the later, was either to fall back upon a System of Law based upon nothing else than the simple Rules and Maxims which were common both to the Home and the Foreign Systems, or to elaborate out of the prevailing Moral Code a novel system of Law seeming to harmonise with the demands of practical Justice. The pursuit of the one method produced the *Jus gentium*, or the Law common to Rome and to the surrounding Nationalities. The pursuit of the other produced the *Jus naturale*, or the Law held to be dictated by the enlightened Moral instincts as conformable to the "Natural" constitution of Man. The Historical connexion of this last creation with the prevalence of Stoicism has been expounded by Professor Maine in a well-known passage.

The Multiplication, the recognised Independence, and the innumerable Relations to each other of States in Modern times make the problem presented by the Variety of Legal Systems, and by the essential absence of any common Supreme Political Authority far more constantly recurrent, and of far more indefinitely enlarged magnitude and perplexity than it ever could have been in the Ancient World. Similar Methods, nevertheless, reposing as of old on a comparative Ethical and Juridical Science, are those most in use for its solution, the only qualification in the free use of such Methods being that due to National Prejudices, to inveterate Custom or to special National Policy.

In the present chapter one side alone of this problem will be discussed,—that arising out of the Fact that the Citizens of one State, either through Travel, Residence, Commercial dealings, or other causes operating in Modern times with ever-increasing frequency and potency, are ceaselessly and inextricably intermingled with the Citizens of another. Thus the same Ethical and Political considerations which give rise to National Laws of Ownership, Contract, Marriage, and Crimes, where all the Persons addressed by the Law are Citizens of the same State, and the Things (if any) lie within the Territory of that State, seem to be of equal force for the purpose of introducing analogous Laws for cases where these latter conditions are only partially or not at all fulfilled. Whether such analogous Systems of Law,—as applicable to alleged claims arising out of transactions between Citizens and Foreigners, or between Citizens with respect to transactions which have taken place Abroad, or in which the Things in dispute are Abroad,—shall or shall not be introduced by way of Supplement to its ordinary Laws by any given State, must depend on the simple Will of the Law-making Authority of that State. The actual Sources (or complex and immediate generative Causes) of such Laws are, in fact, those which fall under the general head of " Judicial Legislation," rather than those which fall under other heads; though, (as in the case of English " Bankruptcy " and " Extradition " Statutes,) Statutory Legislation often plays no inconsiderable part in the same creative work.

From the above general description of the nature of the Topics of Private International Law it is obvious that, first, so far as it exists at all in a State, it is true Law to all intents and purposes, and is binding, like all other Law, on all Executive Officers, Judges, Sheriffs, and the like. Secondly, its existence is due to two diverse causes,—the one, the existence of various Legal Systems, (whether resembling or conflicting with each other,) in different States,—the other, the existence of certain Modifications, more or less extensive and radical, in the Legal System of one and the same State as recognised in different parts of its own Territory. Ready examples of the "Conflict of Laws" produced by the last-mentioned cause are supplied by the case of England, on the one hand, and of Scotland, India, and the British Colonies generally on the other; and by the equally familiar case of the various States forming the American Union.

The Materials of Private International Law, and the nature of the Questions to which it gives rise, are in themselves so intricate and involved that it needs an almost excessive amount of clearness and precision to avoid confusion. It unfortunately happens that, while the subject has been treated by the ablest English, American, and Continental Jurists, this demand has by no means been properly regarded. Principles have been recklessly blended with the detailed application of them; Positive and arbitrary Rules with universal Doctrines; controversies on points of insignificant value with the gravest Moral or Political dilemmas. This has probably been due to the fact that the provinces of the Jurist, the Politician, and the Text-book Writer have never yet been sufficiently distinguished. Thus Writers have endeavoured, and, in fact from the actual state of the Law, have been compelled to endeavour, to personate the three characters at once.

It will serve to promote the clearness here so urgently required if the Rules of Private International Law be made formally, as they are substantially, Supplementary to those composing the National System of Law. For this purpose the National System itself must be presented in somewhat of a Systematic Form. An outline of such a

Systematic Form, as applicable to all possible Systems of Law, has already been presented; and so, in order to sketch out the lineaments of that Supplementary System which comes under the present head, all that has to be done is to follow as closely as possible the map already limned.

All Laws are addressed to *Persons*, and have reference to their *Acts*, either absolutely or in relation to Things. Some Laws impose what have been called "Absolute Duties," that is, Duties not corresponding with Rights vested in Private Persons. Other Laws confer Rights on some Persons, and thereby impose Duties on some or all other Persons. Under a National System of Law, as hitherto considered, all the *Persons* contemplated are Citizens of the State to all intents and purposes, and are amenable to one and the same System of Law. All the *Acts* contemplated are supposed either to be performed within the Territory, or to be performed by Persons under the permanent control of the State, and thus responsible for Acts even done outside the Territory. All the *Things* contemplated are supposed to be within the Territory of the State, or if outside, as on the High Seas, within its permanent Jurisdiction. Now the special hypotheses which Private International Law, as a Supplement to the National System of any State, presupposes are the following :—

1. *Persons* either not Citizens, or, being Citizens, not amenable to the System of Law recognised and administered in part of the National Territory, are, in respect of certain Classes of Rights and Duties, under clearly defined circumstances, authoritatively addressed by the Law as if they were Citizens, or as equally amenable with others to a System of Law to which they are not generally amenable.

2. *Acts* to be done in the Territory of another State, or to be done anywhere by Persons not being Citizens, are forbidden or commanded, discountenanced or favoured by Law.

3. *Things* contemplated as the subject-matter of Law are not necessarily within the Territory of the State nor otherwise under its permanent Jurisdiction.

The application of these hypotheses will be understood by using them in the construction of a System of Private International Law made to correspond minutely with the general System of National Law already investigated. The Mode in which a System of Private International Law, as considered apart from the general System (though there are many strong reasons for treating the two kinds of Law under each successive topic side by side), would be presented is as follows, reference being made solely to the most familiar matters upon which Legislation of any sort, Judicial or Statutory, has hitherto taken place.

A. Laws directly relating to the Constitution and Administration of the State.
    I. Doctrine of Territorial Jurisdiction.
    II. Citizenship.
    III. Domicile.

B. Laws of Ownership.
    I. Things Movable and Immovable or otherwise distributed [*Lex loci*].
    II. Personal Capacity of Owners.
    III. Rights of Ownership [*Dominium*, Servitudes, Mortgages, "Incorporeal Rights" as recognised in different States].
    IV. Modes of Acquiring Rights of Ownership [Sale, Intestate Succession, Testamentary Dispositions, Adjudication, Prescription].

 V. Modes of Protecting Rights of Ownership:
  1. Injunctions, Interdicts.
  2. Actions Civil and Criminal.
C. Laws of Contract.
 I. Persons *outside* the Jurisdiction making Contracts, or Persons within it making Contracts with Persons outside it, or with respect to Things outside it.
 II. Modes by which a Contract is Made [Common distinction of Formal and Material parts; Rules imposed for Political or Moral reasons, or to economise Judicial Labour; Transfer of Rights under a Contract; "Novation." *Lex loci actus*].
 III. Rights accruing through the Making of a Contract [Interpretation, *Lex loci contractus; Mora; Interest*].
 IV. Modes of Enforcing Contracts [*Lex fori*].
D. Laws affecting Special Classes of Persons.
 I. Husband and Wife; Parent and Child [Divorce; Poor Law Settlements].
E. Laws of Procedure [Foreign Judgments; Limitation of Actions; Bankruptcy; Evidence (procurable Abroad); Extradition].

A. LAWS RELATING TO THE CONSTITUTION AND ADMINISTRATION OF THE STATE.

I. *Territorial Sovereignty.*

It is essential to the conception of a Modern State that its Limits should be Physically marked by the lines circumscribing a Definite Territory. How far this conception is accidental or necessary is, for the present purpose, an irrelevant enquiry, though the traces of variation in the conception as afforded by Tribal Communities and by highly Feudalised Societies are, of course, abundantly supplied by Ancient and Middle-Age History. It is only when States multiply, when prevalent Agricultural and Industrial pursuits imply stability in the Possession of Land, and when the Land itself becomes matter of keen competition among rival Populations bordering on each other, that what is called "Territorial Sovereignty" grows into a fixed and immutable idea.

The Logical and Practical Consequences of the dominance of this idea are of the highest importance. They are (1.) that all the Land within the confines of the State is in such a way Owned by the State itself that all Rights of Ownership in it are Conferred by the State alone and can neither be affected, imparted, nor withdrawn by any other State; (2.) that the State is (Morally) entitled to control the Acts of all Persons whether Citizens of the State or not, performed or to be performed within the Territory, while the State may also treat its own Citizens as responsible for all Acts performed elsewhere; (3.) that the Jurisdiction of Courts of Justice and all their Processes, Litigious, Remedial, Preventive, or Executive can only (in the absence of the special license or the indulgence of other States) reach to the Limits of the Territory and no farther. The application of these doctrines to the special case of *Things* as distinguished into "Movable" and "Immovable" will appear further on under a later section.

Such is the Doctrine of "Territorial Sovereignty" in its most rigorous form. It is in the Qualification of the Logical Consequences of this Doctrine that the largest part of Private International Law consists.

II. *Citizenship.*

The conception of a State implies the existence of a strict Relationship of Moral Rights and Duties between the Supreme Political Authority and the Citizens of the State. These Moral Rights and Duties are expressed under such phrases as the Duties of Allegiance and the Rights to Protection on the part of the Citizen, and the Rights on the part of the Supreme Political Authority to Tax the Citizen and to use his services for the National Defence or even for other public purposes.

It is obvious that the greatest inconvenience and the most perplexing conflicts must arise in the event of various Laws existing in different States for determining the Marks of "Citizenship" or "Nationality." A Person might thereby be treated by one State as its Citizen, and therefore as under obligation to abstain from bearing arms against it: and by another State he may be treated as its Citizen also and be compelled to bear arms against the State likewise claiming his Allegiance. This dilemma has not unfrequently been presented in actual experience, and, till the Laws of all States on this subject are in harmony with one another, the possible occurrence of it cannot be obviated.

Two Questions are presented to the Legislator on his attempting to determine the Marks of Citizenship: The one as to what are sufficient and essential Signs of a Person's being a Citizen; the other as to what (if any) are sufficient and essential Signs of a Person's ceasing to be a Citizen. There are three main Methods in use, either singly or in combination with one another, for settling the first question: These are reference (1) to Birth within the Territory, (2) to Parentage, and (3) to the Will of the Person concerned. Certain Presumptions of Law may be made, again, in favour of a conclusion based on the first or the second of these Signs, which may be capable of being rebutted by a distinct expression of Will made at a certain epoch. An instance of this last Method is supplied by the 9th Article of the French *Code Civil,* according to which every Person born of Foreign Parents in France, is entitled, within a year after attaining his majority, to claim the quality of Frenchman, provided that, if residing in France, he declares his intention of fixing his Domicile in the country, or that, if resident out of it, he make his "Submission" to fix his Domicile in it and actually settles there within a year from the Act of Submission.

It is notorious that up to a very recent date the application of the British Doctrine of "*Nemo potest exuere patriam,*" or of Unchangeable Nationality, led to the most harassing consequences, especially in relation to States like the United States, in which the acquisition of a National character is singularly easy. A recent Act has gone far to remedy this special inconvenience, and furthermore, by removing nearly all the disabilities of Aliens, has for most purposes effaced the distinction, in Times of Peace at least, between British Citizens and Citizens of Foreign States.

In enacting Naturalisation Laws and Laws by which Naturalisation effected in one State is recognised in another, so as to prevent a "double Citizenship," the following Principles have to be kept in view; (1) the Notoriety of the Change of Citizenship, to be secured by Public Registration, Public Advertisements, solemn Acts of Public Officials, and the like; (2) consideration for the Will of an adult Person, as ascertained from his Acts, such as actual Residence for a longer or shorter Time, or from general Legal Presumptions founded on the Nationality of his Parents, or on his Service in the Army or Navy, or from like surrounding Facts; (3) the Limitation, on general principles of Public Policy, of the Quality of the Citizenship conferred.

III.—*Domicile.*

It has already been noticed that the existence of Private International Law is due to two distinct and independent groups of Facts. The one group is that implied in a variety of Systems of Law having Co-ordinate validity and existing side by side with each other in different parts of the Territory of one and the same State. The other group is that implied in the mere Co-existence of different States having Systems of Law more or less identical with or varying from each other; in order to promote and favour intercourse between the Citizens of which, the severe Doctrines of Territoriality above described are relaxed, or other special and supplementary principles of Law are introduced into the National Legal Systems of the several States.

On either hypothesis the test of mere Citizenship is unserviceable for the purpose of determining the System of Law to which a Person at the moment of doing or abstaining from a given Act was amenable. In the one case, the Citizenship of all Persons whose Rights and Duties are severally determined by conflicting Legal Systems is the same. In the other, the mere difference or quality of Citizenship may be no guide whatever to the particular System of Law to which a given Act is to be referred.

Nevertheless, it is admitted that every member of a

State is at every moment of his life subject to some clearly defined body of Laws, and that, in the overwhelming majority of cases he is subject to the same body of Laws all his life long. In the small minority of cases in which a Person is regarded as subject to different bodies of Laws at different epochs of his life, some clear ground must be assigned for introducing and for publicly marking the distinction. Such a clear ground is found in the Fact of *Residence*, coupled with the general Intention that the Residence shall be *permanent*. The Legal Conception of what is called *Domicile* is nothing more than this, though for purposes of Judicial use the Terms in which the conception is couched need careful scrutiny and definition.

The reason for selecting Residence as the general test of subjection to a Legal System is partly Historical and partly founded on conclusions drawn from Practical experience. Savigny has investigated with his usual skill and painstaking scrupulousness of historical research the derivation of the modern Doctrine of Domicile from the *origo* and *domicilium* imputed in later Roman Law to those Born in, or having their Places of Business within, the limits of Italian " Urban Communities." But, apart from historical accident, sufficient reason is abundantly found in actual convenience for the adoption of Intentional Permanent Residence as the test of Subjection. The very same reasons in the way of expediency which prop up any System of Law whatever go to prop up the generally binding nature of each System of Law in respect of those Persons who are permanently associated in Trade or in Social Intercourse with the Persons confessedly subject to it. General expectations are naturally raised by the juxtaposition of the Persons without any ready means of distinguishing from moment to moment their several grades of amenability. Certainly, the avoidance of Litigation and the prevention of Frauds are both promoted by the sort of peremptory Presumption which is implied in the use of the test of Domicile.

The particular occasions on which the test will be used in order to ascertain to what System of Law a Suitor is subject will depend on the nature of the Litigation, and this is one of the various points on which almost interminable disputes have arisen between the most eminent Jurists, Text-writers, and Judges. For the present purpose it is sufficient to explain that the *lex domicilii* means the System of Law to which a Person whose Rights and Duties are in question is *for certain purposes* held to be amenable.

The Rules of Evidence for determining the Mental and Physical ingredients of Domicile have been reduced to very considerable Uniformity, though the Application of these Rules is a matter of the highest Practical difficulty, as might be expected from the prominence of the Mental ingredient, and from the admitted possibility of a Person having more Domiciles than one.

B.—Laws of Ownership.

The peculiarity of a Law of Ownership, as distinguished from every other Law, is that it must have reference to Things, and hence universally the Quality of the Things cannot but determine the character of the Laws. This is eminently the case in Private International Law, where the Doctrine of Territorial Dominion over the Land of a State, as exercisable by the State itself and by no other

State, is brought into direct question. It is owing to the peculiar character of Land as a subject-matter of Ownership, that the distinction between Things Movable and Things Immovable is marked in this Supplementary System with even still greater emphasis than in the Main Body of any National System of Law.

The connection between a State and the Land forming its Territory implies the following characteristic circumstances peculiar to Land as a subject-matter of Ownership. First, no Authority but that of the State itself can accord, qualify, or withdraw the Physical Possession of the Land. Secondly, no State can, directly or indirectly, control the action of any other State as to the Limitations imposed on the Transfer or Modification of Rights of Ownership in the Land of the State, or as to the Solemnities to be observed for the purpose of effecting such a Transfer or Modification of Rights as are there alone possible. The general applicability of the Rule of "*Lex situs*" or the "*Lex loci rei sitæ*" to the decision of all Legal questions where the validity of an Act purposing to transfer or to qualify Rights of Ownership in Immovables is involved is one of the most widely-accepted principles of Private International Law. It is obvious that to this *lex situs* must belong the determination of what Things are "Immovables" and what are not, and also what kinds of Rights in Immovables are capable of being created, such as Servitudes, Charges, Liens, Trust Estates, and the like, and what are the Rules applicable to these several Modifications of Rights of Ownership. The actual use in practice of the *lex situs* may indeed be surrounded by almost unforeseen difficulties; as in the case of the *lex situs* demanding a certain kind of Personal Capacity, generically described, in

Owners,—as to their being above the age of Minority, their not being Married Women, their not having been adjudged Bankrupt or convicted of Felony. In these cases, the existence of the Capacity required may be tested either by the *lex situs* or by some other Law, as that of the Domicile of the Person concerned, or even that of the Place where the Action is brought.

As to *Movables*, an almost equally persistent tendency towards the adoption of the *lex domicilii* of the Agent, for determining the validity of Acts purporting to deal with Rights of Ownership in Movables, has prevailed, as towards the adoption of the *lex loci rei sitæ* in respect to Immovables. A variety of grounds might be assigned for the prevalence of this tendency, or rather of this rooted principle, and, among others, the fictitious assumption (which, of course, proves nothing) that all Movables are situated in the place of the Domicile of the Owner. A crowd of explanations have turned round the favourite distinctions developed towards the close of the sixteenth century, of "Real" and "Personal" Statutes, according to which one Class of Laws dealt principally with Immovable Things, and the other class with "Persons." There was a third class styled "Mixed," which was said by some to deal with Acts, by others to deal with Things and Persons at once. According to this division which, as Savigny says, admits of the most opposite constructions and applications, all Rights in Movable Things must be relegated to the Personal Statutes or to the Laws of the Personal Domicile. Mr. Westlake gives the following interesting and more than plausible explanation of the currency of the Doctrine under consideration. He notices that though corporeal chattels are alone truly subjects of

Ownership, they become mixed up in Judicial contemplation with a variety of so-called "Incorporeal Rights," especially when they jointly compose an *Universitas Juris* in Bankruptcy or at Death for purposes of Succession. "It would be intolerable that in these cases the several "corporeal chattels and active credits should be admi- "nistered on principles varying with the casual situation of "each of the former, and with the Seat of each particular "Tort or Contract that might be involved in the latter, "rather than on one uniform rule for the whole body of "Rights dealt with." "When once it is recognised that "rights of Property and of Action are, for many purposes "of transmission, to be grouped together in the character "of wealth, the only point of union which can furnish a "common rule for them, is found in the Person of the "Owner whose wealth they constitute. They are so "grouped together round the Person of their Owner for "more or fewer of these purposes in every System of Law "which exists among civilised men, and therefore, when "they are similarly dealt with in International Law, it can "only be from his Domicile that the rules to be applied to "them must be derived."

In determining the Rules of Law applicable to the Transfer of Movables or Immovables, it is obvious that the Doctrine of invariably applying the *lex loci rei sitæ* in the one case, and the *lex domicilii* in the other, would sometimes lead to Political Inconvenience or Practical Injustice. On this ground certain exceptions have gradually encroached upon the general Judicial Practice, the existence and applicability of which constitute the main source of vacillation and perplexity in this department of Law. Thus in respect to the Sale of Movables, the exact situation of which may be uncertain, as in the case of ships and merchandise, there may be strong grounds for selecting (as is done in some cases) the Law of the Place of Sale or the *lex loci rei sitæ*, if the situation of the Things is also that of the Sale, in preference to the *lex domicilii*. So, again, the strict Rule of the *lex loci rei sitæ*, as applicable to dealings with Immovables needs Modification, when an Owner in one country is, through the absence of the proper machinery, unable to transfer his Land lying in another. To meet such cases, what is called the *lex loci actûs* has been called in to give validity to a Conveyance insufficiently, but approximately, executed by the technical Rules of the *lex loci rei sitæ*.

The only safe or intelligible principles on which the problems of Private International Law, in relation to this part of the subject, can be solved are the following: (1.) Every Person whose Rights or Duties or the validity of whose Acts are in controversy is to be looked upon as directly and generally subject to the Law prevalent in a certain Territory, that is, in his Domicile; (2.) on the grounds of general Policy common to all States, this Law is sometimes looked upon as superseded by some other Law, and in a complicated transaction one body of Laws may apply to one part of it (that is, the Rights, Duties and Acts involved are interpreted in accordance with it), and another body of Laws to another part of it; (3.) in some cases the *lex fori* or the Legal System prevalent in the Territory where Relief is sought at the hands of a Court of Justice will supersede all other Systems, else, by possibility, applicable. This is especially the case where the *lex fori* professes to be based upon purely Moral considerations, as an Usury Law (in some cases) and a Law forbidding Polygamy.

C. Laws of Contract.

The principles just announced, and which are evolved out of even a brief survey of that part of the field of Private International Law which is occupied with the topic of Ownership, are highly serviceable in solving the many complex problems presented by the topic of Contract. It is to be borne in mind that the main key to the difficulties residing in this part of the Law is found in a persistent hold of the principle that the very essence of Private International Law, as a possibility, implies that "*Rights which have once well accrued by the Laws of the appropriate Territory are treated as valid Rights*" everywhere. Thus, in adjudicating upon a Contract in a Court of Justice administering a different System of Law from that to which one or both of the Parties is subject, the question simply is whether or not the Rights and Duties under the alleged Contract did really attach, and what these Rights and Duties are.

Assuming (1) that the Parties have Contracted in the Territory of their common Domicile, the probability that the Expectations of the Parties were directed to the *lex domicilii* is so great as hardly to be capable of being rebutted, and, consequently, the Nature and Extent of the Rights and Duties arising out of the Contract, as well as the Legal Sufficiency of the Authentic Signs of the Contract, can only be determined by reference to that Law.

Assuming (2) that the Place of Contracting is the Domicile of only one of the Parties or of neither, the application of the *lex domicilii*, except by way of determining Personal Capacity, entirely fails. In this case the ordinary device of making a rough Legal Presumption must be resorted to. Such a Presumption usually points to the Place of Making the Contract for the Legal Sufficiency of the Authentic Signs, and to the Place of Fulfilment for the Quality and Extent of the Rights and Duties arising under it. The *lex fori* is always held as a check on the recognition of any Contract, however valid on other grounds, which is discountenanced by the standard of Public Morality prevalent in the State of the *Forum* or even (as in the case of Contracts in Fraud of its own or of Foreign Revenue Laws) by general Political Expediency.

Such is the general nature of the Principles in accordance with which these arduous Questions are solved. It is obvious that the real difficulty is in applying them with any amount of uniformity and precision to the multifarious Classes of mercantile Contracts and tortuous convolutions of Fact which the daily experience of Courts of Justice actually presents.

D. LAWS AFFECTING SPECIAL CLASSES OF PERSONS.

The problems presented by the varying Marriage and Divorce Laws of different Territories are not the least obstinate and sometimes inexplicable ones in Private International Law. The variety in these Laws, owing to the varying Stages and Modes of Civilisation in different States, coupled with the strange Religious and Moral Vagaries that occasionally cloud the clear Legal Relationship, introduce Judicial difficulties of a very peculiar sort. These difficulties are often increased by the Eccentric or Fraudulent Action of the Persons whose Rights and Duties are matters of Investigation.

The value of Private International Law is tested, and the general Principle of the Adhesiveness of Rights and Duties which have once attached demands consistent support, in the case of Marriage, more perhaps than in any other. The claims of Children, the honour of the Parties, and the interests of general Public Morality are all equally concerned in such support being readily conceded by all States. The Questions involved are (1.) the Validity of the Marriage; (2.) the Rights and Duties of the Husband and Wife as respects each other or the Children of the Marriage or other Persons, whether in reference to Rights of Ownership or to those of Personal Security; (3.) the Authentic Signs of a Divorce, and the Rights and Duties consequent upon it.

The question of the Validity of the Marriage itself involves several distinct inquiries as to, first, the Capacity of the Parties, depending, as it may, on the absence of grounds of Disqualification almost universally recognised, such, for example, as a previous and subsisting Marriage, Physical Infirmity or Immaturity, or Consanguinity; or on grounds of Disqualification frequently recognised, but by no means universally, and admitting of the most capricious variations, as Affinity, and Want of necessary Consents. One of the most perplexing questions of International Law is which of these elements ought to be referred to the Law of the Domicile of one or both of the Parties (if their Domicile be one), and which to the *lex loci actus* or Place of the Celebration of the Marriage. It was seen in a previous chapter that some of these elements of Competency do not generally involve the Invalidity of the Marriage by their absence,—such, for instance, as an Informality in obtaining the necessary

Consents. Others, again, as those opposed to Polygamy, are of so strongly disqualifying a potency that in some countries, as in England, no amount of International Courtesy can allow a Marriage to be valid where the Parties are, on this ground, incompetent according to the *lex fori*. Apart from Special Legislation, and subject to the application of the Principles just enounced, the general custom is in all cases to favour the *lex loci actus*. The main Exception introduced is where the Parties, having a common Domicile, have resorted to a certain Territory in order to evade the Rules of Law as to Incapacity existing in the Territory of that Domicile. Such Marriages are often held as invalid in the Territory of the Domicile as being *in fraudem legis*.

But the Validity of the Marriage in any Territory involves, secondly, a Compliance with the necessary Forms or Solemnities imposed by the Law of the Territory. It is an almost universal and obviously convenient Rule to make a Marriage which is Valid as being in accordance, in point of Form, with the Law of any Territory Valid in every other Territory.

As to the Rights and Duties accruing upon the Marriage, these must be dependent on a variety of considerations, such as the Rules as to Guardianship, Conjugal Duty, and Ownership prevalent in the Domicile of one or other of the Parties which, according to the *lex fori*, would be held to be the Domicile of both Parties, in other words, the Domicile of the Marriage. These Rules again, so far as they affect the Ownership of Immovables, or come into conflict with Rules of a Morally imperative sort existing in the *lex fori* or elsewhere, would be qualified by these latter Rules to that extent.

The question of Divorce, carrying with it, as it may, the perplexing consequence of Re-marriage, and bound up as it is with Moral considerations of the utmost moment, has presented peculiar difficulties in the construction of a recognised Scheme of Private International Law. A questionable but obvious Rule for settling the rival claims of the *lex fori* and the *lex loci actus* is that a Divorce, in order to be effective, must be good by both these Systems of Law. The question is complicated, first, by the persistent application of the analogy of the Dissolution of a mere Contract, and, secondly, by the possibly varying Residence or Domicile of the Husband and Wife at the Time of the Divorce. Again, another analogy, by which Divorce is treated as a Remedy or as a Punishment for an Offence, introduces the hypothetical claims of the Law of the Territory where the Offence was committed.

The introduction of any generally admitted Logical Principle in the matter of the Private International Law of Marriage and Divorce has been obstructed by a number of special Causes, such as Ecclesiastical and National Prejudices, peculiar Moral Conceptions and exceptional notions of Policy and Expediency. The result is that for some time to come it must be almost impossible to tabulate the prevalent Rules of Law with any regard to strict Scientific Arrangement.

E. Laws of Procedure.

The general Principle of recognising in all States Rights and Duties which have properly Accrued by the Law of any one State, has a marked application in relation to

Procedure, and especially to what are called Foreign Judgments, whether such Judgments take the form of Decisions upon litigated disputes in Civil or Criminal Cases, or merely follow upon Proceedings of a purely Executive character, as those implied in Bankruptcy; and whether they only relate to Personal Rights, or affect to touch Rights to Things. With respect to the latter class of Judgments it is obvious that while, on the one hand, the advantage of International concert is especially great, the difficulties of it (in view of the variable Situations and Character of the Things forming a Debtor's Estate, in view of the variable Domicile of his Creditors, and in view of the possibly conflicting Jurisdictions) are unusually great. These difficulties are however capable of being solved by Positive Legislation in each country; the result of which usually is to give to Foreign Decrees all the possible Validity which is consistent with (in some cases) a reserved preference for the claims of Domestic Creditors.

The topic of the Extradition of Criminals who have fled from Justice into Foreign countries, is again one which partly belongs to this head. In some respects it more properly belongs to Public International Law, inasmuch as, though the Rights and Duties of Private Persons are directly involved, the Rule of Extradition (where one exists) can be addressed directly only to the Government of a State and only indirectly and through that Government to the Executive Functionaries, bidding them to Surrender the Criminal or to allow the Officials of the Foreign Government to search him out. It is none the less a matter of Public International Law because special Statutes may so far facilitate the action of a Foreign State as to render the interference of the Home Government only formal, if not superfluous.

It is impossible to take leave of this topic of Private International Law without noting that, while in one respect it presents the most hopeful field for the labours of the Jurist, in many other respects it is peculiarly fraught with perplexity and disappointment. It is obvious that the facility of mutual Intercourse and of incessant Communication between the Citizens of different States must, in a great measure, depend upon the readiness with which Courts of Justice in any one State are empowered and prepared to give complete Validity to Rights and Duties wherever and whensoever vested and imposed. No doubt in order to secure this elastic and sympathetic play between the Courts of Justice of different States there is need of the presence of a multitude of Conditions which are as yet notoriously absent. There is needed, first of all, a certain uniform level of Moral Sentiments in the different States. This want is especially experienced in the region of Contract, of Family Relationships, and of Trusts. Secondly, there is needed as great an approach as possible to Formal and Logical Unity in the Legal Systems of the different States. Apart from such Unity, there will always exist the greatest chances of misapprehension as to the real Character and Extent of the Rights and Duties involved, and consequently the largest openings for the operation of Fraud or for the intrusion of Error. Again, there is needed such more directly and consciously Sympathetic Action between the Governments of different States as may induce them to bring the Material and Substantial portions of their several Legal Systems into ever increasing harmony. Such generous and auspicious efforts, indeed, can hardly be looked for with any sanguine hope so long as the Governments of European States are so variously constituted, and the genuine National Sentiment, instead of being trained and fostered to economise itself for the service of Mankind, is degraded into pandering to the pride of a Regal Dynasty or to the selfish vices of luxurious and exclusive Classes. It is only through this directly Sympathetic Action that the Land Laws, the Bankruptcy Laws, and, generally, the Laws having for their object the Punishment of Criminals and the detailed Administration of Justice will be so constructed in each State as to recognise and favour to the utmost degree the operation of like Laws in all States. At present, Private International Law is just sufficiently advanced to present a gleam of the Future, while it is stagnant and chaotic enough to reproduce with curious exactness the heterogeneousness, the unequal development, and the mutual repulsiveness of European States.

CHAPTER XVI.

PUBLIC INTERNATIONAL LAW.

The Science of Jurisprudence has been hitherto treated solely in reference to the Topics supplied by the National System of Law of a single State, or by the Supplementary System usually existing in Modern States for the protection of Rights and the enforcement of Duties, the commanding claims of which are due to an increasing regard for the mutual Intercourse of the Citizens of divers States. Inasmuch, however, as a State itself, through the Supreme Political Authority which may be taken to represent it more or less adequately from moment to moment, has the Capacity of doing many of the same Acts which Individual Persons are capable of doing; and as some of these Acts may be injurious to other States, while others may be beneficial, there is needed for the control of these Acts some cogent Force analogous to that latent in the Moral or Legal Rules found within the limits of each particular State. In a very Primitive stage of general Civilisation, the Intercourse between the Citizens of different States may be so limited and intermittent that this need may scarcely be felt, except at intervals, between neighbouring countries, or except as a consequence of a long series of injurious provocations. Nevertheless, as the notion of Territorial Sovereignty developes itself and assumes a more and more self-conscious form, the general Conception of the Identification of the People with the National Soil must bring about with it the more strictly defined Conception of National Ownership.

The progress of these Conceptions will be all the more rapid because by this time, within the limits of each National System of Law, the Conception of strict Legal Ownership will long have been an inseparable element of the Public Consciousness. With this Conception of the State as an Owner, strengthened as it must be by the sense of continuous Identity which above all else characterises the Population of a true State, will be developed more and more distinctly the notion of the State, first as a Moral Person, then as a Legal Person, and, in a later time, as at once a Moral and a Legal Person. Coincident with, or as explanatory of, the notion of the Personality of the State, there springs into consciousness the Capacity of Voluntary action, of being invested with Legal Rights, and of being liable to Legal Duties. The actual necessities of Political Intercourse, Rivalries of all sorts, Competition for special advantages, disputed Boundaries, Commercial cooperation, force home and give precision to these dawning and almost instinctive anticipations. A new region of true, though imperfect, Law gradually reveals itself, and, as it does so, is instantly claimed by the Science of Jurisprudence. New kinds of Persons, of Things, of Acts, of Rights, and of Duties belong indeed to this region; but the same Moral and Logical constitution of Mankind belongs to one region as to the other. Therefore it is with no more hesitation than is due to the task of investigating a fresh range of Material Facts that the Jurist proceeds at once to his familiar work of analysing Notions, of explaining and restricting Terms, and of Enumerating and Classifying the appropriate Topics.

The above brief observations indicate the necessity and reality both of International Morality and of International Law. It is a misfortune (as was hinted in a previous chapter) that some Writers have confounded these two Systems, just as some Writers have attempted, though with still less plausibility, and, therefore, with less practical danger, to confound National Systems of Morality and of Law by pointing out the Quality of the Sanction as the only or the main Sign of distinction between the two. It is true that the field of International Law exhibits in its earliest phases the same indefiniteness of outline in respect of the adjoining Territory of Morality as is presented at the same stage of National Law. But the demarcation of the two regions gradually acquires an increasing distinctness in International as in National Law, till, in an advanced stage of either, all risk of further confusion is finally at an end as much in the one case as in the other. Technically speaking, no doubt, all the most characteristic constituents of a "Law" in the strictly National sense are obviously absent from International Law. There is no Power bearing even a distant analogy to the Supreme Political Authority of a State. There is no Executive and no Judicial Authority. There is only the feeblest and most irregular form of Sanction. Nevertheless the Rules, such as they are, which constitute the body of International Law are imperative in their character, and purport to control Acts, and not thoughts, sentiments or emotions. When these Rules are appealed to in Courts of Justice, of whatever sort, they are scrutinised and interpreted by principles of Judicial Logic identical with those applied to the Laws composing the most mature National Legal Systems. They are, in fact, inextricably blended with parts of those Systems, insomuch that it is a common Doctrine that the "Law of Nations" is part of the Law of England, and indeed many special Laws are enacted in every State for the sole purpose of supplementing and enforcing the Duties imposed by International Law.

Again, nothing is gained, while much is lost, by constructing a Definition of Law of so inelastic a nature as to exclude the body of Rules known as International Law. There is surely a "Positive" as well as an "Absolute" "International Morality" existing in the Society of European States, which, however intermittent and flickering, nevertheless prescribes the Rights and Duties of States towards each other by reference to a very different and a far finer measuring scale than the very rough one supplied by even the most beneficial Principles of International Law. It is probable, or, at least, it may be sanguinely hoped, that the future History of Europe will discover the prevalence of a Policy of unselfishness and of mutual help, in the prosecution of which the miserable rivalries and antipathies of the Past will be completely forgotten. Each State will then ascertain its own special advantages and permanent drawbacks, whether due to Climate, Situation, Race or Historical antecedents. Each State will likewise recognise freely the superior claims, in one or another direction, of other Members of the European or Cosmopolitan Community. Every State will vie in a noble rivalry with every other to fulfil its own special Vocation and to co-operate with all others in their several efforts to fulfil theirs.

Now the Positive Moral Duties implied in such a

programme (visionary as it may seem to some) are, by their very nature, wholly outside the region of binding Law. And yet it needs no Political horoscope to discern that there is even now swelling up, beneath the restless waves of superficial Diplomacy and misconceptions, a desire, or, at the least, a Sentiment, of International Unity before which all other more antiquated views of Policy must finally succumb. It is in the creation and strengthening of these lofty and humane aspirations that International Law, fixing as it does the notion of Legal Right and Duty on unassailable foundations, has its truest and worthiest purpose. But to dissolve the whole structural substance of that Morality which no State ventures to ignore,—however completely it may, in its Acts, set it at nought,—into the rough Rules tardily invented for the preservation of Territorial Limits and for shewing bare mercy and pity to Prisoners of War, is to sacrifice Fact and Truth for the mere sake of affected and scholastic consistency in the Definition of a Term.

For the purpose of properly estimating the Juridical contents of a System of International Law it is important to examine the general Causes which obstruct the creation of such a System and the Conditions under which alone an efficient System is possible.

In the first place it is obvious that the existence of any System of International Law to which a number of States will professedly adhere presupposes, at the least, some common Moral Sentiments of Justice, Humanity, and Good Faith, as well as some commonly understood Language for the Communication of Ideas and for the conduct of Negotiations. The need of these Ethical or Physical elements is daily experienced in the contact of European

States with distant and imperfectly civilised Communities. The prevalent weakness in the Administration and the vacillation in the Language of International Law, even within the limits of Europe, is due, among other causes, to the unequal rate at which, especially since the Religious rupture of the XVIth Century, the States of Europe have progressed. To take one token of Progress alone, it is evident that the growing predominance in many States of Europe of Popular influences, as opposed to influences of a purely Dynastic or Aristocratic character, must qualify, to an extent hardly yet appreciated, the attitude of Governments in respect of the claims of Neutral Merchants; of the general Expediency of discouraging War and of Restricting its Effects; and of the Moral Duties of relieving the Wounded, of abolishing the Practice of cruel Modes of Warfare, and of observing Treaties with the same scrupulous integrity as is demanded for the Contracts of Private Life. Such States as are less advanced in this direction, and as still cling to the Traditions of a secret, astute, and selfish Diplomacy, cannot be expected to lend their aid to support and to further Doctrines having for their end the complete Equalisation, in respect of Moral Claims, of all Civilised States. The very terms "Right," "Duty," "Good Faith" have a different sound and meaning for a Progressive and for a Stagnant State. No Formal Documents, however solemnly and strictly authenticated, can draw the mutually repellant States together. Here, as in National Law, a commonly diffused Morality must underlie any possible Legal System, though this Morality may afterwards owe its main sustenance and impulse to such a System.

These considerations as to the obstacles to the Rise

of International Law, founded on the unequal Rate of
Progression of different States, introduce a parallel set of
considerations as to the reasons why International Law
does not make more conspicuous and rapid Progress.
The Questions that cause Disputes between States may be
described as being some of them "Political" and some of
them "Legal." It is not possible to assume in what is
called the "Commonwealth" of Nations that the component Nations have as yet assumed any definite or stable
Relations to each other such as recall the Personal Equality
of all Citizens, in respect of purely Legal Capacity, which is,
at least, vaunted in Modern Times as the domestic characteristic of particular States. It may be, and indeed is, a
useful Presumption that all States, whatever their magnitude, their wealth, or their strength, are Equal and Independent. It is none the less admitted in Practice that some
States are weaker than others, that they need the support
of others, and, in fact, that they are in constant danger of
losing altogether their essential attributes as States. It is
none the less freely admitted, or scarcely concealed, that
certain States are ever becoming more and more
discontented with the Limits imposed upon their Power
and are assiduously watching for opportunities of bursting
the barriers which sufficed to confine them at an earlier
and simpler stage. It is not now to the purpose to
consider how far this progressive degradation or aspiration
is due to general and widely operating Causes, and how
far to moral or immoral Qualities in the Population and
in the Government of these several classes of descending
or ascending States. Suffice it to notice that these Changes
of Political Equilibrium are constantly and undeniably at
work in the great Society of States; that they defy

prophetic calculation as to Time, Place or Amount; and that it seems almost hopeless by any System of merely Legal and Formal Rules to withstand the consequences of their natural operation.

Now it is to these real though often obscure and silently working Political Causes that International Disorder and War are, in the generality of cases, to be attributed. The invention of the Doctrine of the " Balance of Power," for the purpose of protecting the Integrity of weak States against the inroads of strong and ambitious ones, was due, in part at least, to a genuinely felt desire to stave off the inevitable action of these Causes and to guarantee for an indefinite time an accidentally selected *status quo*. The numerous Wars which have been waged either in the name of that Doctrine, or in the face of it, have sufficiently established the impotency of any hard and inelastic Theory to set at defiance portentous and inexorable Facts. In more recent times the Doctrine of " Non-Intervention " seemed likely to succeed to the popularity of the older Doctrine; but the close and inextricable links of every Civilised State with every other proved, on the slightest strain, far too strong and precious to be recklessly snapped asunder,—even if modern Commercial Principles, Economic Interdependence, and an ever-widening Conception of the mutual Moral Relations of each Section of Humanity, as parts of a mighty Whole, did not render a general adoption of a Policy of selfish Isolation a lasting impossibility or Anachronism.

The sort of Causes, then, peculiarly of a Political nature, that generate Disputes between States are sufficiently apparent. For these no Remedy can be found in the mere Forms or even the increasingly recognised cogency of International Law. Every State is deeply rooted in its own Past; is indissolubly bound to numerous other States by Ties that can neither be ignored nor relaxed; and has, at any given moment, tendencies, hopes, fears, and expectations, of which an ordinary instinct of Self-preservation or Self-assertion must compel it to take account in its Public Political Acts.

It is to be feared that the most elaborate Arbitration Board that could be invented could only produce a temporary Check or Modification in the career of a State following out its normal Course of Development. Nevertheless the value of such a Check must in itself be great, and the suggestion that has been made of constructing a standing Court of Arbitration of a Representative character, so constituted as to give a varying prominence to every State according to its varying Force, as estimated from time to time by Population, Wealth, or Energy, deserves the most attentive consideration. But the main though hidden and, it may be hoped, temporary Obstacle to the Practical success of all such magnificent Schemes is that only a very few States sincerely desire to maintain the general *status quo*, or are, in fact, enamoured with the prospect of Permanent Peace. At the same time the actual Situation of many of the States of Europe in their Relations to each other is so artificial, and each is, through a long line of antiquated Treaties and vested Claims, so practically dependent on the exact maintenance of those Relations, that, on the one hand, a nervous thrill attends the slightest prospect of Discord, and, on the other hand, there is the greatest possible facility for any ambitious State to excite, when it pleases, the apprehensions of such Discord.

The most hopeful direction in which Permanent Peace

can be looked for is in a few States, themselves possessed of enlightened views, endeavouring, as far as in them lies, (1.) to reinforce the weak Sanctions of International Law by doing their utmost to discountenance Infractions of that Law, even when such Infractions are not prejudicial to their own real or apparent interests; (2.) to take every opportunity to improve the Substance of International Law by introducing a loftier range of Practice; (3.) to make, as opportunity offers, Private Engagements with one another to observe a Course of Conduct generally beneficial to all States; and (4.) to favour in every way the habit of referring Points in Dispute to Arbitration, and to carry out with punctilious Scrupulousness, and against their own Private interests, the Award of the Arbitrators.

The Political Causes which have hindered the Rise and Progress of International Law by keeping up incessant Disputes have now been sufficiently indicated. The Legal Causes having like effects are of a far more simple and manageable kind. They turn upon nothing else than the imperfect Record of Traditional Usages, the correct Interpretation of Diplomatic Documents and Treaties, the Limits of the Application of generally recognised Maxims, and the Logical Conclusions to be drawn either from admitted Facts or from a long line of, possibly, conflicting Judicial Decisions. The general establishment of Admiralty and Prize Courts affords the most signal instance of the possibility of determining strictly Legal Questions in Courts commanding the confidence of all Nations, and with an effect generally recognised as binding on all. This example might be a most fruitful one for the Future, and might share with a more frequent and ready recourse to Arbitration the honour of reducing such causes of International dispute as are of a purely Legal nature to an insignificant magnitude and number.

The main Conditions of International Law as a possibility are threefold: (1.) the Existence of a Number of co-ordinate States generally affecting a certain measure of equality with one another; (2.) the Distinct Independence and Separation from the rest of each of these States; and (3.) a certain amount of mutual Intercourse and Communication between the several States. These Conditions have all been fulfilled in the case of the States which have risen out of the ruins of the Roman Empire. The circumstances which attended the Dissolution of the Roman Empire were in themselves such as to bring about the necessary accomplishment of the first and second of these Conditions. The Tribes which overran the Roman Territory were sufficiently distinct from one another to prevent indefinite fusion, and were sufficiently cohesive and intelligent to appropriate and to absorb the precious Political Institutions which they found on every side of them. How far Feudalism was, throughout, of essentially Barbarous growth, and (as has recently been advocated), nothing more than an universally occurrent phase at certain stages of National Progress, and how far it coalesced with or supplanted or transformed the Municipal and Colonial Institutions of Imperial Rome, are questions difficult or almost hopeless to solve. It is obvious that the Feudal Institutions of Europe which at one time, as M. Guizot has shown, penetrated every corner of the Social Structure, casting the Ecclesiastical, the Municipal, and the Social Relationship of Persons to each other into one and the same mould, must have had a profound influence on the amalgamation of the various Tribes. Mr.

Ward, in his "Enquiry into the Foundation and History of the Law of Nations," has given an interesting and valuable description of the character and operation of this influence. Feudalism implied in its very nature the opposite notions of Dependence and Independence, as well as the correlative conceptions of Moral Duty and of Moral Right. If the Principle also contained in it a Despotic and Aristocratic element, and tended to maintain connections with the Soil which were Personally slavish,—the tradition and consequences of which subsist to this day,—this is no reason for refusing it the distinctive honour of having been a main Instrument in binding the nascent States of Europe together by ties, of which the main virtue is to have left National Independence and Integrity unassailed.

The direct operation of the *Ecclesiastical System of Europe* on the creation and maintenance of the Independence and Union of European States has also been investigated with scrupulous care by Mr. Ward in what is, perhaps, the most striking and important section of his Work. He notices that if the Union of Christendom bound the States of Europe together through the power of Arbitration practically exercised by the Popes, through the prevalence of General Councils of the most strictly Representative character, and through the common Enterprises and humane or fraternal Sentiments of which all States partook alike; on the other hand, the Fact of this very Union indisposed the States of Europe to entertain humane feelings towards the Turk, the Jew, and the Infidel, while it generated, on a collapse, the most widespread and disastrous Religious Wars.

The influence of *Roman Law*, again,—in its threefold

streams of operation through the Canon Law, through the actually surviving Institutions of Imperial Rome, and through the Technical Rules and Legal Principles embodied in the Barbaric Codes,—is not the least momentous of the general Causes which have determined at once the Substance and the Language of the prevalent System of International Law. Professor Maine has described the curious secondary development in later times of the Roman Doctrines of *Jus Gentium* and *Jus Naturæ*, and it needs but to open the great Work of Grotius to discover the Roman vesture in which all his Conceptions of Persons, Things, Ownership, Contract, Injuries, and Crimes are clothed.

It is sufficient thus briefly to notice the leading Classes of special Causes which furnished the indispensable Conditions of the Existence of a System of International Law among the States of Europe. That a large number of other less readily definable Causes co-operated in the same direction,—such as the Discovery of America, the Development of European Commerce with the East, the varied applications of Steam, and the Announcement of the Doctrine of Free Trade,—is known to all, and only needs to be noticed in order to complete the formal survey of favourable influences.

It appears then that in the case of the European States, while certain Causes have operated widely to prevent the complete Development of any highly organised System of International Law, on the other hand certain Conditions with respect to the Independence and the Mutual Relationship of States, without which the Existence of any System of International Law must be impossible, have been satisfied. In order to apprehend the real character of this System as it has been developed under these essential Conditions, and to contrast it with National Law, for the better elucidation of the true character of both, it will be requisite to consider in turn, first, the *Sources*; and, secondly, the *Sanctions* of International Law as existing in the Past and in the Present among the States of Europe.

With respect to the Sources of the European Law of Nations, according to the Definition of the Term *Source* given in the early part of this Work, as the "complex Assemblage of Facts to which the Existence of a given Law is immediately due," it is to be noted that the ambiguity attaching to the use of the word *Source* is productive of even more uncertainty and confusion here than in the region of National Law. In this latter region the Public Documents or Judicial Records to which reference has to be made in order to ascertain the state of the Law are often called Sources of Law, and the word *Source* is also still more loosely applied both to a Custom, whether or not Judicially recognised, and to the Works of Text-writers carrying with them an authority even of the most faint and uncertain kind. But in this case the line is so broad and clear between the meaning of the word *Source* when thus applied to signify the Quarter to which attention has generally to be directed when it is desired to know what the Law is, and its meaning when applied to signify the Generative Facts to which the existence of National Laws is immediately due, that scarcely any practical inconvenience can be apprehended from the thoughtless habit of employing the same word in two wholly different significations. In the region of International Law, on the other hand, the greatest possible doubt prevails as to what are Sources of the Law in either of these senses of the Term, that is, what (in the one sense) are the Documents, Records, published Works, or general Monuments, to which reference has to be made in order to become acquainted with the Rule of Law, and what (in the other sense) are the complex Facts to which these Rules immediately owe their Birth. The danger of confounding these two meanings is all the greater, because in the very inarticulate and chaotic condition in which the Rules of International Law at present exist the two meanings are closely allied, and the standing Document which first declared and so created the Rule of Law is generally the best or the only Evidence of it. True it is that, in enumerating as among the Sources of Law (in the sense of creative Facts) the Custom and Consent of Nations, it is now generally recognised that the Evidence of this Custom and of this Consent is to be sought in the strictly Historical and Formal Records of Practices in War and in Peace, rather than in the casual researches of antiquarians and travellers. So far there is no danger of confusing the meanings of the term *Source*. Other classes of complex Facts to which the Rules of International Law more immediately owe their authority, —such as the almost fabulous Rhodian Laws, the still cited *Consolato del Mare*, the Laws of Oleron, the Maritime Ordinances of certain of the French Monarchs, the Laws of the Hanseatic League, and even the recent Regulations of the United States for the conduct of their Soldiers in the suppression of the Southern Insurrection,—are *Sources* of International Law in both senses of the Term. It is indeed not through the mere Authority of the Writers of these celebrated Documents, but through the clear and unambiguous assertion of great Principles of Moral Justice or of recognised Expediency as contained in them,—coupled with the general Recognition of them, where possible, by successive generations,—that these Principles have been converted into inflexible Rules of International Law. But, where the original Documents exist, it is to them alone that reference must be made in order to know what the Rule is.

As to *Treaties* between two or more States, it is only under peculiar circumstances that they become Generative Causes of International Law and, thereby, *Sources*, in the secondary or derivative sense of being Evidence, of that Law. Where a Principle has from time to time been in debate, the Fact that a certain Number of States agree to Recognise it is likely to give a weight to the Principle very favourable to its being universally adopted. It will certainly, at the very least, carry enormous weight as against the States which have made themselves Parties to its maintenance. The Rules of the Treaty of Paris of 1856 with respect to Blockade, to the Freedom of Neutral Goods, and to the non-employment of Privateers, will be undoubtedly assumed as binding against any Party to the Treaty in the event of its Enemy, even though not a Party to the Treaty, ever confessing an adhesion to the same Principles. Nevertheless, the mere Will of two or more States, testified by their binding themselves Treaty, would not of itself suffice to originate a novel Rule of International Law, even as against themselves. A Treaty would probably only avail to give a lasting Validity of a restricted sort to a Rule of International Law in the case of the Rule itself having long been strongly advocated by a certain Number of influential States, or of its being obviously recommended in the general interests of Humanity and of Political Expediency, and of its not, in the Case that gives rise to it, operating with peculiar Favour to the States who accidentally are the first to bind themselves to its strict observance.

The influence of *Text-writers* as a Source (in a strict sense of the Term) of International Law has been notoriously greater than in any known System of National Law. This has been due to the Fact, which is wholly peculiar to the region of International Law, that at the very Time when it was most chaotic or defective there existed in the States of Europe Systems of National Law of the greatest maturity, as well as of the greatest Ethical and Logical completeness. Thus it needed but the interposition of Writers deeply versed in prevalent Systems of National Law, ambitious in their Moral aspirations, and favoured by the Political circumstances or by the prestige of their own States, to transfer and adapt the accumulated resources of Ages of Legal Speculation, as conducted within the limits of single States, to the novel requirements of an International Policy. This circumstance drew increased force from the Fact that the majority of the more widely recognised Rules of International Law are of such transparent usefulness and Moral dignity that they needed but the spark, as it were, supplied by any Systematic Writer who could win the Public ear in such a way as to inflame the generous and humane Sentiments of the Nations of Europe. This seems to have been the explanation of the rapid and extraordinary popularity of Grotius' Work.

Furthermore, the finer Doctrines of International Law depend, like the bulk of all Law, on little else than the drawing of correct Logical Conclusions from admitted General Rules. It is in this way that the exigencies of modern Politics, both in Europe and in the United States, have given rise to a succession of Text-writers, whose keen judgment and enlightened philanthropy secure to them as great weight in other States as in their own.

The Correspondence of *Diplomatists*, as a Source of International Law, must be treated very much in the same way as Decisions of International Law-Courts, though perhaps with less reverence than these. The value of the Correspondence, like that of a Judicial Decision, lies rather in the presupposed Rule upon which it casts light, than in the Terms or Contents of the Documents or Notes themselves. A competition of Statesmen to prove their own States to be Legally in the Right, or other States to be in the Wrong, must proceed upon some admitted or presumed Principle and Standard of Legal Right and Wrong. In endeavouring to enforce this Principle, it may be that one or another often puts it into distinct Terms for the first time, or else enlarges or contracts a meaning hitherto imputed to it. Whether the view so attained be finally accepted or contradicted, it is likely to be taken thereafter as the Text on which the Principle hangs, and the Authority of the Text will depend on the general importance of the Controversy, on the character and ability of the Diplomatists, and on the dignity of the States concerned. In the case of Decisions of Courts of Justice, much will depend on the character of the Judge, on the general purity of the Court, and on the interests of the State to which the Court belongs as affected by the Decision.

From these general considerations it will appear that the true Sources of International Law are an Accumulation of Circumstances, sometimes stretching over a long period of Time, rather than,—as is often the case in National Law,—a very Few complex Facts operating at definite Epochs; and that in the former more frequently than in the latter sort of Law the Evidence of the Law and the Facts to which the Law is due closely coincide.

There is no more essential question, as bearing on the true nature of International Law, than the Character of the *Sanction* by which it is capable of being enforced,— that is, of the distinct Penalties which an Infraction of a Rule of International Law may possibly entail on the Offender. In fact it is mostly owing to the peculiar Character of the Sanctions of International Law, as contrasted with that of the Sanctions of National Law, that International Law has, by some Writers, been altogether denied the name of Law, and driven over into the bordering field of Morality. It has already been pointed out that the result of any such attempt is at once to annihilate the notion of a true International Morality, and to ignore the essential Legal aspects of International Rules. Nevertheless, it is obvious that one main characteristic of National Law is the Definite outline of the Penalty, and   l but inexorable sequence on the Infraction of any Rule of Law. In the rival System, on the other hand, the Sanctions are indeterminate and shadowy in the highest degree, while the probability of their being actually applied is, in every Case, matter of the merest conjecture. But it is quite as fair to argue from this circumstance that the Definiteness of the Sanction is not essential to the existence of genuine Law as to argue that International Law is not genuine Law because the Sanctions are vague and weak. In order, however, to throw light on all the aspects of International Law, it will be worth while to gather up in a compendious and classified Form all the more or less distinct Consequences, one or other or more of which is likely in different cases to befall the Transgressor of a Rule of International Law. It may be left to further consideration to decide what analogy these Consequences bear to the Sanctions of National Law.

The possible Consequences of a Breach of a Rule of International Law as immediately befalling the Transgressor are the following:—

1. Certain special and distinct Penalties provided by anticipation in the System of International Law itself, and inflicted with or without the interposition of a competent International Court. [Such are Confiscation of Ships for Breach of Blockade, for carrying Contraband of War, and for resisting Search; Death, on account of Persons classified as Non-Combatants interfering in a War as Combatants; Forfeiture for minor Offences.]

2. Unorganised Public Opinion in surrounding States. [Condemnation in the course of the Public Debates of Legislative Assemblies; Criticism in Public Journals and Meetings, and in the pages of current Literary productions.]

3. Organised Public Opinion in surrounding States taking the form of Direct Moral Pressure. [Diplomatic Correspondence, Menaces of Coalitions against the Offending State, or Actual Coalitions with Threats of Hostile Proceedings.]

4. Cessation or Suspension of Intercourse.
5. Direct Physical Pressure short of War. [Reprisals and Retortions.]
6. Certain Definite Penalties appropriate to the Offence, as the taking advantage of a Broken Treaty against the Party Breaking it.
7. War.

Now it is to be noticed with respect to all these Penalties that, with the exception of those of the first-mentioned Class, there is either the greatest amount of Uncertainty as to their ever being inflicted, or else the main or sole Persons (in the sense of International Law) whose Function it is to inflict the Penalty are those very Persons who are the immediate Sufferers by the Breach of Law. All that International Law can do in this case is to prescribe a number of Rules for the sake of Regulating and Moderating the infliction of the Penalty, and, as a matter of fact, a large part of the Rules of International Law is concerned with nothing else than this. As to the more indefinite Modes of punishing Infractions of International Law, some of them,—such as those implied in an unfavourable judgment on the part of the Population of surrounding States,—must always remain uncertain in their Application and Variable in their Value, just as are the popular criticisms abundantly poured upon the Acts of States in their Domestic relations. Others again, such as that indicated in Suspension or Cessation of Intercourse might be employed with far greater frequency and regularity than has yet been attempted. If the Peace, the Prosperity, and the Moral Progress of the States of Europe are directly dependent upon the Growth and Maintenance of

International Law, there can be no more atrocious Offence than for a State consciously to Break the minutest of the clearly ascertained Rules of this System of Law. This being so, it should not be left to the Individual State which is directly injured,—and which may only too probably happen at the moment to be weak, unprepared, or disadvantageously situated,—to Punish the outrage. All the States that care for the Maintenance of International Law should, severally or jointly, instantly Denounce the Act, and should take immediate measures for Suspending Public Intercourse of every kind with the offending State in the event of Reparation not being at once made and of the Act, if recurrent, being desisted from. The difficulty in the way of such decisive measures is, partly, the Paucity of the Rules of International Law that are so widely admitted and so clearly stated as to admit of a Breach of them being simultaneously resented on all sides without delay; and, partly, as has been already intimated, the want of genuine desire of all the leading States of Europe at the present time to support the existing orderly relations of the Society of States. The thought rather is, on the occurrence of a flagrant Breach of Faith, or of a Trespass on Territory, or of an Invasion of National Security, as to what will be the immediate Consequences to each particular State for good or evil of the Act itself, and of the like ulterior Consequences to which these may give rise. Instantly a sense of Self-preservation turns all the National consciousness inwards instead of outwards; and, in the place of a noble competition to be the first to support European Order, even at personal loss, there is a miserable hustling either to take part in a new War or else to edge out of any participation in it with as much saving of Personal Dignity as the unhappy circumstances permit.

These remarks on what are called, by analogy to the stricter Punishments appended to National Laws, the "Sanctions" of International Law, tend to exhibit that Law in its truest aspect as it exists in Modern Times. For some few purposes, especially those of War, the Sanctions are clearly marked and regularly and unfluctuatingly applied. For some few other purposes,—including the Protection of clearly acknowledged Rights, as in the important matters of Ownership, of Treaties, and of general Independence,—the ultimate and only reliable Sanction, infirm as it mostly proves, is War, either waged by the injured State or, in the most favourable case, waged by a few combined States who accidentally find it conducive to their own interests to ally themselves in order to avenge the outrage. For the larger number of Rules, however, including those in support of indefinite Rights not always susceptible of clear description or not important enough hitherto to have claimed it, the only available Sanction is the fluctuating tide of Public Opinion, supported or directed occasionally by the Formal Despatches of the Executive Authority of particular States.

It has been seen that the Conception of International Law reposes on certain Assumptions,—such as the Co-existence of a Number of Independent States, and the sort of Relationship between them which is implied in their having Rights and Duties in respect of one another. In the Development of International, as of National, Law the identical Course of Legal History is travelled over which is implied in the process of giving Form and Precision to Moral Rights and Duties, and of making acknowledged Duties more and more imperatively binding. Thereby are created what are strictly called Legal Rights and Duties. The true nature then of the Independent States, the Existence of which is thus assumed, and the quality, and the extent of the Legal Rights and Duties which their mutual Intercourse implies under a System of International Law, demands careful Investigation in order to exhaust the purport and contents of this kind of Law.

The general notion of a *State* and of all the elements, Physical, Historical, and Ethical, which are pre-supposed in it has been already investigated in the chapter containing " An Explanation of Leading Terms." There are, however, certain Modifications which have to be introduced into the Definitions there given, when the purpose of the Definition is more especially that of considering a State as a member of a Society of States. By following out the obvious analogy presented by the Systems of National and of International Law, the " Persons " in the one System are represented by " States " in the other. But care has to be taken lest, in treating " States " as Legal Persons, and in speaking of the " Personal " Rights and Duties of States, it be forgotten how very forced and unreal the Metaphorical language, in truth, is. In the first place, States are at any given moment treated in International Law as Eternal, and as having neither beginning nor end. In National Law both Persons strictly so-called and fictitious Persons, such as Corporate Bodies, not only are created and die, but certain of the circumstances attending their Origin and Death are matters of the most anxious Legal concern and precise Regulation. So again a State is a composite Moral Whole containing in itself a multitudinous mass of Moral Agents each capable of independently counteracting, thwarting, or forwarding its Corporate ends. Lastly, a State can only act through its Government, and this Government may from time to time undergo all manner of Changes, and be obeyed at different times with very different degrees of perfection by the bulk of the Community. These two last Facts,—for which there is no parallel in a National System of Law,— give rise to Problems which are wholly peculiar to International Law; and if a fallacious analogy be sought for which, in the Prescriptions of any National System, the conclusion must often be perilously misleading. Thus a State is not the " Universal Successor " or Heir of the Persons who, in their capacity of the Political Authority of a State, properly contracted a Public Debt. It is one and the same State from first to last, quite independently of the Change in the Identity of the Persons constituting its Population, and even of the Changes in the Form of Government. So, again, a State may or may not be responsible for the Acts of all its Citizens ; but whether it is so or not cannot be established by resorting to any Analogy supplied by the Relation of a *Paterfamilias* to his Child or Slave, or of a Principal to his Agent. In fact it may be said that it is impossible to exercise too much diligence in guarding against the seductive and ever ready Analogies supplied by the System of National Law nearest at hand. The field of International Law has, in truth, to the great confusion of sound Principles, been overridden by the almost flippant application of such Analogies.

Starting thus with the full recognition of the Fact that a State is *sui generis*, and can only be likened, for a few narrow purposes, to a Legal Person in the sense implied in National Systems of Law, the next question is as to what are the essential Characteristics of a State as a subject of International Law. On every side it is confessed that a State must be "Independent;" but as soon as the word is used, it is breathlessly insisted that very few, if any, States are absolutely Independent, and thus the main Problem presented is as to the Amount of Dependence which is consistent with a State being, or continuing to be, a true Subject of International Law. That the Doctrine of the essential Independence of States is not practically recognised is obvious when, in some quarters, it is maintained that strong States are entitled to force on weak ones the importation of noxious drugs, the tolerance of abominated forms of Worship, and the reception of resident Merchants. Again, it is often doubted whether, in the case of a prolonged Civil War in any State, it may not be justifiable for surrounding States to interfere; and it is by no means an unpopular, as it is a far more plausible, Doctrine that States are entitled to interfere to prevent the existence of Slavery in other States, and to punish a State which indulges its own Citizens with the license of committing Offences condemned by the general Sentiments of Mankind.

With respect to the amount of Dependence of a State, in its outward Relations, which is compatible with its maintaining its position as a Subject of International Law, the several Modes of possible Dependence must first be enumerated. These Modes of Dependence may be based on any of the following Classes of Facts :—

1. Mere *Political Influence* of some other State, due to Historical Associations, to recent Services, to comparative Strength, or to relative Geographical Situation.

2. *Dynastic Connection*, through the Family Relationship of important Members of the Supreme Political Authority in two States.

3. *Constitutional Connection* in the following Forms:—

    (1.) One or more of the Persons composing the Supreme Political Authority for each State being Common to those of both, and the remaining Persons being not Common.

    (2.) A Political Authority Common to both States and a Separate Political Authority for each State respectively, it being understood that for making some Classes of Laws the Common Authority is Supreme for both States, and for making others the Separate Authority in each State is Supreme for that State. [This is nearly a description of the mutual Dependence of the States of the American Union.]

    (3.) A Combination of (1) and (2). [This last represents, with some exactness, the Relations of Hungary and Austria.]

4. *Political and loose Constitutional Connection*, temporary or permanent.

    (1.) Temporary, as by Alliances under Treaties.

    (2.) Permanent, as in the case of permanent "Confederations of States," having a Central Government of a Representative character, its Functions being restricted, as far as may be, to the purposes of the Confederation; or having, as between themselves, a usually nominal though, at times, an effective tie, as in the case of the more advanced British Colonies and the Mother Country.

It may be rather startling, or it may seem at least premature, under the last-mentioned head, to treat British Colonies as a Subject of International Law, and, indeed, the inclusion of them needs some explanation. In the case of these Dependencies it is to be remembered that their Legal Position is only a very imperfect guide to their Political one; that their Political Position is changing almost daily; that the Relationship between such a State as England and the powerful Communities inhabiting the vast Territories which constitute some of its Colonies, is, and must be, an entirely novel one; and, lastly, that the hope of merely governing the inhabitants of those Territories by the simple machinery of Home-made or Home-approved Law is and must be, as to all the more advanced and enterprising of the Colonies, finally abandoned. It is true that many Legal phantoms still stand in the way of a complete recognition of the practical Independence of many of the British Colonies. The main Executive Officer,—who is also the most essential part of the Colonial Political Authority,— continues to be appointed by, and is wholly subordinate to, the Government at Home. The Local Legislatures are held Legally to be entirely subordinate to the Legislature at Home, to the extent that all their Acts can be ignored, and even their Constitution can be abrogated. An Appeal lies from the Colonial Courts to the Privy Council at Home. As a matter, then, of bare Law, any Court of Justice must recognise the complete Subordination of every one

of the British Colonies to the Crown and to the Parliament at Home. Nevertheless, it is notorious that much of what is here described as Legal Fact is Political Impossibility. Silent, but ever more and more outspoken, Political aspirations will gradually, as they become satisfied, lead to their inevitable expression in the Language of concrete Law.

A purely Juridical and Scientific Treatise like this is not the place to discuss the various Schemes which have been suggested in different quarters for a Reconstruction of the Relations, Legal and Political, of England with her Colonies. The main errors of these Schemes, brilliant and attractive as some of them are, is that they overlook the Facts due to the Variety in the Historical, Geographical, and Social circumstances of the different Colonies, and to the Physical distances between them and the Mother Country. Owing to these Facts, the Problem cannot be treated with reference either to experience gathered in the field of Constitutional Law at Home or in that of International Law strictly so called. On the whole, whatever be the Formal or Sentimental tie which will continue to bind her Colonies to England, their Political situation will be far more closely allied to that of Independent States than to that of mere Subject Populations. A full and generous Recognition of this Fact will do much to pave the way towards the gradual evolution of a new Legal Relationship which shall preserve for England and for the Colonies all the Moral and Material advantages of Permanent Union, while guarding jealously for the Colonies the Moral and Political dignity of the most unrestricted Freedom. A new chapter will thus be created in International Law.

Having pointed out the Qualifications needing to be made in speaking of the "Independence of States," the next question presented is as to the *Rights* which the Independence of States, such as it is, presupposes. A clear view of these Rights is, perhaps, the most important Branch of International Law, inasmuch as the only Justification of War (the main topic of the other Branch) is that certain alleged Rights have been invaded, and that War is the sole remaining resource for their Vindication and future Protection. The Rights of States generally may be distributed into those which they have inasmuch as they are States,—and which are common to all States alike,—and into those which States arbitrarily create by Special Engagements between themselves. All the Rights of States may thus be classified :—

I. Rights of States (as such) to :—

    1. Security against *Interference* in their Internal concerns (including the Right to Change the Form of Government).

    2. Security of National *Territory* and in the Ownership of Things.

    3. Security of *Citizens* when travelling or sojourning in the Territory of other States, and complying with the Laws and Regulations of those States.

    4. Security in the use of *Common Things* incapable of being appropriated or not yet appropriated, as the Ocean, certain Navigable Rivers, Unoccupied Territories, and Islands.

    5. Courteous treatment of *Ambassadors* and Political Representatives, and "Comity" generally.

II. Rights created by Special Engagement or *Treaty*.
III. More doubtful Rights than the above are to:—
1. *Self-preservation* even to the partial detriment of other States.
2. *Commerce* with other States.
3. *Extradition* of Fugitive Criminals.

With respect to the more general Class of Rights appertaining to all States as such, while the Rights themselves have been more and more decisively admitted on all sides, the Modifications in the Rights or the Modes of Qualifying certain of the Rights have given rise to far reaching Controversies and, consequently, to War. Thus where a State is confessedly Dependent in some of the respects above catalogued upon another State, the Dominant or Associated State must have certain definite Methods for Enforcing the Connection in case the other Associated or Dependent State is recalcitrant or resents a Special Interpretation of the Terms of the Union. Short of any attempt at forcible compulsion by Hostile measures, a provisional Remedy may be attempted by Occupying Territory; that is, by infringing a general Right of Ownership or of Personal Security, or by Imprisoning the Citizens of the other State travelling in the Territory of the complaining State by way of taking Hostages,—that is, infringing another equally well recognised Right classed under the third head of the above enumeration; or by Reprisals through the Seizure of Ships or Goods belonging to the Citizens of the State complained against, in defiance of Rights classed under the second and fifth heads. In these cases, of course, the proper and regular Enforcement of the Remedy and of its proper Limitations is apt to present as difficult questions as those involved in the justification of the ground of complaint.

With respect to Rights of Ownership in Things, especially in the National Territory, the legitimacy of special Modes of Acquisition has, in former times, been matter of the warmest dispute, and even still is so. When first the New World was opened to European enterprise, a natural struggle occurred for the appropriation of its Territory between the most adventurous and ambitious States of the East,—at that time, Spain, Portugal, France, and England. The arbitrary line suggested by a Pope would necessarily be more satisfactory to a Catholic than to a Protestant Monarch; while the Doctrine of *Occupation* or *Possession* was not in itself very serviceable, inasmuch as even Roman Law itself could not help to decide how much of a mighty Continent was Occupied or Possessed by the sort of *naturalis possessio* which was, of course, all that a few Colonists and Sailors could lay claim to. The Modern Doctrine in the discussion of which the same Continent is involved, usually called the Monroe Doctrine, may be concisely given, as to one part of it, in Mr. Monroe's own words. "The occasion has been judged "proper for asserting that the American Continents, by "the free and independent condition which they have "assumed and maintained, are henceforth not to be con-"sidered as subjects for Colonisation by any European "Power." And the other part of that Doctrine may be given in Mr. Jefferson's words,—"We will not stand in the "way of any amicable arrangement between the [Spanish] "colonies and their mother country; we will oppose, with "all our means, the forcible interposition of any other "Power as auxiliary, stipendiary, or under any other form "or pretext, and most especially their transfer to any other Power by conquest, cession, or acquisition in any other way." The Juridical aspect of this Doctrine is extremely important, as declaring a Limitation on the Acquisition of Rights of Ownership in Territory imposed by a State not in actual Possession of the Territory but claiming to regulate the Conditions of Transfer through a special and self-asserted interest in the welfare of an enormous part of the Earth's surface.

Recent events on the Continent of Europe have given prominence to another series of Questions respecting the Modes of Acquiring Rights of Ownership in Territory hitherto owned by other States. The occasions on which such questions are presented are on two States attempting to interchange with each other portions of their several Territories; or on one selling Territory to another, either for money or for some other "valuable consideration;" or on the conclusion of a War, when it is attempted to make what is euphoniously designated a "Re-adjustment of Boundaries," that is, permanently to annex a portion of Territory belonging to the State worsted in the War to the Territory of the victorious State. Such an Annexation is usually affected to be made on some pretence of Material Guarantees against future Wars, or even of more intangible reasons, such as the Natural Landmarks, or the community of Race, of Language, or of Sentiment between the Inhabitants of the annexed Territory and the Citizens of the annexing State. In India, the English argument in favour of Annexation has been the permanent disorder of the country and the superiority of British to Native Rule. No doubt in the use of any theory of justification there lurks a reference to the primitive Rights of Conquest by which the conquered State lost, or was liable to lose, all independent Rights whatever. The Modern Doctrine that War is only a rough means to obtain a limited End, and must never be persevered in to a greater extent than is needed to obtain this End, must lead to a complete reconstruction of the Rules as to the Acquisition of Territory by Conquest. The Identity of a State with its Territory, of the Population with the State, and of the Government with the Territory and the Population, as recognised more and more distinctly, must tend to render the practice of detaching portions of Territory from a vanquished State more and more an anachronism and alien to the true Moral Conception of National and International Life. A formal concession to the claims of the more Modern Doctrine of the absolute Unity and Integrity of the Territory of a State is often made by the poor and frivolous process of taking the opinion of the Inhabitants through what is called a "Plébiscite." But any such device, useful as it may be by way of a sedative to Public excitement, is illusory and tyrannical in the worst sense of the word, since the Forms of Freedom are simulated to carry out the Ends of Despotism. The existing Population of a Territory cannot for this purpose be taken to represent their Predecessors or their Successors, any more than they can personate the Supreme Political Authority which is still, at the given Epoch, the only true organ of their Will. Nor is such a vital question as that of their Transfer to another State one that can justly and properly be placed before a mixed and ill-informed Population, generally under circumstances the least of all favourable to the exercise of a calm and deliberate choice.

The most important Class of Rights, next to those which are implied in Security from Interference on the part of other States with the Internal Government or the Territory of a State are those which, by analogy with the Contracts of Private Persons, grow out of the Voluntary Acts of States themselves. These Rights are of the greater moment because there are scarcely any other Rights which may not be, and indeed are not, to a great extent Qualified by the existence of the former. By Treaties the Independence of States may be modified; the Territory of a State may within certain limits (which, as it has just been pointed out, are now becoming more strictly defined) be alienated, sold, exchanged, or mortgaged by way of Material Guarantee. By Treaties the rival Rights of two or more States in Things incapable of appropriation may be ascertained and restricted, as in the case of Fisheries and of the Navigation of common Rivers; the fluctuating influence of humane Sentiments on Modes of Warfare may be congealed into Written Rules; and Rights to Commerce, Copyright, or Rights to the Extradition of Prisoners,—otherwise barely recognised, and any way most inadequately determined,—may be subjected to the finest Modifications.

The Possibility of Treaties rests,—like that of Private Contracts,—upon the prevalent Good Faith of States. Were there no ground for the Governments of two States to trust each other, Treaties would be no more than a farcical playing with Solemn Forms and Documents. So far as States fail to abide by their Promises, Treaties generally run the risk of becoming finally discredited. So far as they adhere to their Promises, the field for the operation of Treaties becomes indefinitely extended.

Nevertheless it is obvious that, while a sufficient amount of Good Faith characterises Modern States to render the notion of Treaties much cherished and their use habitual, some of the most important existing Treaties are, in fact, very imperfectly observed. It will assist the exposition of the Juridical Conception of a Treaty between States, as contrasted with a Contract in National Law, to enquire into some of the leading Causes of this Imperfect Observance.

In the first place (1.), Treaties are often made to last for an indefinite Length of Time, during which the Parties to them ordinarily undergo remarkable changes in their circumstances, both in relation to each other and to other States, to which there is no parallel presented in the circumstances of Parties to a Contract in National Law. In order to meet this difficulty, it has been suggested that either no Treaty should be made for longer than a very limited Period,—say Ten Years,—or that, if made for longer than that period, it should be known to be open to Revision at the end of some such Period. The objection to this recommendation is that some Treaties must, from the nature of the case, be intended to endure for a far longer Time than others, and that a prospect of a Revision of them at a short distance of Time would produce the very Insecurity in the tenure of all Rights under them which it is the main purpose of the Treaty to prevent. In the Treaties with Great Britain which followed the Declaration of American Independence, and which had for one purpose, among others, a definite fixing of the relative Claims of American and British Citizens to Fisheries along the coast of Canada and of the adjoining Islands, any prospect of Change after the efflux of a

Definite Period must have seriously qualified the nature of the Rights themselves, and any prospect of a Revision of the Treaties at a fixed Time must have not only had a like effect, but have operated very unfavourably in fostering a restless temper of Political ambition. It should be admitted that just as a single State can Acquire Rights by Prescription or by continued Possession, or by the enduring Consent of other States, so between two States certain Treaties may be made which must be allowed and expected to operate as long as the two States exist. The responsibility incurred in making any such Treaties, and the inexpediency of multiplying them, is sufficiently evident to all.

Another (2.) Cause which leads to the Imperfect Observance of Treaties is the Fact that the most important Treaties, on the strict Maintenance of which the Peace and Order of a complex Society of States depends, are constantly made at the conclusion of a War, in order to ascertain and fix the Relations of the Belligerent States to one another. A professedly Moral Engagement made under such circumstances can hardly fail to lack all the elements of Choice and Freedom which alone can create a Personal sense or a general Recognition of real Responsibility. In all National Systems of Law the presence of "duress," or *vis* and *metus*, are peremptorily held to invalidate the most Formal, and the most apparently Voluntary transactions. When Terms are imposed by a Conqueror, with the terrible alternative to their adoption of a continuance of the War, and when,—as too frequently happens in Times of War,—opinions and feelings in the vanquished or worsted State are violently distracted, any Engagement that can be made as to the Future must always contain the Suppressed Clause that the Treaty is only to operate so long as the weaker State is Physically forced to tolerate its operation. The very consciousness of this latent Infirmity attaching to every Treaty of Peace tends, of itself, to make the customary Terms of such Treaties harder than they might otherwise be. Thus violence begets distrust, and distrust increases the violence; from which terrible series of reactions springs the lamentable phenomenon that while all the existing Relations of the European States have been mainly determined by Treaties of Peace following upon Sanguinary Wars, and depend, for their stability, upon the rigid observance of those Treaties, nevertheless hardly a single State shrinks from Breaking,—or, at the least, from clamorously insisting upon a Revision of,—any one of those Treaties as soon as it seems conducive to its own interests to do so. A Remedy for this Cause of the prevailing Infirmity attaching to Treaties is to be found in multiplying Treaties between States at Peace with each other, and while each is enjoying a considerable measure of Independence and Dignity. Such Treaties would possess all the most hopeful elements of Stability and Cogency, and the States which were Parties to them, instead of writhing under a hard and tyrannical chain,—the memorials of past degradation,—would cherish and honour them with a noble rivalry, as being at once memorials of a worthy ambition and continuing tests of the National Honour.

A third (3.) Cause of the Non-observance of Treaties is undoubtedly to be found in the loose and inaccurate Form in which they are frequently drawn up, in consequence of which there exists no universal Canon of Interpretation which is applicable to them. This Fact is due partly to the Political necessity of the case, and partly to the want of any common Juridical Language equally accepted by all the States of Europe. A Treaty, when once finally agreed upon, is always the result of a series of Compromises,— especially when following upon a War. These Compromises are the product of protracted Negotiations, conducted by a body of men proverbially famous rather for deceiving one another in the politest language than for successfully communicating to one another the real meaning of their language and no more nor less. Those Negotiations again are apt to be violently interfered with by all kinds of special influences and of indirect aims irrelevant to the main points at issue, which yet, however, in the general result, are not and cannot be ignored. Again, while there is an avoidance of purely colloquial Language in framing a Treaty, there is a current dislike to a purely Legal style,—founded no doubt on a reminiscence of the narrow System of Interpretation, vulgarly, though not altogether unjustly, attributed to Professional Lawyers. It thus comes about that the style of a Treaty runs a risk of having the special defects of a home-made Will, and of containing just enough Legal Phraseology to generate disputes, and not enough to clear them up. It is scarcely necessary to say that the true Remedy for this Cause of the Imperfect Observance of Treaties will be found in the general culture throughout Europe of the Study of International Law. The age of Secret Diplomacy is passing away with that of Autocratic Rule. It is probable that the new Era will be marked by a race of great and popular Statesmen, carrying on their Negotiations with Foreign States as far as may be in the light of day and on Principles which do not shun that light, and by a growing

School of International Lawyers who will assist to build up a truly Humane Code, expressed in precise Language, to which the Terms of every International Document will bear explicit or implicit reference.

The notice of the influence of Popular Movements in the present day suggests the last (4.) Cause which need be noticed of the Imperfect Observance of Treaties. It has always, of necessity, been a matter of the utmost solicitude to determine what amount of Ratification, and by what Persons, is necessary in order to impart to a Treaty its binding force. Treaties are necessarily negotiated and executed by Persons who reproduce, in International Law, the character of Agents in National Law. As in the case of such Agents, the Special or General Character of the Representatives has to be taken into account in estimating the degree of their Authority. In all States, Ancient and Modern, the capacity to make binding Treaties with Foreign Powers has been held to rest exclusively in the Executive Authority of the State, though,—as in the case of the share in such capacity possessed by the Senate in the United States,—the Executive Authority has occasionally been, for this special purpose, modified in its Constitution. This remarkable and enormous Function of the Executive has maintained its ground, no doubt, in part from the traditional notions of the mutual Dynastic Relationships of the Monarchical Heads of different States, whereby all Foreign transactions peculiarly adhered to the Prerogative of the Monarch, even where matters of Internal Government had gradually become encroached upon by the People; and partly to the possibility of sudden Emergencies presenting themselves, needing instant settlement by Conventions between States under circumstances in which the

Delay necessary for consulting a Public Assembly, or the Publicity involved in consulting it, would seriously interfere with the accomplishment of the purpose in view. It is possible, however, that the capacity of making important Treaties will, in all States, be more and more taken into its own hands by the Supreme Political Authority. It is much to be desired that this should be the case, not only to ensure more prudent and deliberate Engagements being made, but in such a way to charge the whole Nation with the joint Responsibility as to ensure their being kept.

Next to clearly ascertaining, limiting, and practically enforcing the Rights and Duties of States in the normal conditions of their Intercourse with each other, it is the province of International Law to Modify and Humanise the exercise of the *Right of War*,—at once the most unwelcome Right or, as it ought to be, the most awful Duty which can be cast upon a National Government.

There are two main departments in which International Law introduces, even in the very heat of a widely spread War, the Conception of Rights and Duties of a wholly novel class, and artificial,—or even apparently arbitrary,—in their construction, but having a decisive influence on the Maintenance of the Claims of Humanity. The occurrence of a War between two States cannot possibly be a matter of indifference to other States, and it is as much the interest of the Belligerents themselves as of all other States that the precise Legal Relations of these so-called Neutral States to the Belligerent States should be definitely described and rigidly maintained throughout the War. Thus one main department of the portion of International Law which is appropriate only to Times of War, is concerned with definitely fixing the Rights and Duties of Neutral and Belligerent States in respect to one another.

The other department is concerned with determining what Limitations are to be introduced upon the exercise of the Physical instrumentality implied in War. These Limitations might indeed be, and generally are, expressed under the phrase "Rights and Duties of Belligerents towards each other." There is, however, something incongruous and self-destructive in the importation of the notion of Rights and Duties in this place. The power of Injury which War imparts is so vast and cruel, even when most restricted, that it can hardly, without a shudder at the inconsistency, be denominated by the Term which of all others recalls a Sentiment of Justice, Order, and unswerving Principle. Suffice it, then, to say that the Exercise of the powers possessed by a Nation at War is held by the common Sentiment of Europe to be Limited in a variety of directions, and it is the record of these Limitations which bears somewhat the character of a Catalogue of formal Rights and Duties.

As to the first (1.) department of International Rules having for their object the Mitigation of the indirect Consequences of War to the States not partaking in it, two main Problems have especially engaged the attention of International Lawyers in Modern Times; the one with respect to the Conditions upon which Citizens of Neutral States may be allowed to carry on their ordinary Commerce under circumstances likely to affect the course of the War; and the other with respect to the Liability of the Government of Neutral States for such Acts of their Citizens as, presumably, favour one of the Belligerents more than the other.

The solution of the first of these subordinate Problems,—that as to the claims to Freedom of Trade by Sea,—has, in fact, generally been settled or provisionally handled rather with reference to the prevalent Political Influence or Material Strength of the Neutral State in each particular War, than to any sound Principles based on a careful and unselfish calculation of all the interests involved. It is admitted on all hands that, on the hypothesis of any Duties whatever being imposed upon Neutral States, the Right of Search and the Penalties attaching to the carriage of so-called Contraband of War are logical and irresistible consequences of a recognition of these Duties. It is none the less obvious that the practical exercise of the Right of Search includes the possibility of the most tyrannical and oppressive Acts, against which the Sufferers have no sort of readily available defence. When this Right is combined with a variable and uncertain Tariff of Things " Contraband of War," there is room left open for every form of robbery and despotism to be inflicted upon Victims who have no Personal concern or Responsibility in the War. The recent tendency has been to protect the Claims of Neutrals in these respects to the extent, at least, of rigidly defining the Order of the Proceedings in conducting a Search, of enforcing the intervention of a Prize Court in cases of doubt, and of demanding a public Notification by the Belligerents of what is to be taken as Contraband of War; though, for obvious reasons, the latter Security is a poor one, where the circumstances and scenes of the warlike measures vary considerably during the progress of the War. The recent Rules agreed to by the Parties to the Treaty of Paris, 1856, to the effect that, with the exception of "Contraband of War," the "Neutral Flag is to cover the Merchandise of an Enemy," and that "Neutral Merchandise is not be seized if found under an Enemy's Flag," marked an important step in the same direction, and would seem likely to put a final close to the most celebrated Controversy in the whole region of International Law. This Treaty, it is to be noticed, was not signed by any Representative of the United States, and therefore it may be doubted whether the Doctrines declared in it are as yet universally binding. It is probable that,—though they would be held binding, under all circumstances, against the States which signed the Treaty,—the States which did not sign it would hold themselves free to adopt in any future War such Principles as considerations of Reciprocity or of any other kind might seem to render expedient.

It is to be noticed that the increasing pressure of Neutral Claims as against the Rights of Belligerents, and the consequent Restriction of these Rights, is a sign of the notorious Fact that, during the last half century, the strongest Maritime States,—as England and the United States,—have been occasionally Neutral when other States have been at War. It is true that in the very War that preceded the beneficent Treaty of 1856 England was one of the Belligerent States. But the general pacific Policy of England was well known by her own Statesmen at that epoch, and accordingly, so far as Private interests could affect the character of the Treaty, the influence of England was undoubtedly exerted in favour of the general support of Neutral Claims.

In respect of the second of the subordinate Problems presented by the attempt to give precision to the Rights and Duties of Neutrals,—that is, as to the Amount of the Responsibility of a Government for the Acts of its Subjects,—both the Principles and the Practice are at present in a high degree fluctuating and inconsistent.

It is, on the one hand, scarcely possible for a Belligerent State to draw a sharp line between the Duties of the Subjects of a Neutral Government and the Duties of the Government itself. It lacks the capacity to ascertain both how far the Subjects are acting under the Encouragement or active Co-operation of their Government, and how far the Government is even able, be it ever so willing, to compel its Subjects to co-operate with itself. On the other hand, it is throwing far too great an incubus on a Neutral Government to expect it to maintain such a zealous and unresting Surveillance over its Subjects as absolutely to prevent, by an indefinite extension and a stringent Administration of the Criminal Law, the doing of Acts which may, by possibility, be interpreted to be Breaches of Neutrality. In the present condition of Commerce, no War of any dimensions can take place without introducing the most serious disturbance into the Commercial Relations of numerous Neutral States. As to two States, at least, there is, on their part, a sudden cessation of Demand and Supply of Commodities, on the regular Supply and Demand of which, it may be, the Wealth and general Prosperity of other States to a great extent depend. Furthermore, all at once, there proceeds from the quarter of the same two or more Belligerent States an artificial and spasmodic Demand for those Instruments and Equipments of War in which, owing to their special Situation or to their casual Want of Preparation, they are severally deficient. Such

Things are, in Modern Times, Ships, Guns, Ammunition, and Coal.

It is obvious that through the accidental Neighbourhood of a Neutral State which possesses, or which is peculiarly able to manufacture with speed, the Things of which some one of the Belligerent States happens to stand in need, the Neutral State may, through the Acts of its Citizens, be able to render to the one Belligerent Services of a most vital kind which it may not be possible or convenient to render to the other; or, at least, to render to the other in a measure which shall be, incontrovertibly, equal in value. These difficulties are eminently Modern difficulties, being brought about, or at least largely intensified, through the expansion of Maritime Commerce, the rapidity of Steam Transit, and the comparative feebleness of Governments at the present day when brought face to face with the Private interests of the richest and most influential among their Subjects.

It might be doubted whether, in view of these obstacles, it be possible to continue to impose any Duties whatever on Neutral States, and whether it might not be more expedient to treat the Propinquity, the Resources, or the Favour of a Neutral State as part of the Natural Advantages possessed by a Belligerent State, and upon the possession of which it must be calculated that the event of the War will, among other things, depend. The opposite Doctrine,—upon which the existing Duties of Neutrality rest, and which undoubtedly will, for some time at least, continue to hold its ground,—proceeds upon the Principle of excluding, as far as possible, from the elements of success in War, the operation of Chance. It is held that the essence of War is that it implies a real Struggle between two States, in which all the energy, the endurance, the wealth, the self-sacrifice, the Political sagacity, the Material resources of one State are, through a brief concentrated effort, put into competition with those of another. Though some of these elements of success may be called Accidental,—in the sense that they are not due to the qualities, good or bad, of the Citizens,—they are, nevertheless, part of the very structure of the State itself, and so are properly relevant to the final decision of the issue. On the other hand, the friendly services of States not publicly engaging in the War are Accidental in the sense of being wholly adventitious, incalculable, and such as can,— whichever way the War is decided,—only obstruct the process of drawing any conclusion as to the relative Strength and Moral Fortitude of the Belligerent States. True it is that a lax enforcement of the Duties of Neutrality is almost as injurious to the interests of Permanent Peace as an abrogation of the Duties of Neutrality altogether. The question, then, is presented as to what are the possible Modes in which, under the existing circumstances of the Commercial and Political World, these Duties can be made more generally binding.

The first step must be directed towards impressing, at every opportunity, and especially on the occasion of Making and Renewing Treaties, the Duties of Neutrality upon the attention of the Governments of all States. The next step must be matter partly of the Political and Moral Education of the People in the different States, and partly of specific Internal Legislation in those States. In the way of Internal Legislation, the "Foreign Enlistment Acts" in England and in the United States, and the successive and important Amendments to them are measures of the greatest importance. The only anomaly they present is that, even in their most improved form, attention is almost exclusively restricted to the Enlisting of Soldiers for Service in a Belligerent State, and to the Building and Equipping of Ships suspected of being intended for the use of such a State. In reference to a variety of other large classes of Acts likely to be done by Private Citizens in defiance of the Neutral Duties of the State, no Legislation has yet been attempted, though a growing feeling of dissatisfaction has arisen of late at the recklessness with which Private Citizens in Neutral States have enriched themselves through the sudden Demand created for implements of War by one and another Belligerent State. It is no doubt difficult to draw the line for purposes of Legislation as to what kind of Commerce shall and what shall not be allowed, and it is also still more difficult to execute effectually a Protective Law wholly alien to the rest of the Legal System. War is, however, in itself so enormous an evil that it might well be expected that all humane and patriotic Citizens would co-operate to promote the Observance of any Rules of Law, however anomalous and exceptional, which seemed really to promise the restriction of the Effects, the shortening of the Duration, and the reduction of the Frequency of Wars.

It was said above that the Restrictions imposed by an increasing conscientiousness and by a more and more enlightened sense of general expediency among the nations of Europe upon the extreme exercise of the Physical powers actually in the hands of a Belligerent State, and the corresponding Claims to such a remission or indulgence recognised as belonging to the other Belligerent, could only by a very metaphorical extension of the terms be styled "Duties" and "Rights." Nevertheless the gradual introduction of these Restrictions has marked the main Historical stages in the Development of International Law and, indeed, has been one of the most directly stimulating Causes of that Development in its existing form. The treatment of Prisoners of War,—which at one time knew no mitigation but such as might be due to the accidental tenderness of the Capturer,—gradually progressed to the general Practice of only retaining the Prisoner till he was Ransomed; then to the imposition of Limits upon the exaction of exorbitant Ransoms; and, finally, to the Modern Practice of simply guarding the Prisoners with every show of consideration and even of confidence till an Exchange of Prisoners is possible, or till the end of the War. The general Principles on this head have advanced as far as the severest claims of Humanity could demand, and as far, indeed, as is compatible with the resort to War at all. This statement does not, of course, imply that the Practice is invariably consistent with the Principle.

There are two main Questions presented by this part of the Law, to which the circumstances of Modern Life and the exigencies of Modern Warfare at this time give peculiar importance. There are at present two influences or tendencies struggling with each other in the States of Europe, and they meet face to face in the Problems of International Law which are here alluded to. On the one hand, the whole Industrial and Commercial Life of the People in Modern States exhibits a Division of Labour, a distinct separation in life-long pursuits, or habits of solitary devotion to confined channels of work and to restricted occupations, which, considering the breadth of their operation, is wholly without a parallel in the Past. The tendency of this Class of Facts is to produce an indelible Line of Demarcation between the Professional Soldier and the ordinary Citizen. On the other hand, owing to the perfection to which improved Physical Science has pushed the manufacture of Projectiles and of Artillery generally, and to the extraordinary powers of concentrated action which the Modern facilities of Communication and of Locomotion have brought about, the Profession of a Soldier has been occupying a far larger share of the Public Mind than heretofore, while the demand for unprecedently large Armies has, in default of resorting to the most tyrannical form of Conscription, rendered inevitable a call for the co-operation of the whole Population, or at least of certain parts of it,—chosen by a variety of methods,— not otherwise disposed personally to engage in Warlike occupations.

These contesting tendencies towards a sharp separation of the Military Class and of Military Pursuits from all other Classes and Pursuits on the one hand, and towards a vaster amount of Popular co-operation, voluntary or forced, on the other hand, give rise to certain characteristic Problems in Modern Warfare which, though they are not new in their kind, yet,—in consequence of the extreme intricacy and multiplicity of prevalent Industrial, Commercial, and Social Relations in times of Peace, and of the enormous scale on which, in view of the Wealth and Mechanical Resources of Modern States, War must be carried on,—are far more difficult even of a Theoretical solution than at any previous period.

The ordinary Doctrine of International Law, as stated

in its broadest and simplest form, has for a long time past been that, on the occurrence of a War, every Citizen of one Belligerent State is technically at War with every Citizen of the other Belligerent State. Yet, in order to mitigate the rigours of War, (without interfering with the Trial of the true Issue as properly to be determined by the relative Strength and Fortitude of the two States,) the extension of Warlike operations ought, it is insisted, to be restricted as much as possible, both in respect of the Persons who may be called upon to take an active part in it, and in respect of those who,—from their accidental proximity to the scene of operations, from Residence in the Enemy's country, from habitation of Territory temporarily occupied or merely passed over by the Enemy's troops,—may become, in a peculiar degree, Sufferers from its consequences.

As to the Persons who may be called upon to take part in a War,—though the general Doctrine is firmly established that a sharp Line must be drawn in each Belligerent State between (so-called) Combatants and Non-Combatants, and that each of these Classes of Persons are severally subject to a different body of Rules, by which their Privileges or Exemptions and their Duties are regulated,—yet, under the circumstances above alluded to as characteristic of the recent Methods of Modern Warfare, the drawing of this Line is becoming increasingly difficult or even impossible. The different expedients for raising Armies to which Modern States seem almost compelled to resort have an influence, both direct and indirect, in complete opposition to what was once a course which presented no greater obstacle than might be implied in the indistinct colour of a National Uniform. These expedients take various shapes, but the bearing of all of them is to render a very large majority of the Male population during some years of life, however few, actually component elements of the National Army, and during other years of life constantly available for express Service in the event of a War breaking out, or even liable to stated Services in times of Peace at short and regularly recurring periods. There are very few States, indeed, with any considerable Military Force, which have not already resorted to certain of these expedients, though they obviously admit of the greatest diversity in points of detail and have, accordingly, very various operations on the Public Liberty of the Citizens in the several States.

The effect of this growing Policy on the Doctrines of International Law now under consideration is that, whereas before it might confidently be assumed that every Citizen either was a Soldier or was not, now only a small fraction of the whole body of Citizens belongs to a strictly Professional Class of Soldiers, while the remainder are nearly all Soldiers in a certain sense and to some intents and purposes. Thus the question of practically applying the old and, undoubtedly, beneficial Rules applicable to "Combatants" and "Non-Combatants" respectively becomes one of ever increasing perplexity.

The Question is further involved by another Practice, which has recently been making way, in the very teeth of long-established Doctrines of International Law. The Practice alluded to is that of giving a wide and informal sort of Commission to all Persons, who choose to apply for it, to rise in Arms against an Invader, at the same time claiming for all such Persons the humane amenities

invented solely for the advantage of regular Combatants, with a view to Restricting the Consequences of War. In the case of an Invasion, even when that Invasion is of a strictly Defensive character, it seems almost a spontaneous instinct, and is at least a transgression inviting the utmost indulgence, to resist the progress of the Enemy with the use of any materials that happen to come first to hand. Nevertheless, the Logical consequences of spreading the area of the War must be looked steadily in the face. If for Strategic or Political purposes the Enemy determines to make his way to the Interior, the desultory Resistance of the undisciplined Population is likely only to irritate and delay him, without proportionally affecting the fortunes of the War; while the immunity still needed for all that part of the Population which in no case can, by reason of Age or Physical Infirmity, take part in the War, can no longer be made matter of irresistible Claim. Dr. Arnold, in his "Lectures on Modern History" (p. 160), in an emphatic passage quoted in a valuable paper by Mr. Droop,—to some of whose suggestions reference will shortly have to be made,—gives a stern and much needed lesson on the present topic. He says:—" It is the bounden
" duty of every Government, not only not to encourage
" such irregular warfare on the part of the population, but
" carefully to repress it, and to oppose its Enemy only with
" regular troops, or with men regularly organised and
" acting under authorised officers, who shall observe the
" ordinary humanities of civilised War. And what are
" called patriotic insurrections, or irregular risings of the
" whole population to annoy an invading army, by all
" means ought to be impartially condemned, by whom-

" soever and against whomsoever practised, as a resource
" of small and doubtful efficacy, but full of certain atrocity
" and a most terrible aggravation of the evils of War."

Short, however, of what may be described as a "general rising of the population" *guerilla* bands are occasionally organised for a sudden emergency with the view, generally, of harassing an Invading Enemy, but without any design of using their co-operation in the systematic conduct of the War. The question is presented as to whether such Troops, exempted as they partially will be from the Duties of true "Combatants" on their own side, ought to enjoy the Privileges and Immunities of Combatants on the other side. All that can be said broadly is that the Privileges ought to be proportionate to the Recognition of the Duties, or rather to the clear Evidence afforded of such Recognition. The Public Recognition that such imperfectly organised bodies of troops are held responsible to their own State for conforming to the general usages of modern Warfare must be sought for in some such way as in the wearing of an Uniform, in the presence of an authorised Officer of the Army of their own State, or in a formal Commission. The following practical Rules for this purpose have been suggested by Mr. Droop, after a lucid review and criticism of the various modern Authorities on the subject, in an important paper contributed to the Juridical Society during the progress of the late War between Prussia and France.

"The conditions which Combatants may reasonably
" be required to satisfy, in order to be entitled to the
" same treatment as regular soldiers, may be briefly
" summed up thus:—

"1. They must have an authorisation from an established Government, or from some *de facto* substitute for such a Government.

"2. They must be under the actual control of Officers who are recognised by, and responsible to, the chief military Authorities of the State.

"3. They must themselves observe the Laws of War.

"4. All Combatants intended to act singly or in small parties must have a permanent distinctive uniform, but this is not indispensable for troops acting together in large bodies.

"5. Levies *en masse* of the whole population are legitimate Combatants, provided they comply with the above conditions, but not otherwise."

The full discussion of this concrete Topic of Modern International Law of course belongs rather to systematic Treatises on that subject than to a Treatise on the Science of Jurisprudence. A general description, however, of the nature and results of this Controversy affords the best possible medium for pointing out the precise character of the Rules which form one main department of International Law and for indicating the Principles which underlie their Creation and Administration.

The treatment of Persons who in no sense whatever can be ranked as "Combatants," but who, from accidental Proximity to the scenes of Warlike operations, or from Residence in the Enemy's Territory, or from intermixture otherwise with the Population or Soldiers of the Enemy, are likely to endure in a peculiar degree the inconveniences of Warfare without thereby affecting the destiny of the War, is also becoming, through the special circumstances of Modern States before adverted to, a matter peculiarly inviting the interference of International Law. Many Doctrines on this subject, especially those relating to Merchants Residing in the Enemy's country, or having Goods or Debts, Private or Public, due to them in that country, have long been established with a tolerably general and steady acquiescence. The main points to which recent attention has converged, and an interest of unprecedented amount (due to the advanced Material Civilisation of Modern States) has attached, concern the treatment of the Population of an Enemy's Territory by an Invading Army. This Territory may be temporarily Occupied in such a way that the National Government has lost, during the period of Occupation by the Enemy, all power of enforcing its Laws in that part of its Territory. The Enemy is then the *de facto* Government. Or else the Territory may only be travelled over in the progress of a March, or may be momentarily occupied for some transitory purpose, as for repose of the Troops, or for conducting some hasty Military operation. In the first of these cases, inasmuch as, by the assumption, the Enemy is physically the Master of the field, it is on every ground in the highest degree inexpedient for the Population to continue, on their part, Warlike proceedings, or to engage in desultory Enterprises. It argues no disloyalty in them to their own National Government to recognise fully the existing claims of the Enemy to real Obedience, and even to perfect Good Faith in rendering it. Rather should it be the Policy of the National Government to encourage the Population of the Occupied District honestly to obey the substituted Authority which, for a brief interval, succeeds to the position of the National Government. On such an understanding, and on it alone, it becomes possible (as it becomes Morally imperative) for the Enemy to perform towards the Population the Duties of a provident, intelligent, and humane Government, and so to save it from the miseries of Anarchy on the one hand, and from the licence of a Military Despotism on the other.

The notion of Occupation of the Territory of its Enemy by an Invading Army includes, as has been already seen, both that of a settled Possession for an indefinite though not very short period of Time, and that of a transitory contact merely incidental to the prosecution of more important and ulterior proceedings elsewhere. It is not always easy to draw the line between these different species of Occupation, and it is only of importance to do so because different Practical Questions are presented according as a given Occupation by an Invading Army rather approaches the more settled or more transitory species. In the one case, as has been noticed, the Invaders may have cast upon them the Responsibility of providing a Government for the People, and the obvious consequences of undertaking this task are that the Invaders succeed to all the legitimate Powers previously held and exercised by the National Executive Authority for the purpose of collecting a Revenue, and for carrying out the Administration of Law. The Invaders will also naturally hold themselves entitled to fix the Amount and Mode of Collection of the Revenue, and to make such temporary Changes in the existing Laws as are needed to enforce their own Authority and to provide for the peculiar exigencies of their own situation.

As the Occupation in question approaches to the more transitory species, a new class of Questions comes into consideration, especially in respect of claims to "Preemption" or to make "Requisitions" for the support of the Army from the Inhabitants of the District It is obvious that Claims of this class may involve in their practical enforcement the grossest Military Tyranny and the most unequally distributed Suffering. On the other hand, if Invasion is to be tolerated at all as a necessary incident of War, it would seem hardly possible to banish altogether one of the Conditions without which it could not, in the multitude of cases, be attempted, or at any rate persisted in. All then that can at present be hoped for, is to reduce to Rules as humanely constructed as possible the exercise of the Claim to "Requisitions." It has been well remarked that an Invading Army must at least have the same advantages as to Billeting Troops and to making Requisitions as are possessed by the Armies of the State whose Territory is invaded; else, if there be a want of exact balance between the advantages enjoyed on either side, the sympathies of the Population will always be in danger of being directed, in the long run, in favour of the side from which they suffer least. The system of regular Payment for Supplies afforded to an Army, which is gradually becoming universally adopted (in theory, if not in practice), has many arguments to recommend it, even in the eyes of those who would, on many accounts, be the most reluctant to adopt it. In the first place, it turns to account the prudence and self-interest of the Inhabitants, and tends to render them subservient to the welfare of the Occupying Army (whether Invading or Defending), instead of directly antagonistic to it. In the second place, it tends to secure a regular Supply of Commodities at every point of the route, each District co-operating with the rest, while none are exhausted and none are exempted from Contribution. In the third place, payment, if fair and honest, affords a Common Measure by which to secure an equally humane and considerate treatment of the Inhabitants by the Armies of both the Belligerent Governments, so that the incidental disadvantages incurred by encountering a hostile or irritated Population, the existence of which disadvantages can generally have little effect on the real destiny of the War, are equally avoided by both.

The decided steps that Public Opinion among the States of Europe is now taking in the direction of mitigating the evils of War are exhibited in nothing more clearly than in the terms of the Geneva Convention of 1864, and of the Supplement to it in 1868, as well as in the practical influence these Authoritative expressions of Opinion have already had upon the Practice of War. Twenty-two States signed the original Convention, and among them are found all the important States of the World, with the exception of the United States, Brazil, and Mexico. The revised Convention has been generally acquiesced in, though not formally signed. By the Convention of 1864 the Neutrality of Ambulances and of Military Hospitals was established, and they were placed under the common Protection of both Belligerents. All Persons engaged in tending the Sick and coming to their aid were equally to be treated as Neutrals, and the general duty of tending and curing sick or wounded Soldiers was affirmed. A Flag and a distinctive Badge for those so employed were determined upon. By the Supplementary Convention of 1868 it was agreed that wounded Soldiers, on being healed, ought to be sent to their homes, on condition of not taking up arms again during the War, and the regulations of the previous Convention were extended to the consequences of Maritime Wars. By a Convention in the same year, 1868, at St. Petersburgh, the use of certain explosive balls, supposed to involve extraordinary cruelty, was forbidden. Other Topics, to which Modern International Law is addressing itself, are Restrictions upon the Claim to Bombard open Towns or Villages; to Bombard a Town in any case without previous Notice sufficient to enable all the Non-combatant part of the Population to withdraw; to Bombard a Town in any case further than is strictly necessary for Strategic purposes; and to seize Private Property as Prize of War on taking a Town after a successful Siege or Bombardment. The Consequences that the prevalent voice in favour of making Rules like these and like those of the Convention of Geneva is likely to have on the Conduct and on the Frequency of Wars form a most interesting subject of conjecture. Rules such as these must be dictated by nothing else than by a growing and Popular apprehension of the true meaning of War. The avenues to real Knowledge afforded by the Public Press, and by the attendant machinery for rapidly conveying War Intelligence which it has called into existence, and rendered one of the most noticeable Characteristics of Modern Warfare, cannot but divest War of much of its adventitious Majesty, and tend to exhibit it in all its naked Deformity. This Deformity is none the less to be put out of sight because some of the greatest Moral qualities are occasionally called into exercise in the actual prosecution of War. But even this opportunity of developing virtue is confined to only a limited Class of the innumerable Persons who are called to engage in the conflict.

For the rest a Modern French Novelist has described in sufficiently glaring, though not exaggerated, colours the monotonous, obscure, and almost invariable tale.

It may not be without its use to estimate the probable Effect which the humane influence that International Law has undoubtedly been long exercising, and is now affecting to exercise more than at any previous period, on the Conduct of Wars, is likely to have on their Frequency. It has been seen that the main directions in which International Law interferes, are: (1.) the giving definiteness and precision to the Limits, whether of Time, of Space, or of Personal Responsibility, within which an existing War operates; (2.) by conferring certain Rights on Neutral States, as against Belligerent States, of an increasingly beneficial character to the former, the purpose of which is to allow the usual Commercial relations and transactions of those States to be supported, as between one another, with as little interference as possible by the current War; (3.) by imposing certain Duties on Neutral States, in respect of the Belligerent States, of an increasingly stringent character, the purpose of which is to leave the Issue of the War to be decided, as far as possible, without reference to any other advantages than those inherent in the National Character, Wealth, Structure, and Native (as opposed to accidental) Opportunities of the States at War; (4.) by Restricting the Consequences of War to a portion of the Population of the two Belligerent States, though the process of distinguishing this portion is becoming constantly more arduous, and needs, at the present day, the introduction of some fresh Rules peculiarly adapted to Modern exigencies; and (5.) by imposing on Belligerent States certain arbitrary Limitations in the use of their actual powers, in order to reduce, as far as possible, the wide-spread Personal misery which War must inevitably cause.

That these gradual Modifications in the Practice of War, as carried on in wholly uncivilised countries, have been dictated by a sincere desire to benefit Mankind, and that their operation has largely conduced to that result, it would be irrational to doubt. Nevertheless, if these, or any of these, apparently benevolent Reforms have an effect, however imperceptible and insignificant it be, tending to facilitate Wars, the general advantage gained by them is not wholly unqualified. But even should this be found to be the case, it would be no argument for recurring to the barbaric Practices of a cruel Age. It would only suggest that possibly a distinction has to be made between the real and the apparent value of certain Mitigations, which in themselves seem the most attractive, in the immediate horrors of War, while it affords a warning that it is not sufficient to stop short at efforts, however commendable, to lessen those horrors and not to wrestle manfully with the Problem of the Abolition of War altogether. It is obvious, for instance, that the immediate tendency of some of the most favourite Modern Reforms in the Laws of War is to lessen the cogency of two of the main natural Checks upon the occurrence of War. These Checks are the sentiments and wishes of the States that are likely to be Neutral in the event of a War breaking out, and especially the sentiments and wishes of the Non-combatant part, that is, the overwhelming majority, of the Population of the States on the verge of becoming Belligerents. In the present day, indeed, when Communication of all kinds is so rapid, when Diplomacy is becoming an open and popular

Mode of frank Correspondence instead of a secret and treacherous Art, and, above all, when direct Popular influences are felt so powerfully by even the most concentrated Form of Political Authority, these last-mentioned Checks become almost omnipotent.

If, however, the newer Laws of War are mainly directed to reserving to Neutral States as many as possible of the Advantages they enjoy in times of Peace, and tend to make the Non-combatant part of the Population of a Belligerent State suffer as little as possible from the condition of War,—to that extent, in either case, the habit of indifference to the occurrence of War might seem to be encouraged.

The best answer to these arguments is to be found in the Fact that, in any case, it is only a very small portion of the Non-combatant Population which is directly affected by a current War, and that it is only a very minute class of interests in Neutral States that can be directly affected in a similar way. The tendency of the Rules in question is only to distribute the affliction caused by War equally over the whole Population of each Belligerent State and of Neutral States, so as to exempt as much as possible those in Accidental Proximity to the scene of War from bearing an undue share in the burdens of the War. It may be said also that other Rules, of Modern growth, imposing very strict Duties on Neutrals with respect to furnishing Assistance to either Belligerent, are sufficiently oppressive to Neutrals to turn all their sympathies steadily in favour of Peace. It is further to be added that the intensely strained System of Commercial Credit in Modern Times, on the stability of which nearly all States,—and nearly all Persons in every

State,—have the most vital interest, is in itself quite commanding enough to put out of favour any Practice like that of War, the direct effect of which is to introduce all kinds of Disorder of the most incalculable sort into the operation of the rules of Supply and Demand, and to substitute the sort of reckless selfishness, to which the immediate necessities of Self-preservation are apt to give rise, for the equable and steady current of Honour and Good Faith.

It can scarcely be seriously maintained,—though it has been suggested,—that Care for the Wounded, or the Discouragement of the use of Cruel Implements of War can, by reducing its horrors, tend to promote its Frequency. It may, however, be a matter of question how far the general use, in Modern times, of a highly perfected and widely destructive kind of Artillery leads, by lessening the Duration of Wars and by precipitating the Issue of them, to that consequence. Through the progress of Mechanical and Chemical Inventions, and through the application of Steam Power to Maritime Warfare, a small and temporary advantage in some purely artificial detail may enable one State to take another by surprise in such a way as to paralyse it, up to the point of forcing on its acceptance the most disastrous Terms of Peace. It is then obvious that the degree of excessive Refinement to which the Engines of War are now capable of being brought renders the entrance upon a War with inordinate chances of success a matter of precise calculation, to an extent it never was before. This points to two Conclusions, each of which is unfavourable to the general persistence in War as a Mode of settling International Disputes. One Conclusion is that if the event can be calculated beforehand by the one State, it may be also by the other, and the practical Trial of the Issue thereupon becomes a superfluous and merely ruinous Enterprise. Another Conclusion is that, for all purposes of really testing the relative Moral Weight or even the Physical Powers and Srength of two States, War is more and more decidedly disclosing itself to be an Impotent Method. It was seen in the early part of this chapter that the relative Magnitude and Influence of different States must for a long time to come undergo considerable Changes. The familiar and only too seductive Method for a State to assert its growing preponderancy, in the course of these Changes, is to enter upon a War with its nearest Rival. So soon, however, as it becomes widely recognised that temporary success in a single War depends no longer on the possession of any Morally or Politically significant qualities, but solely on the number of Persons withdrawn from Productive Employments, on the accident of a Mechanical Invention, or on the skilful selection of a fortuitously favourable Opportunity, it cannot be but that a Sentiment unfavourable to War will become universal. There are other phases peculiar to Modern International Law which will co-operate forcibly in the propagation and support of this Sentiment. Such are (1.) more stringent requirements in the matter of Treaty Obligations, coupled with increased wariness in making Treaties and with the habit of communicating a share of the Responsibility they entail to all Persons in the Community; and (2.) greater power of general Pacific Combinations for the purpose of decisively Punishing, by abstinence from all Intercourse with, any Recalcitrant State which forfeits its claim on the Advantages of Society by being treacherous to the Duties which the continued enjoyment of those Advantages implies.

It is not, then, in any Empirical Machinery,—to be constructed no one can say how,—nor in any formal though inefficacious Rules of International Law that the prospects of an " Eternal Peace " are to be sought. They are to be sought in the Concurrence of a Multitude of Conditions, the presence of which is becoming more and more obvious, some of them Moral and spontaneous, others Physical and inevitable. To the latter belong the necessary and sole Modes in which Modern War can be carried on in view of the development of Physical Science and of the copious resources stored up in recent and in forthcoming Mechanical Inventions. To the former Class of Conditions belong (1.) an assured and widely prevalent Belief that the Issues of Wars tend less and less to decide the question of the relative Moral or even Physical preponderance of either of two States; (2.) the construction of a new class of Treaties between States whilst they are free from all pressure from one another or from outside, and whilst contemplating a joint Policy of Mutual Defence or the Recognition among themselves of Rules based on a higher standard of Morality than that as yet otherwise adopted in International Law; (3.) an increased Communication of Responsibility, in all matters of Foreign Policy, to the whole Population of every State, under such wise Restrictions as the inherent incapacities of loose Popular Bodies prescribe; (4.) a general and determined Resolution among all States to hold the Breaking of a Single Clause in a Treaty by any State as a Crime deserving instant and condign Punishment at the hands, not of the immediate Sufferers alone, but of all.

CHAPTER XVII.

GENERAL PROSPECTS OF THE SCIENCE OF JURISPRUDENCE.

There are in the present condition of the European States, and especially in that of England, a multitude of circumstances which combine to make the Study of the Science of Jurisprudence, as that Science has been Systematically examined in the previous chapters, not only a matter of the keenest Interest but little less than an indispensable Necessity.

It is notorious that within the last half century, and not least within the last decade of that period, a Change has been gradually manifesting itself in the Conceptions of Moral and Political Right and Duty as prevalent in the Populations of the several States. It is not the place here either, from an Historical point of view, to investigate the Causes of these phenomena, or, from a Political point of view, to estimate their future Political bearings for good or evil. It is, however, essential for the present purpose to notice and describe the operation of these general Causes on the progress of purely Juridical ideas and on the Formal Structure of Legal Systems.

The Changes here indicated may be briefly characterised as appearing under three widely-spread Forms. The first of these Forms is (1.) an entirely novel attitude of the Supreme Political Authority in respect of the Persons who are the Subjects of that Authority. The second of them is (2.) in some respects the correlative of the former, though having a far wider scope. It is implied in the growing notion of the value and indestructibility of the purely Moral Claims, or so-called Rights, of every Individual Person in the Community, Man or Woman. Corresponding with these Claims there is also becoming more widely and more fixedly entertained a sense of the particular Vocation of every Individual Man and Woman to share in the Duty of contributing actively to the support of the general Life of the Community and of training all their Faculties to the point essential to enable them adequately to perform this continuous work. Side by side with this advancing Sentiment of individual Right and Duty an indefatigable spirit of Association, in every possible shape and for an almost endless variety of objects, is an unmistakable mark of the present era. The power that is latent in this spirit, or almost instinct, of Association is, of course, indefinitely magnified by the numerous Mechanical appliances which, in Modern times, so signally facilitate Locomotion and the rapid intercommunication of Thought.

The third Form (3.) in which the Change which is passing over European Society manifests itself is closely related to the other two and yet is distinctly separable from them. It is implied in the rapid development of notions of Ownership, especially in respect to Land, which are wholly alien from all the deeply-rooted Conceptions to which both the influences of Feudalism and of Roman Law had given birth and continued vitality.

Now looking at all the above Classes of Facts as mere typical Signs of a vast Political Movement, exhibiting itself differently in each country and at different epochs according to the existing preparation for it, it must be anticipated that in no long time the ancient Legal System of every State in Europe will undergo profound Modifications and that these Modifications will all be in one and the same direction. In the actual Progress of these contemplated Changes it is probable that strong Revolutionary passions and reactionary Prejudices partaking of every shade of Ignorance and Selfishness will constantly meet face to face and strive for the mastery. In every State there are materials in the existing heterogeneously-compounded Legal System for any dominant Political Party to rally round. There will be endless and constantly recurring danger in clinging timidly to the mere Language of Laws, however familiar that Language, and to the Formal Institutions of Law, however venerable and majestic. On every side the Cry, indistinct though it be and drowned in other voices, will be for a Reality and Truth such as nothing but the treasury of a permanent and universal Science can impart. The Science of Ethics, laying its foundations in a deep introspection of the Constitution of Man and of Human Society, will have to do its part. But the Science of Jurisprudence, if not more precious than its indispensable colleague, will be even still more obviously and directly in request. In the course of unsettling long-familiar Institutions,—especially when such unsettlement is accompanied by tempestuous storms and depends on the co-operation of a vast number of Persons imperfectly educated and unaccustomed to self-restraint,—large Terms and vague Principles are apt to be bandied to and fro as missiles all the more hostile because their purport seems to put criticism at defiance. The use that was made at important Political Crises in the Past of such phrases as "the Divine Right of Kings," the "Consent of the People," the "Social Contract," and the "Rights of Man," is now clearly understood and appreciated by every sagacious Historical enquirer. There are still sounding on every side phrases which are equally ominous and generally, in the mouths of those who use them, equally destitute of precise meaning. Such are "Constitutional," "Rights of Nationalities," "Labour Representation," Women's Rights," "Establishment" and "Disestablishment," "Rights of Property," and "Communism." Some of these Cries proceed from nothing better than an impotent clamour after some unattainable good of which those who utter them have little distinct Conception. Others of them proceed from a helpless clinging to the Past or from an over-buoyant hope in an invisible Future. Others, again, have the profoundest significance, and no doubt prophetically announce the advent of a Social reconstruction which shall render the Moral Freedom of each Person in the Community compatible, to an extent which has scarcely yet been guessed at, with the Moral Freedom of all.

Inasmuch as all these voices, good or bad, are immediately directed either against the existing Structure of a Nation's Legal System, or some part of it, or against the Mode in which that System, or that part of it, is Administered, it must be at once the most momentous and the noblest Function of the Jurist to interpret *ex cathedrâ* the true meaning of the voice as resident in the actual Language it employs. Whatever his own Political sympathies or antipathies, (and they need not be less warm than those of other men,—and they are likely enough to be more so,—) he has lessons to teach to which all the conflicting Parties will only too thankfully lend an ear. He has first of all to describe strictly and accurately what is the real Nature and Operation of the Laws which are called in question. He has to rescue real Facts from the glowing drapery thrown around them by Popular enthusiasm. If a Monarchical or an Aristocratic phase of Government be resented, it is for him to distinguish between what is essential to all Forms of Government and what is peculiar to the one in question. He has to guard one Political dissentient against a Fanaticism which is blindly rushing upon Anarchy; and he also has to warn another to beware of the spurious Defences of existing Institutions, on grounds which are only accidental to them in their present form, and are equally valid in favour of any Institution whatever of the class under consideration. So, again, if Laws in support of a so-called " Established Church " are denounced, it belongs to the Jurist to point out and enumerate the actual Laws objected to, and possibly to determine the character of the Laws which would be required for their effectual repeal. He would have to show that the term "Establishment,"—as applied to the State Patronage of a special Religious Faith,—has not one meaning but many, and that these meanings vary in different Countries and at different Epochs. Always and everywhere the State Patronage of a Religious Faith will have reference; (1.) to favouring the Profession of the Faith in question by giving certain Civil Advantages or Immunities to the Professors of it; (2.) to instituting, regulating, or favouring a Hierarchy of Ministers whose province it is to recommend the Profession of the Faith, and to conduct the Forms of Public Worship which it contemplates; and (3.) to Protecting the integrity of the Forms of Worship by enforcing their Public and general Use and discouraging the Use of other and rival Forms.

The Patronage of a special Religious Faith implies almost of necessity the presence of certain Laws directed to these several ends. The Jurist will ascertain in what quarter of the Legal System the Laws are to be found. He will perhaps find some of them prescribing the conditions for Membership of the Supreme Political Authority, that is, he will find some of them among the " Laws relating to the Constitution and Administration of the State." He will find others among the special Laws for the regulation of certain Public Corporations; that is, under the head of " Laws Affecting Special Classes of Persons." He will find others having in view the Institution and Maintenance of Ecclesiastical Courts, under the head of "Laws of Procedure." He will find others, again, among "Laws of Ownership;" and others, lastly, among " Laws of Civil Injuries and Crimes."

Surely nothing can tend more decisively to induce a pause, even in the most reasonable haste, than an exhaustive view of all the real difficulties attending a Revolutionary Change. If the Change be valuable, it is not the sight of such difficulties which will daunt its most worthy advocates. Rather will a large-minded and courageous insight into the true nature of those difficulties brace up his energies for the conflict, and enable him to set at defiance the unreal and phantasmagoric difficulties disingenuously placed in his path by his antagonist.

Amidst the existing inequality of Social conditions in respect of Wealth, and the appalling growth of a Pauper-Class in all Modern States, it is not surprising that prevalent Laws of Ownership, especially of Ownership of Land, should have to bear the brunt of every wide-spread Popular Movement. It is for the Political Economist to explain some of the general Causes which have given rise to the Laws of Ownership which most savour of fostering an Inequality of Conditions. It is for the Moral Philosopher to discuss the Moral importance of these Inequalities, and possibly to suggest grounds of consolation (if any) to those who personally suffer from them. But it is the appropriate Function of the Jurist to ascertain and describe what the actual Laws objected to are in truth, and what is the real Range of their Operation. He will be called to distinguish between what is essential to every Right of Ownership as such, and what is the peculiar Characteristic, either in their Nature or their Extent, of the Rights objected to. He may have to point out that the most liberal Theory of Community of Goods that ever was devised implied the Existence of certain Rights of Ownership. Otherwise the Society in which the Practice of the Theory prevailed could have no secure Possession of the Things necessary for their support, as against the violent and selfish Trespassers from without upon its Security; and within the limits of the Society, but for the existence of such Rights, implied if not expressed, the weakest member must be from moment to moment at the mercy of the strongest. In this way, the Jurist teaches, it may be the Quality, but can never be the Fact, of Laws of Ownership against which opposition must be directed. It is equally easy to construct a System of Law which shall favour Individual Ownership, Family Ownership, Village Ownership, or Ownership on a still more broad and Socialistic basis. It is for the Politician ultimately to judge which Mode of Ownership he shall gradually introduce or constantly encourage. But, in search of new and different Laws of Ownership, to decry all Laws of Ownership in themselves is to introduce a barbaric reign of Selfishness and brute Force in the name, it may be, of a most attractive vision of Human Brotherhood.

In an early chapter of this Work it was noticed that the Prevalent Legal Relations of Men and Women to each other in European countries could not be treated as Necessary and Essential. It happens indeed that Laws affecting to regulate the mutual Relations of the Sexes to each other have been, in all countries, more completely determined by unreasoning Instincts, and even by savage Usages, than any other Laws whatever. Owing, also, to the marvellous Tenacity and Complication of Sentiments which at once embarrass this matter, there are no Laws which are so difficult to change. Here, more than anywhere else, the Modes of Feeling of the whole Community have to undergo a decisive alteration before bare Logical reasoning on the subject can be so much as even tolerated. Criticism of the present Law can only avail if accompanied by an ever-widening and deepening Apprehension of the true condition of things which Law promotes and substantiates. In order to bring about a beneficial Change in the Law, a clear and popular Conception must be formed of what is wanted in the Future, together with a precise Recognition of the Limits of the Provinces of Law and Moral Authority to be observed in providing for that Future. The customary Form in which English writers have propounded the Problem involved in the present enquiry has been the following. It has been noticed that in all Countries and all Times (with the rarest exceptions) Woman has been treated, both Socially and Legally, as in nearly every respect Subordinate and Inferior to Man. Public Opinion, Domestic Manners, Political Institutions, and Positive Laws have unanimously stamped and riveted this Conception of the inequality, for nearly every purpose, of the two Sexes. It has been argued upon these Facts that (1.) this Historical Subordination of one Sex to the other was the result of nothing else than a gross and arbitrary Usurpation of Power on the part of the Physically Strong over the Physically Weak; that (2.) whatever actual Differences exist at this day between the Mental and even some of the Physical capacities of Men and Women, all such Differences may reasonably be attributed at least as much to the Fact of such Diversities of Social and Political Treatment as to Difference of Physical Structure, or to any other actual Differences of a less palpable kind; and that (3.) if hereafter Women be treated for the purposes of Law, of Political action, and of Social existence in the same way exactly as Men, the Differences between the Sexes will or may be finally reduced to the smallest appreciable amount.

Now, the Historical Facts assumed in the above reasoning are undoubtedly true, and the Cause found for those Facts in the tyrannical and selfish habits of Men is a "true cause" likewise. There lurks, however, a very serious and pernicious error in the implied, though not always expressed, propositions to the effect that Differences between the Sexes are in themselves an evil, and that the tendency of Equal and Uniform Legislation for the two Sexes is to eradicate those Differences rather than to deepen and to intensify them. It is here contended, on the other hand, that (1.) while the existing Inequality between the Sexes is a cruel and dangerous imposition dating from the most barbarous Times, nevertheless Difference between the Sexes, in the nature, function, and quality of Mind and Spirit, as well as of Bodily Structure, is an element in the constitution of Social Life so precious and excellent that, apart from the plenary Recognition of it, any high degree of Civilisation would be simply impossible. It is here insisted, again, (2.) that Legislation has hitherto erred by confusing the true character of the Differences separating the Sexes, and that only by the greatest attainable Uniformity of Legislation for both Sexes can the essential Differences between them manifest and express themselves in the most effectual and unmistakeable way.

Contrasting a very Primitive state of Society with a highly advanced one, the former is seen to be composed of elements atomic, mutually repulsive, hateful, and hating one another. The latter is pervaded by Facts and Notions implying every degree and kind of Reciprocity of Function, of Mutuality of Sentiment, and of Relationships indefinitely Multiplied in the most Variegated Forms.

These last Facts and Notions are not confined to the grosser fields of Economic Policy or merely Social Co-operation. The whole Life of the Nation, in its subtlest form, hangs in suspense upon them. A thousand kinds of sensibility are kept in assiduous action through nothing else than their prevalence. It is not only that under these Social conditions men and women do more work and do it more quickly and effectually, but that, in and through the very process of working, they learn to experience an indefinite number of mysterious emotions in respect of each other which, in their aggregate, constitute the Cor-

porate energy of the Nation. Politics, Law, Industrial
and Commercial interests, as well as Literature and the
conscious Communication of Thought in all forms, are
only the cloaks and instruments of this magnificent,
though constantly secluded, activity. This illimitable
range of reverberating Sentiments is the most characteristic product and last expression of Social Organisation at
its culminating point. The History of a progressive
Nation is the story of its efforts to reach this. So far as
it has failed to reach this, so far is it yet removed from
the last attainments of Civilisation.

Now it is not saying too much to allege that the main
lever by which a Nation is lifted out of its Primitive
savagery is Difference of Sex. This is the sole discipli-
nary Fact which, in addition to the ruder one implied in
the necessity of Dividing Labour, serves to teach a Primitive Race that Human Society is not a sum of competing
atoms, each servilely reproducing another, but that, rather
resembling a building, a vegetable product, or an animal
body, it is made up of reciprocally operative parts, no
one of which can be dispensed with in the interests of the
whole, and no one of which can dispense with any one
of the rest. In Primitive Marriage and the Birth of
Children, irregular and undisciplined as these Facts are at
the first, lessons are being ever noiselessly taken in,
through the hourly play of the simplest and tenderest
emotions, which become gradually crystallised into National Sentiments, and which nothing short of the most
obnoxious Laws and Institutions can succeed in crushing
out.

It is quite true that in their ignorance Legislators, reflect-
ing too often the worst and not the best Conceptions of

their day, have done what in them lay to confound the true Differences of Sex. These Differences are far too deep and subtle to admit of the application of coarse methods of Legal description and forcing. Every Law or Political Institution that has fixed and perpetuated any Differences between Men and Women, except by way of Recognising Marriage as the foundation of Family Life or by way of Protecting Physical Weakness, has retarded Civilisation. The Truth is, that the Fact of Opposition of Sex, so far from being an evil in itself, is the source, centre, and symbolic Image of all the other Oppositions from the Multiplication of which a Nation grows to maturity. The question of questions for a wise Politician is how to legislate so as to remove all the Physical barriers which impede the free play upon each other of all such Oppositions,—whether the Oppositions be due to contrarieties of Structure, Situation, Disposition, or Competitive interest. Above all, the most diligent care has to be taken that Laws do not help in crystallising the partial and pauperised Conceptions of a passing day. The Politician cannot too anxiously guard himself against the temptation of trying to do by violence what can alone be brought about by the healthy, though systematic, action of native Human forces. His work is to enable and to facilitate, not to hamper and to provoke. Excepting the case of Marriage and of the occasional need of special Protection due to real Physical Weakness, the sole roots of exceptional Legislation for Women have been either a belief in an absolute Inferiority of one Sex to the other, or else a series of impotent efforts to map out, by arbitrary prescription, the several regions of Men's and Women's occupations and interests. In either case the underlying assumptions have been false and disastrous.

In the first place, whatever apparent Inferiority attaches to Women either is only another name for the peculiarity of nervous structure which renders a Woman's true Strength less palpable to the coarse intelligence of the vulgar, or else may be properly attributed to the tyrannical and contemptuous Treatment to which, during the infancy of National Life, Women in all countries have been submitted.

In the second place, it is a hopeless and suicidal effort to attempt to prescribe by Legal Limitations of any kind, direct or indirect, the functions of the Sexes severally. This has sufficiently appeared from considerations of the following description. Those who believe most vehemently in the actual Opposition of the two Sexes to each other, and who look to the innumerable and indefinite Reactions of the two Sexes upon each other as the sole ground and possibility of Civilisation, are entitled to maintain that this Opposition and these Reactions must be allowed freely to exhibit themselves, throughout life, in the most minute and subdivided departments of Thought, of Feeling, and of Action. It is a desertion of this position to attempt rudely to distinguish between one class of matters and occupations as exclusively belonging to Men, and another as exclusively belonging to Women. Even did such a distinction really exist, any effort to express it in Law could only be directed by the coarse estimate of a particular set of Lawmakers, actuated by the Sentiments common in their own Age. The Law, being once made, creates a need for itself, and Men and Women gradually become unfitted for the tasks from which they are forcibly expelled.

The injurious effects of shutting out Women from large regions of interest have told quite as heavily upon Men as upon Women themselves. There are many pressing questions of Social Order and Progress which Men have become incompetent to gaze upon in their true colours, from the life-long habit of never discussing them in the presence of Women, nor hearing them discussed by Women. The result is that vicious Legislation, thus proceeding solely upon Men's view of the matter, goes far to perpetuate itself. Bad Laws are made; the Sexes are driven more and more asunder; and,—in the place of a high Social Unity being perfected through a Development of true Differences and Oppositions,—false or imaginary Differences are intensified, and there are opened up in the middle of the Body Politic startling gaps which nothing short of a wholesale sacrifice of the most cherished and antiquated superstitions about the several functions of Men and Women can ever close.

The above considerations, discursive or desultory as they may at first sight seem, are of essential value, not only to illustrate the deep and subtle relations to each other of the formal Structure and the Material contents of Legal Systems,—that is of Jurisprudence and of Legislation,—but to point out the true and almost empty place which, in the process of the Reconstruction of European Society, the Science of Jurisprudence is destined to occupy. Besides this more general work, the value and influence of which will be rather indirect and silent than obtrusive, there are in Europe generally,—and in some of its States particularly,—certain tasks in relation to Improvements in the Structure and Administration of Legal Systems in which the Jurist already is, or will shortly be, invited to take a prominent part.

Among these tasks is that called *Codification*, which may be described as " the Process of Republishing in an Authoritative and Systematised Form the whole existing Contents of a Legal System." The common notion of *Codification* generally also includes the filling up of accidentally vacant gaps, through fresh Legislation suggested by the Codifier.

It is well known that at the beginning of this century, on the retreat of Napoleon from the German States which he had occupied, the question was seriously debated by the most eminent Jurists of the most illustrious Modern Juridical School whether the Code introduced by Napoleon should or should not form the permanent Basis of a complete Reconstruction of the National System of Law. In discussing this question the Problem has generally been misstated, and the arguments alleged on either side of the controversy in Germany have been either perverted or misunderstood. In the first place, the Problem for Germany was, from every point of view, a Special one. The Political and Social circumstances were Special and have not had their parallel in any other country. The Situation and Structure of the whole Legal System,—consisting as it did, of the several elements of (1.) the Common German Law, created in a great measure out of the Roman and the Canon Law, (2.) the Provincial or Customary Law of the several States, and (3.) the already partially Codified Law (for some States),—were special, and inapplicable for purposes of affording an example elsewhere. In the second place, though the great leaders of the controversy, Savigny and Thibaut, were held to represent respectively the so called " Historical " and "Philosophical" Schools, these epithets must not be pressed so as to import too great a divergence between those eminent men. No doubt it was more consonant with the temper of Savigny to pay deference to irrefragable Historical Facts and to the even course of a self-directed Development. To Thibaut a mere Logical necessity would seem more peremptory in its claims than even the most fixed and inveterate Usages. But both these men were far too erudite to ignore Facts Past or Present, and both of them too patriotic to close their eyes to the glaring needs of their country.

As has been already said, the situation of Germany and the competition of various Systems of Law was, at the Time, peculiar, if not unparalleled. Nevertheless the arguments used by Savigny are, when thoroughly understood, identical with the most valid arguments against Codification in England in the present day. The arguments, in fact, are so strong that nothing but urgent Practical Convenience, with all its losses in point of Theory and of Principle, can suffice to controvert them.

It is true in England as it was in Germany,—and as it has been in all countries in which the System of Roman Law has either never, or has only at some very remote period, been arbitrarily imposed on the Population,—that the existing Legal System has evolved itself directly out of the whole Life, Spirit, Temper, Social Institutions, Language, Religion, and Manners of the whole People. The Character and Modes of this Evolution have impressed themselves not only on the bare Structure of the System, and on the more definite Rights and Duties which it creates, but on its minutest lineaments; on every part of its Administration; on the Logical Methods alone recognised as applicable to its Interpretation; and above all on the Normal Principle of its Growth.

It thus comes about that a thorough comprehension of such a System as the above in all its length, breadth, and infinite ramifications, presupposes a studious devotion of no ordinary kind and extended over a considerable portion of a lifetime. It is obvious that so subtle and multiform a System, breathing, as it does, the very atmosphere of Popular Life such as it is and has been, can only be inspired by long Personal contact with the System in its actual working, and must be misapprehended or entirely lost sight of through the use of any merely Formal description of it, in however skilful Language the description be attempted.

From this will be understood the Class of Objections to Codification,—enforced so strongly by Savigny and applicable to much of English Law in the present day,—founded on the sort of natural antipathy which may be held to exist between Law having its roots mainly in the Customary Usages of the People, and Law professing to represent an exact translation of those Usages into a Written Code. The objection, of course, was far stronger for Germany than it could be for England at this day. It was proposed in Germany to impose on the People an entirely alien Code, not so much as professing to represent, in its Structure or in its Materials, the Native Habits of the People. In England the suggestion simply is to embody the whole existing Law, to whatever Source it owes its existence, in a compendious Written Form, every effort being exerted to make the Language correspond with and reproduce the finest Modifications of the Unwritten Rules.

But another leading Objection to Codification, applicable in a higher degree than the last to the case both of

Germany and of England, is founded on the supposed inherent imperfections of Language as a vehicle for Law. It is held truly that every Law must be General in its character and ready to cover a multitude of Acts which, at the time of making the Law, cannot be specifically described. This is not only because the Modes of counteracting the Will of the Legislator cannot be distinctly foreseen; inasmuch as this is an incident of all Law whatsoever, however expressed,—according to the ancient adage, *Cur crescunt leges, crescit in orbe scelus.* The objection rather proceeds from a belief that the transactions of Mankind are so manifold and the Events so infinitely diversified that the meshes of Written Language are in all cases too large and coarse exactly and unfailingly to include them in the course of the Administration of the Law. It is held that Unwritten Law,—taking the form either of Traditional Principles of Interpretation handed down from one generation of Lawyers and Judges to another; or of silent and implicit Rules obediently followed in a long series of Judicial Decisions; or of multitudinous Popular Usages, recognised with greater or less regularity by Judges in the course of Declaring the Law,—has in the above respects certain inherent and incommunicable Advantages to which no Written Law or Written System of Law can ever pretend. For instance, Unwritten Law of the character just described, not being hemmed in by the somewhat imperious Restrictions of Formal Terms and Grammatical sentences, is said to have a pliability or an elasticity just sufficient to admit of its reaching the most minute Modification in an unforeseen state of Facts without involving any perilous amount of Vacillation and Uncertainty. In the use of this argument it is implied that a Rule of Law may be greater, wider, and deeper than any possible Expression of it; and that either it is capable of being passed on from one generation of Lawyers and Judges to another without any perceptible loss in its true import, or that, where not so capable, it only undergoes such infinitesimally small and delicately graduated Modifications in a beneficial direction as to make this a fresh point of favourable contrast between such an Unwritten Rule and any Written Rule, however skilfully elaborated.

On the other hand, it is alleged that even were the Advantages of Unwritten Law,—as opposed to Written Law,—generally less signal than on the above grounds they are believed to be, still there are to be found in a sole and excessive reliance on Written Law certain inherent Disadvantages which, however much they may be qualified, can never be entirely got rid of. In the first place, Written Law implies the absolute Exclusion of every other class of authoritative Evidence of the Law outside the Written Letter of the Law. This has two important Consequences. One is that no Judge, in interpreting a Rule of Law, can allow himself to be bound in any but the most indirect manner by the Principle of Interpretation adopted by his Predecessors or by his Contemporaries. From this cause is likely to flow, not only indefinite Vacillation in the Construction of Rules of Law, but a corresponding amount of dangerous Uncertainty in the mind of the Public and of Suitors as to the existence and quality of the Rules themselves. This practical inconvenience is said to be much experienced in France; though there are many influences, especially those due to the Works of the eminent Commentators on the Code, which tend to diminish its natural effect.

The other Consequence of this exclusive reliance on

the Written Text is the negative side of the Consequence already noted. If the Judge is not entitled, nor even allowed, to be guided by the Opinions of his Predecessors, by prevalent Modes of Legal Thought, or by a Traditional meaning impressed upon Technical Terms, a strain is put on the power of Verbal Expression which, even under the most favourable circumstances, it is too feeble to support. Language, at the best, is only a very imperfect Medium for the Communication of Thought; and though the Thoughts which ultimately take the Form of Laws are generally of the simplest kind and have reference to the commonest and least perplexed Relations of Mankind with one another, still the Records of every Court of Justice declare the Fact that there is scarcely any Topic productive of more interminable Logical Controversies than the Meaning and Applicability of Laws. It is thus felt that to attempt to comprise the whole bulk of a Legal System within the compass of Written Rules must either result in the introduction (for a vast class of Matters) of that sort of Anarchy which follows from the absence of all certain Rules whatever; or else must reintroduce, under the name of Judicial Interpretation, all the Irresponsibility, without the Regularity and Publicity, incident to the Modes of ascertaining the Law which it is the distinct object of the Code to exclude and suppress.

In the second place, it is alleged that even were a Code a satisfactory Compendium of the existing Law, and were it not open to objections on the score of Uncertainty and Vacillation in its Construction, nevertheless, from its very nature, it opposes a standing Barrier to the natural Development and Growth of Law. However minute and almost insensible the Modification is that is needed in order to meet a constantly recurring set of Facts which the Language of the Code can by no process of Interpretation be made to cover, there is no resource but either to abstain from giving any Judgment whatever, or to refer to the Supreme Political Authority (or to any Delegates they may choose to nominate for the purpose), for a Formal Reconstruction of the Code. The result is said to be that whereas true Law has a Normal and Spontaneous Principle of Growth peculiar to itself, and whereas it is constantly modified by the slowly-changing Necessities and the widening Moral Conceptions of the day, under the freezing influence of a Code it is stiffened and solidified into an unnatural consistency and can only undergo any change whatever by violent and artificial Processes.

The topic of Codification belongs so peculiarly to the province of the Jurist, and the Prospects of the Science of Jurisprudence are so closely bound up with the Method in which the task of Codification is proceeded with, if at all, in this and in other countries, that it has been thought worth while to place in the strongest possible light,— even at the risk of exaggerating,—every one of the arguments that have been employed, in England or elsewhere, by the ablest opponents of Codification. The plausible reasons in favour of Codification, such as those based upon the advantage of discountenancing "Judge-made" Law, of giving Publicity to the Law, and of rendering the Systematic Study of it easy to everybody, are so numerous, and indeed so intelligible to the most superficial thinker, that hardly any English Jurist, himself in favour of Codification, has had the patience or the honesty to make himself complete master of the views of his opponents. The ordinary habit has rather been first to misstate their arguments and then to denounce them on the ground of their being misty or "metaphysical."

The truth is that the above arguments against Codification generally are, in themselves, unanswerable. The question, however, presented in dealing with the special Problem involved in the proposed Codification of the Laws of any given State is not whether any serious Loss is incurred by Codification, but whether the general Gain is likely to outweigh the Loss. This points to the Fact that all abstract arguments on the value of Codification, though interesting from many points of view, are, for practical purposes, entirely beside the mark. On the confession of all, the main Purposes of a Code are to impart to the National System of Law a Greater Accessibility, Definiteness, Formal Organisation, and Compendious Brevity. The degree in which these several requisites are sought after, and are likely to be obtained, must depend on two distinct elements; the one, the actual state of the Existing System of Law which it is proposed to Codify; the other, the Social Habits and Condition of the Population.

As to the first of these elements,—the state of the Legal System,—it is possible that there may be found in the Community at once two or more compact Legal Systems, existing side by side with each other, as in Germany at one period the Roman or Common Law, the Canon Law, and the Provincial Law; or struggling with each other for the mastery, as the English Systems of Common Law and Equity in former days, and, to some extent, even now.

It is scarcely necessary to insist on the convenience and importance of Consolidating and reducing to the greatest attainable Unity such competing or co-existing Systems.

Many Methods have been suggested for performing this Process in England, whether by way of gradual transition to a complete Reconstruction of the whole body of National Law, or by way of effecting such a Reconstruction at once. Such Methods are allowing and requiring every Judge in every Court of Justice to recognise the Rules belonging to both Systems; to employ the Administrative machinery before appropriated to either Court to support Rights owing their origin to either the one Court or the other; and to afford to Suitors the most suitable and efficient Remedies which either of the Systems is capable of affording. This is the Method that has already been adopted by some of the States of North America which have inherited the bifurcated System of English Law. Certain steps have already been made in this direction in England, as is manifested in the concession of a large and increasing Equitable Jurisdiction to County Court Judges; in the permission of the use of so-called " Equitable Pleas " in the Procedure of Common Law Courts; in the extension to those Courts (though in a limited form) of the powerful engine for obtaining Evidence implied in the use of " Interrogatories," previously confined to Courts of Equity exclusively; and in bestowing on Courts of Equity the capacity, long restricted to the rival Courts, of examining Witnesses orally in Court and of trying Questions of Fact by the expedient of referring them to a Jury constituted on the Common Law model. Another Method for Solidifying into one, (to adopt one metaphor), or Fusing, (to adopt another and the more common one), the Systems of Law and Equity in England is to make a series of partial Statutory Changes deemed to be just sufficient to effect the desired purpose, and no more. Such Changes, for instance, would take the form, in some respects, of the "Statute of Uses" of the reign of Henry VIII. The new Statute would enact that, in certain cases where a Legal Right and an Equitable Right,—that is two co-existent Rights, recognised, one of them in one set of Courts, and the other in another set,—had reference to one and the same Thing or Subject-matter, thereupon, after the Statute was passed, one of the Rights should be entirely absorbed in the other and should, for all purposes, lose its independent existence; or (as would more frequently be the case) a series of novel Rights would be substituted, recognisable and enforcible in all Courts whatever. A specimen of the application of this Method may be afforded by an imaginary piece of Legislation containing the following, among other Enactments; (1.) that no Mortgage of Land, attempted to be created after the passing of the Act, have thenceforward the effect of imparting to the Mortgagee any other Rights (as, for example, those of simulated or inchoate Ownership) than are comprehended at the date of the Act in an Equitable Lien, coupled with a Conditional Power of Sale; (2.) that all Rights of Ownership, vested after the passing of the Act, by way of Trust, and for the sole benefit of Persons other than the Trustees, have thenceforward no effect whatever for the purpose of conveying to the Trustee any Right of the nature or name of a Right of Ownership; and that, in order to carry out the purposes of the Trust, certain Special Rights and Duties (based on the existing Law) be accorded to and imposed upon the Trustee as thereinafter more particularly described; (3.) that all Equitable Rights taking the form of Powers of Appointment be thenceforward treated as valid and available Rights in all Courts of Justice whatever, and that the Defective or Fraudulent Execution, or the Non-execution of the Power,—should the existence of the Right come into controversy,—be thenceforward matter of Investigation as much for one Court as for another; (4.) that all Rights of Partners against each other be equally recognised as valid in all Courts of Justice; (5.) that Rights, void through want of giving proper " Notice," or through " Constructive Fraud," or void on other grounds hitherto ascertained on Principles appropriated to Courts of Equity, thenceforward be held void in all Courts, entitled and required, for this purpose, to apply identical Principles in ascertaining their Validity; lastly (6.) that the several Doctrines upon which a Married Woman's " Separate Estate" rests be thenceforward equally recognised in all Courts whatever.

Such a Statute might, none the less, contain Provisions, or be accompanied by another Statute containing Provisions, for a Distribution among the various Courts of Justice of the different Classes of Matters to be severally investigated by each. In this way the existing Division of Labour, which is accidental rather than essential to the opposition of Common Law and Equity, might be retained. To one Class of Courts Questions tolerably simple in their Logical Elements, and in the nature of the Legal Rights involved, might be exclusively reserved. To another Class might be reserved Questions in which a vast number of delicately adjusted and mutually competing Rights come into consideration. Such are questions relating to the more important forms of Commercial Partnerships, to Joint-Stock Companies and Railway Companies in their Transactions with their Shareholders, to the Administration of Wills, to the Execution of Trusts, and to complicated and disputed Accounts. Under the proposed Legislation, though this distribution of Functions might be carried on somewhat in the same way in which it is at present, yet, of course, every Right recognised in one Court, and peculiarly enforcible there, would be recognised as equally valid, both in itself and with respect to all its incidents and consequences, in every other Court.

It has been thought important thus to exhibit with some approach to completeness the working out of the special Method of conciliating and uniting co-existent Legal Systems which is implied in partial Statutory Changes. In no better way could the inherent defects of the Method be made plain and the superior efficiency of the remaining Method,—that of Codification,—be lucidly illustrated.

It is obvious from the above sketch of the Form that any partial Statutory Change must take that its special weakness lies in the constant reference it is compelled to make to existing Legal Notions and Language, however confused, antiquated, or mutually hostile they may in fact be. On the hypothesis upon which this Method of Change rests no further alteration is to be made than is just sufficient to enable the two Systems to be practically worked as one.

The Method of effecting the Combination of two such Systems as those of English Common Law and Equity into one, which is implied in Codification, proceeds on the assumption that where so great and such an organic Revolution is attempted in the National Body of Laws, the opportunity ought to be taken not only to correct at the same time a number of other anomalies and abuses which have long waited the hand of the Reformer, but,—inasmuch as novel Legislation might impart to these abuses and anomalies a fresh vitality,—the Revolution, if not complete, may be only disastrous. The Method of Codification implies a clear description of what a Legal Right is, and of all the actual Rights recognised by Law, as well as of the appropriate Remedies by which they are severally Protected. The Basis of the Code will, of course, be determined by the existing state of the Law. But the Language, the Form, and the Classification, will depend on nothing else than Logical Accuracy and Public Convenience. In this way all that is contradictory, obsolete, or superfluous, vanishes of itself. All that is precious and living not only maintains its ground but comes forth in transparent relief, unencumbered by the unwieldy appanages which have little other purpose than to gratify the taste of the Antiquary or to form a convenient web for concealing the plots of the Legal Charlatan.

The next set of questions that have to be handled, on estimating the expediency of Codifying any given National body of Law, arise out of the existing Relations to each other of the Written and Unwritten Law. There is at present scarcely any country, even where Codification has made the most rapid strides, in which the complete Legal System does not consist of both these elements. In countries like England, where a compact body of so-called Common Law has gradually evolved itself into a singularly homogeneous and rounded System, side by side with which a steady course of continuous Legislation has ever been supplementing, correcting, and invigorating it, the bearing of these two streams of Law on one another is, of course, highly relevant to the decision of the question as to the need or value of Codification. . In some quarters it has been thought that all the advantages both of a consciously organised and of a spontaneously developed System are capable of being reaped from the reciprocal influences of Written and Unwritten Law. However abstractly true this view may seem, the Application of it in any given country must depend on the existing condition of the Authorities of one sort or another to which reference has to be made in order to ascertain for a given Case the state of the Law.

In England it is notorious that the existing condition of the Authorities to which reference has to be made in order to discover the true purport and extent of an Unwritten Rule makes the search in the highest degree laborious and precarious. The Form in which it is anticipated that a Rule sought for, or conjecturally believed to exist, will manifest itself is that which a number of consecutive or contemporaneous Judges must necessarily, it is apprehended, have had in their minds, in order to give the series of Decisions which it is proposed to scrutinise and to collate. This Rule has been called the *ratio decidendi*; and the value of the Method by which it is reached, and the certainty of the Rule itself, depend partly upon the Logical success with which a number of Cases, differing in their outward circumstances, have been compared together with a view to establishing the needful analogy by the Person in search of the Rule; and partly upon the discrimination of the several Judges, in the force of which it is presumed that no one of them would have decided as he did, in relation to the special state of the Facts before him, had the general Rule been different from what it is asserted to be.

Thus the probability of educing a Rule of Law applicable to a novel and possibly complex state of Facts depends not only on the skilful performance of a train of Logical operations, but also upon the combined existence of a number of Facts by no means easy, even under the most favourable circumstances, of Verification. Such Facts are the preservation of voluminous, accessible, and well-reported Decisions of Judges; the actual Litigation in Courts of Justice of a sufficient number of controverted Questions, to bring into clear view, by means of the Decisions upon them, the whole Body of the Law; a sufficient similarity in large Classes of the actually litigated Questions to afford a reasonable basis for argument as to the uniform Rule which underlies all the Decisions in these cases; and, lastly, actual consistency in the minds of all the Judges themselves, both in their Personal Persuasion as to the state of the Law and in their practical application of it.

In England there are said to be 1,300 volumes of Reports of Cases, any one of which may be cited in a Court of Justice in support of an argument as to the conjectural existence of a Rule of Law. There are said to be contained in these volumes 100,000 Cases. Among these, though there are undoubtedly a large number of tolerably uniform Decisions, especially on the more familiar branches of Law, there are also a very large number of other Cases upon which, it is true, authoritative Decisions have been given, but in which,—whether from the imperfection of the Report, or from the complexity of the circumstances, or from the infirmity of the Judges,—the true *ratio decidendi* admits of indefinite disputation. Again, there is a large class of Cases as to which the Law is confessedly unsettled, and is alleged, even by Judges themselves, to be in a condition of progressive Modification or Flux. The real inadequacy of the existing Authorities on Unwritten Law is sufficiently exhibited by these cursory statements. It cannot be said that the current Text-books or professional Treatises on different parts of the Law have hitherto tended much to illuminate or to supplement the original Authorities. With a very few exceptions, (some of them presented within the last few years), these Works have been nothing more than dreary and servile Compendiums, or rather Catalogues, of the original Cases on which alone the Writers have ventured to rely. Without a Definition, without a Dominant Conception either of a single part or,—it need scarcely be said,—of the whole of the National System of Law, the Writers have done what in them lay by their distracted and skeleton-like productions to paralyse the originality of the youthful Student and to dull the energies of the most unflinching Practitioner.

As to the Authorities on Written Law, that is the Statutes of the Realm, their existing condition,—as likely to promote the Unity, Precision, and harmonious Symmetry of the National System of Law,—needs little description or comment. Those that are least wise in their Materials, having been enacted during a thin attendance of Members of both Houses, and having so escaped the incisions consequent upon a sharp Debate, are almost the only ones that preserve any image of Logical Uniformity,—exactly commensurate as that often is with the unrelenting viciousness of their Aims. The truth is that large and Popular Bodies, just in proportion to their Political energy and to the rich variety of their component elements, are disqualified for the task of constructing

Formal Law. There is scarcely an important Statute affecting any of the most precious Rights of Personal Security or of Ownership that has not been hacked and hewed by the alternate victories of contending Factions till, beneath the weight of Repealing, Amending, Supplementing, Re-enacting, and Declaring Statutes, the real Policy and Meaning of the actual Law can scarcely, even with the utmost Judicial pains and sagacity, be disinterred.

It cannot be long before the Legislature of this country consents to relegate the mere Formal department of Legislation either to carefully chosen Committees of either House or to a standing Commission of Professional Lawyers and Jurists. Such a change, so far from importing any abnegation of truly Political Functions, would afford the greatest Security for their not being trenched upon unawares. On any proposition for a Change in the Law, it would be the duty of the supposed Board of Legal Referees to furnish a Report to the Legislature of the exact effect which the proposed Legislative Change would have, not only on the existing Legal System in its Technical aspects, but on the Rights and Duties of every Member of the Community likely to be directly affected thereby. On any Amendment, or series of Amendments, being adopted during the consideration of the Bill, it would again be the duty of the Board to incorporate it or them in the body of the Statute in such a way as to avoid conflicting Clauses and to ensure the preservation of harmony between the new Act and the rest of the Legal System.

This Change, though it looks large and portentous when described in detail, has been already anticipated in practice under circumstances far less favourable to the Political Liberty and Independence of Members of the Legislature than those here contemplated. The influence of Professional Lawyers on the preparation of important measures, especially on those introduced by the Government of the day, secret and irresponsible as are the Modes of its exercise, could not but find a highly advantageous substitute in the publicly recognised Legal Advisers the general employment of whom is here advocated.

On the whole, then, it appears that in fixing attention upon one special Legal System,—that of England,—the state of the Authorities, from which a knowledge both of the Unwritten and of the Written Law is to be obtained, is such that some organic Reform which shall tend to introduce Order, Uniformity, and Lucidity, in the stead of the prevalent Chaos and Anarchy, is now imperatively needed. The need, in truth, is confessed on all sides, and even Public steps have been already taken with a view to introducing or devising a Remedy. Probably the main objection in the present day against a complete Codification of the English Law is to be found quite as much in the experienced difficulty of carrying out such a Work as in any theoretical dislike to its being accomplished. The fact is that the very same considerations which seem to render some Systematised Re-publication of the whole of the Laws of England so commanding a necessity, also render the difficulty of the task little less than insuperable. The Unwritten Law of England has gradually matured itself from two main roots, which naturally lie deep in the Social habits and in the Industrial or Commercial energies of the People.

There is no equally advanced State which contains a System of Land-Laws still reproducing, after all the modifications they have undergone, so many of the Rules and Institutions of Feudalism There is, again, no State (except, perhaps, the United States of America which, in this particular at least, is England's debtor) which has developed so rich, so broad, so just, so exact, a System of Commercial Law as has, within the last hundred years, progressively been built up in this country. If the English Land-Laws seem to defy Codification because of their antiquarian repulsion to any severe Logical process, the English Laws affecting the Transactions of Commerce equally seem to shun it for fear of incurring careless excision and accidental loss.

On these accounts and on a variety of others it is scarcely probable that any comprehensive attempt will be made, for some time to come, at presenting in an uniform Code the whole body of English Written and Unwritten Law. There are, nevertheless, certain manifestations of an unmistakeable character that a movement in this direction is felt to be of the most urgent importance. There is an increasing tendency to pass Acts of Parliament having for their effect the Consolidation of all the previous Acts and even of the Unwritten Rules of Law upon the same subject. There are also signs of a growing desire step by step to construct what is called a "Digest" of large Departments of the Law with a view, confessedly, to ulterior Codification of the whole Law.

The main difficulty in approaching Codification as a Practical measure is naturally experienced at the outset. It is almost impossible to bridge over the two different phases of Legal Thought which prevail in the absence, and under the dominion, of a Code. To those who have long been accustomed to treat Formal Language only as matter of infinite debate,—the broad Principles of Unwritten Law ever coming to their aid to save them from the shipwreck of anarchy which must otherwise be their doom,—the Formal Terms and final Distinctions, which alone are known to a System of wholly Written Law, seem intolerable, and likely to breed the very license they endeavour to suppress. It thus comes about that two Conditions are essential to the construction of a Code, each of these Conditions in some way presupposing the other. There must be, first, a set of Persons competent to construct a Code. This Condition necessarily implies the existence of Persons exempt, through accidental causes, from the current prejudices and antipathies, not to say from the inherent disqualifications, of the large mass of their contemporaries. They must have rather a close and prophetic sympathy with the Future than a regretful yearning after the Past, though they must reverence that Past sufficiently to understand and to reproduce it. The second Condition is the gradual preparation of the Minds of the whole Legal Profession, and through them of the Population at large, for the reception of a Code. This at once introduces a Topic which is becoming every day of increasing interest in this Country, and with which the Prospects of the Science of Jurisprudence are intimately bound up,—that of Legal Education.

It is impossible to estimate the influence which a higher range of Legal Education in England is likely to have in the Future both on the Structure and on the Administration of English Law. The progress of Legal Education contains in itself two distinct elements,—the one having relation to the increased Number of Professional Lawyers who are made the subjects of that Education, the other having relation to the superior Quality of the Education imparted.

It is not worth while for the present purpose to linger over merely transitory Obstacles in the way of affording equal Educational advantages to the whole of the Legal Profession in England,—into whatsoever sub-divisions the Profession may, for purposes of general convenience, continue to be divided. A Political question may, indeed, be interposed as to the Moral Claims of the State to interpose between the Client and his Professional Adviser, with a view to ensure in the latter the amount of Professional competency which is capable of being estimated by Educational Tests. There is, no doubt, in this matter a possibility of making a plausible use of the Doctrines of "Free Trade," and of thereby arguing that the Client can best find out for himself who is most competent to forward his interests, and that, even were he not, that it is not expedient for the State to protect his indolence or ignorance by an arbitrary interference in his favour. The sufficient answer to this class of objections is that the Public Administration of Law has in view far more determinately the General interests of the Community looked upon as an organic Whole than the Private interests and concerns of any particular Persons. The only ground for conferring Rights upon Private Persons is the consideration that it is for the good of all (including the Persons directly benefited) that such special advantages as the Rights comprise should be bestowed upon them. It is, then, of the highest importance to the State that the Public Administration of Law should be conducted with the utmost dispatch, efficiency, and intelligence. These

Conditions depend in a higher degree than upon anything else, upon the Legal acquirements, general attainments, and exact Logical training of the Professional Lawyers in whom, under a mature Legal System, Suitors are compelled to repose their entire confidence.

Furthermore, it is upon the Mental qualities and the acquired Knowledge of the Members of the Legal Profession that all Formal Changes in the Law must ultimately depend,—whether these Changes are introduced through the medium of Judges in the course of Interpreting the Law; through the medium of Statutory Legislation with the help of Professional Lawyers to prepare a draught series of Proposals; or through the medium of a Code dependent, for its Amendments, on the experience, reports, and suggested alterations of those who have to administer or officially to criticise it. On all these accounts it is obviously an irrelevant impertinence for Private Persons to insinuate that the State has no concern in ensuring, by every means in its power, the possession of a minimum amount of Legal accomplishments in every Member of the Legal Profession whom it admits to practise in its Courts.

As to the detailed Methods of carrying out an effective System of Legal Education, they resolve themselves into two parts, the one relating to the proper Topics or Departments of Knowledge to which the Student's atention had best be directed, and to the Order in which these Topics should be successively approached; the other relating to the general Modes, Mechanism, and Times which will form the general basis or groundwork of the Student's whole labours.

To take the last series of questions first; the earliest and not the least important practical enquiry both for the individual Student and for any Authoritative Body of Persons charged with the responsibility of inaugurating an universal System of Legal Education is as to the relative advantages of combining Special Legal Studies with the more General Studies which, on any hypothesis, are their necessary complement, and of fixing, first of all, undistracted attention on the General Studies and subsequently of fixing an equally undistracted attention on the Special Studies. This problem has been practically solved in the Universities of Germany, as well as in the University of London, and, to a certain extent, in the Universities of Oxford and Cambridge, by breaking up the whole assemblage of Special Legal Studies into two parts. Of these parts the one is concerned mainly with the Historical and Philosophical sides of Law, and is invariably made to include Roman Law, the Science of Jurisprudence strictly so called (so far, at least, as that Science has as yet been recognised and developed), and not infrequently International Law. The other part is concerned with the Study of the Technical Legal System of the particular Nation, with the meaning and use both of the simpler and of the more solemn kinds of Legal Documents, with the detailed character of Legal Formalities and of the Procedure of Courts of Justice, and, lastly with the Art of Advocacy and the Methods of handling Evidence.

There is, no doubt, a considerable plausibility and even practical convenience in this broad division. But it has certain characteristic disadvantages which are peculiarly adherent to the nature of the subject under consideration. With respect to all the other Studies forming the general cycle of an aspiring Student's accomplishments,—such as

General History, Geography, Literature, the Physical Sciences, and even what are sometimes called the "Moral" Sciences,—the Student will always have obtained through his mere experience of Life (immature as it yet is) a provisional acquaintance with the general nature and purpose of the Subjects of the Study before approaching the profounder investigation of them. He will thus have his curiosity stimulated, his interrogations ready at hand, and his intellect considerably on the alert. Every step he takes will open out fresh vistas of interest and will require him to turn to the utmost account all his previously acquired knowledge, while inciting him to an indefinite increase of it.

With respect to the Study of Law the case is wholly different. In the life of ordinary Students, from childhood up to manhood, Law is a distant and unknown field. References to its existence are, of course, contained in ordinary Social dialogue, in the Public Journals, and also in Literary and Historical Treatises, Ancient and Modern. But the notions so obtained are far too vague and fleeting to admit of the characteristic distinctions between a Moral and a Legal Rule or between a Legal Rule and a strict Physical Sequence to be firmly and intelligently grasped. Law is primarily and essentially a Concrete Study, and the nature of it can only be apprehended, in its fullest extent, by actual contact with the Concrete Forms in which it manifests its operation. These Forms are not to be sought nor to be found in the tranquil Portico of the Dialectician, but in the agitated atmosphere of the Court of Justice, in the thronged Chambers of a popular Advocate, Conveyancer, Special Pleader, Equity-Draughtsman, or Consulting Counsel. It is here, and nowhere else, that the Student can get the Knowledge of what a Legal Right and Duty really mean in all their length and breadth, with all their minute Modifications, and with reference to all the actual Modes in which they are transferred from one Person to another, or are Protected and Enforced in Courts of Justice. There is a freshness of colour, a vividness, an unapproachable distinctness of outline, which is obtainable through the Material handling and sight of the Documents appertaining to a real Suit as it is actually progressing between a Plaintiff and a Defendant which makes all other Knowledge of the Subject, affected to be procured from mere Books, or second-hand retailers,—however competent and erudite,—little better (for the generality of Students at least) than mere empty and lifeless Rhetoric.

These considerations, then, point to the general necessity of combining, where it is possible, the Study of Law in its most Concrete and Practical shape with that of its Historical and Philosophical aspects. How far this may be possible in the special circumstances in which the leading Universities of the different Countries of Modern Europe are placed, both as to their local situation and their special destination, or how far it may be necessary to create new Institutions for the express purpose of imparting at once a Theoretical and a Practical Legal Training to aspirants to the Profession of Law,—this is not the place to enquire. It is more to the purpose to point out the relative advantages of certain competing and familiar Modes of studying the Theoretical side of Law.

It is a well-known and current aphorism at present that the day of Lectures has gone by and that Books have succeeded to their place. It is true that the temporary function which the Lecturer once discharged, of communicating to his Class the contents of rare Books not accessible to more than a few, has become for ever obsolete. All the Books which are needed for strictly educational purposes, whatever be the subject, are sufficiently open to all. It is also, and consequently, true that a modern Lecture may be simply an anachronism, and may imply nothing more than a dreary mode of imparting, in the most tedious and desultory of ways, the knowledge of a quantity of Facts which the Student can readily find for himself in any ordinary Text-book, or at least which he can easily collect by a judicious use of a number of well-chosen Text-books. In such a case as this, attendance at Lectures is, for the serious Student,—that is for the Student who wishes to economise to the utmost all his opportunities,—a wasteful abuse of time, and the paralysis of his Understanding. The Lecturer teaches him nothing that he cannot get better elsewhere: what is received is received under the greatest disadvantages: no pause is allowed in which to ponder over the truth of successive Propositions, to adjust new Facts to Facts already known, to store away conclusions commodiously in the memory, and generally to conduct that active and energetic intellectual process which is called pre-eminently Thought.

On the other hand, it cannot be denied that a Teacher, himself deeply imbued with the Principles of any single branch of Knowledge, and possessed by a generous and enthusiastic desire for its general cultivation, can do much by his Personal presence that he can do in no other way whatsoever. He can rouse the inattentive and stimulate the weary by the constant exhibition of his own unflagging faith and zeal. He can, by a ready and extemporaneously adopted turn of expression, by colloquial address, by a popular image, by a homely illustration, by a fantastic inversion of language, drive home to the intellect and imagination of his hearers a Conception with which hours and weeks of solitary Study could not imbue them. He can, furthermore, give that Personal Unity to the whole Subject which, in the bewildering maze of Modern publications on all Subjects, every Subject needs. He can direct his hearers to the right Books for them to select, and to the right parts of those Books for them to study in due proportion. He can, as by an electric touch, enable them at once to grasp the final results of his own troublous experience, and so prevent them from ever falling into the snares and quicksands by which his own progress was so seriously and, it may be, almost irreparably retarded. He can, above all, answer questions, adapt his teaching to immediate needs or to exceptional conditions, and present in himself a living example of a Student who has succeeded in the very field in which all his Pupils hope themselves one day to excel.

The value and necessity of Private Study, nevertheless, cannot well be overrated. However competent may be the Lecturer, the Student must read hard and continuously for himself. He must keep himself always a little ahead of that part of the Subject with which the Lecturer is dealing, so as to have those questions ready which he wishes to have answered, and that curiosity stimulated which it is the province of the Lecturer day by day to gratify, or rather to satiate. In order to turn to the best account an Oral Lecture, the insufficiency of Books must have been fully felt, not through Ignorance of Books,

K K

but through an exhaustive Knowledge of them. Whatever the Lecturer may do in directing the way to Books, he cannot be a substitute for them. Lonely intercourse with any Book which is worth thoroughly mastering, questioning, re-reading, and reproducing in new and original forms, is a mode of Education which no devoted Student can ever dispense with.

The general purport of this comparative survey is to establish that the main Problem put before a Student is the wise choice of the best Instructors, both Persons and Books, and of the most efficient ways of making a productive use of them when they are chosen.

Next to the Modes of Study suitable for acquiring a Scientific Knowledge of Law, the special Topics of Study present themselves for consideration. It is needless to urge what the whole course of this Treatise and the peculiar Methods adopted in it have implicitly enforced,—that the Scientific Study of Law involves a larger range of General Knowledge than probably the Study of any other single Subject. The acquisition of this General Knowledge should be the main preparation made by the Student before approaching the Study of Law itself either in its Theoretical or its Practical aspect. It may be noticed by the way that if it be true that Logic, Ethics, History, Political Economy, Social Ethics, and General Politics, are indispensable ingredients in the Training of a Lawyer of the most aspiring class, it is also true that the Study of Jurisprudence will be found to react most felicitously on the Knowledge of those Subjects previously attained. In fact it may be said broadly that the Study of the Science of Jurisprudence, while it demands a more accurate and specific acquaintance with those departments of Knowledge than does any other single Study, does also of itself, by giving point and direction to the acquisition of all that Knowledge, render the most effective aid in rounding off and equipping the Student's mind. As a man becomes a better Jurist, he becomes, of necessity, a more ready and correct manipulator both of Inductive and of Deductive processes of Thought, a more keen discriminator of the nature of Moral Distinctions and of the Relation to each other of the true fields of Moral and Legal Duty, a profounder and more self-restrained Politician, a wiser and better-balanced Investigator of the great leading Facts of Human Life in all their forms. No Student who respects himself will flinch from the Study of Jurisprudence because he is warned that, in order to know well a limited district, he must accustom himself to travel through large outlying districts, and that, in order to be Master of a few things, he must wrestle not altogether unsuccessfully with many things.

As respects the Topics of Study which are of a more strictly Legal complexion, it is sufficient to dwell on the three indispensable elements of Knowledge comprised in (1.) *Roman Law*, (2.) *Foreign Law*, especially Modern Codes, and (3.) *International Law*.

The great advance that the Study of Roman Law has made in England during the present generation might almost seem to supersede the necessity of lauding it as an essential component in a complete Course of Legal Education. The main value of this Study is, of course, not to be found in the Material Contents of the Roman System. These Contents mostly have reference to Institutions which, even in Continental countries, have entirely changed their form or passed away, and in England, never existed. Others were the result of little more than Imperial caprice or, at the best, of a struggling desire to wrench antiquated Rules and Usages so as to promote the ends dictated by advancing Sentiments of Moral Truth and Justice. Nevertheless, the survival of what is called " Dutch Roman Law,"—illustrated as it has been by the genius of Grotius,—in some important British Colonies, and the conspicuous influence of the Language, of the Notions, and of the Divisions, of Roman Law on the Law of Scotland, impart even to the Material Contents of the Roman System a practical value for the English Student which is scarcely, if at all, inferior to that which they have for the Continental one.

The characteristic advantage of the Study of Roman Law is to be found not only, as is generally recognised, in the inexorable Logic which pervades the System, but in the combination of its Organic Completeness with its extraordinary Breadth of Compass. Many other Systems might rival it in one or other of these features, but,—owing to a multitude of causes, connected chiefly with the complex conditions of Modern Civilisation,—there is no single one which can pretend to rival it in both.

The excellence of Roman Law for the purposes of the Jurist is that, broad and capacious as that System is, it can be effectually mastered and grasped as an Organic Whole in a way which no other System of Law (not even those that are exact copies of it) admits of. Besides this eminent advantage, it has the further one of having been laboriously commented upon by the most brilliant line of Jurists and Practical Lawyers the world has seen. The Fact, too, that the Institutes of Gaius and Justinian, in their Arrangement and in their Language, have given form and colour (not to say substance) to every Modern European Code and to the Doctrines of European International Law renders a Knowledge of Roman Law at its fountain head an indispensable acquisition for even a moderately enterprising Student of Law.

This Subject introduces the kindred one of the Study of Modern Codes. So soon as ever the Principles, the main Divisions, and the Language of Roman Law have been absorbed, the Study of modern Codes becomes comparatively easy.

The Study of Systems of Law prevailing in a variety of different countries is, indeed, the most fruitful of all experiences to the intelligent Jurist. The Universal and the Permanent, reappearing everywhere, is at once seen to distinguish itself broadly from the partial and the accidental which varies from State to State. Even strange Systems of Law, as the Mahomedan, the Hindu, and those of very Primitive Communities, enforce, if properly interpreted, the same ineradicable lessons. Government, Marriage, Ownership, Contract, Intestate and Testamentary Succession, Crime, Death, Birth, Fraud, Malice, and Accident are Facts of Human Society which eternally accompany it from its Birth to its Dissolution. Law itself is only one of these Facts, the necessary effect of which upon all the rest, and of the rest upon it, it has been seen to be the peculiar Province of the Jurist to watch and to describe. However monstrous, anomalous, and unaccountable may be the Forms in which the Facts clothe themselves, still those Facts are invariably present and are ever the same. The Jurist, as by the stroke of a magic wand, instantly disentangles them from their barbaric confusion, and presents them in symmetrical order and harmonious beauty. The use, then, to the

Jurist and to the Legal Student, of Codes, Ancient and Modern, Primitive and Advanced, is sufficiently obvious. It happens, indeed, that their Study is peculiarly easy; as the more Systematic ones have been constructed in conformity with one and the same Type, and, with few exceptions, there is to be discovered in them the smallest amount of originality or independent genius. For an Englishman, the New York Codes, actual and projected, will have a special interest as professing to be Digests of different departments of a Legal System closely resembling that of England. This Work is all the more interesting as reproducing less of the Language and Arrangement of the Roman Institutes than is the case with any of the European Codes. The actual success of the performance as a specimen of Technical Codification is more doubtful, though the measure of that success must be estimated, as will have been seen from remarks in a previous part of this chapter, with reference quite as much to the temper, wants, and habits of the People for whose use it is intended, as to the wisdom of its Plan, the precision of its Terms, and the Logical Accuracy of its Subdivisions.

The observations that were made at the commencement of the Chapter on Public International Law will already have suggested the prominent place this Topic must occupy in a general Course of Legal Study. There are, indeed, certain special reasons why an acquaintance with Public International Law should react most favourably both upon the Legal Conceptions and upon the Mental Habits of the Student.

In the first place, Public International Law exhibits Law in the Making; that is, as undergoing the characteristic process of Transmutation from habitual Moral Practices into severely coercive Rules. This process is, in every Nation, slow, tentative, and uncertain, as well as intermittent and even occasionally retrograde. International Law supplies a vivid example, on the largest scale, of this progressive Development going on before our eyes. So also the influence upon the formation of Rules of International Law of Text-writers such as Grotius, Vattel, Kent, Wheaton, and Heffter; of Statute-Law, such as the attempted Regulations of the Baltic Powers representing the 'Armed Neutrality' of 1801; of Commercial Ordinances such as those of some of the French Monarchs; of specific Moral engagements, such as the great Historical Treaties out of which so much of Public International Law is built up; of Judicial Decisions, as those of Sir William Scott in the British High Court of Admiralty; of Authoritative Opinions solemnly maintained, such as those contained in the Despatches of eminent American and European Diplomatists,—all suggest the most valuable and striking illustrations of the Modes in which all Law Grows, and of the laborious Processes through which a vast and compact System of Law is gradually Framed and Fashioned throughout, even to its minutest and most finely articulated details. Again, the Study of International Law brings before the Student's mind more clearly than does any other part of his Studies the essential Nature of Law, properly so called, as implying the Existence of a Supreme Political Authority, and thereby involving the use of such leading Terms as *Nation, State, Government, Political Independence, Citizenship, Nationality,* and the like. These are Terms which, being permanent and universal, essentially belong to the Science of Jurisprudence, and yet the true purport of which can in no way be so well apprehended as by attention to the Distinctions actively enforced in the course of defending points in Controversies arising out of the attempted application of International Law.

But International Law has even a loftier purpose than any of these to serve with the Student. At no point of his Studies does he begin to feel so fully the true Dignity and Value of his Subject as when he is called upon to investigate what Legal Rules for the regulation of Ownership, Contract, Belligerency and Neutrality (the Persons concerned being Sovereign States) can be most conveniently adopted in view of the different Systems of Law prevalent in the several States. The Jurist (to whom the Student betakes himself), in treating so profound a question as this,—involving as it does the life and welfare of countless numbers of Persons,—is found to be doing nothing more than exercising his ordinary Craft. He is discovering Permanence and Universality in the midst of incessant Flux and Variety. He is enforcing the peremptory Dictates of a great Moral Unity in the midst of innumerable distracted Factions. He is tempering the heated passions of men by recalling to their minds Eternal Principles of Moral Right and Justice which no artificial Institutions can transform, nor accidents of War annihilate or obscure. He, whose habitual occupation it is to Study the Laws of every Nation with the view of determining what is Common to all, is never so much at home as when called upon to legislate for all Nations in the name of Principles which no civilised Nation can refuse to recognise. Thus International Law is the most serviceable, the most charming, and the most honourable of the

Pursuits to which the Juridical Student is imperatively urged.

The prospects of the Science of Jurisprudence, especially in England, will depend largely upon a greater familiarity than has hitherto been encouraged in Legal Education with the vast and invaluable Juridical Literature of Germany and France.

It happens, indeed, that in no other department of Knowledge is it so hard to apprehend the best Conceptions hitherto attained, without a familiar acquaintance with German Philosophical language, as in Jurisprudence. Modern Jurisprudence is emphatically a German creation. Kant, Hegel, Hugo, Savigny, Thibaut, Falck, and their laborious and not unworthy successors have stamped their Personality, their Nomenclature, their Ethical tone, their Methods of Philosophical analysis, far too ineffaceably upon the Science of Jurisprudence to be only read at second hand by any Student who would penetrate to the profoundest depths of that Science. The German words used to express the Idea of "Law" are untranslateable, or, if a translation be attempted otherwise than by a long periphrasis, some essential parts of the meaning unavoidably drop out. Germans have thought on Juridical and Ethical subjects in a way not the same as that in which Englishmen and Frenchmen have thought. Hence no English or French Term can be a substitute for some German ones. There are German Ideas which can be thoroughly and adequately mastered through the German language and not otherwise. These Ideas may, indeed, some day be reproduced in the living Thought of a different Nation, English, French, or other; and then new and appropriate Terms will be created to communicate those

Ideas. Till this takes place, old English Terms, convulsively grasped at as substitutes for the Foreign ones, are utterly valueless and only misleading. Hence it must be insisted that, for the Student who wishes to know everything that is known and that can be known about the Science of Jurisprudence, a capacity to read Philosophical German with facility and precision is indispensable.

As to French Writers, the Ideas conveyed by them almost invariably admit of easy and efficient, if not of terse and elegant, rendering in any other Language. The lucidity and chasteness of style, and the fineness of the deductive Logic which every French Legal Writer exhibits in so high a degree, make an acquaintance with French Legal Writing, at the least, a highly desirable, if not an indispensable, accomplishment for the Student. A Modern School of English Writers, with Bentham at their head, possess so many of the characteristic traits of the best French speculators on Ethical subjects, that it is not absolutely essential for an Englishman to travel beyond his own tongue in order to acquire familiarity with French Methods of Thought. Nevertheless, the *Code Napoléon* has played so important a part in the History of Modern Codification all over the Continent, and the Debates of the "*Conseil d'Etat*" which accompanied its formation are of such transcendent interest (considering the Historical Characters who took part in them and the nature of the Problems discussed), that the young Jurist cannot safely dispense with a personal knowledge of French Writers on Law. Furthermore, the Commentators on the Code present a long line of liberal-minded, acute, and erudite men with whom too familiar an acquaintance cannot be made.

At the commencement of this Treatise an almost excessive amount of care was taken to fix with precision the true import of the phrase "Science of Jurisprudence." It was shown at once that such a Science Exists and what its Contents are. It may be serviceable in this place, in direct relation to the wants and difficulties of the Legal Student, to criticise the extremely loose way in which the Term "Jurisprudence" is commonly employed.

The Term "Jurisprudence," in the present State of English Scientific Terminology, suggests, even to the Professional Lawyer, ideas possessing every degree of laxity and indeterminateness. To some the term "Jurisprudence" conveys no more precise meaning than what may be described as "everything that has to do with the Law of a Nation, or (perhaps) any other, if there be any other, kind of Law." To others, the Term means the "Philosophy" of Positive Law; an expression consecrated indeed by Mr. Austin, but which throws the enquirer back on the true import of the Term "Philosophy," and so into one of the most intricate and hopeless questions of Nomenclature that has ever divided the world of Thinkers into an indefinite number of mutually repulsive atoms. To others, again, the Term "Jurisprudence" means nothing more than the process of comparing at leisure the Positive Law of different Countries without having any distinct purpose in instituting the comparison. Or, again, the Term seems to be almost synonymous with "Legislation," and to mean the process of discovering the best Laws to Make, and also the best way of Publishing them in Formal Language so as to secure them most effectually against all chances of erroneous Interpretation. Lastly, the Term

"Jurisprudence" means, for many serious minds, the intellectual process of ascertaining the Place that the phenomenon of Law holds in the constitution of Human Society and in the Development of the Human Race. In this use of the Term the History of Law, Ancient and Modern, the Facts attending the Growth of International Law, the Usages of Barbarians, and the recorded aspirations of Utopists, are held to be the legitimate or the only appropriate matters of interest for the Professional Jurist. The most consistently employed meaning of all is that which is scarcely known in England, though familiar enough to a French ear, according to which it implies the finer shades of Interpretation of a well-acknowledged Rule of Law which are gradually developed in the course of the actual Administration of Law in Courts of Justice.

Such being the flux and plasticity of the luckless Term "Jurisprudence," it cannot be surprising if the young English Student approaches the Science of Jurisprudence with somewhat of a quivering heart and trembling gait. He knows not where he is going and is not quite sure whether he is going, or wanting to go, anywhere. He thirsts for something broader, deeper, more indestructible than anything he can find in Text-books of English Law or in the successive Modifications in the substance of Law itself. He hears of "Jurisprudence," and he has a dim hope that what he is in search of may perchance be there. He draws near, and in the place of a Science, or a Systematic Exhibition of what is Universal and Everlasting, he is often enough regaled with nothing more satisfying than the story of incessant Change, the dreary register of meaningless Variety, the loose guesses of Politicians and Moralists, the reckless verbiage of those who have studied just Law enough to confuse the spontaneous workings of their Conscience, and yet who affect just sensitiveness enough of Conscience to interfere with their unflinching Interpretation of a single Law.

It is sufficient here, in relation to this prevalent confusion of Thought or variety of Expression, to recur to the Definition or Explanation of the Science of Jurisprudence given in the first Chapter of this Work, and which has been consistently adhered to throughout. "The Science of Jurisprudence deals with the Facts brought to light through the operation upon the Fact of Law (considered as such, and neither as good nor bad) of all other Facts whatsoever,—including among these other Facts those resulting in the Creation, and expressing the Historical and Logical vicissitudes, of Law itself."

It is scarcely possible to draw to a conclusion a Treatise dealing with materials so manifold and so complex as does the present one without casting a glance onward to the National Fortunes of the States of Europe in the immediate Future, and without framing certain not wholly conjectural estimates as to the Influence which the Scientific Study and Development of Law is likely to have on those Fortunes. Apart from all the more fleeting, anarchical, and revolutionary manifestations of which symptoms are presented on every side, and upon which, in reference to the possible Political services of Scientific Jurists, some remarks were made at the commencement of the present chapter, there are indications that two opposite Tendencies in respect to the proper Limits of the action of Law and Government will constantly be exhibited in conflict with one another in every State, and that a permanent reconciliation of these Tendencies will only be attained after a long and bitter experience of mistakes and failures.

It may be said generally that the existence of either of these Tendencies or rival Principles implies the acceptance of a number of Common Assumptions which there is reason to hope will become more and more undisputed as they are, in themselves, indisputable. Such Assumptions are, (1.) that the Supreme Felicity and Moral Perfection of all Human Beings, necessarily as yet only dimly shadowed out as an Ideal,—though ever needed in order to correct and purify the search after what is Possible and Real,—depend upon the utmost Expansion and the unmutilated Integrity of National Life and of Family Life; (2.) that the richest Development of which the Human Race is susceptible is to be sought not in a monotonous Uniformity or an endless repetition of identical types, but in Variety, in Contribution, in Reciprocity,—or, in one word, in Organisation; (3.) that the Spiritual, Moral, and Physical Perfection of the Individual Man and Woman is only to be obtained through the concurrence of a number of Conditions of which the influences of Family and of National existence are among the most momentous and the most potent; and, (4.) that the accomplishment of this Perfection (partial as it must be, even according to the most sanguine expectations), not as a rare and thinly-scattered privilege for Some but as a Common and evenly distributed boon for All, is the sole justifiable End of the efforts of the Statesman and of the Legislator. So far there is little difference of opinion among those profounder and more far-sighted

Thinkers whose views, for the present purpose, it is at all necessary to take into account. The difference begins so soon as a Theory of Action is contemplated for the purpose of hastening the attainment of these confessedly-desirable Ends. According to one view, the main or sole aid is to be found in improved Laws and in the more watchful and intelligent Energy of National Governments. According to the other view, it is mainly or solely in what are called Moral or Spiritual efforts, whether isolated and desultory or to a greater or less degree finely organised,— and not in any machinery which must have its momentum in Physical Force,—that confident reliance can be placed.

Between and beyond these competing views there is, of course, a third one, which will probably tend to establish itself with increasing steadiness through the mutual conflicts of the other two. The purport of this view is that an ascertainable distinction can be drawn between the appropriate fields of Law and Government on the one hand, and of Moral Agencies on the other; and that consequences as pernicious are to be apprehended from confounding the two as from neglecting the use of either.

The first of the views above noticed,—that is, the one which tends to enlarge indefinitely the Province of Government,—assumes the truth of one of two alternative sets of suppositions. In accordance with one of these sets of suppositions, it is held that, as Time advances, good Moral Habits are likely to become so fixed and dominant throughout the bulk of the Population that, however widely the Province of Government is extended, the Laws will operate only by way of affording an acceptable stimulus and guide without endangering Public Liberty or inducing general Moral Paralysis. It is further presupposed that the Science and Art of Government and of Legislation will become more and more of a strictly exclusive and Professional character; and that while, on the one hand, the narrow aims and the stolid ignorance of casually chosen Popular Legislators will be entirely away, on the other hand no Official prejudices or Aristocratic tempers will sully the purity and the wisdom of the Persons charged with the responsibility of Government. According to the alternative set of suppositions it is held (and this, no doubt, is the coarser Theory just now current in this country) that the only effective engine for working on Mankind in order to produce the richest results must be that implied in the employment of direct or indirect Physical Pressure, such as is involved in appealing to the Fear of Punishment, that is, of Physical Pain; and that in view of the Ignorance, or the unequal diffusion of Knowledge, to which Man is for a long time doomed, and of the perverse misconception of what conduces to his truest welfare, to which he is and will for a long time be helplessly prone, the wisest and kindest measures to adopt are that those who think they know best what is for the Good of all should use what Physical Force is at their disposal in order to help all to the attainment of that Good by Punishing those who refuse to seek it. These measures will generally be carried out in some such specious name as that of "Popular" or even "Democratic" Government, and by the plausible aid of Persons said to Represent the People, while the favourite argument in support of the Legislation adopted will be that no assault on Public Liberty is intended, but that the Liberty, not to say the Moral Sentiments or scruples of a Few must obviously be immolated in order to secure the liberty, ease, or convenience of the Many.

Those who represent the opposite tendency, that is those who may be characteristically denoted as hostile to the Extension of the Province of Government and to the Multiplication of Laws, and as looking with most hope to the wise use of Moral Influences of all sorts, may be said to deny the validity of every one of the hypotheses assumed on the other side. As to the first class of these hypotheses, they say that it is of no practical value to rely on the advent of a Time when good Moral habits will be as widely prevalent as they are now the reverse, because the essential difficulty of the Problem consists in the actually existing state of Society at this day and in the Moral torpor and inanition to be found on every side. If a Theory of Government only professes to meet National evils by creating a glowing vision of a Time when that evil does not exist, the Theory has no lesson of any practical interest to impart to the present Age.

As to the second class of the hypotheses relied upon in support of the advantages to be derived from Extending the area of Law, it is urged, by way of answer, that it should be the main work of the enlightened Statesman to enact, to amend, to repeal, or to abstain from enacting Laws, not with the object of appealing to the brute fears of his Fellow-Citizens, but with the object of dispelling these fears and of helping towards a final triumph over them. The phrase "Public Liberty" means not the License of the Many coupled with the Degradation of a Few, but the Liberty of Every one, including the meanest and the humblest,—to the full extent that is compatible with the general Liberty of All the rest. The only limitations on this enjoyment of Liberty are applicable in cases where it is established by a Public Judicial Investigation that it has already been abused. Consistently with these broad and general Principles, it is open to the Legislator to construct a Catalogue of Rights and Duties for the special and limited purposes indicated sufficiently in the previous parts of this Treatise. The creation of Artificial Crimes, and the consequent reckless onslaughts upon Public Liberty, form the most perilous temptation to which a modern Statesman is exposed. The ignorance and the unhappy perverseness of the bulk of the Population is still so considerable in Modern States, that they present no barrier against the most enticing and hazardous Political Experiments, while they offer the most ready though treacherous arguments for the stern necessity of having recourse to those Experiments. The inevitable result is general paralysis of Moral Responsibility; Executive tyranny in obscure places and practised especially on Classes of Persons unable to attract Public attention for their defence; a servile habit of reliance on Government for the instant remedy of every evil,—including those which are the direct consequences of voluntary vice or self-indulgence; and the existence of a wide-spread network of Police-inspection and *Espionage*, sapping the essential vital force of a free, self-reliant, and self-respecting National Life.

Out of these two opposing views there is a Theoretical, if not yet a Practical, issue to be found in one which contains the truth of both and the error of neither. According to this view Law and Government are indeed potent and majestic instruments, but,—like others employed in the Material world,—they are precious, or indeed are other than noxious, only when used in their proper Place and within their proper Limits. The proper Place and Limits, in any State, cannot be wholly determined by abstract considerations, but must have reference to the circumstances, traditions, and Institutions prevailing at a given time in that State. Nevertheless some such abstract considerations as the following will not be without their use in fixing generally the true Place and Limits of Law and Government when contrasted with those of what may be called purely Moral and Spiritual Forces.

The purpose of Law is to maintain and to fortify Public Morality and not to create and invent it; to give solidity and permanence to the essential Relationships on which National Life depends, and not to be the fountain of their vital energy; to secure for every Man and Woman, through the creation of Rights and Duties, a clear and open space for unrestricted action, within which they are free to develope all their faculties without hindrance or intrusion from without; and to uphold the security of such Institutions as the voluntary efforts of Mankind may devise or adopt as seeming to them best calculated to quicken, to develope, and to invigorate the Moral aspirations of the Race.

It will be admitted on all sides that the highest degree of Perfection and of Moral Enfranchisement that Man can reach is in having the largest number of his faculties and emotions in the fullest exercise and flow, and with the least necessary restraint from without or from within. It will be admitted, too, that Man only discovers the use of his faculties and brings his highest emotions into play through Intercourse with his Brother-Man; that the more intense and extended is this Intercourse, the more adequately developed he may become and he ought to become; and that there exists somewhere a true and Common Canon or Standard of action,—inflexible in itself and yet withal admitting of the nicest adjustments and the most exquisite modulations,—for all Members of the Society, which the more habitually each Member adopts, the vaster is the expansion of which his own nature is capable, and the less is the chance or the need of interruption by others; and which the more habitually all men adopt, the more freely and harmoniously the general machinery of Social Intercourse works. This Canon or Standard of action is hard indeed to discover, and particular Societies may spend long Ages in unavailing tentative efforts to discover it. The Modes of its Discovery or even the prior question whether, in any strict sense of the term, it be a matter of Discovery at all, are not proper to the present discussion. It is sufficient to notice as a Fact that some Nations seem for a time to approach this Discovery nearer and nearer, and then to remove indefinitely far away from it; some to stagnate,—neither approaching nor moving away; some, in their constantly progressive History, to show hopeful signs of ever more and more nearly attaining to it. This Canon or Standard of action,—including here under the term *action* all the thoughts and feelings that give it life and worth,—is Absolute Morality. It is only the feeble Image or the mechanical scaffolding of this that is designated by the phrase "National Law."

It is obvious that the attendant Image will constantly be improving in quality and in efficiency according as the manifestation of the Reality it follows becomes increasingly distinct. In this way Law, though never reaching further nor deeper than to the control of outward Acts, tends even within these limits to become more and more nearly the exact expression of the highest and most refined Reason of the People, while, on the other hand, its operation becomes more and more invisible and is scarcely recognised as other than a Mode of benevolent Guidance and Aid. Law in this last form characteristically stands forth as the ever-present and incarnate Witness of that ultimate Morality of which itself is at best no more than the Symbol and the Counterpart. It comes home with an awful directness to every Man and Woman in the Public recognition of Family Relationships, in the distribution of Property, in the frame-work of Government, in the Formal arrangement of Contracts, and in the correction of outward Wrongs. In doing this it keeps ever testifying of the tender and intimate concern that Each one has in the Wills and Actions of Every other one, and that the State, embodying in itself the whole National Past, Present, and Future, has in the conduct of All. It reminds him ever and anon of an infinitely deeper and higher Rule than itself, which, without National danger or ruin, cannot be broken. It helps him to work onward in order to promote, both in himself and among those about him, the dominion of that higher Rule, by guarding him against the constant solicitations that will beset him, in the life of every day, to selfishness, thoughtlessness, and contempt of his Brother-Man.

It is not, then, in Law nor in Government that hope must be placed for the direct culture of a Nation's true Vitality. It is in Moral and Spiritual efforts,—whether expressed in solitary and silent influences, or in highly Systematised Organisations,—that a firm and tranquil confidence can alone be reposed. It is these alone which can deal with the true springs of Human Action and can penetrate to the mysterious workings of the Human Conscience. It is from these alone, and from the Everlasting Truths which it is their province to enforce and to represent, that Man can draw all the inspiration he needs for Action, all the assurance he needs to give him a steady trust in the enduring value of his Work, all the consolation he needs to support him against the vicissitudes he must encounter. In a word, it is to these direct Inspirers of Human Virtue and Energy that Law itself must turn in order to find at hand a race of Citizens whose dearest concern it will be to Obey, to Cherish, and to Reform it.

INDEX.

	PAGE
Abduction, Ground of Laws relating to	243
Accession, where Classed	157
,, Meaning and Juridical Import of	159, 160
Accessories and Principals (in Crimes), Law relating to	300
Account, Procedure for Enquiry into Matters of	322, 323
Acté d'Accusation, Critical Notice of the French	329
Actions, Nature and Policy of Laws relating to Limitation of	346, 347
,, Laws determining the proper Parties to	348, 349
Act and Event, Explanation of Terms	93
,, Marriage viewed as an, rather than as an Event	94
,, Death ,, ,, ,, ,, ,, ,, ,, ,,	94
,, Bankruptcy ,, ,, ,, ,, ,, ,, ,,	94
,, Elements of a Criminal	298
Acts, Interpretation of, by Ethical considerations	32
,, Character of: how open to Misconstruction	33
,, alone affected to be controlled by Law	75
Adjective Law opposed to Substantive Law by BENTHAM	283
Adjudication involved in the idea of Law	3
,, where Classed	157
,, Juridical Import of, in respect of Ownership	169
Adjunctio, Meaning of	160
Administrators, Law relating to	262
,, Modes of their Appointment	271
Admiralty Courts, their International Character and Importance	400
Adultery, Place of Laws relating to certain forms of, in a Scheme of Criminal Law	301
Advocacy, Functions of Lawyers as to	278
Advocates, Laws relating to	276–280
Affinity, Ground of Laws relating to	211, 212
Affreightment, Contract of, under what head Classified	216, 227
Age, Difference of: a Fact on which Science of Jurisprudence depends	12
,, Old, a Fact impairing Moral Responsibility	85
Agency, a Fact artificially restricting Moral Responsibility	85, 90
,, Nature of Contract of	223, 225
Agents as Contractors	191–193

INDEX.

	PAGE
Alienation in Life and in Death: where Classed	157
,, ,, ,, Juridical Import of	163-169
Aliens as Owners	146
,, as Contractors	193, 194
Allegiance, Juridical Import of Duties of	374
Alliances as Grounds of Mutual Dependence of States	417
Ambassadors, Rights of States to Courteous Treatment of their	420
American Union, Description of Mutual Dependence of States of	417
Annexation of Territory as a Mode of Acquiring Rights of Ownership	423
Appeal, Court of, for Criminal Cases	341
Apprenticeship, Nature of Contract of	223-225
Arbitration, Juridical Nature of	323
,, Modes of Constructing International Board of	399
,, Importance of referring International Disputes to	400
Arbitrator, his Functions	323
Armed Neutrality, The, of 1801: its Influence on the Formation of Rules of International Law	503
Army, Rules regulating the Conduct of an Invading or Occupying	447, 443
ARNOLD, Dr., his views on Irregular Risings in an Invaded Territory	442
Artillery, Improvements in, as affecting the Frequency and Duration of Wars	440, 454
Assault, Right of Actions for, under what head Classed	290
Assaults, Place, in a Scheme of Criminal Law, of Laws relating to	301
Assets in Bankruptcy	10
,, ,, ,, Laws regulating the Distribution of	345
Assignees in Bankruptcy, Laws Regulating the Appointment of	345
Attainder as resulting in Forfeiture	170
Attempts to commit Crimes are illustrations of Inchoate Responsibility	83
,, ,, ,, ,, Defined, and Contrasted with Consummate Crimes	299, 300
Attorneys, Laws relating to	276-280
AUSTIN, Mr., his use of the Term Jurisprudence	507
,, ,, his use of the Distinction between "Primary" and "Secondary" or "Sanctioning" Rights	283
AUSTRIA: Description of its Constitutional Relation to HUNGARY	417
Authority, The Legislative, Distinguished from the Executive	105, 106
,, ,, Supreme Political: Explanation of Phrase	74, 107
,, ,, ,, ,, cannot enjoy Rights nor be liable to Duties	77
,, ,, ,, ,, Analysis of Elements of	108
,, ,, ,, ,, Rights and Duties of Members of	110
,, ,, ,, ,, Modes of Change of	115
Award, Nature of Arbitrator's	323
Bailments, Nature of	151, 152, 202, 203
,, Distinguishable from Sale	222
Balance of Power, Nature of Doctrine of	398

INDEX.

	PAGE
Bankruptcy, what is implied in a Law of	10
" viewed as an Act rather than as an Event	64
" a Mode of Acquiring Rights of Ownership by Adjudication	169
" as a Mode of Minimising Loss	207, 208
" Nature of Acts of	209, 245
" Place of Topic of	344, 345
" Assignees in	345
" Distribution of Assets in	345
" as a Topic of Private International Law	388
" Fraudulent: Place of Law relating to, in a Scheme of Criminal Law	301
Barristers, Law relating to	276–280
BENTHAM, Mr., his sagacious Measures rendered possible by the insulation of English Law	15
" " opposes "Substantive" to "Adjective" Law	283
" " his use of the Term "Informative Suppositions"	330
" " his Terms "Principal" and "Evidentiary"	333
Bigamy, Ground of Laws relating to	243
" Place, in a Scheme of Criminal Law, of Laws relating to	301
Billeting Troops, Rules for the Regulation of	448
Bills of Exchange, Nature and Incidents of	88, 206, 227, 228
Birth, a Fact on which the Science of Jurisprudence depends	12
Blasphemy, Place, in a Scheme of Criminal Law, of Laws relating to	300
Bombardment, Laws controlling	450
Bond, Operation in English Law of a	211
Breach of Blockade, Punishment for	410
" " Contract opposed in English Law to a Tort	284, 285
" " International Law, Consequences of	410
Burglary, Place, in a Scheme of Criminal Law, of Laws relating to	301
Capital Punishment, its Juridical Aspects	311–313
" " Evidence before Commission on	357–360
Carrier, A, Nature of his Rights	151, 152
Cases, Condition of Reports of, in England	484, 485
"Case Law" in England, what	58
Cestuique-Trust, Description of	267
Chancellor (The English), his Executive Functions	322
Chancery, Jurisdiction of Court of, as to Trusts	268
Character, Evidence of, its Nature	313–316
" As a Ground of Suspicion	338
Children, Rights of Action for Injury to, where Classed	291
Citizenship, its Nature and Import	374–376
Civil Injuries and Crimes, Place and Import of Laws of,	100–102, 283, sq.
" " distinguished from Crimes	286, 287
" " Laws relating to	287
Classification of Laws, what based on	26, 37
" " " based on Quality of Persons	26, 27

INDEX.

	PAGE
Classification of Laws based on Interposition of a Thing	26, 27
,, ,, ,, on Basis of Rights	66
,, ,, ,, various Bases of	96
,, of Crimes, its Place in a Scheme of Criminal Law	300
,, of Punishments, ,, ,, ,, ,, ,,	301
Code, Analogy of an International, to a Body of Moral Prescriptions	46
,, An International, how it resembles the Phenomena of National Law	47
,, main Purposes of a	477
,, Napoléon, The, its Services in the History of Modern Codification	506
Codes, Modern, as a Topic of Legal Education	499, 501, 502
,, New York, their Interest and Value	502
Codification a Source of Law	53
,, Meaning and Import of the Term	469, 470
,, History of, in Germany	472
,, The Question of in Germany, as contrasted with that in England	471–473
,, General Objections to	473–477
,, Methods of effecting	482
,, Special reasons for, in England	483–489
,, of English Law, Practical Difficulties attending	487, 489
Coining, Laws relating to, their Place in a Scheme of Criminal Law	300
Collegia, as Persons	81
Colonies, their Political Relation to the Mother-Country	418
,, the British, their Relation to the Crown and to Parliament	418, 419
,, ,, Criticism of Schemes for the Reconstruction of their Relation to England	419
Combatants and Non-combatants, Penalties affecting	440
,, ,, ,, Practical Difficulties in distinguishing	440, 444
Comity, Rights of States to	420
Command, Definition of a	73
Commerce, Doubtful Rights of States to	421
,, Present Condition of, as Affecting Wars	435
,, of Neutrals with Belligerents	437
Commercial Tribunals as Exceptional Remedies	342
,, ,, in Relation to Bankruptcy	344
,, Credit as Influencing the Frequency of Wars	452, 453
Commission, Practice of giving a, to Persons in order to resist Invader	442, 443
Commixtio, Meaning of	160
Common Law, Convenience and Modes of Fusion of, with Equity	478–483
Communauté, System of, prevailing on the Continent	247
Community of Goods implies Laws of Ownership	463
"Compassing the Death of the King" is an illustration of Inchoate Responsibility entailing Punishment	83

INDEX. 523

	PAGE
Compensation for a Civil Injury, Modes of obtaining	206, 207
„ „ „ Place of Laws assigning Measure and Mode of	341
Compositions with Creditors, Laws Relating to	345
Compulsion, a Fact impairing Moral Responsibility	85
Concealment, as a Ground of Suspicion	339
Confederation of States, Nature of a Permanent	417, 418
Confession of Crime, as a Ground of Conviction	339
Confiscation of Ships, as a Penalty for Breach of Blockade	410
Conflict of Laws, Examples of	369
Confusio, Meaning of	160
Consanguinity, Ground of Laws relating to	242, 243
Consent of Friends, as a Condition of Marriage	241
'*Consolato del Mare*' as a Source of International Law	405
Constitution of the State, Laws relating to the, their Place	97, 98
„ „ „ „ Distribution of	103
Constitutional Law, its Place	97, 98, 102
„ „ Distribution of Topics of	103 sq.
„ Morality, meaning and criticism of Phrase	104, 105
Constructive Fraud, a Fact artificially held to impair Moral Responsibility	85
„ „ Explanation of Doctrine of	274, 275
„ „ Application of Doctrine to Contractors under Duress	189
Contraband of War, Penalties for carrying	410
Contract, Mental as contrasted with Formal, Elements of	12
„ a Rudimentary Fact on which the Science of Jurisprudence depends	13
„ Idea of, latent in that of Ownership	63
„ Historical and Real Place of Laws of	99
„ Laws of	176 sq.
„ Analysis of Judicial Elements in Laws of	176
„ End of Laws of	178
„ Phenomenon of, as a Social Characteristic	177
„ Mode of Development of	177, 178
„ Complete Explanation of Term	179-181
„ Relation of a, to a Conveyance	165, 166
„ Persons who Make	181-194
„ Acts by which the Making of a, is signified	194-200
„ Rights Accruing through the Making of	201-208
„ how Dissolved	211, 212
„ Rights to Dissolution of, where classified	211
„ Injuries to Rights under a	283, 291
„ Private International Laws of	383, 384
Contracts, Classification of	213-220
„ Implied, ambiguous uses of Phrase	199, 200
„ of Affreightment	216, 227
„ of Assurance	216, 226

	PAGE
Contracts, of Guaranty	226
,, of Indemnity	216, 226
,, Relating to Negotiable Securities	216, 227
,, In View of Marriage	215–218
,, ,, Sale	219, 220
,, Subsidiary, attending Sale	221
,, Certain, have the notion of Sale underlying them	222, 223
,, of Warranty, as Subsidiary to a Sale	221
Contraventions, Délits, and Crimes: Nature of Division of Offences into in France	302
Contributory Negligence, its Juridical Nature	328
Convention of Geneva of 1864 and of 1868, Nature and Purport of	449
,, of St. Petersburgh, Purport of	450
Conveyance, A, its Relation to a Contract having for its Object a Sale	221
,, ,, its General Relations to Contract	165, 166
Conveyancing, Functions of Lawyers as to	278
Copyhold Estate, under what head Classified	149
,, ,, what Rights implied in	149, 150
,, ,, Mode of Conveyance of a	164
Copyright, Nature of	140, 141
,, Rights of Action for Piracy of, where Classified	291
Corporate Bodies, Laws relating to Certain	261
Corporation, a Person	61
Corporations as Owners	147
Corpus Delicti, Meaning of Expression	336
Cour de Cassation in France	341
Courts, Admiralty: their International Character and Importance	400
,, Prize: their International Purposes	400
,, of Appeal for Criminal Cases	341
,, of Justice, Laws for their Establishment	320
,, ,, ,, their various Characters and Purposes	321
,, ,, Probate: their Executive Functions	322
,, ,, ,, their Constitution, and what it implies	322
,, ,, Chancery: their Jurisdiction as to Trusts	268
,, ,, Equity, Distinguished from Prætorian Court at Rome	320
,, ,, Law and Equity: Suggested Statute for affording identical Remedies in	480 sq.
Creditors, Relief from Claims of, in Bankruptcy	345
,, Compositions with, in Bankruptcy	345
Crime, A, Definition of	286
,, ,, Distinguished from a Civil Injury	286, 287
,, ,, Analysis of Elements of	290
Crimes, Laws of Civil Injuries and, Place and Import of	100–102
,, ,, relating to	297
,, Consummate, Distinction between them and Attempts to Commit Crimes	299
,, Classification of, its Place in a Scheme of Criminal Law	300
,, Concurrent, as Affecting Punishment	301

INDEX. 525

	PAGE
Crimes, Mischief of Creating Artificial	514
Criminal Liability, at what Age it commences by English Law	86
„ Act, its Elements	298
„ Cases, Court of Appeal for	341
„ Pleading, Juridical Character of	328
„ Procedure, Conflicting Theories of	349 sq.
Cross-examination, Claims of Rival Suitors in respect of	339, 340
„ „ „ Prosecutor and Prisoner in respect of	339
Culpa Lata, Levis, and *Levissima*, Distinctions between	203, 204
Curator, Purposes of his Appointment	260
„ *Prodigi*, Policy of Institution of	260
Customs, Recognition and Adoption of, a Source of Law	52
Damages, Vindictive, Nature of	211
Death, a Fact on which the Science of Jurisprudence depends	12
„ viewed as an Act rather than as an Event, in case of Homicide	94
„ The Punishment of, its Juridical Bearing	311–313
„ „ „ In Relation to Prerogative of Pardon	352, 356
„ „ „ Evidence before Capital Punishment Commission concerning	357–360
Decisions of International Courts, a Source of International Law	408
Declarations, as a Ground of Suspicion	338
Deed, English, as a Mode of Transfer	164
Definition of Leading Terms, a Topic of the Science of Jurisprudence	49
Délits, Contraventions, and *Crimes*, Nature of Division of Offences into, in France	302
Demurrer, Juridical Nature of a	325
Dependence of a State, its Limitations and Modes	416, 417
Depositary, A, Nature of his Rights	151, 152
Digest, Signs of Attempting a, in England	488
Diligence, Want of, what	203, 204
Diminutio Capitis, as a Mode of Forfeiture	170
Diplomatists, Correspondence of, a Source of International Law	408
Disobedience to Law, Act of, must be Intentional	4
Disposition as a Ground of Suspicion	338
Dissolution of Contract, Rights to, where Classified	211
Distress, Nature of Laws of	345, 346
Divorce, Law of, what Elements it involves	10
„ Nature and Policy of Laws of	252–257
„ Modes of Legislating with respect to	256, 258
„ Court, Mode of Pleading in the English	327, 328
„ Rules in Private International Law respecting	384–387
Domicile, Nature and Juridical Import of	376–378
Domicilii, Lex, Meaning of	378
Dominium, Nature and Incidents of	148, 149, 151
Donatio Mortis Causâ, Import of	167
Dsoor, Mr., his views on Irregular Warfare by Population of an Invaded Territory	412

	PAGE
Droop, Mr., his views on Modes of Distinguishing Combatants from Non-combatants	444, 445
Drunkards as Contractors	187
Duress, Persons under, as Contractors	188, 189
Duties imposed by Law without Rights being conferred, Certain	65
„ Absolute, not included in Mr. Austin's Divisions	283, 284
Duty, Explanation of Term	76–79
„ A, how far it presupposes a Right	76
Easements, Nature of	150, 151
„ under what head Classified	149
Ecclesiastical Corporations, Laws relating to	281
„ System of Europe: its Influence on International Law	402
Education Laws, under what head Classified	249
„ of Children, Who Legally Responsible for	248, 257
Educational Corporations, Laws relating to	281
Eleemosynary „ „ „ „	281
Embezzlement, Prosecution for, a Mode of Protecting Rights of Ownership	175
Emphyteusis, Rights implied in	149, 150
Error, a Fact Impairing Moral Responsibility	85, 87
Equitable Pleas: their Historical Import	327
„ „ Recent Permission of Use of, in Common Law Courts	479
„ and Legal Rights, Suggested Statute for Recognising in one and the same Court	480
Equity, a New Series of Legal Principles	13
„ administered by a New Set of Officials	13
„ an Instrument of Legal Reform	15
„ a Source of Law	52
„ Notion of, in relation to the Law of Trusts	264
„ Courts of, how distinguishable from Prætorian Court at Rome	329
„ Convenience and Modes of Fusing, with Common Law	479–482
Escheat as a Mode of Forfeiture	170
Espionage, a Vicious Consequence of Multiplying Crimes	514
Established Church, Nature of Laws in Support of	460, 461
Establishment (Church), Juridical Import of Term	460, 461
Estates, Copyhold, Rights implied in	149
„ Fee-simple „ „ „	148
„ Tail „ „ „	149
„ Usufructuary „ „ „	149
Ethical Science, Relation of, to Science of Jurisprudence	25, 29, 30–34
Ethics and Social Ethics: how far they can be treated independently of each other	35
Event, Explanation of Term	93, 94
„ Bankruptcy, when regarded as an	94
„ Death „ „ „ „	94
„ Marriage „ „ „ „	94
Evidence of Acts involved in Idea of Law	3

INDEX. 527

	PAGE
Evidence of Character, its Nature	313–316
" Circumstantial	332–339
" Classification of Kinds of	331, 332
" Direct	332–335
" of Experts	308
" Expediency of Laws Regulating Admission of	330
" Laws Regulating, included in Laws of Procedure	102
" Medical, in Cases of Lunacy	308
"Evidentiary" Facts: their Nature and Juridical Import	334–339
Exculpation, Grounds of	301, 303
" Classification of Grounds of	289
Execution of Sentence, Laws relating to	341
Executive Authority: Meaning of Phrase, and Distinction from Legislative Authority	105, 106, 117
Executive Authority, Functions of	117
" " Component Elements of	117, 118
" " Analysis of Laws Regulating	121
" " Laws providing Securities against Abuses by	119, 120
" " Its Special Functions in the Ratification of Treaties	430, 431
Executors, Laws relating to	262, 270
" Rights of Action for Injuries committed by: where classified	201
Experts, Evidence of	308
Extenuating Circumstances, History and Import of the Verdict of, in France	341, 358, 379
Extortion, Place, in a Scheme of Criminal Law, of Laws relating to	301
Extradition, Doubtful Right of States to	421
" Doctrine of, in relation to Political Offences	392
" of Fugitives Accused of Murder	390
" Place of Topic of	388
" Treaties, their General Nature	392
Extraordinaria, System of Procedure at Rome, its Historical Import	326
Extraordinary Remedies, Place of Laws providing	342
Fact, Questions Involved in Trial of Issues of	329
Factory Acts, under what head Classified	249
Family Life, what Embryonic Juridical Facts it implies	20
Father and Child, Laws relating to	235, 245, 247, 250, 257, 258
Fear as a Ground for Suspecting an Accused Person	339
Fee-simple Estate, meaning of Phrase	148
Felonies and Misdemeanors, Historical Nature of the Division	302
Felons as Owners	147
Feoffment as a Sign of Transfer	164
Feudalism, its Influence on the Creation of International Law	401
" M. Guizot's Account of the Prevalence of, in Europe	401
" what was implied in its very Nature	402
Fiction, Legal, Professor Maine's Theory respecting	13
" " A Source of Law	52

	PAGE
Fideicommissa, their History in relation to the Law of Trusts	263, 266, 270
Fideicommissarius, his Functions	267
Fiduciarius, how Appointed	270
„ his Functions	267
Fiscus, a Person	81
„ whether a Person or a Thing	142
Fisheries in Canada, Treaties Regulating Disputed Claims to	426
Fixtures, under what head Classified	135, 136
Forgery, Place, in a Scheme of Criminal Law, of Laws relating to	301
Forfeiture, where Classed	157
„ Juridical Import of, as a Mode of acquiring Rights of Ownership	170
„ As a Penalty in International Law	410
Foreign Law as a Topic of Legal Study	490, 501, 502
"Formulary" System of Procedure at Rome, its Juridical Nature	325, 330
Fraud, Analysis of the state of Mind implied in, a Main Department of Juridical Enquiry	12
„ a Fact impairing Moral Responsibility	85, 87
„ Import and Illustrations of	84, 88
„ on what Ground it relieves the Person pleading it	83
„ Regulation of Legal Consequences of	88, 92
„ Constructive, Explanation of	92
„ „ a Fact artificially held to impair Moral Responsibility	85
French Writers, their value to the Juridical Student	503
Fruits of Crime, Carrying off, as a Ground of Suspicion	339
Geneva, Conventions of, 1864 and 1868, Nature and Purport of	449
German Philosophical Language, Value of Acquaintance with, to Juridical Students	505
„ Words to express Idea of "Law" untranslateable	505
Germany, Use to Juridical Student of Juridical Literature of	505
Government, a Fact on which the Science of Jurisprudence depends	12
„ Rudimentary Form of, how accounted for	21
„ Formal Creation of, how explained	20
„ Notion of, contemporaneous with that of Law	97
„ Science of	93
„ and Direct Moral Forces, Contending Theories as to their several Provinces	511, 517
Grotius, Explanation of Popularity of his Work	407
„ Roman Vesture of his Work	408
Growth of Law, Mode of, as Affecting Question of Codification	476, 477
Guaranty, Contract of	216, 226
Guardian and Ward, Foundations of Relationship	259, 260
„ „ „ Laws relating to, under what head Classed	235, 258
„ „ „ Scheme of Laws relating to	262
Guardianship of Children, Who Legally Responsible for	248, 257
„ „ „ Modes of Providing for	260, 261

INDEX. 529

	PAGE
Guardianship of Lunatics	260, 261
Guerilla-bands, Nature of, and Rules respecting	444, 445
Guizot, M., his Account of the Feudal Institutions of Europe	401

Hæreditas, a Person 81
" whether a Person or a Thing 142
HANSEATIC League, Laws of, as a Source of International Law . 405
Health, Rights to Enjoyment of Conditions of 288
Historical Methods, Identical, for some purposes, with Logical Methods 18
" School, as opposed to Philosophical School in GERMANY 471, 472
History, Science of, recognises Facts already reduced to Scientific Form 16
Homicide, Difficulties attending Verbal Description of . . 357–360
HUNGARY; its Constitutional Relations to AUSTRIA . . . 417
Husband and Wife, Laws relating to, under what head Classed 235, 236
" " " Distribution of Topics of Laws relating to . 236
" " " Description of Moral and Legal Relationship of 236–239
" " " Signs of Creation of Relationship of . . 239–243
" " " Rights and Duties Accruing as between . 243–252
" " " Signs of Termination of Legal Relationship of . 252
" " " Rights of Action for Injuries to, where Classed . 291
" " " Rules of Private International Law respecting 385–387

Idiocy, a Fact Impairing Moral Responsibility 85
Ignorance, Regulation of Legal Consequences of 88
" of Law, Presumption against 89
Immorality, Contracts Void on Ground of 228
Imprisonment, Rights of Action for False, where Classed . . 290
Imputability, Legal, Three Distinct Sorts of Capacity needed for . 84
Incest, Ground of Laws forbidding 243
" Place, in a Scheme of Criminal Law, of Laws relating to . 301
Indemnity, Contract of 216, 226
Independence of States, Limitations of Doctrine of . . . 416, 417
" " " Rights presupposed in . . . 420, 421
Independent, Meaning of a State being 416, 417
INDIA, English Argument in favour of Annexation of Territory in . 423
Infamia, its Operation in Roman Law 276
Infancy, a Fact Impairing Moral Responsibility 85–87
" as Operating on Capacity for Ownership . . . 144, 145
" " " " " Making Contracts . 184–186
Infants as Contractors 184–186
" Guardianship of 260, 261
" Infirmative Suppositions," BENTHAM's Use of Expression . . 336
In Fraudem Legis, Doctrine of 380
Injunction, a Process for Protecting Rights of Ownership . . 174
" Nature of Process of 174, 342
" Inquisitorial" System of Criminal Procedure as opposed to "Litigious" System 349, 350
Insanity, a Fact Impairing Moral Responsibility . . . 85–87

M M

530   INDEX.

	PAGE
Insanity, as operating on Capacity for Ownership . . . 144, 145	
" as operating " " " Making Contracts . . 154, 157	
" as a Ground of Exculpation 290, 306–309	
Instruments of a Crime in the Possession of the Accused, as a Ground of Suspicion 338	
Insurance, Interpretation of Contracts of 206	
" Fire, Liability of Company in Case of Insurer's Negligence . 207	
" Life, Implied Conditions in Contract of 203	
" Marine, Grounds of Exemption from Liability under Contract of 206	
Intemperance, a Fact Impairing Moral Responsibility . . 85–87	
Intention, Analysis of, a Main Department of Juridical Enquiry . 12	
" " " a Criminal 298	
Intercourse, A Cessation or Suspension of, as Penalty for Breach of International Law 411, 412	
Interdict, a Process for Protecting Rights of Ownership . . . 174	
" Process of 342	
Interest, Payment of, under Contracts, how Determined . . 210, 211	
Interference, Rights of States to Security against 420	
International Law, its Nature and Origin 391, 392	
" " Code of, Alleged Analogy of a, to a Body of Moral Prescriptions 46	
" " Effect of, on History of Law . . . 45–47	
" " Sources of 46, 404–409	
" " General Character of Sanctions of . . 47, 409	
" " its Sanctions Described and Enumerated . 409–413	
" " its Conditions as a Possibility . . . 401–404	
" " Private . . . . 306 sq.	
" " Public . . . . 391 sq.	
" " " how it illustrates the Essential Nature of all Law 502	
" " " Concern of the Jurist with . . 503, 504	
" " " its Function in Legal Education . 501–504	
" " " Opposed to International Morality . 393–395	
Interpretation, Theory of 63	
" True Import of, as a Process 59, 60	
" Complete Meaning of Term as part of a Judicial Process 59	
" Judicial, an Instrument in Legal Reforms . . . 15	
" Processes of, as Essential Sides of the Phenomenon of Law 40	
" of Acts, its general bearing on Legal Classification . 29	
" Extensive or Restrictive, a Source of Law . . . 52	
" how Affected by Mode of Publication of Laws . 54	
" of Treaties, Obstacles to Universal Canon of . 428, 429	
" Difficulties of, as Affecting the Question of Codification 474–476	
Interrogatories in Procedure, their Origin and Nature . . 339, 340	

	PAGE
Interrogatories, Extension of Use of, to Courts of Common Law.	479
Intoxication, Necessaries Supplied during Fit of	87
Invasion, Irregular Resistance to, by Population	442–444
Invention as a Mode of Acquiring Rights of Ownership: where Classed	157
„ Juridical Import of	161
Issues of Law and of Fact, Modes of Trial of	328, 329, 340
JEFFERSON, Mr., his Statement of the Monroe Doctrine	422
Judicial Decisions, a Source of Law	58
„ Separation, Policy of Permitting a	256
Jurisprudence, a Science	1, 4
„ What Constitutes the Science of	4–8
„ Extension and Enrichment of Science of	9
„ Science of, Dependent on Growth of Positive Law	12
„ „ „ Ultimately Dependent on Facts of Human Life and of Natural World (as Age, Sex, Birth, Death)	12
„ „ „ Description of	18
„ „ „ Emphatically a German Production	504, 505
„ „ „ True Import of Phrase	507–509
„ „ „ General Prospects of	457 sq.
„ A System of, how Distributed	44
„ Mr. AUSTIN's Use of Term	507
„ Various Uses of Term	507
Jurist, Functions of a	6–8, 18, 19, 20, 504
„ The, his Concern with Systems of Foreign Law	501
Juries, Policy of requiring Unanimity from	363–365
Jury, Trial by, its Juridical Aspects	328, 330, 363
Jus ad Rem does not always precede a Conveyance	165
„ in Re, under what head Classed	149
„ „ Rem, Historical Import of Phrase	127
„ Rerum, its Historical opposition to Jus Personarum	126, 127
„ Personarum „ „ „ Rerum	126, 127
„ in Personam, Historical Import of Phrase	127
„ Gentium, its Bearing on Private International Law	366, 367
„ „ „ „ Public „ „	403
„ Naturale „ „ „ Private „ „	366, 367
„ Naturæ „ „ „ the History of Public International Law	403
Justice, Courts of, Laws for the Establishment of	319 sq.
„ Natural, Interest of Phrase to Jurist	31
Kidnapping, Place, in a Scheme of Criminal Law, of Laws relating to	301
"King, The, can do no Wrong," Import of Phrase	118
Language, A Fact on which Science of Jurisprudence depends	12
„ is reinforced from Observations of the Vulgar	17
„ Inherent Difficulties of	55

INDEX.

		PAGE
Language of Law, how affecting its Administration		31, 32
,, its Imperfections as affecting the Question of Codification		474, 475

Law, Nature of 2
— Various Uses of the Word 70
,, of God; Natural; Moral 70
,, Explanation of Term 7
,, and Morality, Real Connection of 77, 78
,, Affects to Control Acts alone 74, 75
,, Interpretation of . . . . . . 3, 50 sq.
,, Sources of, involved in Idea of Law 3
,, ,, ,, Investigation of . . . . . 50 sq.
,, ,, ,, Enumeration of Possible 52
,, ,, ,, Time of First Appearance of . . . 22
,, Notion of, how Developed 24
,, Not an Isolated Social Phenomenon 18
,, Growing Fixity and Distinctness of 19
,, the Expression of Moral Order demanded by the People . 21
,, not the Sole Cause of Human Society . . . 35
,, Fact of, presents itself in Two Aspects . . . 41
,, Phenomena of, Distributed under their Main Heads . . 27
,, Three Essential Aspects of 49
,, Any particular System of: how Analysed . . . 42
,, of Persons opposed to Law of Things 27
,, of Persons 90, 100
,, of Things 10
,, "Public and Private." Criticism of Opposition . . 98
,, Growth of Positive, Determined by National Progress . 12
,, "Case," in England: what 58
,, Condition of relations of Written and Unwritten, in England 483-487
,, Common, Convenience and Modes of Fusing it with Equity 479-482
,, ,, (English) an Example of Formation of Certain Sources of Law 52
,, of "Torts," its Place 101
,, Relating to Husband and Wife . . . . 236 sq.
,, ,, ,, Parent and Child . . 235, 245, 247, 250, 257, 258
,, ,, ,, Guardian and Ward 235, 258
,, Constitutional, its Place 97, 98
,, Systems of Foreign, as Sources of Law 52
,, Foreign, as a Topic of Legal Study . . . 499, 501, 502
,, Private International, its Nature . . . . 366 sq.
,, Public ,, ,, ... 391 sq.
,, ,, ,, Functions of, in Legal Education . 501-504
,, ,, ,, Sources of . . . 46, 404-409
,, ,, ,, its Effect on History of Law . . 45-47
,, Primitive: what it is the key to 48
,, of Murder laid down in McNaughten's Case . . . 33
,, Trial of Issue of 340

INDEX. 533

	PAGE
Law and Morality: Contending Theories as to their respective Provinces	510–517
,, Written and Unwritten: their several Qualities as Affecting the Question of Codification	473–475
,, German Words to express Idea of, Untranslateable	505
Laws of Nature, Interest of Phrase to Jurist	31
,, Written: on what they depend for their Special Value	56
,, Unwritten, Sources of	58
,, Written and Unwritten, Relative Values of	59, 474, 475
,, Various Bases of Classification of	26, 27, 96
,, Relating to the Constitution and Administration of the State: their Place	97, 98
,, ,, ,, ,, Distribution of 103 sq.	
,, of Ownership, Purpose and Place of	99
,, of Contract	176 sq.
,, ,, ,, Historical and Real Place of	99
,, Affecting Special Classes of Persons, Place of	100, 230 sq.
,, of Civil Injuries and Crimes, Place of	100–102, 283
,, ,, Crimes	297 sq.
,, ,, Procedure	317 sq.
,, ,, ,, their Place	100–102
,, Relating to Advocates	276–280
,, ,, ,, Attorneys	276–280
,, ,, ,, Barristers	276–280
,, ,, ,, Certain Corporate Bodies	281
,, ,, ,, Notaries Public	276–280
,, ,, ,, Proctors	276–280
,, ,, ,, Solicitors	276–280
,, ,, ,, Trustees	262–276
,, ,, ,, Writers to the Signet	276–280
,, of Evidence, their Expediency	330
,, Examples of Conflict of	369
,, Private International, respecting Ownership	378–382
,, ,, ,, ,, Contract	383, 384
,, ,, ,, Affecting Special Classes of Persons	384–387
,, ,, ,, respecting Procedure	387–389
Leading Terms, List of	48, 49, 71
,, ,, Explanation of	69–95
,, ,, Created by the Sentiments of the People	69
Lectures: their Function in Legal Education	495–497
Legal Education: its Prospects in England	490 sq.
,, System, a Skeleton, Leading Principles of	61, 62
,, ,, Basis of Distribution of a	67
,, ,, Leading Divisions of a	67
Legis Actiones: their Nature	324
Legislation, Direct and Conscious	13
,, the most effective instrument in Changing the Law	13
,, Rudimentary Form of, how accounted for	21

534   INDEX.

	PAGE
Legislation, Stage of Conscious, when it is reached	24
„ Science of, how related to Jurisprudence	37
„ Judicial, a Source of Law	52
„ Statutory, a Source of Law	53
Legislative Authority, Meaning of Phrase, and Distinction from Executive Authority	105, 106
Legislator, Will of, how discovered	53
Legitimatio per subsequens Matrimonium, Policy of	250, 251
Legitimation of Children	250, 251
Letting and Hiring, Nature of Contract of	222
Lex Aquilia, Action under, a Mode of Protecting Rights of Ownership	175
„ *Domicilii*, Meaning of	378
„ *Fori*, Meaning and Application of	382, 384, 387, 388
„ *Loci Actus*, Meaning and Application of	382, 386, 387
„ „ *Rei Sitæ* „ „ „ „	379–382
„ *Situs*, Meaning of	379, 380
Libel in relation to Doctrine of Privilege	293, 294
Libels, Indecent, Place in a Scheme of Criminal Law, of Laws relating to	300
„ Malicious	301
Liberty, Public, what it imports	513, 514
Lien, as a Mode of Minimising Loss	207, 208
Limitation of Actions, Nature and Policy of Laws relating to	346, 347
"Litigious" System of Criminal Procedure, as opposed to "Inquisitorial" System	349, 350
Loan, Contract of, as Distinguishable from Sale	222
Locatio Conductio, Nature of Contract of	151
Logical Methods, Identical, for some purposes, with Historical	18
Lunatics as Owners	144, 145
„ „ Contractors	187, 188
„ Guardianship of	260, 261
Lunacy—see Insanity	
McNaughten's Case, Law of Murder laid down in	33
Maine, Professor, to what his Speculations owe their Importance	11
„ „ his Theory respecting Equity	13
„ „ „ „ „ Legal Fictions	13
„ „ „ Theories of Ownership	123, 124
„ „ „ Theory on Laws of Contract	176, 177
„ „ „ „ of the *Jus Naturale*	367
„ „ „ Description of the Development of *Jus Gentium* and *Jus Naturale*	403
Maintenance of Children, who Responsible for	248, 257
Malice, Analysis of, a main Department of Juridical Enquiry	12
„ Definitions of Term	305, 306
„ Actual, Meaning of Phrase	305, 306
„ Aforethought „ „ „	305, 306
„ Implied „ „ „	305, 306
„ Legal „ „ „	305, 306

	PAGE
Malice, Modes of Defining, in relation to Murder	359-361
Malicious Arrest, Rights of Action for, where Classed	200
,, Injury to Property, Rights of Action for, where Classed	200
,, Libel, Place in a Scheme of Criminal Law, of Law relating to	301
,, Prosecution, Rights of Action for, where Classed	200
Mancipatio, as a Sign of Transfer	164
Mandamus, Nature of Remedy by	342
Mandatary, Nature of his Rights	151, 152
Manslaughter, Law of, its Place in a Scheme of Criminal Law	301
,, Its varying Qualities	316
,, Difficulties attending its Distinction from Murder	357, 360
Marriage, a Fact on which the Science of Jurisprudence depends	13
,, Presupposes the Existence of Law	80
,, Primitive, as a Mode of National Training	467
,, Policy of Laws in Support of	463
,, a Fact artificially held to Impair Moral Responsibility	85
,, as Operating on Capacity for Ownership	144-146
,, when treated as an Event and when as an Act	94
,, not a Contract	216
,, Contracts in view of	215-218
,, Settlements, Law relating to Trustees of	270
,, Place, in a Scheme of Criminal Law, of Offences relating to	301
,, Fraudulent Evasion of Laws of, its Place in a Scheme of Criminal Law	301
,, Private International Laws respecting	385-387
Married Women as Owners	145, 146, 245-247
,, ,, ,, Contractors	190
Maxims, Legal, a Source of Law	52, 58
Medical Evidence in Cases of Lunacy	308
Métayer Tenancies, Rights implied in	140
Mill, Mr., his Criticisms of Mr. Austin's Divisions	283, 284
Minister of Justice, Policy of instituting a	351-353
Minors as Owners	145-147
,, under 25, Guardianship of	200
Misdemeanors and Felonies, Historical Nature of Divisions	302
Mistake, Analysis of, a Main Department of Juridical Enquiry	12
,, a Fact Impairing Moral Responsibility	85-87
Monroe Doctrine, Mr. Jefferson's Statement of	422, 423
,, ,, as stated by Mr. Monroe	422
Moral Responsibility, Terms Respecting Qualifications of	82
,, ,, Assumptions involved in	83
,, ,, Capacities essential to the Idea of	83
,, ,, Classification of Facts which are held to Impair	84, 85
,, ,, as shared between Principal and Agent	90
Morality, its Relation to Law	77, 78, 514-516
,, and Law (International) Contrasted	303-305
,, Constitutional, Meaning and Criticism of Phrase	104, 105
,, Absolute, true Import of Phrase	515, 516

536 INDEX.

	PAGE
Mortgage, Contract of, Assimilated to Contract In View of Sale	223
,, Suggested Mode of Fusing Rules in Equity and Common Law respecting	480
,, Aspect of, in Courts of Common Law and of Equity	269
Mortgagee, Nature of Rights of a	151, 152
,, Claims of a, in Common Law and in Equity	269, 270
Mortgagor, his Rights in English Law	152, 153, 269, 270
Mortmain, Effect of Laws of, on Law of Trusts	268
Motive, Analysis of, a Main Department of Juridical Enquiry	12
,, of an Accused, as Ground of Suspicion	338
Municipal Corporations, Laws relating to	281
Murder, its Place in a Scheme of Criminal Law	301
,, Presumptions made in applying Law of	305, 306
,, English Law of, as laid down in McNaughten's Case	33
,, Suggestions for Novel Definition of	357–360
,, Evidence before Capital Punishment Commission with respect to Crime of	357–360
Mutiny Act, Place of, in Legal System	120

NAPOLEON, his Indirect Influence on the Discussion of Codification in Germany	471
National Character, made up of what Elements	22
Nationality, Juridical Import of Term	375
, Mode of Determining, in FRANCE	375
Nations, Law of, said to be part of the LAW OF ENGLAND	344
"Natural" Agents as opposed to other Things	129
Naturalisation, Import of Laws of	375, 376
Nature, Laws of, Interest of Phrase to Jurist	31
,, "Law of," a Source of Law	52
Negligence, Analysis of, an important Department of Juridical Enquiry	12
,, Distinct Grades of	203, 204
,, Contributory, its Juridical Nature	328
Negotiable Securities, Contracts relating to	216, 227
Neutral Claims, Development and Nature of	434–438
,, ,, Grounds of Enforcing	436
,, ,, Modes ,, ,,	436, 437
,, Flag and Merchandise, Rules of Treaty of Paris respecting	433, 434
"Neutrality, The Armed," of 1801, its Influence on the Formation of Rules of International Law	503
NEW YORK Codes, their Interest and Value	502
Non-Combatant Population, Effects of War upon, as influencing Frequency of Wars	452, 453
Non-intervention, Recent phases of Doctrine of	308
Notaries Public, Laws relating to	270–280
Notice, Juridical Import of, in respect of Dishonour of Bill of Exchange	200
Novatio, its Operations	212
Noxalis Actio, its Nature as a Mode of Compensation	207
Nuisance, Rights of Action for, where Classed	290

INDEX. 537

	PAGE
Nuisances, Public, Place of Laws relating to, in a Scheme of Criminal Law	300
Obligation, Natural, Meaning of Phrase	200
Occupancy, Meaning of, as a Juridical Fact	157, 158
Occupation, Doctrine of, in International Law	422
OLERON, Laws of, as a Source of International Law	405
Opportunity to do a Criminal Act, as a Ground of Suspicion	338
Outlaws as Owners	146, 147
„ „ Contractors	193
Outlawry, as affecting Rights of Ownership	170
Own, Persons who	5, 143
Owned, Things	5, 128
Ownership, Function of Jurist in ascertaining Meaning of	462, 463
„ A Fact on which Jurisprudence depends	13
„ Quality, not Fact, of, a Proper Matter for Political Dispute	462, 463
„ General Nature of Fact of	122, 123
„ Progressive Vicissitudes of Fact of	123
„ Object and Place of Laws of	90, 125, 127, 128
„ Laws of	122 sq.
„ Distribution of Laws of	124, 125
„ Laws of, Implied in Theories of Community of Goods	463
„ Injuries to Rights of, under what head Classed	288, 290
„ Enumeration of Modes of Protecting Rights of	174
„ Development of Notion of, as affecting Progress of Jurisprudence	458
„ Professor MAINE's and Sir JOHN LUBBOCK's Speculations concerning	123, 124
„ Private, International Laws of	378–382
„ not a Creature of Antecedent Law	4
„ Notion of Individual, of Slow Growth	5
„ Individual, an Organic Element of Social Development	10
„ Exercise of Capacity of (Possession)	6, 153, 154
„ Fact of, begins or ends on the happening of what Events	5, 154
„ Rights of, explained	147, 148
„ „ „ as between Husband and Wife	245, 247
„ „ „ „ „ „ „ Various Species of	246, 247
„ „ „ „ „ Parent and Child	248–250
PALEY's and AUSTIN's Theories concerning Promise	205
Pardon, Prerogative of, its Nature and Policy	352–357
Parent and Child, Laws relating to	235, 236
PARIS, Treaty of, of 1856, Effect of Rules of	400, 433, 434
Parties to Actions, Law Determining the Proper	348, 349
Partnership, Nature and Elements of Contract of	226
Patent Right, Nature of	140, 141

538 INDEX.

	PAGE
Patent Right, Rights of Action for Infringement of, where Classed	291
Paterfamilias, his Rights of Ownership	132
Pawnbroker, Nature of his Rights	151, 152
Peace, Modes of Favouring, and Prospects of a Permanent.	399, 400, 456
Perjury, Laws of: their Place in a Scheme of Criminal Law	300
Person, Modern Notion of a	46
,, Explanation of Term	70, 80
,, Various Uses of Term	80
,, Distinction of a, from a Thing	79–81
,, Moral Responsibility of a, as a Ground for the Conception of Legal Relationship	12
,, Was the Roman Slave a	80
,, A "Fictitious" or "Artificial"	81
,, A Corporate Body is a Legal	81
,, A State as a	414, 415
Personal Rights, Distinction between, and Real Rights	27
,, Property, History of, and Distinction from Real Property	134, 135
,, Security, Rights to: under what head Classed	288, 290
,, "Statutes," "Real," and "Mixed," Meaning of expressions	380
Persons, The Classes of, contemplated by every Law as such	25
,, Quality of, as a Basis of Classification of Laws	26
,, Law of, opposed to Law of Things	27
,, ,, ,,	96, 100
,, Laws Affecting Special Classes of	230
,, ,, ,, ,, ,, their Place	100
,, who Own, Classification and Description of	143–147
,, ,, Make Contracts	181
,, Use of Term in Public International Law	414, 415
Philosophical School in Germany as opposed to the Historical	471, 472
Physical Science, Relation of, to Science of Jurisprudence	25
,, ,, Use of to Jurist	29
,, ,, Effect of Progress of, on War	440
Pignus, Nature of Contract of	151
Place, a Fact on which the Science of Jurisprudence Depends	12
Pleading, Functions of Lawyers as to	278
,, its Nature and Varieties	325–328
Pleas, Various Modes of Presenting or Joining	325–327
,, Equitable, Extension of Use of, to Common Law Courts	479
Plébiscite, Process of Resorting to a, characterised	424
Pledge, Distinguishable from Sale	222, 223
Political Authority, Supreme, Explanation of Phrase	74
,, ,, ,, cannot enjoy Rights nor be liable to Duties	77
,, Crimes, their Nature	360, 361
,, Economy recognises Classes of Facts already reduced to Scientific Form of	16
,, ,, its Relation to the Science of Jurisprudence	36
,, Science ,, ,, ,, ,, ,, ,, ,,	25

INDEX. 539

| | PAGE |

Politics, General, Science of, recognises Facts already reduced to Scientific Form 16
   „   „   „ of, what it comprehends 34
Possessio Naturalis and *ad Interdicta*, Meaning of . . . 153, 154
   „   „ how applicable in International Law . . 422
   „ *Civilis*, Meaning of 154
   „ *ad Usucapionem*, Meaning of 154
Possession, Juridical Import of 153, 154
   „ Usages and Contracts in reference to, on a Sale . 220, 221
Power of Appointment, Suggested Statutory Changes in Equitable Jurisdiction over 480, 481
Prætorian Jurisdiction at Rome Distinguished from that of Courts of Equity 320
Pre-emption, Rules regulating Claims to, on the part of an Occupying Army 448
Preparations for a Crime, as a Ground of Suspicion . . . 338
Prerogative of English Monarch, Import of Term . . . 111
   „   „ Pardon, its Nature and Policy . . . 352–357
Prescription, Explanation of 162, 163
   „ where Classed 157
   „ Policy of Laws of 347
"Primary" Rights, their Nature as opposed to "Secondary" Rights 289, 290, 291
Principals and Accessories in Crimes, Law relating to . . 300
   „   „ Agents, Nature of Mutual Relations of . 193, 224
Prisoners of War, Progressive Mitigation of Treatment of . 439
Private International Law, its Nature . . . . 360 sq.
   „   „   „ its Materials and their Classification 369–372
   „   „   „ its Existing Condition and Prospects 389, 390
   „ Law, as opposed to Public Law, Criticism of Phrase . 98
Privilege, Explanation of Term in Reference to Defamation . 293, 294
Privileges of Members of English Parliament, Illustrations of, and Meaning of Term 111, 112
Prize Courts, their International Character and Importance . 400
Probate, Court of, its Executive Functions generally . . 322
   „   „   „ Functions in Appointing Administrators . 271
   „   „   „ Modes of Pleading in the . . . 327, 328
Procedure, Framing Rules of, a Source of Law . . . 52
   „ Laws of, Meaning and Place of 100, 102
   „   „   „ Matters dealt with by 319
   „   „   „ 317
   „ Criminal, Conflicting Theories of . . . 319 sq.
   „ Private International Law concerning . . 387–389
Proctors, Laws relating to 276–280
Profession, Legal, an Engine for Adapting Law to National Exigencies 13–15
   „   „ Habits of Mind of a 14
Professional Lawyers, Laws relating to Classes of . . 276–280

		PAGE
Property, an Abused Expression		4
,, Individual Interest in, as contrasted with Family Interest in		12
,, Real and Personal, History and Meaning of Distinction between		134, 135
Promise, PALEY's and AUSTIN's Theories of		205
Prosecutor, Policy of Instituting a Public		351, 352
Psychological Science, in relation to Science of Jurisprudence		25, 29
Public Law, Criticism of Phrase		98
,, International Law		391 sq.
Punishment, Juridical Aspects of		309–313
,, Idea of, is involved in Idea of Law		3
,, Place of Laws regulating Assignment of		341
,, Fear of, as an Instrument of Government		512
Quasi ex Contractu, Import of Obligations so called		199
,, Delict, Meaning and History of the Expression		205, 206
Rape, Law relating to, its Place in a Scheme of Criminal Law		301
Ratification, its Application to the Contracts of Agents		192
,, of Treaties, Modes of, criticised		430
Ratio Decidendi, Meaning of Phrase		58, 484
,, ,, Mode of Eliciting the		484, 485
Real Rights, Distinction between, and Personal Rights		27
,, Property, History and Meaning of its Distinction from Personal Property		134, 135
Religious Faith of Parents, as Legally Affecting Education of Children		249
Remedies, Extraordinary, Place of Laws Providing		319, 342
Reports of Cases, Condition of, in ENGLAND		485, 486
Reprisals, as Penalties for Breach of International Law		411, 421
Reputation, Rights to, under what head Classed		288, 290
Requisitions, Rules regulating Claims to make, on the part of an Army		448
Res Fungibiles and Res Non-fungibiles, Nature of Distinction described		138, 139
,, Mancipi and ,, Nec-mancipi, Nature of Distinction described		135
,, Singulæ ,, Universitas Rerum ,, ,, ,, ,,		120, 142
Residence, Fact of, as Implied in Domicile		377
Responsibility, Moral, Allegation of, Involved in Idea of Law		3
Restitutio in Integrum, Operation of, upon Contracts		213
Retortions, as Penalties for a Breach of International Law		411
RHODIAN Laws, as Sources of International Law		405
Right, Explanation of Term		76–79
,, A, presupposes a Corresponding Duty		76
,, of Search		433
,, ,, Action for Civil Injuries		200
Rights, Distinction between Real and Personal		27
,, of Ownership, Explanation of Phrase		147, 148
,, ,, ,, in National Territory		422
,, Vested and Contingent, Explanation of Phrase		172, 173

INDEX. 541

	PAGE
Rights, "Primary," their Nature as opposed to "Secondary" Rights	283
,, "Sanctioning"	66, 283
,, "Secondary"	66, 283
,, to Conditions of Health	288, 290
,, ,, Personal Security	288, 290
,, ,, Reputation	288, 290
,, of States Classified	420
,, of Way, under what head Classed	150
,, and Duties of Belligerents	432
,, ,, ,, ,, Neutrals	434
Robbery, Law relating to, its Place in a Scheme of Criminal Law	301
ROMAN LAW, its Influence on Modern International Law	402, 403
,, ,, its Province in Legal Education	499, 500
,, ,, in SCOTLAND, its continuing Influence	500
,, ,, Dutch, its survival in some English Colonies as adding Interest to its Study	500
Sale, not a Contract	210
,, Contracts in view of	210, 220
,, Subsidiary Contracts attending	221
,, Notion of, underlies the Notion of certain other Contracts	222, 223
"Sanctioning" Rights	66, 283
,, ,, their Nature as opposed to "Primary" rights	283
Sanctions, their Nature in Public International Law	409, 410, 413
,, in Public International Law Enumerated	410, 411
,, ,, ,, ,, Modes of enforcing	411-413
SAVIGNY, his Researches into Doctrine of Domicile	377
,, his Position in the Discussion on Codification in Germany	471-473
Science, a, Description of	16
,, of Jurisprudence, Definition of	18
,, ,, Statical and Dynamical view of	43, 44
,, Ethical, its relation to Jurisprudence	25, 26
,, of Government ,, ,,	38
,, of Legislation ,, ,,	37
,, Physical ,, ,,	25, 26
,, Psychological ,, ,,	25, 26
,, of Political Economy ,, ,,	36
,, Political, what it Comprehends	34
Search, Penalties for resisting	410
,, Right of	433
"Secondary" Rights as opposed to "Primary" Rights	283, 290, 291
Seditions, Conspiracies, and Libels viewed as Political Crimes	301
Senatus Consultum Macedonianum, its Purport	185
Sentence, Laws relating to, their place	341
,, ,, ,, Execution of	341
Séparation des Biens, Policy of	256
Servitudes, under what head Classified	149
,, Nature of	150, 151

	PAGE
Set-off, its Juridical Nature	328
Sex, Difference of, a Fact on which Science of Jurisprudence depends	12
„ „ Qualifying Moral Responsibility	85, 86
„ „ Grounds of Recognising, in Laws	464–470
Sexes, Laws Regulating the Relations of the	464–470
Slander, Rights of Action for, where Classed	290
„ of Title, Action for, a Mode of Protecting Rights of Ownership	175
Slavery, LORD MANSFIELD's Opinion on	78
„ Abolition of, how operating on History of Law	45–47
Social Ethics, Science of, recognises Facts already reduced to Scientific Form	16
Soldier, Professional, Tendency to oppose the, to the Citizen	430–441
Solicitors, Rights of Action for Injuries committed by, where Classed	291
SOMMERSETT's Case	78
"Source" of Law, Definition of Term	52
Sources of Law, Notion of, involved in Idea of Law	3
„ „	49
„ „ Explanation of Phrase	50
„ „ Time of First Appearance of	22
„ „ Proximate Causes of parts of Legal System	51
„ „ Enumeration of	52, 53
„ International Law, Meaning of Phrase	404, 405
„ „ „ Character of	46
„ Unwritten Law in England, what	58
Sovereignty, Territorial, its Nature and Import	372, 373
Special Classes of Persons, Laws affecting	230
„ „ „ Injuries to Rights appertaining to	288, 291
Specification, where Classed	157
„ Meaning of	159
State, Explanation of Term	71–73
„ Definition of a, in International Law	414–416
Station in Life, as a Ground of Suspicion of an Accused Person	338
Status, Conception of	231–235
Statute of Frauds, its Policy and Import	197
„ of Limitations, Debt barred by	200
„ Suggestion of a, for Fusing Law and Equity	480
Statutes, English, Existing Condition of	486, 487
„ „ Suggestions for Improvements in Formal Enactments of	487, 488
„ "Real," "Personal," and "Mixed," Meaning of Expressions	280
Stipulatio, Capacity of Articulation essential to	184
Stoppage in Transitu, as a Mode of Minimising Loss	207, 208
ST. PETERSBURG, Convention of, of 1868, its Purport	449, 450
"Substantive" Law, Opposed to "Adjective" Law, by BENTHAM	283
Suicide, Laws relating to, their Place in a Scheme of Criminal Law	300
System, Legal, Leading Principles of a skeleton	61, 62

INDEX. 543

	PAGE
Terminology, Legal, Promoted by Legal Profession	14
Terms, Leading, List of	46
,, ,, Definition of, a Topic of the Science of Jurisprudence	49
,, ,, Need and Use of clear Intuition of Meaning of	49
Territorial Sovereignty, its Nature and Import	372, 373
Territory, National, Rights of Ownership of States in	422
,, ,, ,, ,, ,, ,, International Questions as to Modes of Acquiring	422–424
,, Enemy's, Treatment and Occupation of, by an Invading Army	446–449
Testamentary Method, what it involves	7, 8
,, Disposition, Political Grounds of recognising a	167, 168
Text-Writers, Influence of, as a Source of International Law	407
Theft, Laws relating to, their Place in a Scheme of Criminal Law	301
THIBAUT, his Position in the Discussion on Codification in Germany	471, 472
Thing, Interposition of a, a Basis of Classification of Laws	26, 27
,, Explanation of Term	79, 80
Things, Corporeal and Incorporeal, their Distinction	139–142
,, Destructible and Indestructible	6
,, Divisible and Indivisible	6
,, Enjoyable by one Person or by more than one	6
,, Law of, Opposed to Law of Persons	27
,, ,, ,,	96
,, Movable and Immovable	6, 129, 131
,, ,, ,, ,, Described and Classified	131–138
,, ,, ,, ,, Rules respecting, in Private International Law	379, 382
,, Owned, Modes of Distributing	128, 129
,, Perishable and Imperishable	6
,, Treated as Persons	81
Threats, as a Ground of Suspicion of an Accused	338
Time, a Fact on which the Science of Jurisprudence depends	12
Title, Various Meanings of Term	171, 172
,, how the Term is best Used	172
Torts, Law of, its Place	101
,, Opposed in English Law to Breach of Contract	284
Trade or Property Marks, Place, in a Scheme of Criminal Law, of Laws relating to	301
Tradition, as a Sign of Transfer	164
Treason, Place, in a Scheme of Criminal Law, of Law of	300
,, viewed as a Political Crime	361
,, Constructive, Place, in a Scheme of Criminal Law, of Law of	300
,, Misprision of ,, ,, ,, ,, ,, ,, ,, ,, ,,	300
Treaties, on what their Possibility rests	425
,, their various Purposes	425
,, Modes in which they become Sources of International Law	406, 407
,, the Making and Upholding of, a Condition of lasting Peace	455, 456

	PAGE
Treaties, Causes of Imperfect Observance of	429–431
,, Ratification of, Suggestions for Regulating	430, 431
,, of Extradition, their Nature	382
Treaty of Paris of 1856, Effect of Rules of	406, 433, 434
,, Rights of States created by	421
Trespass, Rights of Action for, where Classed	290
Trial of Issue of Fact	329
,, ,, ,, Law	340
,, by Jury, its Juridical Aspects	328, 330, 363
Tribunals, Commercial, Nature of, as Exceptional Remedies	342–344
Troops, Rules for regulating the Billeting of	418
Trust, a Fact Artificially Qualifying Moral Responsibility	85, 91
,, Juridical Nature of a	263–265
,, Elements in the Conception of a	263, 264
Trustees, Moral Responsibility of, how measured	91
,, why Treated as a "Special Class" of Persons	265
,, Laws relating to	262–276
,, their Rights and Duties	272–275
,, Modes of Enforcing Duties of	275
,, Rights of Action for Injuries committed by, where Classed	291
,, Suggested Statutory Changes in Equitable Jurisdiction over	480
Trusteeship, Description of the Relation implied in	267
,, Modes in which it takes its Rise	268–272
Trusts, Principle of, as Affecting Capacity of Ownership	145
,, Constructive, Meaning of Phrase	269

Unanimity of Juries, General Policy of requiring the	363–365
Uniform, a National, as a Mode of Distinguishing Combatants from Non-Combatants	441, 444, 445
UNITED STATES OF AMERICA, Nature of Constitution of	104, 114, 120, 417, 430
,, ,, ,, Amendments ,,	114
,, ,, ,, their Relation to the Treaty of Paris of 1856	434
Universitas Rerum opposed to *Singulæ Res*	142
,, *Juris*, as a Ground of the Rules in International Law Affecting Movables	381
Universities, their Province in Legal Education	493
Usucapio, as a Form of Prescription	162
Usufructuary Estates, Rights implied in	140, 151
Usufructus, under what head Classified	151
Usus, ,, ,, ,,	151
Utility, Recognition of General, a Source of Law	52

Vaccination Laws, under what head Classified	249
Vested and Contigent Rights, Nature and Import of the Distinction	172, 173
Vigilantibus non Dormientibus subvenit Lex, Meaning of	347
War, as a Penalty for Breach of International Law	411
,, The Sole Legal Justification of	420

	PAGE
War, Limitations on Powers possessed by a Nation at	431, 432
" Rules for Mitigation of Consequences of	432
WARD, Mr., his Enquiry into the Foundation and History of the Law of Nations	402
Wards, Rights of Action for Injury to, where Classed	291
Warranty, Contracts of, as attending Sale	221
Way, Rights of, under what head Classified	150
WESTLAKE, Mr., his Theory of Private International Law of Movables	380, 381
Will, an Element in Moral Responsibility	82, 84
" how far present in cases of Infancy and Insanity	83
Will, A, what it involves	7
" Juridical Elements of	168, 169
" its Formalities	8
" Made during a Lucid Interval	84
" Nuncupatory, Import of	167
Wills, Laws relating to Suppression or Mutilation of, their Place in a Scheme of Criminal Law	301
Women, Laws regulating Relations of Men and	464–470
" Married, as Owners	145, 146, 245–247
" " as Contractors	190
Words, Changing significance of	55, 476
Wounded, Rules providing for Care of the Sick and, in War	449, 454
Writers to the Signet, Laws relating to	270, 280
Written and Unwritten Law, their respective Qualities as Affecting the Question of Codification	472–476
" " " their State and Relations in England	483–487

WORKS BY JOHN STUART MILL.

PRINCIPLES of POLITICAL ECONOMY, with some of their Applications to Local Philosophy:—
    Library Edition (the Seventh), 2 vols. 8vo. 30s.
    People's Edition, crown 8vo. 5s.

On REPRESENTATIVE GOVERNMENT:—
    Library Edition (the Third), 8vo. 9s.
    People's Edition, crown 8vo. 2s.

A SYSTEM of LOGIC. Seventh Edition. 2 vols. 8vo. 25s.
    STEBBING'S ANALYSIS of MILL'S SYSTEM of LOGIC. Second Edition, revised, in 12mo. price 3s. 6d.
    KILLICK'S STUDENT'S HANDBOOK of MILL'S SYSTEM of LOGIC, lately published, in crown 8vo. price 3s. 6d.

An EXAMINATION of Sir WILLIAM HAMILTON'S PHILOSOPHY, and of the Principal Philosophical Questions discussed in his Writings. Third Edition, revised. 8vo. 16s.

DISSERTATIONS and DISCUSSIONS, POLITICAL, PHILOSOPHICAL, and HISTORICAL; reprinted from the Edinburgh and Westminster Reviews. Second Edition, revised. 2 vols. 8vo. 24s.

DISSERTATIONS and DISCUSSIONS, POLITICAL, PHILOSOPHICAL, and HISTORICAL; reprinted chiefly from the Edinburgh and Westminster Reviews. Vol. III. 8vo. price 12s.

UTILITARIANISM. Third Edition. 8vo. 5s.

On LIBERTY:—
    Library Edition (the Fourth), post 8vo. 7s. 6d.
    People's Edition, crown 8vo. 1s. 4d.

The SUBJECTION of WOMEN. The Third Edition. Post 8vo. price 5s.

ENGLAND and IRELAND. Fifth Edition. 8vo. 1s.

CHAPTERS and SPEECHES on the IRISH LAND QUESTION. Crown 8vo. price 2s. 6d.

PARLIAMENTARY REFORM. Second Edit. 8vo. 1s. 6d.

INAUGURAL ADDRESS at the UNIVERSITY of ST. ANDREWS. Second Edition, 8vo. 3s. People's Edition, crown 8vo. 1s.

A FRAGMENT on MACKINTOSH; being Strictures on some Passages in the Dissertation by Sir James Mackintosh prefixed to the Encyclopædia Britannica. By JAMES MILL. 8vo. price 9s.

ANALYSIS of the PHENOMENA of the HUMAN MIND. By JAMES MILL. A New Edition, with Notes, Illustrative and Critical, by ALEXANDER BAIN, ANDREW FINDLATER, and GEORGE GROTE. Edited, with additional Notes, by JOHN STUART MILL. 2 vols. 8vo. price 28s.

London: LONGMANS, GREEN, and CO. Paternoster Row.

Van Der Hoeven's Handbook of ZOOLOGY. Translated from the Second Dutch Edition by the Rev. W. CLARK, M.D. F.R.S. 2 vols. 8vo. with 24 Plates of Figures, 60s.

The Harmonies of Nature and Unity of Creation. By Dr. G. HARTWIG. 8vo. with numerous Illustrations, 18s.

The Sea and its Living Wonders. By the same Author. Third Edition, enlarged. 8vo. with many Illustrations, 21s.

The Subterranean World. By the same Author. With 3 Maps and about 80 Woodcut Illustrations, including 8 full size of page. 8vo. price 21s.

The Polar World: a Popular Description of Man and Nature in the Arctic and Antarctic Regions of the Globe. By the same Author. With 8 Chromoxylographs, 3 Maps, and 85 Woodcuts. 8vo. 21s.

A Familiar History of Birds. By E. STANLEY, D.D. late Lord Bishop of Norwich. Fcp. with Woodcuts, 3s. 6d.

Insects at Home; a Popular Account of British Insects, their Structure, Habits, and Transformations. By the Rev. J. G. WOOD, M.A. F.L.S. With upwards of 700 Illustrations engraved on Wood. 8vo. price 21s.

Insects Abroad; being a Popular Account of Foreign Insects, their Structure, Habits, and Transformations. By J. G. WOOD, M.A. F.L.S. Author of 'Homes without Hands' &c. In One Volume, printed and illustrated uniformly with 'Insects at Home,' to which it will form a Sequel and Companion. [*In the press.*

The Primitive Inhabitants of Scandinavia. Containing a Description of the Implements, Dwellings, Tombs, and Mode of Living of the Savages in the North of Europe during the Stone Age. By SVEN NILSSON. 8vo. Plates and Woodcuts, 18s.

The Origin of Civilisation, and the Primitive Condition of Man; Mental and Social Condition of Savages. By Sir JOHN LUBBOCK, Bart. M.P. F.R.S. Second Edition, with 25 Woodcuts. 8vo. 16s.

The Ancient Stone Implements, Weapons, and Ornaments, of Great Britain. By JOHN EVANS, F.R.S. F.S.A. 8vo. with 2 Plates and 476 Woodcuts, price 28s.

Mankind, their Origin and Destiny. By an M.A. of Balliol College, Oxford. Containing a New Translation of the First Three Chapters of Genesis; a Critical Examination of the First Two Gospels; an Explanation of the Apocalypse; and the Origin and Secret Meaning of the Mythological and Mystical Teaching of the Ancients. With 31 Illustrations. 8vo. price 31s. 6d.

An Exposition of Fallacies in the Hypothesis of Mr. Darwin. By C. R. BREE, M.D. F.Z.S. Author of 'Birds of Europe not Observed in the British Isles' &c. With 36 Woodcuts. Crown 8vo. price 14s.

Bible Animals; a Description of every Living Creature mentioned in the Scriptures, from the Ape to the Coral. By the Rev. J. G. WOOD, M.A. F.L.S. With about 100 Vignettes on Wood. 8vo. 21s.

Maunder's Treasury of Natural History, or Popular Dictionary of Zoology. Revised and corrected by T. S. CONSEN, M.D. Fcp. 8vo. with 900 Woodcuts, 6s.

The Elements of Botany for Families and Schools. Tenth Edition, revised by THOMAS MOORE, F.L.S. Fcp with 154 Woodcuts, 2s. 6d.

The Treasury of Botany, or Popular Dictionary of the Vegetable Kingdom; with which is incorporated a Glossary of Botanical Terms. Edited by J. LINDLEY, F.R.S. and T. MOORE, F.L.S. Pp. 1,274, with 274 Woodcuts and 20 Steel Plates. Two PARTS, fcp. 8vo. 12s.

The Rose Amateur's Guide. By THOMAS RIVERS. New Edition. Fcp. 4s.

Loudon's Encyclopædia of Plants; comprising the Specific Character, Description, Culture, History, &c. of all the Plants found in Great Britain. With upwards of 12,000 Woodcuts. 8vo. 42s.

Maunder's Scientific and Literary Treasury; a Popular Encyclopædia of Science, Literature, and Art. New Edition, in part rewritten, with above 1,000 new articles, by J. Y. JOHNSON. Fcp. 6s.

A Dictionary of Science, Literature, and Art. Fourth Edition, re-edited by the late W. T. BRANDE (the Author) and GEORGE W. COX, M.A. 3 vols. medium 8vo. price 63s. cloth.

Chemistry, Medicine, Surgery, and the Allied Sciences.

A Dictionary of Chemistry and the Allied Branches of other Sciences. By HENRY WATTS, F.C.S. assisted by eminent Scientific and Practical Chemists. 5 vols. medium 8vo. price £7 3s.

Supplement, completing the Record of Discovery to the end of 1869. 8vo. 31s. 6d.

Contributions to Molecular Physics in the domain of Radiant Heat; a Series of Memoirs published in the Philosophical Transactions, &c. By JOHN TYNDALL, LL.D. F.R.S. With 2 Plates and 31 Woodcuts. 8vo. price 16s.

Elements of Chemistry, Theoretical and Practical. By WILLIAM A. MILLER, M.D. LL.D. Professor of Chemistry, King's College, London. New Edition. 3 vols. 8vo. £3.
PART I. CHEMICAL PHYSICS, 15s.
PART II. INORGANIC CHEMISTRY, 21s.
PART III. ORGANIC CHEMISTRY, 24s.

A Course of Practical Chemistry, for the use of Medical Students. By W. ODLING, M.B. F.R.S. New Edition, with 70 new Woodcuts. Crown 8vo. 7s. 6d.

Outlines of Chemistry; or, Brief Notes of Chemical Facts. By the same Author. Crown 8vo. 7s. 6d.

A Manual of Chemical Physiology, including its Points of Contact with Pathology. By J. L. W. THUDICHUM, M.D. 8vo. with Woodcuts, price 7s. 6d.

Select Methods in Chemical Analysis, chiefly Inorganic. By WILLIAM CROOKES, F.R.S. With 22 Woodcuts. Crown 8vo. price 12s. 6d.

Chemical Notes for the Lecture Room. By THOMAS WOOD, F.C.S. 2 vols. crown 8vo. I. on Heat, &c. price 5s. II. on the Metals, price 5s.

The Diagnosis, Pathology, and Treatment of Diseases of Women; including the Diagnosis of Pregnancy. By GRAILY HEWITT, M.D. &c. Third Edition, revised and for the most part re-written; with 132 Woodcuts. 8vo. 24s.

Lectures on the Diseases of Infancy and Childhood. By CHARLES WEST, M.D. &c. Fifth Edition. 8vo. 16s.

On Some Disorders of the Nervous System in Childhood. Being the Lumleian Lectures delivered before the Royal College of Physicians in March 1871. By CHARLES WEST, M.D. Crown 8vo. 5s.

On the Surgical Treatment of Children's Diseases. By T. HOLMES, M.A. &c. late Surgeon to the Hospital for Sick Children. Second Edition, with 9 Plates and 112 Woodcuts. 8vo. 21s.

Lectures on the Principles and Practice of Physic. By Sir THOMAS WATSON, Bart. M.D. Physician-in-Ordinary to the Queen. Fifth Edition, thoroughly revised. 2 vols. 8vo. price 36s.

Lectures on Surgical Pathology. By Sir JAMES PAGET, Bart. F.R.S. Third Edition, revised and re-edited by the Author and Professor W. TURNER, M.B. 8vo. with 131 Woodcuts, 21s.

Cooper's Dictionary of Practical Surgery and Encyclopædia of Surgical Science. New Edition, brought down to the present time. By S. A. LANE, Surgeon to St. Mary's Hospital, &c. assisted by various Eminent Surgeons. 2 vols. 8vo. price 25s. each.

Pulmonary Consumption; its Nature, Varieties, and Treatment : with an Analysis of One Thousand Cases to exemplify its Duration. By C. J. B. WILLIAMS, M.D. F.R.S. and C. T. WILLIAMS, M.A. M.D. Oxon. Post 8vo. price 10s. 6d.

Anatomy, Descriptive and Surgical. By HENRY GRAY, F.R.S. With about 410 Woodcuts from Dissections. Sixth Edition, by T. HOLMES, M.A. Cantab. With a New Introduction by the Editor. Royal 8vo. 28s.

The House I Live in; or, Popular Illustrations of the Structure and Functions of the Human Body. Edited by T. G. GIRTIN. New Edition, with 25 Woodcuts. 16mo. price 2s. 6d.

The Science and Art of Surgery; being a Treatise on Surgical Injuries, Diseases, and Operations. By JOHN ERIC ERICHSEN, Senior Surgeon to University College Hospital, and Holme Professor of Clinical Surgery in University College, London. A New Edition, being the Sixth, revised and enlarged; with 712 Woodcuts. 2 vols. 8vo. price 32s.

A System of Surgery, Theoretical and Practical, in Treatises by Various Authors. Edited by T. HOLMES, M.A. &c. Surgeon and Lecturer on Surgery at St. George's Hospital, and Surgeon-in-Chief to the Metropolitan Police. Second Edition, thoroughly revised, with numerous Illustrations. 5 vols. 8vo. £5 5s.

Clinical Lectures on Diseases of the Liver, Jaundice, and Abdominal Dropsy. By C. MURCHISON, M.D. Physician to the Middlesex Hospital. Post 8vo. with 25 Woodcuts, 10s. 6d.

Todd and Bowman's Physiological Anatomy and Physiology of Man. With numerous Illustrations. VOL. II. 8vo. price 25s.

VOL. I. New Edition by Dr. LIONEL S. BEALE, F.R.S. in course of publication, with numerous Illustrations. PARTS I. and II. price 7s. 6d. each.

Outlines of Physiology, Human and Comparative. By JOHN MARSHALL, F.R.C.S. Surgeon to the University College Hospital. 2 vols. crown 8vo. with 122 Woodcuts, 32s.

Copland's Dictionary of Practical Medicine, abridged from the larger work, and throughout brought down to the present state of Medical Science. 8vo. 36s.

Dr. Pereira's Elements of Materia Medica and Therapeutics, abridged and adapted for the use of Medical and Pharmaceutical Practitioners and Students. Edited by Professor BENTLEY, F.L.S. &c. and by Dr. REDWOOD, F.C.S. &c. With 125 Woodcut Illustrations. 8vo. price 25s.

The Essentials of Materia Medica and Therapeutics. By ALFRED BARING GARROD, M.D. F.R.S. &c. Physician to King's College Hospital. Third Edition. Sixth Impression, brought up to 1870. Crown 8vo. price 12s. 6d.

The Fine Arts, and *Illustrated Editions.*

Grotesque Animals, invented, described, and portrayed by E. W. COOKE, R.A. F.R.S. In Twenty-Four Plates, with Elucidatory Comments. Royal 4to. price 21s.

In Fairyland; Pictures from the Elf-World. By RICHARD DOYLE. With a Poem by W. ALLINGHAM. With Sixteen Plates, containing Thirty-six Designs printed in Colours. Folio, 31s. 6d.

Albert Durer, his Life and Works; including Autobiographical Papers and Complete Catalogues. By WILLIAM B. SCOTT. With Six Etchings by the Author and other Illustrations. 8vo. 16s.

Half-Hour Lectures on the History and Practice of the Fine and Ornamental Arts. By W. B. SCOTT. Second Edition. Crown 8vo. with 50 Woodcut Illustrations, 8s. 6d.

The Chorale Book for England: the Hymns Translated by Miss C. WINKWORTH; the Tunes arranged by Prof. W. S. BENNETT and OTTO GOLDSCHMIDT. Fcp. 4to. 12s. 6d.

The New Testament, illustrated with Wood Engravings after the Early Masters, chiefly of the Italian School. Crown 4to. 63s. cloth, gilt top; or £5 5s. morocco.

The Life of Man Symbolised by the Months of the Year in their Seasons and Phases. Text selected by RICHARD PIGOT. 25 Illustrations on Wood from Original Designs by JOHN LEIGHTON, F.S.A. Quarto, 42s.

Cats and Farlie's Moral Emblems; with Aphorisms, Adages, and Proverbs of all Nations: comprising 121 Illustrations on Wood by J. LEIGHTON, F.S.A. with an appropriate Text by R. PIGOT. Imperial 8vo. 31s. 6d.

Sacred and Legendary Art. By Mrs. JAMESON. 6 vols. square crown 8vo. price £5 15s. 6d. as follows:—

Legends of the Saints and Martyrs. New Edition, with 19 Etchings and 187 Woodcuts. 2 vols. price 31s. 6d.

Legends of the Monastic Orders. New Edition, with 11 Etchings and 88 Woodcuts. 1 vol. price 21s.

Legends of the Madonna. New Edition, with 27 Etchings and 165 Woodcuts. 1 vol. price 21s.

The History of Our Lord, with that of His Types and Precursors. Completed by Lady EASTLAKE. Revised Edition, with 13 Etchings and 281 Woodcuts. 2 vols. price 42s.

Lyra Germanica, the Christian Year. Translated by CATHERINE WINKWORTH. with 125 Illustrations on Wood drawn by J. LEIGHTON, F.S.A. Quarto, 21s.

Lyra Germanica, the Christian Life. Translated by CATHERINE WINKWORTH; with about 200 Woodcut Illustrations by J. LEIGHTON, F.S.A. and other Artists. Quarto, 21s.

The Useful Arts, Manufactures, &c.

Gwilt's Encyclopædia of Architecture, with above 1,600 Woodcuts. Fifth Edition, with Alterations and considerable Additions, by WYATT PAPWORTH. 8vo. price 52s. 6d.

A Manual of Architecture: being a Concise History and Explanation of the principal Styles of European Architecture, Ancient, Mediæval, and Renaissance; with their Chief Variations and a Glossary of Technical Terms. By THOMAS MITCHELL. With 150 Woodcuts. Crown 8vo. 10s. 6d.

History of the Gothic Revival; an Attempt to shew how far the taste for Mediæval Architecture was retained in England during the last two centuries, and has been re-developed in the present. By C. L. EASTLAKE, Architect. With 48 Illustrations (36 full size of page). Imperial 8vo. price 31s. 6d.

Hints on Household Taste in Furniture, Upholstery, and other Details. By CHARLES L. EASTLAKE, Architect. New Edition, with about 90 Illustrations. Square crown 8vo. 18s.

Lathes and Turning, Simple, Mechanical, and Ornamental. By W. HENRY NORTHCOTT. With about 240 Illustrations on Steel and Wood. 8vo. 18s.

Perspective; or, the Art of Drawing what one Sees. Explained and adapted to the use of those Sketching from Nature. By Lieut. W. H. COLLINS, R.E. F.R.A.S. With 37 Woodcuts. Crown 8vo. price 5s.

Principles of Mechanism, designed for the use of Students in the Universities, and for Engineering Students generally. By R. WILLIS, M.A. F.R.S. &c. Jacksonian Professor in the Univ. of Cambridge. Second Edition; with 374 Woodcuts. 8vo. 18s.

Handbook of Practical Telegraphy. By R. S. CULLEY, Memb. Inst. C.E. Engineer-in-Chief of Telegraphs to the Post-Office. Fifth Edition, revised and enlarged; with 118 Woodcuts and 9 Plates. 8vo. price 14s.

Ure's Dictionary of Arts, Manufactures, and Mines. Sixth Edition, re-written and greatly enlarged by ROBERT HUNT, F.R.S. assisted by numerous Contributors. With 2,000 Woodcuts. 3 vols. medium 8vo. £4 14s. 6d.

Encyclopædia of Civil Engineering, Historical, Theoretical, and Practical. By E. CRESY, C.E. With above 3,000 Woodcuts. 8vo. 42s.

Catechism of the Steam Engine, in its various Applications to Mines, Mills, Steam Navigation, Railways, and Agriculture. By JOHN BOURNE, C.E. New Edition, with 89 Woodcuts. Fcp. 8vo. 6s.

Handbook of the Steam Engine. By JOHN BOURNE, C.E. forming a KEY to the Author's Catechism of the Steam Engine. With 67 Woodcuts. Fcp. 8vo. price 9s.

Recent Improvements in the Steam-Engine. By JOHN BOURNE, C.E. New Edition, including many New Examples, with 124 Woodcuts. Fcp. 8vo. 6s.

A Treatise on the Steam Engine, in its various Applications to Mines, Mills, Steam Navigation, Railways, and Agriculture. By J. BOURNE, C.E. New Edition; with Portrait, 37 Plates, and 546 Woodcuts. 4to. 42s.

A Treatise on the Screw Propeller, Screw Vessels, and Screw Engines, as adapted for purposes of Peace and War. By JOHN BOURNE, C.E. Third Edition, with 54 Plates and 287 Woodcuts. Quarto, price 63s.

Bourne's Examples of Modern Steam, Air, and Gas Engines of the most Approved Types, as employed for Pumping, for Driving Machinery, for Locomotion, and for Agriculture, minutely and practically described. In course of publication, to be completed in Twenty-four Parts, price 2s. 6d. each, forming One Volume, with about 50 Plates and 400 Woodcuts.

Treatise on Mills and Millwork. By Sir W. FAIRBAIRN, Bart. F.R.S. New Edition, with 18 Plates and 322 Woodcuts. 2 vols. 8vo. 32s.

Useful Information for Engineers. By the same Author. FIRST, SECOND, and THIRD SERIES, with many Plates and Woodcuts. 3 vols. crown 8vo. 10s. 6d. each.

The Application of Cast and Wrought Iron to Building Purposes. By the same Author. Fourth Edition, with 6 Plates and 118 Woodcuts. 8vo. 16s.

Iron Ship Building, its History and Progress, as comprised in a Series of Experimental Researches. By Sir W. FAIRBAIRN, Bart. F.R.S. With 4 Plates and 130 Woodcuts. 8vo. 18s.

The Strains in Trusses Computed by means of Diagrams; with 20 Examples drawn to Scale. By F. A. RANKEN, M.A. C.E. Lecturer at the Hartley Institution, Southampton. With 35 Diagrams. Square crown 8vo. price 6s. 6d.

Mitchell's Manual of Practical Assaying. Third Edition for the most part re-written, with all the recent Discoveries incorporated. By W. CROOKES, F.R.S. With 188 Woodcuts. 8vo. 28s.

The Art of Perfumery; the History and Theory of Odours, and the Methods of Extracting the Aromas of Plants. By Dr. PIESSE, F.C.S. Third Edition, with 53 Woodcuts. Crown 8vo. 10s. 6d.

Bayldon's Art of Valuing Rents and Tillages, and Claims of Tenants upon Quitting Farms, both at Michaelmas and Lady-Day. Eighth Edition, revised by J. C. MORTON. 8vo. 10s. 6d.

On the Manufacture of Beet-Root Sugar in England and Ireland. By WILLIAM CROOKES, F.R.S. With 11 Woodcuts. 8vo. 8s. 6d.

Practical Treatise on Metallurgy, adapted from the last German Edition of Professor KERL'S *Metallurgy* by W. CROOKES, F.R.S. &c. and E. RÖHRIG, Ph.D. M.E. 3 vols. 8vo. with 625 Woodcuts, price £4 19s.

Loudon's Encyclopædia of Agriculture: comprising the Laying-out, Improvement, and Management of Landed Property, and the Cultivation and Economy of the Productions of Agriculture. With 1,100 Woodcuts. 8vo. 21s.

Loudon's Encyclopædia of Gardening. comprising the Theory and Practice of Horticulture, Floriculture, Arboriculture, and Landscape Gardening. With 1,000 Woodcuts. 8vo. 21s.

Religious and *Moral Works.*

The Outlines of the Christian Ministry Delineated, and brought to the Test of Reason, Holy Scripture, History, and Experience, with a view to the Reconciliation of Existing Differences concerning it, especially between Presbyterians and Episcopalians. By CHRISTOPHER WORDSWORTH, D.C.L. &c. Bishop of St. Andrew's, and Fellow of Winchester College. Crown 8vo. price 7s. 6d.

Christian Counsels, selected from the Devotional Works of Fénelon, Archbishop of Cambrai. Translated by A. M. JAMES. Crown 8vo. price 5s.

Ecclesiastical Reform. Nine Essays by various Writers. Edited by the Rev. ORBY SHIPLEY, M.A. Crown 8vo.
[*Nearly ready.*

Authority and Conscience; a Free Debate on the Tendency of Dogmatic Theology and on the Characteristics of Faith. Edited by CONWAY MOREL. Post 8vo. 7s. 6d.

Reasons of Faith; or, the Order of the Christian Argument Developed and Explained. By the Rev. G. S. DREW, M.A. Second Edition, revised and enlarged. Fcp. 8vo. 6s.

Christ the Consoler; a Book of Comfort for the Sick. With a Preface by the Right Rev. the Lord Bishop of Carlisle. Small 8vo. 6s.

The True Doctrine of the Eucharist. By THOMAS S. L. VOGAN, D.D. Canon and Prebendary of Chichester and Rural Dean. 8vo. 18s.

The Student's Compendium of the Book of Common Prayer; being Notes Historical and Explanatory of the Liturgy of the Church of England. By the Rev. H. ALLDEN NASH. Fcp. 8vo. price 2s. 6d.

Synonyms of the Old Testament, their Bearing on Christian Faith and Practice. By the Rev. ROBERT B. GIRDLESTONE, M.A. 8vo. price 15s.

Fundamentals; or, Bases of Belief concerning Man and God: a Handbook of Mental, Moral, and Religious Philosophy. By the Rev. T. GRIFFITH, M.A. 8vo. price 10s. 6d.

An Introduction to the Theology of the Church of England, in an Exposition of the Thirty-nine Articles. By the Rev. T. P. BOULTBEE, LL.D. Fcp. 8vo. price 6s.

Christian Sacerdotalism, viewed from a Layman's standpoint or tried by Holy Scripture and the Early Fathers; with a short Sketch of the State of the Church from the end of the Third to the Reformation in the beginning of the Sixteenth Century. By JOHN JARDINE, M.A. LL.D. 8vo. 8s. 6d.

Prayers for the Family and for Private Use, selected from the Collection of the late Baron BUNSEN, and Translated by CATHERINE WINKWORTH. Fcp. 8vo. price 3s. 6d.

Churches and their Creeds. By the Rev. Sir PHILIP PERRING, Bart. Late Scholar of Trin. Coll. Cambridge, and University Medallist. Crown 8vo. 10s. 6d.

The Truth of the Bible; Evidence from the Mosaic and other Records of Creation; the Origin and Antiquity of Man; the Science of Scripture; and from the Archaeology of Different Nations of the Earth. By the Rev. B. W. SAVILE, M.A. Crown 8vo. 7s. 6d.

Considerations on the Revision of the English New Testament. By C. J. ELLICOTT, D.D. Lord Bishop of Gloucester and Bristol. Post 8vo. price 5s. 6d.

An Exposition of the 39 Articles, Historical and Doctrinal. By E. HAROLD BROWNE, D.D. Lord Bishop of Ely. Ninth Edition. 8vo. 16s.

The Voyage and Shipwreck of St. Paul; with Dissertations on the Ships and Navigation of the Ancients. By JAMES SMITH, F.R.S. Crown 8vo. Charts, 10s. 6d.

The Life and Epistles of St. Paul. By the Rev. W. J. CONYBEARE, M.A. and the Very Rev. J. S. HOWSON, D.D. Dean of Chester. Three Editions:—

LIBRARY EDITION, with all the Original Illustrations, Maps, Landscapes on Steel, Woodcuts, &c. 2 vols. 4to. 48s.

INTERMEDIATE EDITION, with a Selection of Maps, Plates, and Woodcuts. 2 vols. square crown 8vo. 21s.

STUDENT'S EDITION, revised and condensed, with 46 Illustrations and Maps. 1 vol. crown 8vo. 9s.

Evidence of the Truth of the Christian Religion derived from the Literal Fulfilment of Prophecy. By ALEXANDER KEITH, D.D. 37th Edition, with numerous Plates, in square 8vo. 12s. 6d.; also the 39th Edition, in post 8vo. with 5 Plates, 6s.

The History and Destiny of the World and of the Church, according to Scripture. By the same Author. Square 8vo. with 40 Illustrations, 10s.

The History and Literature of the Israelites, according to the Old Testament and the Apocrypha. By C. DE ROTHSCHILD and A. DE ROTHSCHILD. Second Edition. 2 vols. crown 8vo. 12s. 6d.
Abridged Edition, in 1 vol. fcp. 8vo. 3s. 6d.

Ewald's History of Israel to the Death of Moses. Translated from the German. Edited, with a Preface and an Appendix, by RUSSELL MARTINEAU, M.A. Second Edition. 2 vols. 8vo. 24s. Vols. III. and IV. edited by J. E. CARPENTER, M.A. price 21s.

England and Christendom. By ARCHBISHOP MANNING, D.D. Post 8vo. price 10s. 6d.

The Pontificate of Pius the Ninth; being the Third Edition, enlarged and continued, of 'Rome and its Ruler.' By J. F. MAGUIRE, M.P. Post 8vo. Portrait, price 12s. 6d.

Ignatius Loyola and the Early Jesuits. By STEWART ROSE. New Edition, revised. 8vo. with Portrait, 16s.

An Introduction to the Study of the New Testament, Critical, Exegetical, and Theological. By the Rev. S. DAVIDSON, D.D. LL.D. 2 vols. 8vo. 30s.

A Critical and Grammatical Commentary on St. Paul's Epistles. By C. J. ELLICOTT, D.D. Lord Bishop of Gloucester and Bristol. 8vo.

Galatians, Fourth Edition, 8s. 6d.
Ephesians, Fourth Edition, 8s. 6d.
Pastoral Epistles, Fourth Edition, 10s. 6d.
Philippians, Colossians, and Philemon, Third Edition, 10s. 6d.
Thessalonians, Third Edition, 7s. 6d.

Historical Lectures on the Life of Our Lord Jesus Christ: being the Hulsean Lectures for 1859. By C. J. ELLICOTT, D.D. Fifth Edition. 8vo. 12s.

The Greek Testament; with Notes, Grammatical and Exegetical. By the Rev. W. WEBSTER, M.A. and the Rev. W. F. WILKINSON, M.A. 2 vols. 8vo. £2. 4s.

Horne's Introduction to the Critical Study and Knowledge of the Holy Scriptures. Twelfth Edition; with 4 Maps and 22 Woodcuts. 4 vols. 8vo. 42s.

The Treasury of Bible Knowledge; being a Dictionary of the Books, Persons, Places, Events, and other Matters of which mention is made in Holy Scripture. By Rev. J. AYRE, M.A. With Maps, 15 Plates, and numerous Woodcuts. Fcp. 8vo. price 6s.

Every-day Scripture Difficulties explained and illustrated. By J. E. PRESCOTT, M.A. I. *Matthew* and *Mark*; II. *Luke* and *John*. 2 vols. 8vo. price 9s. each.

The Pentateuch and Book of Joshua Critically Examined. By the Right Rev. J. W. COLENSO, D.D. Lord Bishop of Natal. Crown 8vo. price 6s.

PART V. Genesis Analysed and Separated, and the Ages of its Writers determined 8vo. 18s.

PART VI. The Later Legislation of the Pentateuch. 8vo. 24s.

The Formation of Christendom. By T. W. ALLIES. PARTS I. and II. 8vo. price 12s. each.

Four Discourses of Chrysostom, chiefly on the parable of the Rich Man and Lazarus. Translated by F. ALLEN, B.A. Crown 8vo. 3s. 6d.

Thoughts for the Age. By ELIZABETH M. SEWELL, Author of 'Amy Herbert.' New Edition. Fcp. 8vo. price 5s.

Passing Thoughts on Religion. By the same Author. Fcp. 3s. 6d.

Self-examination before Confirmation. By the same Author. 32mo. 1s. 6d.

Thoughts for the Holy Week, for Young Persons. By the same Author. New Edition. Fcp. 8vo. 2s.

Readings for a Month Preparatory to Confirmation from Writers of the Early and English Church. By the same. Fcp. 4s.

Readings for Every Day in Lent, compiled from the Writings of Bishop JEREMY TAYLOR. By the same Author. Fcp. 5s.

Preparation for the Holy Communion; the Devotions chiefly from the works of JEREMY TAYLOR. By the same. 32mo. 3s.

Bishop Jeremy Taylor's Entire Works; with Life by BISHOP HEBER. Revised and corrected by the Rev. C. P EDEN. 10 vols. £5. 5s.

'Spiritual Songs' for the Sundays and Holidays throughout the Year. By J. S. B. MONSELL, LL.D. Vicar of Egham and Rural Dean. Fourth Edition, Sixth Thousand. Fcp. price 4s. 6d.

The Beatitudes. By the same Author Third Edition, revised. Fcp. 3s. 6d.

His Presence not his Memory, 1855. By the same Author, in memory of his SON. Sixth Edition. 16mo. 1s.

Lyra Germanica, translated from the German by Miss C. WINKWORTH. FIRST SERIES, the *Christian Year*, Hymns for the Sundays and Chief Festivals of the Church; SECOND SERIES, the *Christian Life*. Fcp. 8vo. price 3s. 6d. each SERIES.

Endeavours after the Christian Life; Discourses. By JAMES MARTINEAU. Fourth Edition. Post 8vo. price 7s. 6d.

Travels, Voyages, &c.

Six Months in California. By J.G. PLAYER-FROWD. Post 8vo. price 6s.

The Japanese in America. By CHARLES LANMAN, American Secretary, Japanese Legation, Washington, U.S.A. Post 8vo. price 10s. 6d.

My Wife and I in Queensland; Eight Years' Experience in the Colony, with some account of Polynesian Labour. By CHARLES H. EDEN. With Map and Frontispiece. Crown 8vo. price 9s.

Life in India; a Series of Sketches shewing something of the Anglo-Indian, the Land he lives in, and the People among whom he lives. By EDWARD BRADDON. Post 8vo. price 9s.

How to See Norway. By Captain J. R. CAMPBELL. With Map and 5 Woodcuts. Fcp. 8vo. price 5s.

Pau and the Pyrenees. By Count HENRY RUSSELL, Member of the Alpine Club. With 2 Maps. Fcp. 8vo. price 5s.

Hours of Exercise in the Alps. By JOHN TYNDALL, LL.D., F.R.S. Second Edition, with Seven Woodcuts by E. Whymper. Crown 8vo. price 12s. 6d.

Westward by Rail; the New Route to the East. By W. F. RAE. Second Edition. Post 8vo. with Map, price 10s. 6d.

Travels in the Central Caucasus and Bashan, including Visits to Ararat and Tabreez and Ascents of Kazbek and Elbruz. By DOUGLAS W. FRESHFIELD. Square crown 8vo. with Maps, &c., 18s.

Cadore or Titian's Country. By JOSIAH GILBERT, one of the Authors of the 'Dolomite Mountains.' With Map, Facsimile, and 40 Illustrations. Imp.8vo. 31s. 6d.

The Playground of Europe. By LESLIE STEPHEN, late President of the Alpine Club. With 4 Illustrations on Wood by E. Whymper. Crown 8vo. 10s. 6d.

Zigzagging amongst Dolomites; with more than 300 Illustrations by the Author. By the Author of 'How we Spent the Summer.' Oblong 4to. price 15s.

The Dolomite Mountains. Excursions through Tyrol, Carinthia, Carniola, and Friuli. By J. GILBERT and G. C. CHURCHILL, F.R.G.S. With numerous Illustrations. Square crown 8vo. 21s.

How we Spent the Summer; or, a Voyage en Zigzag in Switzerland and Tyrol with some Members of the ALPINE CLUB. Third Edition, re-drawn. In oblong 4to. with about 300 Illustrations, 15s.

Pictures in Tyrol and Elsewhere. From a Family Sketch-Book. By the same Author. Second Edition. 4to. with many Illustrations, 21s.

Beaten Tracks; or, Pen and Pencil Sketches in Italy. By the Author of 'How we spent the Summer.' With 42 Plates of Sketches. 8vo. 16s.

The Alpine Club Map of the Chain of Mont Blanc, from an actual Survey in 1863—1864. By A. ADAMS-REILLY, F.R.G.S. M.A.C. In Chromolithography on extra stout drawing paper 28in. × 17in. price 10s. or mounted on canvas in a folding case, 12s. 6d.

History of Discovery in our Australasian Colonies, Australia, Tasmania, and New Zealand, from the Earliest Date to the Present Day. By WILLIAM HOWITT. 2 vols. 8vo. with 3 Maps, 20s.

Visits to Remarkable Places: Old Halls, Battle-Fields, and Scenes illustrative of striking Passages in English History and Poetry. By the same Author. 2 vols. square crown 8vo. with Wood Engravings, 25s.

Guide to the Pyrenees, for the use of Mountaineers. By CHARLES PACKE. Second Edition, with Maps, &c. and Appendix. Crown 8vo. 7s. 6d.

The Alpine Guide. By JOHN BALL M.R.I.A. late President of the Alpine Club. Post 8vo. with Maps and other Illustrations.

Guide to the Eastern Alps, price 10s. 6d.

Guide to the Western Alps, including Mont Blanc, Monte Rosa, Zermatt, &c. price 6s. 6d.

Guide to the Central Alps, including all the Oberland District, price 7s. 6d.

Introduction on Alpine Travelling in general, and on the Geology of the Alps, price 1s. Either of the Three Volumes or Parts of the *Alpine Guide* may be had with this INTRODUCTION prefixed, price 1s. extra.

The Rural Life of England. By WILLIAM HOWITT. Woodcuts by Bewick and Williams. Medium 8vo. 12s. 6d.

Works of Fiction.

Yarndale; a Story of Lancashire Life. By a Lancashire Man. 3 vols. post 8vo. price 21s.

The Burgomaster's Family; or, Weal and Woe in a Little World. By CHRISTINE MÜLLER. Translated from the Dutch by Sir J. G. SHAW LEFEVRE, K.C.B. F.R.S. Crown 8vo. price 6s.

Popular Romances of the Middle Ages. By the Rev. GEORGE W. COX, M.A. Author of 'The Mythology of the Aryan Nations' &c. and EUSTACE HINTON JONES. Crown 8vo. 10s. 6d.

Tales of the Teutonic Lands; a Sequel to 'Popular Romances of the Middle Ages.' By GEORGE W. COX, M.A. late Scholar of Trinity College, Oxford; and EUSTACE HINTON JONES. Crown 8vo. price 10s. 6d.

Hartland Forest; a Legend of North Devon. By Mrs. BRAY, Author of 'The White Hoods,' 'Life of Stothard,' &c. Post 8vo. with Frontispiece, 4s. 6d.

Novels and Tales. By the Right Hon. BENJAMIN DISRAELI, M.P. Cabinet Editions, complete in Ten Volumes, crown 8vo. price 6s. each, as follows:—

LOTHAIR, 6s. VENETIA, 6s.
CONINGSBY, 6s. ALROY, IXION, &c. 6s.
SYBIL, 6s. YOUNG DUKE, &c. 6s.
TANCRED, 6s. VIVIAN GREY, 6s.
CONTARINI FLEMING, &c. 6s.
HENRIETTA TEMPLE, 6s.

Stories and Tales. By E. M. SEWELL. Comprising *Amy Herbert*; *Gertrude*; the *Earl's Daughter*; the *Experience of Life*; *Cleve Hall*; *Ivors*; *Katharine Ashton*; *Margaret Percival*; *Laneton Parsonage*; and *Ursula*. The Ten Works complete in Eight Volumes, crown 8vo. bound in leather and contained in a Box, price TWO GUINEAS.

Cabinet Edition, in crown 8vo. of Stories and Tales by Miss SEWELL:—

AMY HERBERT, 2s. 6d. | KATHARINE ASHTON, 2s. 6d.
GERTRUDE, 2s. 6d. |
EARL'S DAUGHTER, 2s. 6d. | MARGARET PERCIVAL, 3s. 6d.
EXPERIENCE of LIFE, 2s. 6d. | LANETON PARSONAGE, 3s. 6d.
CLEVE HALL, 2s. 6d. | URSULA, 3s. 6d.
IVORS, 2s. 6d. |

A Glimpse of the World. Fcp. 7s. 6d.

Journal of a Home Life. Post 8vo. 9s. 6d.

After Life; a Sequel to the 'Journal of a Home Life.' Post 8vo. 10s. 6d.

The Giant; a Witch's Story for English Boys. Edited by Miss SEWELL, Author of 'Amy Herbert,' &c. Fcp. 8vo. price 5s.

Wonderful Stories from Norway, Sweden, and Iceland. Adapted and arranged by JULIA GODDARD. With an Introductory Essay by the Rev. G. W. COX, M.A. and Six Illustrations. Square post 8vo. 6s.

The Modern Novelist's Library. Each Work, in crown 8vo. complete in a Single Volume:—

MELVILLE'S DIGBY GRAND, 2s. boards; 2s. 6d. cloth.

———— GLADIATORS, 2s. boards; 2s. 6d. cloth.

———— GOOD FOR NOTHING, 2s. boards; 2s. 6d. cloth.

———— HOLMBY HOUSE, 2s. boards; 2s. 6d. cloth.

———— INTERPRETER, 2s. boards; 2s. 6d. cloth.

———— KATE COVENTRY, 2s. boards; 2s. 6d. cloth.

———— QUEEN'S MARIES, 2s. boards; 2s. 6d. cloth.

TROLLOPE'S WARDEN, 1s. 6d. boards; 2s. cloth.

———— BARCHESTER TOWERS, 2s. boards; 2s. 6d. cloth.

BRAMLEY-MOORE'S SIX SISTERS OF THE VALLEYS, 2s. boards; 2s. 6d. cloth.

Becker's Gallus; or, Roman Scenes of the Time of Augustus. Post 8vo. 7s. 6d.

Becker's Charicles: Illustrative of Private Life of the Ancient Greeks. Post 8vo. 7s. 6d.

Tales of Ancient Greece. By the Rev. G. W. Cox, M.A. late Scholar of Trin. Coll. Oxford. Crown 8vo. price 6s. 6d.

Poetry and The Drama.

Ballads and Lyrics of Old France; with other Poems. By A. LANG, Fellow of Merton College, Oxford. Square fcp. 8vo. price 5s.

Thomas Moore's Poetical Works, with the Author's last Copyright Additions:—
Shamrock Edition, price 3s. 6d.
People's Edition, square cr. 8vo. 10s. 6d.
Library Edition, Portrait & Vignette, 14s.

Moore's Lalla Rookh, Tenniel's Edition, with 68 Wood Engravings from Original Drawings and other Illustrations. Fcp. 4to. 21s.

Moore's Irish Melodies, Maclise's Edition, with 161 Steel Plates from Original Drawings. Super-royal 8vo. 31s. 6d.

Miniature Edition of Moore's Irish Melodies, with Maclise's Illustrations (as above), reduced in Lithography. Imp. 16mo. 10s. 6d.

Lays of Ancient Rome; with Ivry and the Armada. By the Right Hon. LORD MACAULAY. 16mo. 3s. 6d.

Lord Macaulay's Lays of Ancient Rome. With 90 Illustrations on Wood, Original and from the Antique, from Drawings by G. SCHARF. Fcp. 4to. 21s.

Miniature Edition of Lord Macaulay's Lays of Ancient Rome, with Scharf's Illustrations (as above) reduced in Lithography. Imp. 16mo. 10s. 6d.

Southey's Poetical Works, with the Author's last Corrections and copyright Additions. Library Edition. Medium 8vo. with Portrait and Vignette, 14s.

Goldsmith's Poetical Works, Illustrated with Wood Engravings from Designs by Members of the ETCHING CLUB. Imp. 16mo. 7s. 6d.

Poems. By JEAN INGELOW. Fifteenth Edition. Fcp. 8vo. 5s.

Poems by Jean Ingelow. With nearly 100 Illustrations by Eminent Artists, engraved on Wood by DALZIEL Brothers. Fcp. 4to. 21s.

A Story of Doom, and other Poems. By JEAN INGELOW. Third Edition. Fcp. price 5s.

Bowdler's Family Shakspeare, cheaper Genuine Edition, complete in 1 vol. large type, with 36 Woodcut Illustrations, price 14s. or in 6 pocket vols. 3s. 6d. each.

Horatii Opera, Library Edition, with Copious English Notes, Marginal References and Various Readings. Edited by the Rev. J. E. YONGE, M.A. 8vo. 21s.

The Odes and Epodes of Horace; a Metrical Translation into English, with Introduction and Commentaries. By Lord LYTTON. With Latin Text. New Edition. Post 8vo. price 10s. 6d.

The Æneid of Virgil Translated into English Verse. By JOHN CONINGTON, M.A. Corpus Professor of Latin in the University of Oxford. New Edition. Crown 8vo. 9s.

Rural Sports &c.

Encyclopædia of Rural Sports; a Complete Account, Historical, Practical, and Descriptive, of Hunting, Shooting, Fishing, Racing, &c. By D. P. BLAINE. With above 600 Woodcuts (20 from Designs by JOHN LEECH). 8vo. 21s.

The Dead Shot, or Sportsman's Complete Guide; a Treatise on the Use of the Gun, Dog-breaking, Pigeon-shooting, &c. By MARKSMAN. Fcp. with Plates, 5s.

A Book on Angling: being a Complete Treatise on the Art of Angling in every branch, including full Illustrated Lists of Salmon Flies. By FRANCIS FRANCIS. New Edition, with Portrait and 15 other Plates, plain and coloured. Post 8vo. 15s.

Wilcocks's Sea-Fisherman: comprising the Chief Methods of Hook and Line Fishing in the British and other Seas, a glance at Nets, and remarks on Boats and Boating. Second Edition, enlarged, with 80 Woodcuts. Post 8vo. 12s. 6d.

The Fly-Fisher's Entomology. By ALFRED RONALDS. With coloured Representations of the Natural and Artificial Insect. Sixth Edition, with 20 coloured Plates. 8vo. 14s.

The Ox, his Diseases and their Treatment; with an Essay on Parturition in the Cow. By J. R. DOBSON, M.R.C.V.S. Crown 8vo. with Illustrations, 7s. 6d.

A Treatise on Horse-shoeing and Lameness. By JOSEPH GAMGEE, Veterinary Surgeon, formerly Lecturer on the Principles and Practice of Farriery in the New Veterinary College, Edinburgh. 8vo. with 55 Woodcuts, 15s.

Blaine's Veterinary Art: a Treatise on the Anatomy, Physiology, and Curative Treatment of the Diseases of the Horse, Neat Cattle, and Sheep. Seventh Edition, revised and enlarged by C. STEEL. 8vo. with Plates and Woodcuts, 18s.

Youatt on the Horse. Revised and enlarged by W. WATSON, M.R.C.V.S. 8vo. with numerous Woodcuts, 12s. 6d.

Youatt on the Dog. (By the same Author.) 8vo. with numerous Woodcuts, 6s.

The Dog in Health and Disease. By STONEHENGE. With 73 Wood Engravings. New Edition, revised. Square crown 8vo. price 7s. 6d.

The Greyhound. By the same Author. Revised Edition, with 24 Portraits of Greyhounds. Square crown 8vo. 10s. 6d

The Setter; with Notices of the most Eminent Breeds now extant, Instructions how to Breed, Rear, and Break; Dog Shows, Field Trials, and General Management, &c. By EDWARD LAVERACK. With Two Portraits of Setters in Chromolithography. Crown 4to. price 7s. 6d.

Horses and Stables. By Colonel F. FITZWYGRAM, XV. the King's Hussars. With 24 Plates of Woodcut Illustrations, containing very numerous Figures. 8vo. 15s.

The Horse's Foot, and how to keep it Sound. By W. MILES, Esq. Ninth Edition, with Illustrations. Imp. 8vo. 12s. 6d.

A Plain Treatise on Horse-shoeing. By the same Author. Sixth Edition, post 8vo. with Illustrations, 2s. 6d.

Stables and Stable Fittings. By the same. Imp. 8vo. with 13 Plates, 15s.

Remarks on Horses' Teeth, addressed to Purchasers. By the same. Post 8vo. 1s. 6d.

Works of Utility and General Information.

Modern Cookery for Private Families, reduced to a System of Easy Practice in a Series of carefully-tested Receipts. By ELIZA ACTON. Newly revised and enlarged; with 8 Plates, Figures, and 150 Woodcuts. Fcp. 6s.

Maunder's Treasury of Knowledge and Library of Reference: comprising an English Dictionary and Grammar, Universal Gazetteer, Classical Dictionary, Chronology, Law Dictionary, Synopsis of the Peerage, Useful Tables, &c. Fcp. 8vo. 6s.

Collieries and Colliers: a Handbook of the Law and Leading Cases relating thereto. By J. C. FOWLER, Barrister. Second Edition. Fcp. 8vo. 7s. 6d.

The Theory and Practice of Banking. By HENRY DUNNING MACLEOD, M.A. Barrister-at-Law. Second Edition, entirely remodelled. 2 vols. 8vo. 30s.

M'Culloch's Dictionary, Practical, Theoretical, and Historical, of Commerce and Commercial Navigation. New Edition, revised throughout and corrected to the Present Time; with a Biographical Notice of the Author. Edited by H. G. REID, Secretary to Mr. M'Culloch for many years. 8vo. price 63s. cloth.

A Practical Treatise on Brewing; with Formulæ for Public Brewers, and Instructions for Private Families. By W. BLACK. Fifth Edition. 8vo. 10s. 6d.

Chess Openings. By F. W. LONGMAN, Balliol College, Oxford. Fcp. 8vo. 2s. 6d.

The Law of Nations Considered as Independent Political Communities. By Sir TRAVERS TWISS, D.C.L. 2 vols. 8vo. 30s. or separately, PART I *Peace*, 12s. PART II. *War*, 18s.

Hints to Mothers on the Management of their Health during the Period of Pregnancy and in the Lying-in Room. By THOMAS BULL, M.D. Fcp. 5s.

The Maternal Management of Children in Health and Disease. By THOMAS BULL, M.D. Fcp. 5s.

How to Nurse Sick Children; containing Directions which may be found of service to all who have charge of the Young. By CHARLES WEST, M.D. Second Edition. Fcp. 8vo. 1s. 6d.

Notes on Hospitals. By FLORENCE NIGHTINGALE. Third Edition, enlarged; with 13 Plans. Post 4to. 18s.

Notes on Lying-In Institutions; with a Proposal for Organising an Institution for Training Midwives and Midwifery Nurses. By FLORENCE NIGHTINGALE. With 5 Plans. Square crown 8vo. 7s. 6d.

The Cabinet Lawyer; a Popular Digest of the Laws of England, Civil, Criminal, and Constitutional. Twenty-third Edition, corrected and brought up to the Present Date. Fcp. 8vo. price 7s. 6d.

Willich's Popular Tables for Ascertaining the Value of Lifehold, Leasehold, and Church Property, Renewal Fines, &c.: the Public Funds; Annual Average Price and Interest on Consols from 1731 to 1867; Chemical, Geographical, Astronomical, Trigonometrical Tables, &c. Post 8vo. 10s.

Pewtner's Comprehensive Specifier; a Guide to the Practical Specification of every kind of Building-Artificer's Work: with Forms of Building Conditions and Agreements, an Appendix, Foot-Notes, and Index. Edited by W. YOUNG, Architect. Crown 8vo. 6s.

Periodical Publications.

The Edinburgh Review, or Critical Journal, published Quarterly in January, April, July, and October. 8vo. price 6s. each Number.

Notes on Books: An Analysis of the Works published during each Quarter by Messrs. LONGMANS & Co. The object is to enable Bookbuyers to obtain such information regarding the various works as is usually afforded by tables of contents and explanatory prefaces. 4to. Quarterly. *Gratis.*

Fraser's Magazine. Edited by JAMES ANTHONY FROUDE, M.A. New Series, published on the 1st of each Month. 8vo. price 2s. 6d. each Number.

The Alpine Journal; A Record of Mountain Adventure and Scientific Observation. By Members of the Alpine Club. Edited by LESLIE STEPHEN. Published Quarterly, May 31, Aug. 31, Nov. 30, Feb. 28. 8vo. price 1s. 6d. each Number.

Knowledge for the Young.

The Stepping Stone to Knowledge: Containing upwards of Seven Hundred Questions and Answers on Miscellaneous Subjects, adapted to the capacity of Infant Minds. By a MOTHER. New Edition, enlarged and improved. 18mo. price 1s.

The Stepping Stone to Geography: Containing several Hundred Questions and Answers on Geographical Subjects. 18mo. 1s.

The Stepping Stone to English History: Containing several Hundred Questions and Answers on the History of England. 1s.

The Stepping Stone to Bible Knowledge: Containing several Hundred Questions and Answers on the Old and New Testaments. 18mo. 1s.

The Stepping Stone to Biography: Containing several Hundred Questions and Answers on the Lives of Eminent Men and Women. 18mo. 1s.

Second Series of the Stepping Stone to Knowledge: containing upwards of Eight Hundred Questions and Answers on Miscellaneous Subjects not contained in the FIRST SERIES. 18mo. 1s.

The Stepping Stone to French Pronunciation and Conversation: Containing several Hundred Questions and Answers. By Mr. P. SADLER. 18mo. 1s.

The Stepping Stone to English Grammar: Containing several Hundred Questions and Answers on English Grammar. By Mr. P. SADLER. 18mo. 1s.

The Stepping Stone to Natural History: VERTEBRATE OR BACKBONED ANIMALS. PART I. *Mammalia*; PART II. *Birds, Reptiles, Fishes.* 18mo. 1s. each Part.

INDEX.

ACTON's Modern Cookery.................... 10
ALLIES on Formation of Christendom 15
ALLEN's Discourses of Chrysostom 16
Alpine Guide (The) 17
——— Journal 20
AMOS's Jurisprudence 5
ANDERSON's Strength of Materials 9
ARNOLD's Manual of English Literature .. 6
Authority and Conscience 11
Autumn Holidays of a Country Parson 7
AYRE's Treasury of Bible Knowledge...... 15

BACON's Essays by WHATELY 5
——— Life and Letters, by SPEDDING .. 4
——— Works........................... 5
BAIN's Mental and Moral Science 8
——— on the Senses and Intellect........ 8
BALL's Guide to the Central Alps........ 17
——— Guide to the Western Alps 17
——— Guide to the Eastern Alps 17
BAYLDON's Rents and Tillages 11
Beaten Tracks 17
BECKER's Charicles and Gallus 18
BENFEY's Sanskrit-English Dictionary 6
BERNARD on British Neutrality 1
BLACK's Treatise on Brewing............. 10
BLACKLEY's German-English Dictionary .. 6
BLAINE's Rural Sports 19
——— Veterinary Art 19
BLOXAM's Metals.......................... 9
BOOTH's Saint-Simon..................... 5
BOURNE on 39 Articles................... 14
BOURNE on Screw Propeller 13
——— 's Catechism of the Steam Engine.. 13
——— Examples of Modern Engines .. 13
——— Handbook of Steam Engine 13
——— Treatise on the Steam Engine... 13
——— Improvements in the same 13
BOWDLER's Family SHAKSPEARE........... 18
BRADDON's Life in India................. 16
BRAMLEY-MOORE's Six Sisters of the Valley 18
BRANDE's Dictionary of Science, Literature, and Art............................ 19
BRAY's Manual of Anthropology 7
——— Philosophy of Necessity 7
——— On Force 7
——— (Mrs.) Hartland Forest........... 17
BREE's Fallacies of Darwinism 10
BROWNE's Exposition of the 39 Articles... 15
BRUNEL's Life of BRUNEL 4
BUCKLE's History of Civilisation 2
——— Posthumous Remains 7
BULL's Hints to Mothers................. 20
——— Maternal Management of Children. 20
BUNSEN's God in History................. 3
——— Prayers 14

Burgomaster's Family (The) ....
BURKE's Vicissitudes of Families........ 6
BURTON's Christian Church 3

Cabinet Lawyer........................... 20
CAMPBELL's Norway 16
CATES's Biographical Dictionary 4
——— and WOODWARD's Encyclopædia 3
CATS and FARLIE's Moral Emblems 12
Changed Aspects of Unchanged Truths 7
CHESNEY's Indian Polity 2
——— Waterloo Campaign 2
Chorale Book for England 12
Christ the Consoler...................... 14
CLOUGH's Lives from Plutarch........... 2
COLENSO on Pentateuch and Book of Joshua 15
COLLINS's Perspective................... 13
Commonplace Philosopher in Town and Country, by A. K. H. B................ 7
CONINGTON's Translation of Virgil's Æneid 18
——— Miscellaneous Writings 7
CONTANSEAU's Two French Dictionaries.. 6
CONYBEARE and HOWSON's Life and Epistles of St. Paul......................... 14
COOKE's Grotesque Animals 12
COOPER's Surgical Dictionary 11
COPLAND's Dictionary of Practical Medicine 12
COTTON's Memoir and Correspondence 4
Counsel and Comfort from a City Pulpit .. 7
Cox's (G. W.) Aryan Mythology 3
——— Tale of the Great Persian War 2
——— Tales of Ancient Greece 17
——— and JONES's Romances....... 17
——— Teutonic Tales... 17
CREASY on British Constitution 2
CRESY's Encyclopædia of Civil Engineering 13
Critical Essays of a Country Parson..... 7
CROOKES on Beet-Root Sugar.............. 11
——— 's Chemical Analysis............ 11
CULLEY's Handbook of Telegraphy 13
CUSACK's Student's History of Ireland 2

D'AUBIGNÉ's History of the Reformation in the time of CALVIN 2
DAVIDSON's Introduction to New Testament 15
Dead Shot (The), by MARKSMAN 19
DE LA RIVE's Treatise on Electricity 9
DE MORGAN's Paradoxes 7
DENISON's Vice-Regal Life 1
DISRAELI's Lord George Bentinck 4
——— Novels and Tales 17
DOBSON on the Ox 19
DOVE's Law of Storms 9
DOYLE's Fairyland 12
DREW's Reasons for Faith 14
DYER's City of Rome 3

22   NEW WORKS published by LONGMANS and CO.

Eastlake's Gothic Revival 13
———— Hints on Household Taste 13
Eaton's Musical Criticism and Biography 6
Eden's Queensland........................ 16
Edinburgh Review 20
Elements of Botany 10
Ellicott on New Testament Revision.... 15
———'s Commentary on Ephesians 15
———————————————— Galatians 15
———————————— Pastoral Epist. 15
———————————— Philippians,&c. 15
———————————— Thessalonians 15
————'s Lectures on Life of Christ 15
Ericusen's Surgery 11
Evans's Ancient Stone Implements 10
Ewald's History of Israel 15

Fairbairn's Application of Cast and Wrought Iron to Building 13
——————— Information for Engineers 13
——————— Treatise on Mills and Millwork 13
——————— Iron Shipbuilding 13
Faraday's Life and Letters 4
Farrar's Chapters on Language 6
——————— Families of Speech 7
Fitzwygram on Horses and Stables 19
Fowler's Collieries and Colliers 10
Francis's Fishing Book 19
Fraser's Magazine...................... 20
Freshfield's Travels in the Caucasus 16
Froude's English in Ireland 1
——————— History of England 1
——————— Short Studies 7

Gamgee on Horse-Shoeing 19
Ganot's Elementary Physics 9
——————— Natural Philosophy 9
Garrod's Materia Medica 12
Giant (The) 17
Gilbert's Cadore 16
——————— and Churchill's Dolomites 16
Girdlestone's Bible Synonyms 14
Girtin's House I Live In 11
Gledstone's Life of Whitefield 4
Goddard's Wonderful Stories 17
Goldsmith's Poems, Illustrated 18
Goodeve's Mechanism..................... 9
Graham's Autobiography of Milton...... 4
——————— View of Literature and Art ... 2
Grant's Ethics of Aristotle............. 5
——————— Home Politics................... 2
Graver Thoughts of a Country Parson.... 7
Gray's Anatomy.......................... 11
Griffin's Algebra and Trigonometry 9
Griffith's Fundamentals 14
Grove on Correlation of Physical Forces .. 9
Gurney's Chapters of French History 2
Gwilt's Encyclopædia of Architecture 13

Hartwig's Harmonies of Nature.......... 10
——————— Polar World 10
——————— Sea and its Living Wonders.... 10
——————— Subterranean World 10
Hatherton's Memoir and Correspondence 2
Hayward's Biographical and Critical Essays 6
Herschel's Outlines of Astronomy....... 7
Hewitt on the Diseases of Women 11

Hodgson's Time and Space................ 7
——————— Theory of Practice 7
Holland's Recollections................. 5
Holmes's Surgical Treatment of Children.. 11
——————— System of Surgery 11
Horne's Introduction to the Scriptures .. 15
How we Spent the Summer................. 16
Howitt's Australian Discovery........... 17
——————— Rural Life of England 17
——————— Visits to Remarkable Places 17
Hübner's Pope Sixtus the Fifth 4
Humboldt's Life.......................... 4
Hume's Essays............................ 9
——————— Treatise on Human Nature........ 9

Ihne's History of Rome 8
Ingelow's Poems 18
——————— Story of Doom 18

James's Christian Counsels............... 14
Jameson's Legends of Saints and Martyrs.. 12
——————— Legends of the Madonna 12
——————— Legends of the Monastic Orders 12
——————— Legends of the Saviour........ 12
Jamieson on Causality 5
Jardine's Christian Sacerdotalism 14
Johnston's Geographical Dictionary 8
Jones's Royal Institution 4

Kalisch's Commentary on the Bible...... 6
——————— Hebrew Grammar............... 6
Keith on Destiny of the World........... 15
——————— Fulfilment of Prophecy.......... 15
Kerl's Metallurgy, by Crookes and Röhrig 14
Kirby and Spence's Entomology........... 9

Lang's Ballads and Lyrics 18
Lanman's Japanese in America 16
Latham's English Dictionary 5
Laughton's Nautical Surveying........... 9
Laverack's Setters 19
Lecky's History of European Morals 3
——————— Rationalism.................... 3
——————— Leaders of Public Opinion....... 4
Leisure Hours in Town, by A. K. H. B. 7
Lessons of Middle Age, by A. K. H. B. 7
Lewes's Biographical History of Philosophy 3
Liddell & Scott's Greek-English Lexicon 6
Life of Man Symbolised.................. 13
Lindley and Moore's Treasury of Botany 10
Longman's Edward the Third 2
——————— Lectures on History of England 2
——————— Chess Openings................. 20
Loudon's Encyclopædia of Agriculture 14
——————— Gardening 14
——————— Plants 10
Lubbock's Origin of Civilisation 10
Lytton's Odes of Horace................. 18
Lyra Germanica 12, 16

Macaulay's (Lord) Essays................. 3
——————— History of England .. 1
——————— Lays of Ancient Rome 19
——————— Miscellaneous Writings 7

NEW WORKS PUBLISHED BY LONGMANS AND CO.   23

Macaulay's (Lord) Speeches	5
———— Works	1
Macleod's Principles of Political Philosophy	5
———— Dictionary of Political Economy	5
———— Theory and Practice of Banking	10
McCulloch's Dictionary of Commerce	10
Maguire's Life of Father Mathew	4
———— Pius IX.	15
Mankind, their Origin and Destiny	10
Manning's England and Christendom	15
Marcet's Natural Philosophy	9
Marshall's Physiology	12
Marshman's History of India	2
———— Life of Havelock	5
Martineau's Endeavours after the Christian Life	16
Massingberd's History of the Reformation	3
Mathews on Colonial Question	2
Maunder's Biographical Treasury	5
———— Geographical Treasury	9
———— Historical Treasury	3
———— Scientific and Literary Treasury	10
———— Treasury of Knowledge	10
———— Treasury of Natural History	10
Maxwell's Theory of Heat	9
May's Constitutional History of England	1
Melville's Digby Grand	18
———— General Bounce	18
———— Gladiators	18
———— Good for Nothing	18
———— Holmby House	18
———— Interpreter	18
———— Kate Coventry	18
———— Queen's Maries	18
Mendelssohn's Letters	4
Merivale's Fall of the Roman Republic	3
———— Romans under the Empire	3
Merrifield's Arithmetic and Mensuration	9
———— Magnetism	
———— and Evers's Navigation	8
Meteyard's Group of Englishmen	4
Miles on Horse's Foot and Horse Shoeing	19
———— on Horses' Teeth and Stables	19
Mill (J.) on the Mind	5
Mill (J. S.) on Liberty	5
———— Subjection of Women	5
———— on Representative Government	5
———— on Utilitarianism	5
———— 's Dissertations and Discussions	5
———— Political Economy	5
———— System of Logic	5
———— Hamilton's Philosophy	5
Miller's Elements of Chemistry	11
———— Inorganic Chemistry	9
Mitchell's Manual of Architecture	13
———— Manual of Assaying	14
Monsell's Beatitudes	16
———— His Presence not his Memory	16
———— 'Spiritual Songs'	16
Moore's Irish Melodies	18
———— Lalla Rookh	18
———— Poetical Works	18
Morell's Elements of Psychology	6
———— Mental Philosophy	6
Mossman's Christian Church	3
Müller's (Max) Chips from a German Workshop	7
———— Lectures on the Science of Language	5
———— (K. O.) Literature of Ancient Greece	3
Murchison on Liver Complaints	12
Mure's Language and Literature of Greece	2
Nash's Compendium of the Prayer-Book	14
New Testament Illustrated with Wood Engravings from the Old Masters	12
Newman's History of his Religious Opinions	5
Nightingale on Hospitals	20
———— Lying-In Institutions	20
Nilsson's Scandinavia	10
Northcott on Lathes and Turning	13
Notes on Books	20
Odling's Course of Practical Chemistry	11
———— Outlines of Chemistry	11
Owen's Comparative Anatomy and Physiology of Vertebrate Animals	9
———— Lectures on the Invertebrata	9
Packe's Guide to the Pyrenees	17
Paget's Lectures on Surgical Pathology	10
Pereira's Elements of Materia Medica	12
Perring's Churches and Creeds	14
Pewtner's Comprehensive Specifier	20
Pictures in Tyrol	16
Piesse's Art of Perfumery	14
Playfair-Brown's California	16
Prendergast's Mastery of Languages	6
Prescott's Scripture Difficulties	15
Present-Day Thoughts, by A. K. H. B.	7
Proctor's Astronomical Essays	8
———— Orbs around Us	8
———— Plurality of Worlds	8
———— Saturn	8
———— Scientific Essays	9
———— Star Atlas	8
———— Star Depths	8
———— Sun	8
Public Schools Atlas	8
Rae's Westward by Rail	16
Ranken on Strains in Trusses	13
Rawlinson's Parthia	2
Recreations of a Country Parson, by A. K. H. B.	7
Reeve's Royal and Republican France	2
Reichel's See of Rome	14
Reilly's Map of Mont Blanc	17
Rivers's Rose Amateur's Guide	10
Rogers's Eclipse of Faith	7
———— Defence of Faith	7
Roget's Thesaurus of English Words and Phrases	6
Ronalds's Fly-Fisher's Entomology	19
Rose's Loyola	15
Rothschild's Israelites	15
Russell's Pau and the Pyrenees	16
Sandars's Justinian's Institutes	5
Sanford's English Kings	1
Savile on Truth of the Bible	15
Schellen's Spectrum Analysis	8
Scott's Lectures on the Fine Arts	12
———— Albert Durer	12
Seaside Musing, by A. K. H. B.	7
Seebohm's Oxford Reformers of 1498	2

Sewell's After Life	17
—— Glimpse of the World	17
—— History of the Early Church	5
—— Journal of a Home Life	16
—— Passing Thoughts on Religion	16
—— Preparation for Communion	16
—— Readings for Confirmation	16
—— Readings for Lent	16
—— Examination for Confirmation	16
—— Stories and Tales	17
—— Thoughts for the Age	16
—— Thoughts for the Holy Week	16
Shipley's Essays on Ecclesiastical Reform	16
Short's Church History	3
Smith's Paul's Voyage and Shipwreck	14
—— (Sydney) Life and Letters	4
—— Miscellaneous Works	7
—— Wit and Wisdom	7
—— (Dr. R. A.) Air and Rain	8
Southey's Doctor	6
—— Poetical Works	18
Stanley's History of British Birds	9
Stephen's Ecclesiastical Biography	4
—— Playground of Europe	16
Stepping-Stone to Knowledge, &c.	20
Stirling's Protoplasm	7
—— Secret of Hegel	7
—— Sir William Hamilton	7
Stockmar's Memoirs	1
Stonehenge on the Dog	19
—— on the Greyhound	19
Strickland's Queens of England	4
Sunday Afternoons at the Parish Church of a University City, by A. K. H. B.	7
Taylor's History of India	2
—— (Jeremy) Works, edited by Eden	16
—— Text-Books of Science	8
Text-Books of Science	9
Thirlwall's History of Greece	2
Thomson's Laws of Thought	5
—— New World of Being	7
Thudichum's Chemical Physiology	11
Todd (A.) on Parliamentary Government	1
—— and Bowman's Anatomy and Physiology of Man	12
Trench's Realities of Irish Life	2
Trollope's Barchester Towers	18
—— Warden	18
Twiss's Law of Nations	20
Tyndall's Diamagnetism	9
—— Faraday as a Discoverer	4
—— Fragments of Science	9
—— Hours of Exercise in the Alps	16

Tyndall's Lectures on Electricity	9
—— Lectures on Light	9
—— Lectures on Sound	9
—— Heat a Mode of Motion	8
—— Molecular Physics	11
Ueberweg's System of Logic	7
Ure's Dictionary of Arts, Manufactures, and Mines	13
Van Der Hoeven's Handbook of Zoology	10
Vogan's Doctrine of the Eucharist	16
Watson's Geometry	9
—— Principles and Practice of Physic	11
Watts's Dictionary of Chemistry	11
Webb's Objects for Common Telescopes	6
Webster & Wilkinson's Greek Testament	15
Wellington's Life, by Gleig	4
West on Children's Diseases	11
—— on Children's Nervous Disorders	11
—— on Nursing Sick Children	20
Whately's English Synonymes	8
—— Logic	5
—— Rhetoric	5
White and Riddle's Latin Dictionaries	6
Wilcocks's Sea Fisherman	19
Williams's Aristotle's Ethics	5
Williams on Consumption	11
Willich's Popular Tables	20
Willis's Principles of Mechanism	13
Winslow on Light	9
Wood's (J. G.) Bible Animals	10
—— Homes without Hands	9
—— Insects at Home	10
—— Insects Abroad	10
—— Strange Dwellings	9
—— (T.) Chemical Notes	11
Wordsworth's Christian Ministry	16
Yarndale	17
Yonge's History of England	1
—— English-Greek Lexicons	6
—— Horace	18
—— English Literature	6
—— Modern History	3
Youatt on the Dog	19
—— on the Horse	19
Zeller's Socrates	3
—— Stoics, Epicureans, and Sceptics	3
Zigzagging amongst Dolomites	15

www.ingramcontent.com/pod-product-compliance
Lightning Source LLC
Chambersburg PA
CBHW031935290426
44108CB00011B/570